FICTION
OF THE
FORTIES

FICTION
OF THE
FORTIES

Chester E. Eisinger

Phoenix Books

THE UNIVERSITY OF CHICAGO PRESS

CHICAGO AND LONDON

15912

FOR

MARJORIE

LIBRARY OF CONGRESS CATALOG CARD NUMBER: 63-20904
THE UNIVERSITY OF CHICAGO PRESS, CHICAGO & LONDON
THE UNIVERSITY OF TORONTO PRESS, TORONTO 5, CANADA
© 1963 BY CHARLES E. EISINGER
PUBLISHED 1963. FOURTH IMPRESSION 1967
PRINTED IN THE UNITED STATES OF AMERICA

ACKNOWLEDGMENTS

I would like to thank the following individuals and publishers for permission to reproduce the photographs used on the jacket of this book: Dos Passos, by Sylvia Salmi, McCullers, by Louise Dahl Wolfe, courtesy Houghton Mifflin Company; Farrell, courtesy Doubleday & Company; Trilling, by Sylvia Salmi, Gordon, by Willard Starks, Stegner, by James Hall, Bellow, by Joseph Zimbrolt, courtesy Viking Press; Shaw, by Richard L. Simon, Schulberg, by Bob Smallman, Bowles, by Ahmed el Yacoubi, Stafford, by Erich Hartmann, Capote, by J. R. Roustan, Warren, by Peter Fink, Clark, courtesy Random House; Morris, courtesy Atheneum Publishers; McCarthy, by James West, courtesy Farrar, Straus and Cudahy; Algren, by Nick Cox, courtesy Angel Island Publications.

PORTIONS of this book have appeared in *Accent, College English, Pacific Spectator, Southwest Review,* and *University of Kansas City Review.* I gratefully acknowledge permission to use them here, where they appear in revised form. I wish also to acknowledge a summer grant from the Purdue Research Foundation and receipt of funds for typing from the Department of English at Purdue University. I want to thank Joanna Comen for her intelligent typing of the book. My colleague Harold H. Watts read the entire manuscript; it owes a great deal to his learning and good taste. My indebtedness to various scholars and critics can only be partially recognized in the footnotes. I have drawn upon many others, who are not named there. But the largest contribution to this book has come from my wife, who made it possible.

CONTENTS

CHAPTER ONE   INTRODUCTION: THE SHAPE
OF THE FORTIES   1

CHAPTER TWO   THE WAR NOVEL   21
Background: The War Behind the Fiction   21
Patterns of Despair   28
Patterns of Affirmation   44

CHAPTER THREE   NATURALISM: THE TACTICS
OF SURVIVAL   62
The Meaning of Naturalism in the Forties   62
The Survivors   64
New Voices, Negro and White   70
Nelson Algren: Naturalism as the Beat of the Iron Heart   73

CHAPTER FOUR   FICTION AND THE LIBERAL
REASSESSMENT   86
The Day of the Locust for the Liberal Spirit   86
The Collapse of Marxism   87
Traditional Liberalism   94
    Budd Schulberg: The Popular Voice of the Old
        Liberalism
    Irwin Shaw: The Popular Ideas of the Old Liberalism
    The Popular Fiction of the Old Liberalism
The New Liberalism   117
    John Dos Passos and the Need for Rejection
    Granville Hicks and the Painful Process of Reconstruction
    Mary McCarthy as the Sceptical New Liberal
    Lionel Trilling and the Crisis in Our Culture
A Critique of the New Liberalism   144

CHAPTER FIVE THE CONSERVATIVE
                IMAGINATION   146
Neo-Conservatism and the Idea Vacuum   146
James Gould Cozzens: The Pennsylvania Voice of
    Aggressive Aristocracy   150
The True Religion and Conservatism   171
Southern Conservatism   177
    William Faulkner: Southern Archetype
    Caroline Gordon: The Logic of Conservatism
    Andrew Lytle and Peter Taylor: Conservative Fiction
        in Tennessee
    Robert Penn Warren: The Conservative Quest for
        Identity
A Critique of Conservatism   229

CHAPTER SIX THE NEW FICTION   231
The New Fiction Defined: The Triumph of Art   231
The New Fiction and the Gothic Spirit   235
    Truman Capote and the Twisted Self
    Carson McCullers and the Failure of Dialogue
    Eudora Welty and the Triumph of the Imagination
    Paul Bowles and the Passionate Pursuit of
        Disengagement
The Children of Henry James   289
    The Two Worlds of Jean Stafford

CHAPTER SEVEN IN SEARCH OF MAN
                AND AMERICA   308
The Fiction of the Forties and the Existential Crisis   308
Walter Van Tilburg Clark: Amid Confusion, The
    Triumph of Nature   310
Wallace Stegner: The Uncommitted   324
Wright Morris: The Artist in Search of America   328
Saul Bellow: Man Alive, Sustained By Love   341

APPENDIX: FICTION OF THE FORTIES   363

NOTES   368

INDEX   385

CHAPTER ONE

INTRODUCTION: THE SHAPE OF THE FORTIES

The nineteen forties was the Age of Prose Fiction. It was also the Age of Survival and the Time of Hesitation. Whatever it is called — and some have even called it the Age of Criticism — fiction was the principal literary form of the decade, and fiction revealed more about the forties than did any other kind of literature — more than criticism, even more, I am constrained to say, than sociology. The novelists and the short-story writers of the period tell us now more about the hesitations that beset men then and more about the struggle for survival than other investigators. They speak to us not only about the elementary struggle for life, but about the possible survival of the individual identity, about the survival of the writer as artist. They penetrate more deeply into the secret recesses of the period than poets or critics or sociologists. For novels are the mirror of their age, as Flaubert has said. They reflect for us the inner face of their time and the impulses and conflicts, both conscious and unconscious, that contain its history. To read the novels of the forties is to commit oneself to the stream of that history. But fiction will lead us beyond a knowledge of the time; it will lead us also to a sense of the self afoot at that time. If it may be said that self-knowledge is the ultimate goal of all experience with the arts, then I submit that fiction, during the forties, was the chief and best way to achieve that goal. Self-knowledge was the subject that writers most persistently pursued. They wrote about it and sought it for themselves. And it was what the reader might find as his most satisfying reward in their work. The fiction writers of the forties, then, carried forward the crucial quest for an understanding of our lives as social creatures and as individual human beings. They undertook to do what John Peale Bishop, speaking of Hemingway, said that fiction writers should do: "It is the mark of the true novelist that in searching the meaning of his own unsought experience, he comes on the moral history of his time."

To assert that the special value of studying the prose fiction of the forties lies in its capacity to expand and deepen our understanding of that time and of ourselves is to have made, surely, a large claim. I should like to follow with another, equally large. Every addition to contemporary literature alters the face of our total literature and affects the nature and meaning of our literary tradition. As that tradition helps us to understand the present, so the present enables us to understand the past out of which the tradition comes. The totality of our literary history is constantly changing, of course. Such changes mean that we must be alive always to the need for re-evaluating and regrouping our writers. We must affirm the continuity of American literary history, but we must also acknowledge the changing contours of that history. It is my hope that increased attention to the literature of the twentieth century will eventually bring about a rewriting of our literary history that will reflect in its proportions the relative importance and quality of twentieth-century writers. With their work the world has come to recognize fully the claims of our literary culture. And it is from about the beginning of the forties that ours has been acknowledged as first among literatures in the English language. This book is a modest contribution to that work of revision as it is carried on within the overarching pattern of our literary tradition.

That pattern has always been divisible, and in the twentieth century we have tended to see the decades as units in our literary history, since 1919, 1929, and 1939 each mark an end and a beginning. This method of division may be extended to the forties. How the limits of this decade may be established and what gives

the forties its distinctive character, as the twenties and the thirties have theirs, are questions to which I now turn.

The social-political criteria we may use to establish terminal
points for the forties are certainly as compelling as those Scott
Fitzgerald used in dating the twenties from the May Day riots of
1919 to the stock market crash of 1929. Fitzgerald apparently felt
that such events had a relevance in marking out a period in our
culture, a period even in our literature. The same may be said
for the criteria presented here for the forties. The two events of
smashing impact that attended the death of the thirties and the
birth of the forties were the Nazi-Soviet Pact of 1939 and the outbreak of the war in Europe a short time after, a war the United
States entered in 1941. The pact signaled the failure, nay the
death, of Marxism in this country, a Marxism that had nourished
social idealists of the non-Communist left as well as party members. The war revealed, in the career of fascism, a capacity for
evil in human beings that struck at certain optimistic psychological assumptions commonly made in our liberal democracy. It cast
doubt upon the potential for survival of that democratic culture
that had come to us from the humanistic Renaissance and the
Enlightenment. It numbed the individual conscience, inducing
nihilism and acquiescence in the loss of human identity. All these
consequences of both the pact and the war were to have an effect
upon the fiction of the forties.

For the end of the forties the historian Eric Goldman has made
a strong case for 1949, viewing it as a year of shock and a turning
point. It was the year that Americans were forced to recognize
the East-West division of the world, based on power parity and
maintained in precarious balance. It was the year that conservative, even reactionary, forces appeared to assume command in
American life. In August it was conceded that the Communists
had won China. In September the Soviet Union announced that
it had the atomic bomb. In that year the Alger Hiss case seemed to
put an entire generation of liberals on trial and to find them
guilty. For Hiss was made to represent the liberal who was in
fact a traitor to his country. The theory of conspiracy — the notion that liberals, Socialists, and Communists were engaged in a
gigantic plot to subvert democratic institutions — was about to

emerge as a political instrument of the American Right. This theory summarized all our uncertainties and fears. But if 1949 seems too deliberately of a piece with the terminal dates of earlier decades, then perhaps 1952 will serve as the year in which a period of our history came to an end. With the election of President Eisenhower in that year, the American people seemed to surrender up their problems; they deposited them at the feet of the wise father figure and hoped he would resolve them. It was a turn to the right. It was a turn away from a challenge to mind and will. The people seemed to surrender more than social responsibility. What marks and makes the end of the period is a spiritual and intellectual abdication. The emergence of the political right and the failure of liberalism were to affect fiction profoundly in our decade.

Literary criteria also helped to define the forties. The thirties may be said to have crested with the publication of *The Grapes of Wrath* in 1939, certainly the finest statement of the social indignation and faith in the common man that marked the sociological fiction which dominated that decade. This kind of fiction went into a chilling descent immediately thereafter. The forties opened with the publication of first novels by Robert Penn Warren (*Night Rider*, 1939), Walter Van Tilburg Clark (*The Ox-Bow Incident*, 1940), and Carson McCullers (*The Heart Is a Lonely Hunter*, 1940) which all bear one meaningful similarity: although they show an interest in social issues, they turn away from these issues to find their real center in moral-ethical problems, or in what concerns the inward, private being. This shift in emphasis begins at once to reveal a characteristic tendency of fiction in the forties.

Two other matters figure in establishing beginning points for the decade: one concerns death and the other inception. The death of talent in the old giants of American fiction marked an ending and made a new beginning necessary. Thomas Wolfe was in truth dead before the decade opened. Steinbeck, Hemingway, Farrell, and Dos Passos had all run their talents into the shallows. And the death of James Joyce and Virginia Woolf in 1941 was symbolic of the passing of experimentalism in the fiction of the entire English-speaking world. An era closed with death, with the decline of talent and the disappearance of innovation. The inception, the beginning, is in criticism. In 1941 the school of criticism that had been long in the making issued its manifesto in John Crowe Ransom's *The New Criticism*, which launched in the forties a critical movement that colored the literature of the decade.

This evidence suggests what ended with the thirties and began with the forties. It is more complicated to establish what ended, in literature and particularly in fiction, around 1950. For the forties seemed to run indiscriminately into the fifties. Many of the writers who give the fiction of the forties its distinctive life, writers like Saul Bellow, Wright Morris, Jean Stafford, and Warren, went right on publishing into the next decade. The forties may be said to end, then, not with the close of many careers, but with a body of idea or a mode of writing exhausted. Or the forties end with a movement launched and established, through its achievement in the decade, as a recognized way of fictional expression.

For example, the war novel, naturalism, and the fiction resting on the stereotypes of social liberalism were all, by the end of the decade, worn out or completed as *literary movements*. The conservative imagination, on the other hand, finally won a secure place in this period as a part of the landscape of American fiction. Likewise the Southern Renaissance, although it had long been unfolding, had assumed by 1950 its definitive shape. The new fiction was fully developed during the forties and may well have burned at its brightest point as the decade turned. The quest for the self was intensified in the fiction of this decade in such a way as to assume the proportions of a movement. Some literary modes inherited by the forties virtually passed away in the course of the decade, while what was initiated in the period became an ongoing concern in American literature and did not necessarily end with the period. It follows that in many ways the forties was a period of transition, but, I submit, a reasonably well defined entity, as periods in literary history go, and a convenient one. But since no one expects the birth and death of literary ideas or tendencies to accord neatly with the calendar, in my discussion of the fiction of the forties I shall take the liberty of ranging from 1939 to 1952 or 1953. Such latitude seems to be sanctioned by what the various criteria have yielded in establishing limits for the period.

If prose fiction, as I have suggested, helps to explain these years, if it brings us to an understanding of the reality of the period, the reverse is also true: the culture of the time helps to explain the fiction. When I speak of culture I mean the total social and historical experience, the ideas, the beliefs, the customs, the psychology, the art, the assumptions — everything that gives the time its special tone. It is necessary to understand the culture in which the writer lived in order to understand fully what he wrote. Of the usefulness of this relationship between the writer and his culture I am convinced. A quick profile of the culture of the forties, especially as it bears upon the writer, will point up this usefulness, I trust, and provide a helpful background to the discussion of the fiction in later pages.

The cultural life which the writer found everywhere about him in the forties was marked by incoherence and uncertainty. He had to examine the possibilities for literature in a universe of fragmented beliefs where a multiplicity of values or none at all had long ago replaced a unified world view. The fragmentation of belief did not take place in the forties, but the decade was heir to it, heir to the failure of world views or systems of belief by which men could live. As these views and systems began to break up — and certainly they had been in the process of doing so at an accelerated rate ever since the introduction of Darwinian science — men found themselves confronted either with discredited or fragmented ideological or philosophical conceptions. Science had failed to answer all questions and indeed had created intolerable and insoluble problems. The bourgeois world of eighteenth-century rationalism and nineteenth-century economic liberalism could no longer answer to the needs of anguished twentieth-century man: the shortcomings of overconfident reason and the muddled inadequacies of free enterprise had become shockingly apparent to him.

It follows that the culture of the forties could offer the writer neither an ideology nor a faith that might sustain him. The available ideology of the previous decade had been Marxism, but the treachery of Russia had moved the writer to take the first quick step toward disenchantment with political philosophy and with politics. This disengagement was to mark much of the creative work throughout the decade. Social revolution could no longer appeal to the writer when he saw that the efforts to change the world for the better, in politics and in literature, had brought down upon us varieties of totalitarianism abroad and regimentation at home. Liberalism, not precisely an ideology to be sure, seemed equally fruitless in the light of events. Rebellion and reform were unacceptable tactics, and many writers saw no alternative but to withdraw from the political scene, that is, as artists to turn their attention elsewhere. But neither did religion offer a satisfactory refuge. Few writers seemed affected by the more or less spurious religious revival that began during the war, although many were attracted to religious conceptions. For the most part, however, they were unable to make a serious religious commitment. They managed a suspension of disbelief and a yearning tentativeness with respect to religion, but these attitudes resulted only in bringing them to an uneasy halfway house between faith and scepticism.

In sum, the radical disunity that marked men's lives created spiritual and intellectual turmoil. Men could not find or accept a set of common assumptions. The writer had to ask himself: can I, under these circumstances, find a way to communicate with others, or should I give up and keep silent? The writer chose the first alternative, chose to live as a writer. He refused to fall silent even though he felt alienated. In fact, he capitalized on the disjunctions of his culture. His survival constitutes a small triumph over that culture.

To turn now from idea and belief to society. In the forties, the culture offered the writer a society in which chaos was balanced against a factitious kind of order. The war brought chaos. It had a disrupting effect upon the life of the writer, as it did upon the lives of everyone else. It forced upon him a sense of the contingency of life and confronted him with the surrealistic disorder of history. It left him with the implacable horror of the atom bomb, with the possibility that the human race might be wiped out. It confronted him with the reshuffled power relations among the nations, a situation in which he saw the possible destruction of the Western world and the humanistic ideals that had been born there. But on the social and political scene in the United States the war made for a rationalization of social forces that imposed order upon the total society during the decade. The war brought about conscription, censorship, discipline, in short, the ruthless use of governmental powers for the total organization of society. And these developments were justified and continued in the postwar world in the name of national survival, as we faced the world-wide Communist threat. Fear of communism at home led to attacks on leftists of every kind and finally to the great security psychosis which prepared the way for the eruption of Senator McCarthy. The consequence of this repressive climate of opinion was the virtual elimination of dissent. Extreme views, not simply with respect to the political spectrum but in any area, almost disappeared. All shades of opinion slid toward the center.

This world of bureaucratized society, victimized by the manipulative techniques of mass media, was inhabited by the new white-collar man and the man in the gray flannel suit. The little white-collar man, according to C. Wright Mills, was estranged from his community and his society; he was alienated from his work and his self. The citizen in the gray flannel suit was a more co-operative victim of conformity than the white-collar man. The best dressed gravedigger of individualism in American history, the man in the gray flannel suit found his more or less happy place in the leviathans of our society. He was an organization man in any one of the corporate structures erected by government, business, or labor. There he sought security — the kind embodied in group hospitalization plans and retirement provisions — and status. His anxieties about economic stability often contributed to his fears about political security. And his status aspirations, which demanded that his attitudes be "right," killed the impulse toward intellectual adventure and nourished the fear of any deviation from the dead center. A society so organized was as grave a threat to the life of the writer as the chaos in the realm of ideas. It threatened his existence as an individual, as indeed it threatened the precious individualism of all men.

The winds of doctrine that swirled through the cultural air of the forties blew up three controversies that had a profound effect upon writers and intellectuals. The first of these began as the decade opened, with the publication in 1940 of *The Irresponsibles*, by Archibald MacLeish. This book initiated the debate on literary nationalism. The irresponsibles, MacLeish claimed, were the writers and scholars who had failed to defend Western civilization against the onslaught of fascism. They suffered from a disease which is the surrender of the mind and the will, and they were going to lose the things they loved because of the purity of their detachment and objectivity in regarding and using them. Writers, MacLeish said, must make a total commitment to their society. So saying, he tied together literature and society in an indissoluble knot.

In 1944 Bernard De Voto published *The Literary Fallacy*, in which the announced intention was to cut the knot. As De Voto defined it, this fallacy judges the nature of a culture, its values and its content, by means of its literature. His point was that the work of representative writers of the twenties was not a trustworthy guide to an understanding of the twenties. But then, much in the MacLeish vein, he went on to argue that such writers were responsible for an American literature that has been "a betrayal of our culture." Later in the book he agreed with MacLeish's indictment of American literature: it has failed, he claimed, to safeguard democracy and failed in respect for democratic man. The implication of this second point is that if writers had understood the democratic experience, then their work would have been a valid index to their time. Under such happy circumstances one could judge a democratic society by its literature. But this is the literary fallacy, and it is now De Voto who is guilty of it. The net effect of De Voto's confused book was to give support to MacLeish's position. De Voto's knife proved too dull for the knot. Van Wyck Brooks, in two essays on primary literature and coterie literature, which he brought together in his *Opinions of Oliver Allston* in 1941, joined with MacLeish and De Voto by calling for the life-drive in literature, for immersion in the American past, for recognition of progress and the goodness of man, in short, by advocating a positive and constructive literature of America. With the statements of these three critics, the new nationalism was firmly established in the forties. Fiction was to be self-consciously democratic and anti-fascistic in the service of national goals.

The reply to the view that literature must serve the state might well begin with a comment by André Gide: "Il me paraît aussi absurde d'incriminer notre littérature au sujet de notre défaite qu'il l'eût été de la féliciter en 1918, lorsque nous avions la victoire . . . ." Similar views were expressed in the United States, where the reaction to the new nationalism brought into the market place for discussion important aesthetic and intellectual questions. It was maintained that the writer as such had no responsibility during wartime. It was argued that cultural nationalism destroys the critical spirit. It was said that art is not specifically American; art speaks for mankind. Nationalism endangers detachment and moral discriminations. Dwight Macdonald, whose voice was the loudest and most frequently heard in opposition, announced that "Kulturbolschewismus Is Here." He saw in this unleashed Americanism the danger of an official line on literature which would lead inevitably to censorship and book burning. The new nationalism had emerged with a totalitarian flavor, he thought, as a consequence of the breakdown of the bourgeois order and the impotence of any progressive revolutionary force. Malcolm Cowley thought that on the evidence the nationalists were wrong in attributing the outbreak of war to the picture of decadent America given by American writers. Most of the writers widely discussed in Germany before the war, he reported, showed America as powerful and expansive and her soldiers as brave.

In the late forties, literary nationalism found other voices and other emphases, although its essential Americanism remained. *Fortune, Life, The Catholic World*, John Chamberlain, and J. Donald Adams, in the years from 1947 to 1949, all complained bitterly that current fiction was misrepresenting America by overemphasizing unpleasant aspects and by its general air of negativism. Thus our fiction was misleading foreigners, who would come to underrate our spirit and ability. We ought, they agreed, to have optimistic novels full of positive thinking in which business men were the heroes.

Those who wrote war novels, naturally, were most susceptible to the pressures of the new nationalism. And critics were most sensitive to its implications when they assessed such books. Edmund Wilson, in reviewing *Apartment in Athens*, felt that Glenway Wescott had sacrificed his talent to the erroneous notion that fiction had to help win the war. And the journalistic furor over the depiction of the good Nazi in Steinbeck's *The Moon Is Down* was further evidence of the disquiet critics felt in the shadow of the nationalistic spirit.

It seems safe to guess that writers of all sorts would feel reluctant to write social-political fiction when its conditions and criteria are imposed upon them. The experience of the Communist party in America was that it could not long dictate to writers the political ideas and psychological assumptions that were to go into their work. Writers must have reacted in the same way to the official line of the new nationalism. The withdrawal of many writers in the forties to an apolitical stance is a result in part of this rejection of a "given" political line. The spirit of opposition, the quest for living alternatives, withered in the forties under its impact. The new nationalism must take its place as a real force in the general political disenchantment of the period.

It follows that the new criticism and the new fiction, insofar as they postulate indifference or hostility to fictional engagement with political ideas or the social-political scene, draw encouragement from the literary consequences of the new nationalism. At the same time, it must be said that the later expression of that nationalism attacked many of the attitudes inherent in the new fiction. If the apolitical imagination was safe, the negative imagination was not. When the new fiction turned away from an empirical view of reality where social problems might be viewed, it did not attract the attention of patriotic or moralistic critics. But when it revealed the degeneracy of man and espoused a sweeping nihilism, it became distasteful to the self-righteous custodians of the arts. It did not, then, win approval from nationalistic critics. It crept unnoticed into the forties, so to speak, while the nationalists were busy chastising a more obvious enemy who already held the ground — the social-political writers.

The intellectual battle lines during the forties took on a new conformation when Sidney Hook began the failure of nerve controversy in the *Partisan Review* in the first months of 1943. This is the second doctrinal debate to which I want to call attention. Liberalism as an intellectual temper, as faith in intelligence, he noted mournfully, was on the defensive; theology and metaphysics were on the rise. This change in the hierarchy of intellectual values and systems represented a flight from responsibility which

Hook called the new failure of nerve. The primary evidence for this failure was the loss of confidence in the scientific method, which was being displaced, in his view, by an irresponsible subjectivism. Others joined Hook in asserting the claims of naturalism, positivism, and science. John Dewey and Ruth Benedict attacked the degrading view of man that followed from an acceptance of original sin. Dewey denied that naturalism can be equated with materialism and that our plight — the rise of dictatorship and the denial of rights and freedoms everywhere in the world — is a consequence of belief in naturalism. Others attacked Kierkegaard for a renunciation of life and Gerald Heard and Aldous Huxley for an irresponsible mysticism.

The real issue in this controversy, it quickly became evident, was the adequacy of science as the basis for a total philosophical position. Hook and the others had felt the challenge to the dominance of science before they spoke up. In the replies to their statements they were made to feel the challenge even more sharply. A typical response came from Philip Wheelwright. The methods of science were not applicable to the insights which constitute the real basis of human wisdom, he said. Love, moral urgency, or reverence cannot be understood by reference to the canons of science. In dealing with literature, philosophers of science were incompetent to discuss phenomena described in terms of imagination, intuition, vision, or revelation. In general, the human capacity for experience exceeded the limits of any area that science might legitimately claim to explain. The debate was inconclusive. But it had, in any case, the effect of showing how far liberalism, associated with the rational-scientific mind as it was, had slipped from its dominant intellectual position of only a few years before, and how much it stood in need of modification if it were not to be abandoned. In questioning the authority of science, furthermore, the controversy succeeded in opening the possibility for the pursuit of truth by non-objective and non-empirical modes of inquiry. In other words, it resulted in a new authority for literature and religion, especially in the literature of sensibility as opposed to the literature of ideas. In the forties the latter led a hand-to-mouth existence, while the emergent and more powerful kinds of fiction rested on some kind of tradition or, like the new fiction, drew upon the subjective resources of the writer.

A third controversy bears directly on the writing of fiction. It concerns the death of the novel. Discussion of this matter was not limited to the forties or to the United States, but it engaged Americans during that decade. Ortega y Gasset and T. S. Eliot had both declared the novel dead and had buried it beneath the weight of their authority. They had asserted it was a literary genre that had worn itself out; it had exhausted its supply of subjects and its capacity for technical experimentation, and it could no longer present us with original forms. Joyce and Woolf were indeed dead; they had left no sons whose reach exceeded the grasp of the parent.

Yet novels, as we know, continued to appear in the forties. Novelists met in symposia to assert that the novel was still alive and to draw comfort from the concerted denial of its death by their still palpably warm and quick colleagues. Some critics, like Lionel Trilling, said that the novel was not dead, but he made such a good case for its numerous maladies that he might better have been silent on this matter. But the novel did survive, and its survival did not depend on a continuous development of techniques in fiction. People continued to write fiction because they felt a need to confront, even if they could not resolve, the moral and social tensions of their culture and of their lives.

The culture of the forties, then, indeed of the United States in almost its total history, does help to explain its fiction, as I have said. For in searching out a reason for the novelist's survival and his continuing effort, one comes upon the view that multiplicity and fragmentation have had not a baneful but a beneficent influence upon creativity in America. The writer has had to make his own choices, has always had a field of possibilities. He has never had to bend to an official dogma, and in modern times he has not had the security of a unified world view. He has been forced to enjoy, if that is the proper word, the dreadful freedom of multiplicity. In our history we have had a constantly recurring pattern of polarities, as Max Lerner is only one of several to point out, which has demanded the resolution of conflicting views and impulses or has made necessary an allegiance to one view rather than another. And the American novelist throughout our history has been aware of these tensions in his culture. The fructifying tradition of the American novel, in the opinion of its recent historians, rests upon the very disunities and disorders of American life. Many of our best novels achieve their form and their energy, they point out, from the perception of radical disunities like the opposition between Europe and America, tradition and progress, liberalism and tradition, acquisitive economics and benevolent wealth, a series of polarities very similar to those Lerner lists. The American novel of the forties belongs to such a continuous historical stream: it is confronted with the antinomies of our culture as the work of previous generations has been. Its writers have felt, perhaps, more gravely threatened and more thoroughly harassed than their forebears. But its writers have discovered that what was difficult was not impossible. Deprived of peace and unity, they found compensation and opportunity in turbulence and change. One of them, Ralph Ellison, has testified that the novel, far from dying, thrives under such conditions. In the absence of common ground and a pervasive public myth, the novel is free to create its own world.

But the novel did not survive in complete freedom. For the origins of the novel helped to determine its character in the forties. And the culture of America once more helps to explain its fiction. The novel emerged as a literary form with the birth of the modern world. It belonged to the bourgeoisie, and it had an affinity with science. It turned its attention almost at once to money, property, and manners, the chief concerns of the middle class. Its original tradition was observational, realistic, and analytical, as it drew its habits of mind and its mode of discourse from science.

A literary form of this kind should have been perfectly at home in America from the beginning. One would be justified, on the face of it, in assuming its normal development in a country whose founders, in New England, were middle-class Protestants; in a country where, presently, Mr. John Locke became the chief philosopher, with all his intellectual energies bent toward the problem of defining and securing the bright idea of private property; in a country where the Enlightenment, with all its faith in reason and science, in nature's laws and the sovereignty of man, constitutes the heart of our heritage. And indeed such a normal development took place. The American novel has dealt with property, money, and manners in a realistic way. The forties is heir to this realistic tradition.

And it is heir to another tradition as well. For American fiction has been a divided stream. Strangely, given the nature of American culture as I have sketched its origins above, the gothic and symbolic have played a part in American fiction almost from the beginning. The seeds of these literary modes also lay in those origins. Out of the quest for property on the frontier, for example, came the loneliness and terror of the gothic. Out of the Puritanism came the idealism which made a symbolic interpretation of experience thoroughly understandable. Critical opinion in recent years, in pointing out the distinction between the novel and the romance, has demonstrated that the romance as fiction is gothic and symbolic, antirealistic and melodramatic. It has insisted that most American fiction is written as parable and its real life is internal. It has shown how the power of blackness pervades much of nineteenth-century fiction. The forties is heir to this tradition, too. Indeed, often one has the impression that critics feel this is the only tradition at work upon modern American fiction.

But the realistic stream of American fiction cannot be neglected, even though it is clad in habiliments less seductive to the contemporary critical eye. James Fenimore Cooper may have been a myth-maker, but his Littlepage trilogy is solid realism. He is himself a divided writer, belonging to both streams; and both require attention. The same is true of James. He is the author of such conventionally realistic novels as *The American* and *The Portrait of a Lady*, but he is also the author of such ghostly and terror-ridden stories as "The Turn of the Screw" and "The Jolly Corner." And in the forties a writer like Jean Stafford, in whose work the Jamesian shadow is frequently seen, can be wholly explained neither in terms of the dark psychological terror she evokes nor in terms of the acutely observed drawing room she so caustically inhabits. Or when one thinks of Cozzens, where the complex self-division does not seem to appear, one searches for his ancestors in the line of the American novel defined by Ellen Glasgow and Edith Wharton and William Dean Howells and John De Forest.

The symbolic and gothic stream began with Charles Brockden

Brown. In the nineteenth century Poe, Hawthorne, and Melville contributed to it, artists whose deepest spiritual needs, whose intimacy with the terrors of darkness and death, demanded and found symbolic expression. The American tradition which they initiate and carry forward survives in the forties in the work of writers like Paul Bowles and Truman Capote and Carson McCullers, where we see the world of flight, childhood terror, estrangement, and perverted love. We can understand the writers of the forties better for the light that has been thrown upon their predecessors, for the way, in fact, that their predecessors have been identified for us.

Not to labor the point further, then, I should say that the American novel has mirrored two great areas of our national experience. It has behaved like the English and French novel of the nineteenth century part of the time, adhering to the rational-scientific-Protestant-democratic cultural conformation of which it was a part and a product. It has, in short, a realistic tradition upon which to draw. It has behaved, at other times, like the other self, the haunted self, of that culture, the self that had its being underneath the surface of the culture. It has divided in two, and both its parts are still with us in the forties.

While it is accurate enough to see the forties as issuing from this double-pronged tradition, the literary influences, the culture heroes, that at once strike the eye are those who appeal to the gothic and pessimistic impulses, the symbolic and formalistic impulses at play in this generation of writers. The conditions of life for these writers made them, and make us, more sensitive to these particular influences than to those of another kind. The new criticism helped powerfully to enshrine James and Flaubert as models of style and form in the writing of fiction. The work of Cassirer and Susanne Langer on symbolism helped to account for the wide interest in Hawthorne and Melville and for the often perfervid symbolic reading of literature, a tendency which I think clearly affected the writing of some fiction in the forties. Closely allied to this tendency was the exploitation of myth in fiction, encouraged by the example of Joyce and Eliot and possibly influenced by the growth of the myth-ritual school of scholarship. Kafka offered himself as a model of the tortured imagination caught in endless nightmare. Kierkegaard, Buber,

and Tillich gave new life to troubling questions of moral ambiguity and revived interest in the doctrines of original sin and
the Fall.

If these models and ideas were new to the forties — new in the
sense that they were not operative in the thirties or the twenties —
they still did not produce an avant-garde fiction. The forties was
not a period of experimentation in prose. The air of pessimism
induced by the cultural milieu was not encouraging to experimentation. The pessimism of the culture heroes that the period
had chosen seemed to overbear whatever stimulus to avant-gardism those figures might have given. Experiment and innovation
demand the possibility of maintaining extreme positions, a climate agreeable to dissent. Such a climate, as we have seen, did
not exist. Conservative influences in the forties were destructive
of the fascination with change that makes possible a thrust toward
the new and untried in social attitudes as well as in literary forms.
Bohemianism, from which avant-gardism springs, was in the same
ill repute as old-fashioned liberalism, and neither could withstand
the challenge of respectability, which arose in reaction to them.

Other miscellaneous observations may be made about the fiction of the forties. As it was not a fiction of innovation, neither
was it a fiction of broad and generous affirmation. As it was not
a heroic time, we do not find in the writer's imagination a figure
of heroic proportions: the fiction of the forties reveals and confirms the death of the hero. But we do get the full-blown emergence of the child and a preoccupation with childhood. With the
end of innocence comes the yearning for innocence. The dream
of Eden drives the writer's imagination back to the years before
knowledge came to corrupt the soul and complicate the world.
At the same time the end of innocence — or the ending of it, the
act itself — takes on the fascination of dreadful and inevitable
novelty in the American experience, and many writers, thus
compelled, return to the theme repeatedly.

These remarks, while they may be suggestive, do not adequately
frame the fiction of the forties, which demands a pattern much
as the total culture does. Among the possibilities is a regional
framework, in which the fiction is seen as provincial. The difficulties in this scheme of arrangement are that it is not sufficiently
comprehensive, since not all the fiction of the period falls into

regional divisions; and it is misleading, since it does not discern the distinctions in fiction having the same regional provenance. Another possibility is the chronological approach. This would demonstrate the emergence of some kinds of fiction in the decade and the decline of others; it would show the impact of the war on the number of books published. But since much of what chronology has to offer may be seen in a simple table, I have appended such a table at the end of this book and chosen another and more meaningful arrangement. I have divided the fiction of the forties into six sections: the war novel, the fate of naturalism, the new liberalism, the conservative imagination, the new fiction, and the search for man and America. In discussing this fiction, I shall devote myself to the novels, considering, with few exceptions, only those short stories written by novelists.

The war novel, generally speaking, is more important as an historical phenomenon than as an artistic achievement. The variety of ways in which writers responded to the war — their pervasive sense of nihilism, their desperate affirmation, their withdrawal from society and politics — tells us a great deal about the culture of the forties. But since the intrinsic literary merit of the war novel is not great, since the books that came directly out of the war did not herald a renaissance in American letters comparable to the flowering of the twenties, unfavorable judgments have rained down on the entire decade. These judgments, the product of unjustifiable expectations, stand in need of revision. I think we must try to see the war novel of the second war, and all the fiction of the forties, as a product of its own time with its own historical accumulations and cultural tensions to cope with.

Naturalism is the literary god that failed in the forties. Leslie Fiedler has contended that the period was concerned with establishing alternatives to naturalism in a revolt of offended sensibility against crudities of style and excesses of feeling. His view helps to explain the rise of the new fiction, and there, the evidence seems to show, the pessimism of the forties found an outlet in nihilism that overwhelmed consciousness. The impersonal and deterministic qualities of naturalism, rarely accepted fully and objectively by earlier writers, were unpalatable in the forties to the naturalists themselves. Insofar as naturalism survived, it did so, paradoxically, by trying to redeem man, by giving the individual a new importance, by obeying, in short, a major impulse in much of the fiction of the forties.

The sections on the new liberalism and the conservative imagination present two varieties of response to the social and literary culture of the forties. The creative imagination retreated from the frontiers of social revolution, or even social meliorism, and began the painful process of redefining its social assumptions or of asserting with new vigor ideas that had hitherto played a mild and unnoticed part in fiction. Some liberal writers saw that if society no longer fit the liberal formula, then the formula had to be altered. They recognized the collapse of old style, nineteen-thirties liberalism and accepted the lessons learned from the betrayal of Russia, the rise of totalitarianism, and the war. They revised their political ideas, curbed their social aspirations, took a more pessimistic view of man, and still, in the face of all the disabilities which burdened liberalism, asserted a new but now sobered liberal spirit. Conservative writers demonstrated a new assurance in a period more hospitable to them than any other in the twentieth century. The conservative resources of our political heritage and of our traditional way of life, buttressed by a new acceptance of religious ideas and institutions, if not of religious faith, were fully exploited in the fiction of this period. But even in the literature re-assessing liberalism or engaging the conservative mind, one finds a fundamental concern for individual man and a feeling, perhaps a conviction, that all social enterprises are valid only as they assist the assertion of selfhood. The shift in emphasis from society to man, in writers rooted self-consciously in society and engaged at first hand with it, is further indication of that major impulse toward a man-centered fiction that I have just mentioned.

The new fiction, which emerged in the forties, rejected public experience. It is here that one sees the full force of the writer's alienation from his society. It is here that one sees most clearly the writer's reliance on his private vision, out of which he spins the substance of his fiction. The war drove the writer to withdrawal; the social and political scene served to confirm the wisdom of his retreat. The literary influence of both the new criticism and the tradition of romance in the American novel also accounts for the rise of the new fiction. The fine writing and the preoccupation with technique, represented by the new criticism, had its impact on the followers of Henry James, the writers of the new novels of manners. The heavy cargo of symbol and myth shrouded in a gothic ambience, represented by the tradition of romance, made the new fiction positively glow in its distorted brilliance and extravagant decadence.

Finally, the search for man and America, for man in America, is the most quixotic literary enterprise of the decade. For it was conducted in the face of the gigantic conspiracy of history and society to eliminate man. With all forces thus conspiring to destroy the self, fiction set about recording the survival of the self. Its writers understood that its most sacred aim was self-discovery — for themselves and for their readers. Their most desperate, urgent, and yet heartening maneuvers were undertaken in the search for the self, ways of fulfilling the quest for identity or of consummating the process of individuation in the urge toward self-knowledge. The historic charge, the function, of literature has always been to uncover the self. But few periods in history have made the imperatives of that responsibility so difficult to obey. In virtually all the chapters that follow I shall have occasion to remark how fiction of all kinds in the forties confronted this problem of the survival of the self. And the final chapter I shall devote to the question of man's search for identity in America.

CHAPTER TWO

THE
WAR
NOVEL

BACKGROUND: THE WAR BEHIND THE FICTION

Colonel Cantwell is not sanguine about war novels. Some sensitive boys who have had three or four days of combat will write books, but dull books if you've been there yourself, he tells Renata. Others will write quickly and opportunistically, and inexactly. Everyone will write his book, and we might possibly get a good one. So Hemingway in *Across the River and Into the Trees.* He is accurate, mostly. Everyone — everyone and his brother, one is tempted to say — wrote a war novel. Some of these books were dull but a great many were competent. Many were written by men who had not before published a novel and have not since. We have had some good ones: *Guard of Honor,* by James Gould Cozzens; *The Naked and the Dead,* by Norman Mailer; *The Gallery,* by John Horne Burns; *The Gesture,* by John Cobb. We have had many that were less than good but either more than competent or of special interest, like those written by Irwin Shaw, Robert Lowry, John Hawkes, James Jones, Vincent McHugh, John Hersey, and Glenway Wescott. But I think none of the books written about the second World War will have the continuing vitality or the cultural importance of the fiction Hemingway wrote after the first war.

Hemingway epitomizes the response his generation made to that war. He mastered its violence by reducing it to aesthetic form. He was the poet of its virtues and its terrors. He created and lived the code by which men went to war and survived it or died in it: tight-lipped courage, physical prowess and manual skills, ready confrontation of physical danger. When he retreated from war it was to surrender neither the code nor the aesthetics of recording with immediacy and honesty how it really was. He retreated only from the phony abstractions of nobility, honor, and patriotism. It was the act of a disillusioned and frustrated idealist. The anticipatory sense of adventure and excitement, of the possibility for fulfilment, had soured in the mouth. This same curve — up to excitement and down to disillusionment — he had shared with others. Malcolm Cowley testifies in *Exile's Return* that the writers and intellectuals who served in various ambulance corps during the first war subjected themselves to a heady stimulation. We took, as it were, several extension courses, he says, which "taught us courage, extravagance, fatalism, these being the virtues of men at war; they taught us to regard as vices the civilian virtues of thrift, caution and sobriety; they made us fear boredom more than death. . . . The War," he continues, "created in young men a thirst for abstract danger. . . . There were moments in France when the senses were immeasurably sharpened by the thought of dying next day, or possibly next week." The dangers of the war "made it possible to write once more about love, adventure, death." Then later the flame of excitement dimmed. Disappointment, rebellion, utter rejection, moral and spiritual collapse marked the memorable books that came out of the first war, books like *Three Soldiers, In Our Time* and *A Farewell to Arms*, and *The Enormous Room*.

The postwar generation of Hemingway, Dos Passos, and Cummings brought the literature of disenchantment to a very high level. Out of the interaction between the chemistry of their genius and the war came the impressive books that launched their careers. And it was their success that became the curse of the postwar generation of writers in the forties. Critics waited breathlessly but not quietly for the young artists to cast off their uniforms and take up their magic pens, assuming by some quaint analogy to physical laws that the same cause, war, will produce the same results, first-rate novels about the war, written in the same way. These critics suffered from a kind of cultivated blindness: in their orientation toward the twenties, they had prepared themselves for a literature about the war like the literature of the first war. Many young artists, not knowing any better, disregarded their own chemistry and refused to examine the truth of their experience through their own eyes. They tried, instead, to answer to the expectations of the critics. Or if not that, they tried quite self-consciously to see their war as an earlier one had been seen twenty-five years before. This expectation on the part of the literary world and this imitation on the part of the young writers did much to rob the war novel in the forties of originality and freshness of vision and technique.

Hemingway redivivus in the war novels proved to be Hemingway half-baked and half-dead. The trauma of violence and horror in war which he knew, others had come to know. This was a constant in the war experience. But significant differences between Hemingway's time and the forties are easy to find. The twenties emerged from the innocent idealism of Progressivism and the Wilsonian new freedom, from the public avowal of public acts based on principle, to a reality quite suddenly and shockingly different in its unprincipled chaos. Ideals and principles so recently found to be inadequate and inapplicable nevertheless lingered in the consciousness of the writer of the lost generation and gave to his sense of disenchantment the force and pain of a real and anguished loss. The forties was heir to the disillusionments not only of the first war but of the depression and the second war. Innocence thrice violated makes only a spurious protest when it finds the world wicked. The recorded disillusionment of the war novelists in the forties, accordingly, was robbed of much of its strength.

Before the peace of Versailles, Cowley's young men had gone to war with a sense of high excitement and Hemingway's young men with the military virtues that are much the same as the elements of the code. But writers of the later generation did not share in this kind of excitement and did not admire war virtues. Times had changed. No one expected, or wanted to be embarrassed by, moral heroics. In fact, it was said that America did not provide the moral resources necessary to withstand, as one of the risks of war, the terrors of captivity. Survival, not the thought of danger and death, was what preoccupied young Americans. In war we saw the triumph of those civilian virtues Cowley had spoken of.

Americans have always resented the discipline of the armed forces, the special privileges of officers, the interference with one's freedom of movement. It was true of both wartime periods that Americans, as Denis Brogan wrote, were not merely not military; they were anti-military. In the first war there was still some response to the romantic conception of war and the warrior, if not to a military conception. The retreat from romance may be measured in the difference between the recruiting picture of the jaunty doughboy in the first instance and Bill Mauldin's wearily cynical and lugubrious cartoon characters in the second. A drab pall covers the general attitude of Americans toward the second war. An analysis of service men's attitudes, *Studies in Social Psychology in World War II*, shows that most men looked upon the war as a defensive or national necessity. It was a detour without context in the national life. It was a forced disturbance of the normal patterns of personal life. Most men failed to achieve a satisfactory relationship with the military organization or a reasonable understanding of their own role in the nation's war aims. They made no personal commitment to the war. It is not surprising to find that most men were not eager for combat. They wanted jobs in the military organization that would not expose them to injury or death. During basic training the men recognized the necessity for learning two kinds of behavior: expedient, or that which pleased their superiors, regardless of the rules; and proper, or that which was acceptable to their fellows. In discussing their officers, enlisted men were less critical of incompetence than they were of special privileges enjoyed by that group. At the end of the war, three-fourths of the enlisted men questioned agreed that most officers had been more concerned with promotion than with doing a good job. Promotion, the prevailing opinion had it, was primarily but not exclusively dependent on what the men delicately called brown-nosing. Most men, it may be concluded, made a cynical and uneasy adaptation to their military environment and regarded their military careers as a suspension of real life activities. If the war novelist did not actually share in these attitudes of the majority, he did live among them or observe them in some way. They were a part of the climate of his sensibility.

Another difference between the two generations is found in the changing nature of war itself. The trench warfare of 1917

Complexity &
fantastic and —

was very different from the blitzkrieg tactics of the second war. By using war as an instrument of policy, as Quincy Wright observes in his *A Study of War*, the totalitarian states in the forties had forced the other nations into a more complete organization than ever before of their resources, economy, channels of opinion, and government structure for the purpose of fighting a war. Totalitarian states had succeeded in imposing their own policies and practices upon the others. The doctrine of total war was the result, accepted by fascism and the democracies to an unparalleled extent. Wright quotes Hans Speier and Alfred Kahler: "War always concentrates and reveals the potential forces of collective life as they are embodied in the given social organization." The preparation for war, they say, necessitates disastrous sacrifices of human values. Add to all this the vast geographical scope of the second war and the overwhelming technological complexity of arms and armaments, of organization, none of which had been matched in the earlier conflict. It is clear that war becomes less comprehensible than ever before: it defies the single intelligence that would embrace and order it. Before it, the writer's imagination understandably quails. The writer sees that the individual has to struggle constantly against the impersonality of his military organization and the meaninglessness of his activity. The war and the military take their proper place as prime forces working toward the depersonalization of modern man.

In the light of these encouragements to silence and the sweet sleep of the tongueless singer, what did the writer do? He wrote, and produced, paradoxically, a large body of work about the war, as I have said, of reasonably high competence. No other war in American history has been so fully recorded in fiction, from a purely quantitative point of view. And writers covered all aspects of the war on all fronts: combat in the army, the navy, the air force; the activities of service and headquarters troops; the problems of command; the period of training in boot camp or air base; the merchant marine during the war; the liberation and the aftermath of the war in Europe; the problems of the home front in America. The generic use of the term war novel applies to books dealing with any of these subjects.

And when the writer wrote, how did he write? Some writers imitated Hemingway. It has been claimed that Hemingway perfected the language of war, that his style and his manner were peculiarly appropriate to combat, and writers naturally fell back on the remembered rhythms of his language, which had given them, possibly, their first idea of war. Those who imitated Hemingway — Vance Bourjaily, Gore Vidal, Robert Lowry are among them — did not often penetrate beyond the manner. They did not try to record combat as the real thing experienced by one who was there; or when, infrequently, they did try, they did not succeed. They did not seek in writing about the war to purge themselves of the war's effects, as perhaps Hemingway did, if we accept Philip Young's conjecture. They did not, like Hemingway and Crane, too, in *The Red Badge of Courage*, find themselves obsessed with the conquest of fear, and so feel compelled to render the experience of war with vivid accuracy as a meaningful gesture in their own lives. Other writers, like Norman Mailer and James Jones, drew upon the naturalistic tradition in American letters. I am speaking now not of the philosophy of naturalism but of the style. Some of these books showed a cultivated and deliberate contempt for the resources of language, and others appear to have been badly written out of sheer inability to do any better. In general the prose contribution of the war novel, like its originality in all formal matters, was minimal.

And what did the war novelist write about? The writer was constantly tempted by the new nationalism. It had seemed to call for a propaganda art. But even those who were theoretically opposed to nationalism and propaganda in art found themselves coming forward with anti-Fascist positions embedded, says Kenneth Burke, in the very form and style of what they wrote. "For it had become too undeniably obvious that political actions and passions are a major aspect of 'reality' as now constituted. Where motives are vigorously actual, there are the themes of art." From the non-Communist left came the claim that war was a frustrated social revolution and the writer should give it no support. From the disengaged critic came the claim that the writer has no special responsibility during wartime except to himself as an artist.

But the non-Communist left and the critic could not check the patriotic urge. Inevitably there appeared rhetorical war novels and war novels with democratic saints. They constitute a part of what I shall call the patterns of affirmation. This is one of two

major divisions of the war novel that I wish to make. The curious
feature of these two manifestations of affirmation is that the novels
in which they appear rely far more upon the pieties of democracy
than upon serious analysis of political or ideological positions.
These novels do not render in imaginative terms and in the lives
of their characters the dramatic conflict of the felt idea. They
share in the traditional weakness of the novel of ideas in America.
The characters in these novels, and their authors too, had little
understanding of the sweep of history and little feeling for a cool,
long view of the destinies of all nations.

The war novelist was sensitive to injustice and compassionate
toward those who were wronged or victimized by the military
machine. The engagement of his mind and his emotions with the
problems of what have been called the ritualistic victims of our
culture — Negroes and Jews — is a mark of his indebtedness to
the thirties. The social attitudes he brought to questions of prejudice or to the status of the underdog, who is the enlisted man in
this case, were preformed for him in the decade of social protest
literature in which he may have grown up. The rebellion against
mindless, arbitrary authority, which had been directed against
the police in the thirties, was directed, in the war novels, against the
officer class. The patterns of despair, which is the second major
division of the war novel, emerged in part as the frustration of
social idealism in the light of triumphant brutal authority or of
the meaningless military machine. Much of the nihilism in the
war novel, but not all, results from a recognition that democratic
and humane conceptions, the currency of the thirties learned in
that period or taken from it, could not survive in the armed forces
and during wartime.

The war novel, then, has a kind of split personality. On the one
hand it is driven to savage attack because the perceived reality
falls short of the democratic and humane ideal, and on the other
it feels compelled to praise the democratic virtues and the United
States. It is this split which gives me the framework for my discussion of the war novel when I divide it largely, but not finally,
into two groups: those revealing patterns of despair and those
showing patterns of affirmation. In the first group I shall begin
with those novels about the war and the armed forces that reveal
the blank face of nihilism. Then I shall treat those books which

ise out of the frustrated democratic idealism I have mentioned and issue in a politics of despair. I shall close this first section with the novels that make a contrast between America and Europe for the purpose of criticizing Americans and their total ethic and praising the warmth and vitality of Europe. The patterns of affirmation, the second group, give us rhetorical novels and those with democratic saints. In addition, the war novel appears as a novel of ideas in the clash between democracy and fascism. Finally there are the novels in which characters grow to maturity, in which men are regenerated and come to self-knowledge. Two novels worthy of comment do not fall clearly into either of these large groups, and I shall not force them in. One is neutral and objective and the other contains both patterns.

PATTERNS OF DESPAIR

One American critic was so carried away by Hemingway's apparent conversion to democratic orthodoxy in *For Whom the Bell Tolls* that he claimed this novel announced the end of despair and futility for American writers. The emergence of the new lost generation that wrote about the war is alone enough to challenge, if not to invalidate, this assertion. The most obvious response to the war, one might have predicted, would be imitative and nihilistic. Young novelists especially might be expected to speak with someone else's voice and to summon up untapped stores of outraged indignation at the regimentation or oppression of the armed services and the all-too-human conduct of the men in them. These writers are not concerned with reform of institutions or men. What they see is only a confirmation of the cynicism which they had cultivated as the indispensable condition of their seeing at all.

Typical of this violated sensitivity is Vance Bourjaily in *The End of My Life* (1947).[1] This is a novel about four young American volunteers in the British ambulance corps. The protagonist quotes *The Waste Land* and "The Hollow Men." In the college scenes he acts like an F. Scott Fitzgerald sophomore, and

[1] As a general practice, a title is followed by date of publication at that point in the book when a work of fiction is to be discussed. No effort is made to date the first appearance in print of individual short stories, but dates of publication are given for volumes of short stories.

at the end of the book he behaves like a condemned Dos Passos hero. Throughout, he talks, as do his companions, like a mixture of early Faulkner and Hemingway. He suffers from prewar neuroticism, the result of growing up with the knowledge that the war is coming. Dislocated and disoriented by the total insecurity of his position, he is like Saul Bellow's dangling man. But instead of losing himself in the anonymity of the army, this young man gives in to amorality and an uncontrollable urge toward destruction which is tantamount to a death wish. The book is colored by a deep distrust of human beings and by the conviction that the army brutalizes men, forcing them into a life-denying regimentation. The novel is derivative and gauche, of course, but even in these qualities, and in what it says, it speaks for many in its generation. It tries to convert psychological and sociological truths into imaginative truth, but something factitious and something posed and mannered stand in the way.

Williwaw (1946), by Gore Vidal, presents another variety of despair, one found in the purposelessness in the lives of soldiers who do not fight. This novel attempts, in the Hemingway manner, to record accurately and simply the observed scene, as if only physical detail were of real importance because only it can be trusted. One senses a ritualistic tone in the recorded act, as if the act were an end in itself and as if the integrity of the act were all that men had. And, indeed, Vidal's men have little more; they are stupefied with boredom as they run their ship from one point to another in the Aleutians. When the ship encounters a big wind, the second mate murders the chief engineer. Nothing comes of this crime. Vidal does not investigate questions of evil, sin, punishment, morality. It is as if he denies the pertinence of such questions or the possibility of facing them with any salutary results. Life is in the observed but unexamined act.

Other novelists see the war as incomprehensible and meaningless. It is fought by bone-weary troops whose commanders, especially those in the rear, are opportunistic, incompetent, pompous, and cowardly. War leads to the total corruption of man. Any attempt to maintain his ethical standards, should he have any to begin with, only maims a man. "The confusion of a whole civilization," as Gordon Merrick puts it in *The Strumpet Wind*, prevents man from finding himself or from being true to himself. Man can never conquer his enemy, because the enemy is within him in his intellectual and appetitive failures. The wages of war are death and lead directly to the collapse of humanity. In the kind of world which we have made, no expiation of our sins is possible. Perhaps the most fearful and widespread component in this dreary fabric of disenchantment is the conviction that war and the army develop a sadistic, killer-instinct in decent young American men. Judgments about a man's worth in the army are based on his ability to kill, as if to illustrate Kenneth Burke's remark, made in 1950, that texts involving the imagery of killing are typical today.[2]

One of the few successful novels of despair about the war, in my opinion, is a brutal little book, *Casualty* (1946), by Robert Lowry. Written out of a cold fury and with grim economy, it makes its point by understatement and a savagely bitter irony. Its success lies in its controlled passion and in the way Lowry faces up, logically and honestly, to the consequences of his assumptions. In a world where virtually every character is self-seeking and hypocritical, where everything is sordid and nothing has meaning, then even death is meaningless. These assumptions are brought to their chillingly inevitable end by characters who, though they are in the army, do nothing — do not fight or plan the war. They are merely the insensate pawns of a destructive chance. These characters engage only in make-work processes because, Lowry seems to say, if we are to see the whole meanness of war and the men in the war, then we can only see it through men who do nothing.

The army is pictured as an institution that fakes everything. It forces men into hypocrisy because they cannot live up to the military code. Its officers are ambitious only for self-aggrandizement — for promotion and prestige — and they are generally weak and unintelligent. They are without principle, co-operating hap-

[2] Some of the novels that display the patterns of despair upon which I have drawn for the above paragraph are *Night Journey* (1950), by Albert Guérard; *Day Without End* (1949), by Van Van Praag; *The Freebooters* (1949), by Robert Wernick; *World Without Heroes* (1950), by Arthur C. Fields; *A Convoy Through the Dream* (1948), by Scott Graham Williamson; *The Street of Seven Monks* (1948), by William Woods; *The Strumpet Wind* (1947), by Gordon Merrick; and two which I shall discuss later in another context, *The Naked and the Dead*, by Norman Mailer, and *The Brick Foxhole*, by Richard Brooks.

pily with Italian Fascists although their official duty is to disseminate democratic propaganda. The army robs all men of life; they are dead because the army deprives them of will. They must be blank and inhuman, they must be nobody, they must think nothing and stand for nothing, if they are to adapt to the army. Those who act alive or human are of no use. Decent human gestures are impossible in the army. In sum, "The army brings out the worst in everybody." The protagonist in this novel, disgusted by the pettiness with which a meaningless breach of discipline is treated, gets drunk, has a nauseating experience with a whore — an experience in which life is death — and then staggers into the street to be run down by a six-by-six. He is a casualty.

Lowry conveys his attitudes in a bitterly realistic way, which is the case with most of the nihilistic writers. The importance and the interest of *The Cannibal* (1949), by John Hawkes, is that it goes beyond realism. Hawkes has chosen to express his feeling for the dislocations of the modern world, of the world of war, in a surrealistic way, and in so doing has found an appallingly appropriate mode. Surrealism deserts the ordered, rational world of experience because reason has failed both as an instrument of order and of comprehension. It plunges below the empirical world of solid fact in the conviction that reality lies in the subconscious. Frederick Hoffman has defined surrealism as "an attempt to bring directly to consciousness the revelation of the unconscious being." Hawkes makes such an attempt in *The Cannibal*, where a nonsequential illogic dominates the presentation of events, the fears and fantasies of childhood color the gruesome action, desperate but futile flight is an important motif, and a pall of horror lies over all. The novel belongs, then, to the Kafka tradition — an American's view of Europe to put beside Kafka's *Amerika*.

The problem in surrealistic fiction is to create out of the disconnected episodes and out of the discrete symbols some comprehensible and unified vision. Not statement — that is asking for something surrealism is not prepared to yield. Hawkes succeeds well enough in conveying a generalized sense of sterility, destruction, futility, rapine, madness, and depravity which is total in its nihilism and apocalyptic in its force. The main line of the story contributes to this end, dealing, as it does, with a German conspiracy to murder a single American soldier who oversees about a third of conquered Germany and thereby to free and re-create the nation once more. Individual episodes like the riot in the insane asylum or the pursuit, by the mysterious Duke, of the already corrupted child in the bombed-out theater where the projector casts a blurred picture to no audience also contribute. It is a considerable achievement for Hawkes to have created in such gruesome and absolute proportions this unity of mood.

But the book reaches beyond a consistent mood to a full integration of Western disorder, a disaster born of the history and politics and the racialism of Europe. Hawkes does not succeed in this quest for an over-all unity that would give a larger significance to his book. He treats the Germany of 1914 and of 1945, obviously in an effort to weave past and present together and to show the continuity of Germanic blood madness and the persistence of Germanic dedication to lust, leader, and land. But he is not able to transcend the incoherence that his method imposes upon him. He has sought a goal incompatible with his means. Or again, the ephemeral quality of his symbols — carved crucifixes immobilized in pain, for example — denies him the power and the authority to deal with the universal collapse of religious faith. The result is that *The Cannibal* is full of strikingly effective passages which reveal a disaster-ridden and cloacal imagination of genuine merit. They make the book an original contribution to American nihilistic war literature. But their excellence in isolation is the very characteristic that deprives the book of any claim to high importance.

The pessimism of frustrated democratic idealism, another pattern of despair, often seems masochistic in the war novel. Some writers seemed to lash themselves over the failures of men in the armed forces to behave like decent Americans on Main Street who harbored no prejudices against black men or foreigners and who saw to it that everyone had an equal chance. It is, of course, a naïve view of what happens on Main Street. To these writers it is a matter of shocked surprise that those who wield power in the army, on whatever level, behave like Fascist gangsters or petty grafters, or that the liberation does not at once produce liberty and happiness for all. Others write from a deeper initial cynicism about America. Richard Brooks, in *The Brick Foxhole* (1945), sees the army as the product of its society. In our society the law is, Kill or be killed. We call this rugged individualism or the American way. By attacking the 100 per cent American as native Fascist in the army, Brooks is able to write a violent indictment of an American culture that had discarded the humane spirit of justice and tolerance which sustains democracy.[3]

This criticism of America finds its most trenchant expression in Norman Mailer's *The Naked and the Dead* (1948). Here we have a systematic analysis of the neurotic disabilities induced in Americans by the culture from which they spring. In Mailer's view, the United States is a seedbed of psychic insecurity. But this is only the beginning of Mailer's pessimism. For him, naturalism becomes the literary mode of despair; for him, the political history of the American soldier, of America itself in the postwar world, is harshly apparent in the revealed helplessness of the liberal-leftist spirit and the emergent aggressiveness of native fascism; for him, the moral history of the army is the story of spiritual corruption. At the center of this novel is a dramatic conflict of political philosophies which constitutes the most thoroughgoing and sophisticated discussion of political issues to be found in any war novel and which, indeed, makes *The Naked and the Dead* one of the few successful novels of ideas to be written in the entire decade. The pessimism of frustrated democratic idealism finds its fullest expression here.

Mailer manages his criticism of America by introducing a device called "The Time Machine," which enables him to flash back to the civilian life of his characters. He explains their actions and their attitudes in the army as the products of social determinants at home. Among the psychological problems created by the society, the most obvious is racial and religious discrimination. In a dominantly Anglo-Saxon, white, Protestant culture, all minority groups bear the special psychic burden of being outsiders, while those who share only marginally in the dominant culture find their compensations in the superiority and hatred they may manifest toward the minorities. While Mailer may fairly be criticized for the overly systematic and unimaginative way in which he makes these points and the deliberate way in which he as-

[3] Other novels of political disillusionment are *The Liberators* (1946), by Wesley Towner, and *The Crusaders* (1948), by Stefan Heym.

sembles and manipulates the characters who will illustrate his ideas, his documentation of his view is nevertheless impressive. We are made to feel the force of the Mexican sergeant's sense of alienation from the others. We are able to see the genuine pathos of Goldstein, who is strong and efficient, naturally optimistic and gregarious; yet he is obsessed with the feeling that anti-Semitism dictates the relationships of all men with him, and he finds his good spirits and his self-confidence dissolving.

Another source of anxiety and frustration in American life is the demands of a virile sexual idea that most men cannot meet. The entire range of questions dealing with sex-fulfilment as life-fulfilment will possess Mailer in later books. Here he shows how easy it is to fail in the sexual aspects of the marriage relationship in America and how the sense of such failure eats away at the manhood of his characters. The single standard, monogamous ideal is also beyond the powers of his characters to sustain. Failure in either of these patterns robs men of will or reduces them to indulgence in meaningless peccadilloes which cannot give them the psychological satisfactions they need. As success in sex is an ideal, so is success in one's economic life. Again, demands are made that men cannot meet. Characters like Gallagher and Brown are the victims of frightening economic pressures at home which are surely to be related to the insecurities and failures of their sex lives. Polack, to a degree, has escaped economic failure, but he has done so only by going outside legitimate business channels. He is a petty racketeer and the shoddiest product of American urban life. Mailer's indictment is whole and uncompromising.

Given this kind of civilian society, what can be the moral history of men in the army? It is that the army will confer power and position upon mediocrities at best and upon vicious sadists at worst. These military leaders, ex-sergeants and former managers of chain stores, are dishonest and unprincipled; they attain to hardly a shallow intellectuality. They have warped the minds and talents of the younger men in the army and have made them spiritually sick. The disillusionment that has eaten away the ideas of heroism and patriotism rolls out of the poisoned mouths of these officers, as it comes from the society as well. All the forces of moral disintegration combine to account for the episode which reveals the deepest urge toward violence and debasement in human beings: the men violate the corpses of Japanese soldiers found in a cave, Martinez smashing the head of one to pocket the gold teeth.

The political history of the American soldier — in fact, more *politica* than this, of the contemporary world — is written in the unequal contest between General Cummings, who is in command of the American forces on the Pacific island where the story takes place, and Lieutenant Hearn. General Cummings is a proto-Fascist, and Hearn is a confused liberal. The political issues are largely in the hands of these two, but two other characters, named Roth and Red Valsen, also contribute to Mailer's analysis.

Mailer has made of General Cummings a figure who has all *Cummings* the fascination and power of evil itself. A soundly trained military man, he is a brilliant tactician with real qualities of leadership and capacities for organization. He possesses an intuitive sense of what to do in any military situation. With it all, he is a romantic intellectual who strives to grasp the philosophic truth behind obvious propositions of political and military life. This formidable man believes that the reactionaries of the world are on the threshold of a new day. Power concentration is the chief phenomenon of the twentieth century, and fascism is simply the organization of power, directed by men who strive for omnipotence, which is man's deepest urge. In order to achieve the goal, the masses must be made subservient to the power machine. The instrument of enslavement is the fear ladder, on which every man will fear the man above him. Cummings advocates not only an hierarchical class structure in which the upper class will self-consciously develop the appropriate prejudices and assumptions. But he insists also that if an army is to fight well, the officers, by means of the fear ladder, must break the spirit of the men. The men must hate and fear the officers; they must be made to feel the superiority of the officers.

Although General Cummings is made to apply these ideas to a military situation, it is clear that Mailer has in mind a broader referent. We see this in two analogies that Cummings draws. He says that decline is more rapid in time than is growth, and that the curve showing this phenomenon is like the curve of sexual

excitement or the curve of a projectile. The social meaning of
these speculations is that the inertia of the mass blunts the upward leap of a culture. The doctrine is reminiscent of Ortega y
Gasset's theory of the revolt of the masses, which holds that the
masses, in their clamor for status, have watered down and
degraded the culture they inhabit. Purification and re-estab-
lishment of the culture must be accomplished by the restoration
to power of an elite who will exercise aristocratic controls over
society. For General Cummings, this is the desirable shape of
the future.

For Mailer, it is a prophecy of doom that he faces with reluctant but stark honesty. Roth, the sensitive pseudo-intellectual, is
utterly ineffectual in withstanding the power structure of the
army. Red Valsen, a Thoreauvian individualist, is also crushed.
Red had been a hobo with a dimly conceived vision of complete
independence. "I won't take no crap from nobody," he says. But
the lines of authority in the army and the ambition of stronger
men break him completely. The only man of mind and spirit
who might oppose Cummings' view is Lieutenant Hearn. He,
however, is the confused liberal who has not been able to think
through his own position or to find solid ground upon which to
stand. He is the victim of the typical liberal guilt feelings at his
own advantages of wealth and education. Mailer is criticizing
here the liberal sentimentality about egalitarianism which refuses
to admit the possibility of real differences in men. Hearn, in his
discussions with the general, cannot accept the prerogatives and
prerequisites of caste, although Cummings lays before him every
temptation to do so. But Hearn can only take a negative position
of recalcitrance, for he is unable to defend rationally the vague
conviction that democratic man will survive and that power may
be administered equitably. Caught between the hard and realistic
view of the general and his own sceptical hesitation about any
final commitment, Hearn finds himself in the old dilemma of the
liberal: he is in suspension and immobilized. The prey of his
own uncertainties and of the general's arguments, he is actually
killed because of Sergeant Croft. Croft figures as the superb instru-
mentation of Cummings' theories. He is the other strong character in the novel. It has been said that Mailer discovered while he

was writing *The Naked and the Dead* what he had not known before he wrote it, namely, that liberalism was dead. He thought that he ought to defend liberalism, but Hearn and Valsen as its champions turn in his hands into indefensible victims. Cummings and Croft dominate the book.

But in this novel nobody wins. Mailer's pessimism is implicit in the naturalistic literary philosophy that he chose as the very ground upon which his book would stand. The dominant view of experience here is that an over-all futility marks man's every effort. The role of accident in human life is so much more important than that of individual will, mind, or skill that life appears to be meaningless. It is a naturalistic irony that Cummings should devote all his brilliant talents to his campaign to win the island from the Japs only to see victory come through accident, through the blundering efforts of a stupid subordinate, and through a weakness of the Japs that he had done nothing to induce. And it is a naturalistic horror that Croft should lead a reconnaissance behind the Jap lines that discovers nothing and yields only intolerable suffering and senseless loss of life. It is a naturalistic cliché that an insensate world of nature should challenge and defeat man, as Mount Anaka does provoke and conquer Croft, who sacrifices his men and himself to a blind compulsion to climb the mountain. He fails. Although it adds nothing to the pessimism of the book, I should remark that the speech Mailer gives to his characters is in the naturalistic tradition. It has the coarseness and monotony of the vulgate at its most scatalogical level. It seems accurate, as in general Mailer's observation of Americans is.

The serious ideological content of the novel is, on the whole, satisfying, especially as Mailer has made it an integral part of his action, dramatizing it in the conflict between Hearn and Cummings. But one troubling question remains. How can we have as a real threat Cummings' view of a *willed* future and a controlled society in a naturalistic context that assures us that experience is meaningless because chance is all? Only if the coming of fascism is itself regarded as the inevitable wave of the future can we reconcile the basic determinism of the novel with the general's attitudes. One might also object to the flat characters who people the book, almost all of them mechanically conceived in accordance

[handwritten marginalia: unless you see people as free-willed — this round]

with the determinism of the novel. Nevertheless, *The Naked and the Dead*, on balance, is a major achievement among war novels and a remarkable effort for so young a novelist.

To the politics of despair, which Mailer grounds in part on the inadequacies of American society, we may now add another variety of despair — that induced by Europe. The war novelists stood appalled at what Americans had done to Europe, and they were humiliated but at the same time morally revitalized by the endurance and the vibrant sense of life that they observed in Europeans. In both these ways the novelists criticized, by explicit and implicit comparison, their own country and people. The image of Italy was especially fascinating to American writers. Italy seemed to mean everything to them that France had meant to an earlier generation. It seemed to offer compensations for all the shortcomings of America. After the first World War, the intense attachment to Europe and the rejection of America had led to a sizable expatriate movement, which Malcolm Cowley has charted in the classic pattern of exile and return. First the charm and culture of Europe cause alienation from home; then when the wonder of it all wanes, the emigrés come back to try to integrate themselves into American life once more. After the second World War, Europe clearly exerted the same kind of attraction, and the American artist rejected with equal fervor his own country where his place was marginal and his attachments enfeebled. But curiously enough no substantial expatriate movement among writers and intellectuals took place. These people did return sporadically to Europe, but only a few lived there continuously.

Some of the changes that marked the two wars and some of the dissatisfactions with America are seen in Robert Coates's *The Bitter Season* (1946). The novel is of interest because it is written by an expatriate of the twenties about the home front during the second World War. For the protagonist of this novel, the gaiety of Europe had been enthralling in the twenties, and there, surrounded by beauty and intoxicated by the heady cosmopolitan air, he had fallen in love. And now, during the second war, he is having another love affair, this time in the United States with a refugee from Europe. The novel suggests the decay of Europe, a place where love can no longer flourish. And it suggests, in this bitter season, that America is not really hospitable to love but is just the bearable alternative to an intolerable Europe.

In the war novels of the younger writers the Europeans, to make a composite portrait, are human beings who have learned how to suffer. Paunchy, balding men are heroic in their endurance, even though they are not well nourished on orange juice, like their American allies. Italians and Yugoslavs are open and warm in their affections. Their folk culture is genuine. The common man in France is full of sullen resentment at his betrayal, and shame too, but he is grimly determined that France shall be reclaimed from the Nazis. The Americans, by contrast, assume that they are superior to the crude natives by virtue of higher hygienic standards and an Anglo-Saxon heritage. They are, as a consequence, ostentatious and patronizing. They are rich by European standards, and they are pleased to monopolize European women. The novelists generally shrink from the grossness and intolerance they attribute to their American characters. It is worth noting that the principal critics of America in the thirties had been liberals and Marxists. Those who inherited this tradition in the forties, like Irwin Shaw and Albert Maltz, fill their war novels with orthodox democratic affirmations and find no finally harsh word to say about America. It is the essentially apolitical novelists who have revived this international theme, giving a new twist to the Jamesian contrast between the cultures of the Old World and the new.[4]

In the two novels by Alfred Hayes, *All Thy Conquests* (1946) and *The Girl on the Via Flaminia* (1949), Americans are responsible for the corruption of Italy. They have failed to live up to the promises of democracy. They came into Italy on a flood tide of optimism, bringing the liberation. But they have left only frustration and disappointment. Hayes is not original in his stylized judgments: Americans are rich in material goods; they are peasants with technological educations; their women are without passion. Beneath these destroyers who came in the guise of libera-

---

[4] In this paragraph I have drawn from the following novels: *Tomorrow Will Sing* (1945), by Elliott Arnold; *Primer for Combat* (1942), *Avalanche* (1944), and *1939* (1948), by Kay Boyle; *A Bell for Adano* (1944), by John Hersey; *A Time To Go Home* (1951), by William C. Fridley; *Face of a Hero* (1950), by Louis Falstein; and the book by Robert Lowry.

tors, Italy lies in ruins. Its symbols of grandeur, the Colosseum and the Forum, are rendezvous for whores and the dispossessed. Its aristocracy is degenerate. In the episode in which an American forces his Italian mistress to abort her baby, Hayes suggests that the Americans are attacking the very sources of life itself in Italy. Hayes's hostility to America is unmitigated. His bitterness about Italy is, it seems, a measure of his love for that country, destroyed by war and by its benefactors.

John Horne Burns, in *The Gallery* (1947), exploits the expatriate theme most fully and commits himself most completely to Europe. The central strategy of his book is the juxtaposition of America and Europe, of Americans and Italians. In Burns's comparisons, as in Hayes's, the Old World is always superior. To be sure, it is dirtier, it is softer (its men, especially), it is, in American eyes, less moral or downright immoral, but it knows intimately levels of experience never known to Americans. For Burns, experience is more immediate there and understanding of life more profound. Like other war novelists, Burns is convinced that suffering has a salutary effect upon character, and he makes it account for the greater sensitivity and the greater depth of the Italians. The machine-made civilization of America has removed the possibility of pain and thus robbed men of humanity. In Italy, one finds a greater sense of vitality and a larger capacity for love, a more noble sadness and a graver dignity. Confronted with the European experience, the American is seized with self-doubt and a sense of inferiority. As Burns rather crudely puts it, his Chaplain Bascom, a primitive Baptist from South Carolina, ". . . knew at last that there are other forces in the world than the fists of a red-blooded American man." Other Americans who accept Italy, like the Jewish cab-driver or Michael Patrick, fulfil their need for love or music, for responses of sensitivity.

Reading this book, one thinks both of James and Dos Passos. What Paris was for Strether in *The Ambassadors*, the place where he came alive and recognized once for all that one must live, Naples is for Burns and those characters he makes admirable. The cult of experience, which Philip Rahv thinks begins with Strether's famous declaration in the garden, links James and Burns, even as their international literary strategy links them. The similarity may be pushed further, for both rest, not upon the exploitation of idea, but upon the felt quality of experience. In method, however, Burns's book shows the influence of what Joseph Warren Beach has called the collective novelistic technique of Dos Passos. Burns alternates sections called Promenades and Portraits. The first are reflections on the adjustment of Americans to foreign cultures; the second contain the narrative. The central place in the book is the Galleria Umberto, where most of the characters are seen at one time or another. But the real unity of the novel lies in the contrapuntal play of acceptance and rejection with respect to Italy. For the characters who accept, a new dimension is given to life and experience. For those who reject, all the latent meanness and inadequacies encouraged by an American training and environment prove disastrous. The final meaning of the book lies in the tragic shortcomings it sees in America.

Some books stubbornly resist classification as novels of despair or of affirmation, but they are few in number. I should like to comment on two such works, *A Walk in the Sun* (1944), by Harry Brown, and *From Here to Eternity* (1951), by James Jones. Brown's novel is perhaps the most objective effort in the Hemingway manner to record how it really was in the second war. His pragmatic soldiers look upon the war as a dirty job that must be done, and in a bare, lean prose they conduct the business of war in casual half-tones. Mind and heart are deliberately numbed, for there must be no overt recognition of the danger of combat and no attempt to evaluate the meaning of the war. These men understand that war is chance; Brown tries to endow them with grace under pressure. Facing hardship and danger, they nevertheless wear the mask of indifference. Their conversation is a kind of mechanical patter, a persiflage coming off the well-worn top layers of the mind. Brown's unpretentious novel was conceived certainly in reaction against the immense scale of the war which, he must have felt, would resist any comprehensive panoramic treatment. His narrow range is a recognition of how little one could honestly apprehend of the war.

From Here to Eternity falls — I should like to say between two stools, on its face — in both camps: it contains patterns of despair and patterns of affirmation. This immensely popular novel, which has more interest as a cultural phenomenon than as a literary work, is basically romantic in an adolescent way. The stream of romantic rebellion in the novel produces the despair; the stream of sentimentalized and perverse romantic acceptance of the army produces the affirmation.

The major theme of the novel is rebellion against all forms of social compulsion in the modern world and against any necessary or coercive obedience to social forces. The army as an institution and the middle class as the repository of certain life-attitudes and values are the foils upon which the romantic anarchists in the novel impale themselves. They recognize that in the army, where men are counted in the mass, the individual man has no meaning and individualism has virtually no chance for survival. They recognize that in the army, since honor died a victim of the machine age, it has been necessary to resort to fear to control men. The military establishment centralizes power by exploiting fear at every level. This is practically the same argument that Mailer had made in his novel. Jones is less interested, however, in making an analysis of the idea than he is in attacking it. His characters do not bend to the imperatives of the power structure in the army. On the contrary, resistance becomes the essential mode of their beings. Jack Malloy is the model character for this anarchism which insists that a man's responsibility to himself comes before the need or demands of the group. Malloy is a reader of Whitman, whose individualism has bitten deep into him, and a practitioner of Thoreau's doctrine of civil disobedience. Prewitt and Maggio are his respectful followers. In opposing authority, they invite death, not deliberately perhaps, but in obedience to a sucidal impulse which is eventually stronger than anything else in either of them. Prewitt has refused to allow the army to channelize his talents and his energies: he tries to find fulfilment as a bugler and resists the pressure to join the boxing team. But in the unequal contest between the individual and the institution he is overwhelmed. His only recourse is to demonstrate that he can take it, that he has the endurance and the courage to absorb all the punishment that he provokes. This is not so much a death wish as a glorification of the downtrodden and abused who somehow assert their superiority to authority by forcing it into its most brutal manifestations. The hero thus becomes the dispossessed rebel with no stake in the society; he can afford to carry his resistance to every coercive force to its ultimate conclusion, which is death.

The attack upon the middle class in the novel may well begin with its language, which is conceived as a gesture of romantic rebellion. The painfully honest reportage of soldiers' speech is not simply a realistic technique for the grim rendering of army life as Jones knew it. The language is a means by which Jones spits in the eye of middle-class respectability, asserting his right to any form of uninhibited expression that suits him. He repudiates middle-class values by trying deliberately to shock his readers, much as an adolescent boy breaks rules in order to challenge parental authority. Another facet of Jones's offensive against the middle class is seen in the affair of Sergeant Warden with Karen Holmes, the wife of his company commander. This affair is essentially an attack upon the virility of a decadent bourgeois who cannot hold his woman against the powerful sexuality of this he-man from the lower depths. Warden's class allegiances are emphasized when he refuses to accept a commission which would automatically promote him to the middle class. And his superiority to middle-class values is demonstrated in the cynical but ambiguous scene when he breaks off with Karen because he will not be trapped by her middle-class demands for status.

The affirmative note in the novel arises from a perversity and sentimentality that are grounded in the primitive conception of maleness which runs throughout the book. Despite the heavy attack mounted against the army in the documentation of its injustices and brutality, of the ignorance and ineptitude of its leadership, Jones appears to love the army, and he makes Prewitt and Warden love it. And they love it at their own level as professional army men. It is this conception of himself and of his own place that makes Warden turn his back upon apparent self-interest — promotion and a "respectable" woman — and remain where he is. These same notions of virility and place are at work in Prewitt. He leaves the girl he loves, with whom he has been hiding out as a deserter and a murderer, because the war has started and he must take his proper place as a fighting man. Women and love, romantic love, are less important than the army. The army is the perfect setting for a drinking, brawling, screwing life. Jones glorifies the men who live this life and who joyously welcome combat with the Japanese. The paradox of the novel is the paradox of maximum freedom for individualistic expression of fundamental maleness within the framework of iron limitation and discipline imposed by the army. Jones seems to want it both ways, and for this reason he stands between the nay-sayers of despair and the yea-sayers of affirmation.

PATTERNS OF AFFIRMATION

As the war novel appeared in the forties, the current generalization about it centered on the warmed-over pessimism and the forlorn nihilism that I have just discussed. One had the impression that all the war novels fell into the same dead-end of hopelessness. The novelist had no cause to affirm; he was fighting a crusade without a cross, as someone said. But as a matter of fact a considerable number of war novels responded to the demands of the new nationalism with a general and undiluted glorification of the armed services and its leaders or with a flattering version of the democratic ethic and the democratic hero. Others spoke out boldly in the language of religion and love and in the accents of moral consciousness. These books were marked by a determination to face the religious and philosophical issues brought urgently to the fore by the war. Their authors turned in upon themselves, confronting the problems of personal identity and of man's relation to God. Or they probed the mysteries of man's inner resources in an effort to discover the springs of personal growth, and of individual and moral survival in periods of crisis.

The emergence of patterns of affirmation cannot be explained simply as a resurgence of patriotism. In view of the disorder and sorrow of the war period, where, it might be asked, did the writer find the intellectual sanctions and the moral strength to write the novel of ethical sensibility and affirmation? I do not refer to easy, sentimental affirmations, but to hard-won assertion that is always fully conscious of the cost in moral travail of any moral achievement. One source of strength for the writer was the renewed interest in James and Conrad, in this case especially in the quality of spiritual discernment with which they endowed characters who recognized always the stern limitations that life places upon moral fulfilment. A related source was certainly the need for love or faith that the writer felt. It was a time when religious and subjective values had, of course, an increasing appeal to men. W. H. Auden expressed an awareness of this need in a poem called "September 1, 1939," where he wrote, "We must love one another or die. . . . May I . . . Show an affirming flame." And what made such sources operative in a time of intense trouble, I suggest, may be explained by Kenneth Burke's idea of *circumferences*.

In *A Grammar of Motives* Burke is discussing the question: can a man perform a "good" act in a "bad" situation? He argues that ". . . a man is not only in the situation peculiar to his era or to his particular place in that era. . . . He is also in a situation extending through centuries; he is in a 'generically human' situation; and he is in a 'universal' situation." Burke continues by observing that in times of adversity

. . . one can readily note the working of the "circumferential" logic, in that men choose to define their acts in terms of much wider orbits than the orbit of the adversity itself. The "solace of religion," for instance, may have its roots not in a mere self-deception, whereby one can buoy himself up with false promises or persuade himself that the situation is not bad when it is so palpably bad; but it may stem from an accurate awareness that one can define human nature and human actions in much wider terms than the particularities of his immediate circumstances would permit; and this option is not an "illusion," but a fact, and as true a fact as any fact in his immediate circumstances.

The writers of the "affirmative" novels chose something wider than the orbit of adversity.

The rhetorical war novel is one that is unblushingly patriotic in intention, written to persuade us that the war was a noble effort. These novels justify the brutality of the war by arguing that fighting against the nation's enemies somehow completes a man; the only effective rebuttal to brutality is brutality. They justify the submersion of the individual will by declaring that the collective will is an instrument for positive good in a war situation. As for the individual, he will come to see that the habit of obedience brings contentment. They admire without apology the athleticism of the military hero. They regard the officer class as a well-trained, competent corps. The top brass are tenderly concerned for the welfare of the men and will sacrifice them only in order to shorten the war. The habit of command has given them dignity. These novels honor the men who were bred and trained for war and are now able to lead the nation in fighting it.[5] Sartre has a passage in *Existentialism* in which he speaks of the anguish the military commander feels when he sends men to their death and of the dreadful burden of responsibility to these men. Some of the rhetorical novels deal with this problem, but no one of them examines it with the same profound realization of the human dilemma that Sartre expresses.

The best-known novel in this group is *The Caine Mutiny* (1951), by Herman Wouk. This book is a justification of the navy way, an attempt to find the justice of life within the framework of naval law and practice. Lieutenant Greenwald tells us what the war is all about: it is fought to stop the enemy from slaughtering human beings; it is won by a devoted officer class, trained before it broke out; our enemy is the man who destroys confidence in the country's military leadership. If we accept these premises, we must accept the proposition that the law of the navy is good and just because it is the enabling instrument in the achievement of these aims. In the novel, Maryk and Keith, the characters we are asked to like and admire, come into conflict with the law. If Wouk is to be true to his premises, these men should be destroyed. But in fact they escape real punishment. Herman Melville, writing about another navy in an earlier time, understood in *Billy Budd* that when the good man broke the law he had to be killed in order to confirm the majesty and rightness of that law. Wouk allows Keith to become captain of the "Caine" and to claim the girl he loves.

These final results are the components of Hollywood reality, but as a serious commentary on the problem of reconciling the good man with the good and necessary institution they represent intellectual failure and moral cowardice. They suggest that rhetorical motives play too large a part in this novel and perhaps, also, that Wouk is pandering to his notion of public taste. Both these points are reinforced by the way Wouk treats Lieutenant Keefer, the intellectual in his novel. The navy distrusts Keefer

[5] Examples of such novels are *East of Farewell* (1942), by Howard Hunt; *Mask of Glory* (1949), by Dan Levin; *Melville Goodwin, USA* (1951), by J. P. Marquand; *Command Decision* (1947), by William Wister Haines; and Falstein's *Face of a Hero*.

largely because he is an intellectual, and its judgment is borne out when he shows himself to be a troublemaker who is cowardly and unfit for command. The navy, however, has advanced Keefer's brother, who is less bright and sensitive, a simple tool, and finds its judgment vindicated when the brother turns out a hero. The anti-intellectualism of this book is cut from the same cloth as that sanctioned by De Voto and MacLeish and leads to the same demand for the suspension of critical intelligence.

The rhetorical novel tends to be either simple-minded or shrewdly calculating, and perhaps aesthetically and intellectually dishonest. Many of the novels in which the democratic saints appear read like the chronicles of simple-minded hagiography, and they are, of course, painfully sincere. The Italian-American appears in three or four of these books as the standard-bearer of liberty, giving of himself freely to help the Europeans and telling the varnished truth about democracy in America. The democratic saint is not susceptible to original sin. He is only a two-dimensional representation, after all, of the sort carried through the streets in some minor festival. Other saints appear in the guise of junior officers who talk about their willingness to fight and suffer for what men believe in or gentle intellectual types who read Plato on the battlefield and spout the truisms of the liberal democratic faith. In Irwin Shaw's *The Young Lions*, Noah is a kind of Jewish saint, martyred at the end in the cause of humanity everywhere.[6]

This talk of saints calls to mind Walt Whitman, the patron saint of democracy. His spirit broods over the proud affirmations of these novelists. His presence is never more keenly felt than in Vincent McHugh's *The Victory* (1947), where it is explicitly acknowledged. At the heart of this novel are themes that Whitman habitually exploited: the vigorous joy of expansionism, the emotional appeal of international brotherhood, the dignity of the individual human being, and the viability of democracy. Jason Crane is McHugh's democratic saint, conceived as an archetypal American. He is an indigenous product of the West who is thrust

[6] Representative novels in which saints appear are *A Bell for Adano*, by John Hersey; *The Strange Land* (1950), by Ned Calmer; *A Time To Go Home*, by William C. Fridley; and *Tomorrow Will Sing*, by Elliott Arnold. *The Young Lions* is discussed in chap. iv with Shaw's other work.

forward to endure the trials that will test the best that the American culture can produce. Jason is well-equipped for the task. Likened to Daniel Boone by McHugh, he possesses the daring and fighting qualities of a southwestern badman, the inventiveness of a Franklin, and the democratic soul of a Jefferson. He is frankly conceived as a mythopoetic character. Leading native guerrilla forces against the Japanese, he is the instrument of a new manifest destiny that aims at spreading the democratic doctrine and helping the people of the world to freedom and well-being. To the mute accompaniment of Whitman's "Salut au Monde" and "Passage to India" he succeeds.

McHugh is a link in that chain of writers that has included Stephen Vincent Benét, Steinbeck, and Melville, all of whom have charted the westering drive of Americans. All have felt that the ultimate destiny of America will carry us into the Pacific world. McHugh relates the American movement into the Pacific during the war to the "broad stream of American movement in the pace of time" and to the "stream of the American spirit itself." The victory ship to which the title refers is symbolic of the hope in this benevolent and disinterested imperialism. It is symbolic also of the migratory spirit characteristic of this latter-day manifest destiny. The action of the novel includes the search for a missing brother, a quest designed to signify the brotherhood of all men. Jason demonstrates this brotherhood theme among the natives of the Pacific island, who call him *gatsong*, which means buddy or partner.

For the navy hierarchy in the Pacific, the Enormous Presences who think their urine is like wine, McHugh has an undiluted hatred. It matches their own contempt, as he sees it, for the ordinary service man. He regards the distinctions between officers and men as a denial of the spirit of brotherhood. Giving obedience to military authority, McHugh says, produces a moral discord in most Americans. Their will is pre-empted as they squeeze themselves into a dictatorial way of life. Their desire to escape into freedom is so strong that they can never be at ease in the service. At the same time they regard the war as a job to be done, and thus they give grudging acquiescence to the conditions that make it possible to do the job.

Although he is contemptuous of the officer class and aware of the tensions in enlisted men, McHugh has written an essentially "happy" war novel. No other that I know is as deeply involved in the American past. No other expresses such warmth of love for the country and its people. Like Whitman and Wolfe, McHugh wants to embrace all of America. And like them he is incapable of emotional discriminations. *The Victory* is not a profoundly imagined book, and it is often careless and contrived, but it is of genuine interest in finding the American past a source of affirmation and optimism during the war.

The democratic saint, of course, fought the Nazi or Japanese devil. In his triumph, the novel of affirmation finds another form of its expression. For his triumph is proof of democracy's superiority over totalitarianism. This kind of novel had to treat the enemy, which necessitated an imaginative grappling with the character and ideology of Fascists and of democrats. Now clearly the Fascist dogma lends itself to packaging, because it is a more or less coherent ideology; its essence is the bald statement of its propositions. Democracy, as anyone knows who has tried to explain it, is a felt thing resting only partially upon its ideas and institutions. The American novelist of ideas had not in the past been able to give us a democratic literature of lasting interest, Lionel Trilling has said, and is not now writing such fiction. We have established no live sense of active, reciprocal relation between our fiction and our heritage of democratic ideas, nor do we get, Trilling argues, a sense of largeness, cogency, and transcendence from it. These difficulties with democracy are clearly apparent in the war novel, where writers do somewhat better with a more easily comprehended fascism. But the historical inadequacy of the novel of ideas persists; it is only the writers who draw upon the liberal-leftist tradition of the thirties who enjoy any success at all in treating political ideas.

Surrendering the critical stance that the liberal left had taken with respect to American democracy up to the war, writers like Albert Maltz and Irwin Shaw now find blessings in the American way they had hitherto been blind to, especially as that way is compared to the Nazi way. In *The Cross and the Arrow* (1944), Maltz invokes Whitman, using as an epigraph from the poet a passage which tells us that evil fades away and good becomes immortal. Its relevance is found in the claim that even in infested

Germany there is the possibility of good. When the German worker-hero of this novel realizes that he individually must share in the collective guilt of his nation, he repudiates Naziism. Maltz puts his faith in the endurance of human dignity and also, perhaps, in the essential right-mindedness of the proletariat. He assumes that human nature, being essentially good if not actually perfectible, can only flourish under democracy. This Whitmanian optimism, I must say, appears tenderminded and anachronistic in a world that has produced the existentialists, who see the shallow bourgeois notion of human dignity as an astigmatic delusion.

The Cross and the Arrow and *The Young Lions* both rest on the assumption that society determines character. Their picture of the Germans is therefore a condemnation of Naziism. They agree that it eats out the moral fiber and leads inevitably to moral disintegration. They agree that it makes men love lechery as much as killing and war. Its normal channels of action employ suspicion, cheating, and deceit. Its principal political tactic is opportunism. Its soldiers are debased and its ordinary, decent people made into murderers. One must admire the thorough documentation in both novels of the case against the Nazis, but one can only deplore the mechanical air of the examination and the editorializing tone with which Maltz and Shaw handle abstractions. This much can be said for them: they knew what they were for and what they were against; they knew that fascism must be destroyed and the good society created.

Incidentally, some writers tried to escape the Manichaeism of the war in which the Jap or the German is satanic and the American is heroic. Germans were seen as good or bad, or the single man was seen as at once good and bad. A passage in Sartre's *What Is Literature?* suggests that this objective attitude is possible only to those who have not been face to face with the enemy on the battlefield or as a conquered people subjected to occupation. William Woods, in *The Edge of Darkness* (1942), and John Steinbeck, in *The Moon Is Down* (1942), both deal with the German occupation of Norway, and both try to picture Germans as soft and brutal, as loving and hating war. Clifton Fadiman and James Thurber attacked *The Moon Is Down* because its Nazis were not tough, and the *New Republic* wrote an editorial condemning the

soft portrait of the Germans in Steinbeck's book. The imperatives
of patriotism clearly counted for more than aesthetic or psychological considerations in such criticism.[7]

To turn now to the novels of genuine affirmation, which make
the antinomy to the nihilism of Lowry and Bourjaily. These books
are aware of the same crushing forces in the army and the war
itself that those writers see as death-dealing. But the response of
these novels is different, resting on a conviction that the human
spirit is indomitable. No faceless corporate entity can finally ex-
tinguish the individual, they say, and they derive an ultimate
validity for their argument from the intense honesty with which
they confront all the difficulties of their affirmations. These novels
are concerned with the possibilities for individual, willed action.
They insist upon the integrity of the individual, who must not lose
a sense of his self, his own identity, or permit the mass-will of the
army as institution to overwhelm him.

In these novels the individual finds himself through an act of
love or in the growth of his sense of engagement with the magnetic
chain of humanity or in his realization of a sense of community
or brotherhood. Some characters voluntarily return to the war,
a gesture of individual immolation in obedience to some inner
need for personal definition which can only be satisfied through
sacrifice of the self to something larger than the self and outside
of it. Some characters find that the act of love is an indispensable
enabling act in their lives. The act of love is some self-denying
heroic deed; it carries man beyond a desire for mere survival and
dissolves the cowardice and guilt that lurk in his soul. When man
achieves such an act he is released to participate passionately and
fully in life. Some characters grow out of a self-centered, almost
solipsistic state toward responsible involvement in the human
dialogue.[8]

[7] Other novels dealing with the enemy are *Beach Red* (1945), by Peter
Bowman, which gives a simplistic view of the Japanese as murderous little
creatures who are moved to self-immolation by the mad doctrine of emperor
worship; Hayes's *All Thy Conquests*, which makes a genetic study of the
Italian Fascist; and *All Night Long* (1942), by Erskine Caldwell, in which the
Germans are perfect beasts and the Russian partisans are simply perfect.

[8] Representative novels of affirmation upon which I have drawn are *Valley
of the Sky* (1944), by Hobert Skidmore; *An Act of Love* (1948), by Ira Wolfert;
The Wine of Astonishment (1948), by Martha Gellhorn; *Interval in Carolina*

In John Hersey's *The Wall* (1950) we have the documentary novel of contemporary history combined with an effort to get at a timeless theme — the indestructibility of the universal human spirit. Hersey's point in this novel, I take it, is that it is possible for men to achieve their full stature as human beings in a time of deep suffering and deadly peril. This achievement is charted in the growing sense of responsibility felt by the characters of good will for the survival of the group as a group, and as a Jewish group, since this is a novel about the Jews in the Warsaw ghetto. The course of such growth varies with the characters. Rachel Apt moves in a straight line from troubled insignificance as the ugly duckling to guerrilla leader, fulfilled in love as well as in leadership. Dolek Berson, the drifter, undergoes a long process of trial and error before he finally awakes to his courageous destiny. Pavel Menkes, the baker, clings to his atomistic individualism for a long time before he is willing to accept the burden of united action. Felix Mandeltort, in a sense in the service of the Germans, begins by betraying his own people; later he attains peace of mind and composure when he learns that he must accept collective responsibility. Thus he returns to the ghetto when he might have escaped, and there he dies a hero's death.

The regeneration of man is not entirely the result of crisis in *The Wall*. Hersey resorts to two traditional institutions as aids to this process: the family and religion. Since the Germans have killed so many people in the ghetto, or deported them, family units are fairly well destroyed. People of congenial interests therefore come together in groups corresponding to the family and participate in reciprocal relationships necessary to such a group. The warmth of these human associations is increased by the religious ritual that many families engage in. For some of the characters, religion is a new interest, and their spiritual renaissance is a cause of their new claim to human dignity. This search for strength in an ancient religious tradition lends a significant coloration to Hersey's book with respect to the ethical and religious emphases in the intellectual life of the forties.

As Hersey's people oppose traditional Judaism to the Nazis,

(1945), by William Abrahams; *Passing By* (1947), by Elliott Merrick; *Beachhead on the Wind* (1945), by Carl Jonas; and *The Strange Land*, by Ned Calmer.

so Glenway Wescott opposes to the Nazis traditional Greek values. One would suppose that Wescott, who had never been in Greece, chose that country as the setting for *Apartment in Athens* (1945) because its values are most completely antithetical to the Nazi way. Thus the conflict between the Greek and German characters is lifted to the plane of conflict between polar ideas of civilization. In two set pieces, Wescott offers us the political testament of Helianos, his middle-class Greek intellectual, and of Captain Kalter of the occupying Nazi force. Wescott's analysis of the enemy is more anthropological than political, more concerned with the culture characteristics of the German race than with the nazification of the Germans. The Nazis in this novel are mystical worshippers of war and force, with ever the gleam of world conquest in their eyes. Kalter explains that Germany is superior to other nations in making war. The people are indifferent to the outcome, for war is the best part of life and offers the ideal way to die. Kalter believes in the German way of life: love of government and orderliness, confidence in the Germans. The German has substituted for heaven the immortality of his nation; when he dies he finds his reward and vindication in the survival of the nation and the knowledge of its eventual triumph. Yet Wescott avoids an oversimplified picture of the German. Helianos perceives the ambivalence of the German character. Germans are mystical but also scientific, love culture but also war.

The Greeks, for their part, draw their strength from classical symbols and myths, which are Wescott's most illuminating instruments in the treatment of this contrast. When ailing and ignorant Mrs. Helianos, a plaintive bourgeoise, stares out of her window at the Acropolis after her husband's arrest, she is inspired by the grandeur and stubbornness of that citadel, and her own figure quite unconsciously takes on an attitude expressive of its qualities. The bare rock of the Acropolis, which has stood for centuries, gives Mrs. Helianos a feeling of the eternity of Greece. Remembering what her husband has told her about it, she is sustained by the sense of tradition, of intellectual pursuit, of beauty emanating from it. At another point in the novel she tells her children the story of Procrustes and of the demon of daymare and the Furies. It is a recall, in mythic form, of the fierce spirit of the Greeks. Out of the past come those violent barbaric conceptions which temper the reasonableness of the modern Greek and which promise resistance to tyranny.

From such sources comes the strength of the Helianos family, whose members were not meant to be strong. For although they are essentially unheroic, paradoxically enough they give a heroic account of themselves. Aided by their tradition, they fall back upon the resources of the inner being. Even in the performance of routine tasks as they retrench under the whip of the Nazis, their spirit expands. Helianos is a timid man, averse to physical action, willing to compromise. He is ready to give the devil more than his due. He cannot engender the righteous indignation Ruskin so much admired. Yet this quiet little man, falsely accused and expertly tortured, goes to his death like a martyr in the heroic tradition of the resistance. Sartre, who knew about resistance movements and torture at first hand, documents the meaning of Helianos' act, in a comment upon the French resistance. ". . . most of the resisters," he writes, "though beaten, burned, blinded, and broken, did not speak. They broke the circle of Evil and reaffirmed the human — for themselves, for us, and for their very torturers. They did it without witness, without help, without hope, often even without faith. For them it was not a matter of believing in man but of wanting to." Each man in such a situation, as Saint-Exupéry put it, was his own witness.

Helianos' hypochondriacal wife emerges from her traumatic experiences with a re-educated mind and a strengthened body. At the end she is planning to betray a German major to his death and to throw her own children into the resistance movement. Greece is resurgent in her and her daughter Leda. In a way, it is justifiable to say that Wescott has made a humanistic reply to MacLeish's cry of irresponsibility. But perhaps more may be said without fear of rhetorical excess: Wescott has tried to find what resources of spirit and mind the individual could call upon in the forties.

As Wescott deals with the individual capacity to expand, a lesser known writer, Leon Statham, faces the problem of man's discovery of his own identity in an effort to survive during the war. The problem in *Welcome, Darkness* (1950) is much the same as that in Conrad's *Lord Jim*, and in fact the resemblance between the two books is close in other respects. Statham begins with a quotation from Ortega y Gasset: "Man is constantly getting lost; but being lost is actually a dramatic privilege and not an evil. When lost, the man who has faith turns himself into an instrument of orientation to guide him and to return him to himself." Very similar is Stein's dictum in *Lord Jim*: "In the destructive element immerse." Jim's salvation comes only when he subjects himself to the supreme test, when he is ready to give up his life to sustain his notion of his own identity.

In Statham's novel Omar Mills welcomes darkness, the destructive element, as the testing time. He feels guilt and fear, for he has murdered a man; and he must face the problems of pride and leadership as well as the imminence of torture and death. From his trials, his darkness, he emerges as a whole man who knows himself because he has been able to expiate his sins. So intense were these trials, which he survives, that he is now equipped to live in the modern world, for he can face any darkness. While the social aspects of this novel are subterranean, it is clear that Statham conceives of life in society as barbarous and killing. The group of officers in the story who try to escape together from the Japanese-held Philippines may be taken as a microcosm of society. The group dissolves in petty jealousies and hatreds and reveals the insubstantiality of co-operative social action, which men resort to only when it is necessary for the survival of life. Statham wishes to say, I believe, that social patterns have collapsed and man can continue to exist as man only by virtue of his inner resources.

It is the moral and psychological crises that are important in this novel. They are resolved in a way suggestive of religious solutions, especially since Mills's principal act of expiation is to assume, in all humility, the Christian duty of saving another man. Yet when Mills finally casts off the darkness, he is not in a triumphant mood. He soberly recognizes the high cost of self-conquest and the need for the hard, interior strength that man must bring to life.

The concern with ethical modes of action in secular terms is best demonstrated among the war novels in *The Gesture* (1948), by John Cobb (the pseudonym of John C. Cooper, III), and *Guard of Honor*, by James Gould Cozzens. Both books deal with the problem of race relations, but the point of attack is moral and philosophical. I shall discuss *Guard of Honor* in another place as an example of ethical realism; here I want to consider *The Gesture* as an example of the romance of ethics.

It is organized around an examination of the varieties of moral experience. Each of the principal characters takes his own particular view of responsibility and brings to bear his own kind and degree of moral courage. Major Harris, the commanding officer, is a stiff-necked, unlovable man of principle. His principles are related to social action with respect to questions of leadership and responsibility in a democracy. Harris believes that because he has the advantages of education and social position he is qualified to lead, that, in fact, these advantages impose the burden of leadership upon him. Accordingly, he thinks that some men are better fitted to lead than others; these are the officers and gentlemen. This is a denial of democratic egalitarianism and of the spirit of barrack-room camaraderie. Yet Harris is really fighting to serve and save democracy, not only from the external enemy, but from the proto-Fascists within. Having lost his faith in God, he expresses his morality in this social gospel. Since man must believe in something, Harris believes in the welfare of mankind, and to this end he devotes himself. In the novel, therefore, he tries to integrate white and Negro troops in order to end segregation, but he fails. In the end, he undertakes a dangerous secret mission that another flier should have carried out, and he is killed. This is the gesture that gives the story its title.

Cobb treats Harris with an illuminating irony. The good man is accounted a prig and a snob, and with some justice, because Harris, clinging to his principles, never seems quite human. What is said of Ferrovius in *Androcles and the Lion* is true of Harris: "There are men in whose presence it is impossible to have any fun: men who are a sort of walking conscience." An even more devastating irony is that the good man fails in social action. He does not succeed in ending segregation or on his secret flight. For the selfless and dedicated man, the best intentions produce disastrous results. Evil comes out of good, the inverse of the irony in *All the King's Men* where, for Willie Stark, good comes out of evil. Yet the irony is not pervasive, for Harris reveals in conversation that he seeks self-knowledge. He realizes that a man must know himself and fight himself, and he achieves both goals, as his final self-immolating gesture indicates. As Susanne Langer reminds us, Freud taught that human behavior is a language and every movement a gesture. Symbolization, she says, is both an end and an instrument. Harris' gesture is the symbol of his principles, which are his instruments, and of his attained self-knowledge, which is his end.

Apotheosis of mankind, however, is far from Cobb's aim. He is obviously of the opinion that man is a flawed creature, and if the portrait of Harris does not make this sufficiently clear, then the treatment of the other characters does. Harris functions in the novel as the point of reference from which the other characters fix their moral attitudes.

Whipple, the bombardier, is like Harris in that he comes from an established family. But he hides or minimizes his background because aristocratic differentiation, like extraordinary achievement, represents, in the eyes of his fellow officers, a violation of the democratic code. Moral superiority is suspect and its consequence is alienation from the group, the fate Harris suffers. Whipple chooses the warm glow of comradely acceptance and approval and refuses to defend the moral austerity of Harris. His choice is symptomatic of his general moral failure. His place in the moral scheme of things is amply demonstrated in the way he takes refuge in the army's structure — he does only what he is ordered to do. In this way he is absolved of personal responsibility. He never finds the courage to live the life of principle.

Mulrooney, the navigator, is also an educated man of good family. He has, he says, standards of behavior. This background enables him to understand Harris's moral qualities, but it is not sufficient to make him support Harris actively. Spiritually lost, Mulrooney suffers from a moral blackout, and while he is still able to perceive the difference between good and bad, his moral will is paralyzed and he cannot act. He does his own job, although he is really afraid to make a searching inquiry into why he bothers to do even that. The operations officer reveals another variety of moral experience. A completely ordinary person, he is insecure in a position of authority. Nothing in his life prior to the war has prepared him to understand the problems of leadership and responsibility the war thrusts upon him. He is a man of good will who is frustrated because American life had offered no clear-cut moral standard for him to refer to in crisis.

When Whipple tells us at the close of the book that psychiatric treatment had rid him of his sense of guilt but that the psychiatrists had not exorcised his moral flaws, we can understand the farthest reaches of the problem Cobb is trying to deal with. He is not interested in simply opposing common sense and expediency to principle. This book has a moral life of its own because Cobb poses his problem against the frank recognition of human imperfection and limitation. He senses the full difficulty of the moral life lived on a naturalistic plane, where motive and reward must be spun out of a man's inner being. The quintessence of humaneness is in man standing alone, making the decision he must make to affirm his respect for himself and others as men. Cobb is asserting the nobility of moral aspiration in the face of obstacles inherent in the character of man.

The interpretation of morality in the war novel, as everywhere in the fiction of the forties, is predominantly secular. Here and there a religious tone is to be detected, but only one thoroughgoing religious novel came out of the war, as far as I have been able to discover. This was *The Weight of the Cross* (1951), by Robert Bowen. A Catholic novel, it considers the question, phrased by Father Mapple in *Moby-Dick*, of rebellion and obedience: "And if we obey God, we must disobey ourselves; and it is in this disobeying ourselves, wherein the hardness of obeying God consists." For Tom Daly has rebelled against his father, the captain of his ship, and the Church. He has spurned every form of earthly authority. He is a murderer. He is, in short, the degraded, sinning Catholic of the type who breathes so painfully in the pages of Graham Greene. Like Greene's characters, he can never finally break with his religion, and he suffers from a terrible sense of guilt. He endures the dark night of the soul and comes in the end to live by the dogma as the inescapable way of life.

The dreadful struggle to find himself and return to his faith begins for Tom when he admits that it was no more than a desire to kill that led him to murder two Japanese soldiers. This is confession, and it is the beginning of redemption. Then Tom and his companion are captured by the Japanese and tortured. A

Japanese sergeant asks Tom if he is a Christian. It is a test, for if Tom answers yes the Jap may kill him, and if no, he will appear to have denied his faith to save his life. He has been saying that he hates Catholics, all Christians, presumably. Yet, for reasons he cannot understand, he answers yes, and then he says he felt absolutely safe for the first time in his life. He now knows that he believes in God. The next step in his absolution is the knowledge of love, for man and for God. Because men are brothers he loves his friend and, in a self-sacrificial act in which both men are crippled, saves his life. He loves a Filipino in the prison camp. Love is necessary because "Life begins with a pang and ends with an agony and . . . no man is strong enough to live it alone."

For Hemingway, in *To Have and Have Not*, where Harry speaks similar words, and in *For Whom the Bells Tolls*, this doctrine meant the acceptance of the brotherhood of man and the possibility of concerted social action. In the context of Bowen's novel it reveals men's interdependence as part of their total dependence on God. But Tom has not loved the Filipino wholeheartedly. When the Filipino dies, his name remains on the roll, and he must be accounted for. Each morning it is necessary to dig up his grave to expose his face. Tom does the task: it is his penance for a want of trust in man. Through it he loses his sense of guilt. He puts on the crucifix the Filipino had given him, for he has earned it, and the "weight of the cross was very light on his chest." Near the end of the novel, when Tom has conquered his paranoia and when he feels cleansed of sin and guilt, he thinks that the event that brought him back to faith could not have occurred by chance. "There was a plan in all of it that was greater than he could make out, a force that seemed to guide his every move. . . . He grasped no more of its scope or purpose than the simple fact that it controlled him. . . ." And so finally it is a cosmic teleology that dictates Tom's fate.

Although the end of the novel is inevitable, given the religious assumptions it rests upon, Bowen drives his character so far into the depths of degradation that the release, known and anticipated before we come to it, is a welcome escape from tension. While the order of events leading to absolution appears contrived, the thrill of redemption, especially of a character so close to damnation, persuades us to overlook much of the artificiality. Bowen makes his strongest appeal, however, with his tough-minded view of life as pain endured, believing that men must subject themselves, as Hawthorne put it, ". . . to earth's doom of care and sorrow, and troubled joy." Whether this be a religious view or a Catholic view is of no moment. It is the sobering truth generalized enough for this generation of men to whom it is addressed. When, after an incredibly difficult struggle with himself, Tom walks out of the Japanese prison at the end of the novel, he is absolved of guilt but he is not triumphant. He walks under the grim knowledge that all human beings carry a heavy burden of sin, and he knows what it is to have been in deadly conflict with oneself.

What Tom gives up, as a result of this conflict, is the individual self in the recognition of God. And so we come back to the theme of rebellion and obedience. As rebellion against authority in the interest of idiosyncratic, and criminal, action gives way to the acceptance of authority, Tom comes to feel that people have to be told what to do. Command does not include explanation. "The one in charge is above right and wrong anyway because he makes them." And he is apart from men. The passage suggests that submission of the individual will to God ought to be symbolized in the submission of the will to those in authority here on earth. Tom comes, in fact, to this view, and even willingly accepts the authority of his Japanese captors.

In the end we can return with profit, I think, to the circumferential logic of Kenneth Burke. It helps to explain those novels in which social problems appeared to be the primary interest, but where in reality the conflicts and choices involved moral issues and questions about the nature of man. While some novelists chose to make their affirmations by dealing with the public and immediate aspects of the war, others chose a far different circumference. These circumferences show a variety appropriate to a democratic literature, in that no particular value system — pragmatic, humanistic, Christian — has been agreed upon. But there has been limited agreement among the novelists of affirmation to go in quest of value rather than to deny its existence or validity. The heightened moral consciousness in these writers, even where there is no well-defined moral referent, and the temperate optimism about man reveal a way of apprehending experience that is soberly hopeful. The contrast posed is not to the negativism of the twenties alone but to the heirs of that negativism in the war novels of the forties. The contrast, further, to the social determinism of the thirties is in the man-centered focus of these ethical novels. They give a distinctive and unexpected tone to the novel of the second World War.

CHAPTER THREE

NATURALISM: THE TACTICS OF SURVIVAL

THE MEANING OF NATURALISM IN THE FORTIES

The history of American fiction in the twentieth century is marked at its beginning by a surge of interest in naturalism. Indeed, it was in this period the dominant literary mode, influenced by the theory and practice of Zola, appropriate to a period of growth for strangely new and important forces in the national life like science, industrialization, and urbanism. It produced one of the giants of American literature in Theodore Dreiser. Carried forward by Dreiser's contemporaries and successors, it became one of the continuing forces in American fiction. In the thirties especially, when a literature of social relevance, of social protest, absorbed the creative energies of writers, naturalism was the most respected and firmly established way of writing. Yet in the forties, after a reasonably lengthy and distinguished career and on the heels of such intense cultivation in the preceding decade, naturalism found itself struggling to survive. Such a dramatic turnabout in literary history deserves explanation.

The ground for literary naturalism was broken, it is obvious, with the advent of Darwinian science; it was fertilized as a result of the increase in technology and urbanization that came from scientific progress in general. Literary history has long recognized how science marked the naturalistic writer, turning him toward determinism and mechanism and inducing in him a pessimistic bias, and how unsteadily he maintained these beliefs and attitudes, which were often diluted by a kind of social idealism. Science marked the naturalist, further, by convincing him that reality was accessible to those who used the methods of scientific investigation. The dispassionate observer of the external world had only to record objectively what he saw in order to capture the quintessential, the only, reality. Everything was on the surface and was visible to the naked eye. As Philip Rahv has said, naturalism in effect took reality for granted. But during the forties, the crucial question for scientists and writers alike was precisely this matter of the nature of reality. As I have indicated earlier, it was as a result of increasing dissatisfaction with materialistic philosophies, in good part associated with the rejection of Marxism, that a debate developed over the nature of reality. In the shift away from materialism to an interest in Kierkegaard and other religious writers, fiction saw an opportunity to turn inward to examine the spiritual aspects of being, which were regarded as a valid part of reality. The entire development of psychoanalysis also exerted its influence in the same direction, attributing reality to what was indwelling and hidden. The main drift of the fiction in the forties — a turning inward to the self — is perhaps explained by this shift in how reality was conceived; and such a shift also may explain why the writer deserted naturalism.

Furthermore, the naturalist has always had to face certain failures of technique which were made obvious in an age of criticism that began to frame an aesthetic for fiction. The principal technical dilemma that naturalism found inescapable came from the presuppositions of its philosophy: its task was to record fully and honestly a life without plan and to capture objectively undefined social experience; but its discipline was art and its form the novel, which demanded selectivity, definition, and arrangement. In denying that discipline, naturalists were found guilty of what Yvor Winters has called the fallacy of imitative form. In trying to imitate the formlessness of experience, they had surrendered to matter instead of mastering it. The contempt for aesthetic means traditionally expressed by naturalistic writers was, of course, no valid escape from the dilemma they faced in reconciling life and art. And the bad writing which marked their books was still another reason for rejecting them in a period when writers and critics were so self-consciously aware of stylistic considerations.

Logically, naturalism should not have survived the world of nineteenth-century industrialism and science which produced it. But logic does not govern the writer's approach to his material nor does it remove social maladjustments that might arouse a writer's indignation or compassion. Naturalism lingered, then, into the forties, but its hold on life was marginal. It was a survivor from an earlier time; it did not make a vital and lasting impact on the fiction of this decade. Individual naturalistic novels, like Mailer's *The Naked and the Dead*, stand out, nevertheless, as genuine contributions to American fiction and belong, in historical time at least, to this period. And at least one naturalistic novelist, Nelson Algren, came to the full maturity of his powers in the forties. A history of the fiction in this decade cannot ignore naturalism, but does it no injustice by viewing it through the small end of the telescope: curiously enough, such a perspective brings it into proper relationship with the total body of fiction in the forties.

THE SURVIVORS

As the decade opened, one could not easily have predicted the dismal fate of naturalism, for it had a tradition to build upon in America and a successful past immediately behind it. But it seems to be the case that some writers in the forties lived on as though time had a stop, in fact had stopped before the forties came. They lived on what they were in the thirties, or what they had learned then, or on what they had started then and had to complete later. These are the survivors, the writers who clearly belonged to an earlier time: James T. Farrell, Erskine Caldwell, and Richard Wright. Farrell, in fact, was mid-way through his Danny O'Neill tetralogy when the decade opened. He persisted throughout this period with that honest persistence that seems to be one of his chief virtues. He affords us, accordingly, a beginning point for our discussion of naturalistic fiction.

During the forties Farrell completed the O'Neill series with *Father and Son* (1940) and *My Days of Anger* (1943) and began the Bernard Carr series with *Bernard Clare* (1946) and *The Road Between* (1949), in addition to publishing other work. The second series seems a continuation of the first, since at the end of

My Days of Anger, Danny O'Neill leaves Chicago for New York to become a writer, liberated from all the forces that at once both shackled and shaped him — religion and the Church, family, friends, neighborhood — and *Bernard Clare* opens with Bernard in New York, liberated from these same forces, which he has left behind in Chicago, trying to become a writer. The four volumes I have named, although belonging to different series, represent a continuing enterprise for Farrell throughout the decade.

The comprehensive pattern in the two volumes of the tetralogy, *Father and Son* and *My Days of Anger,* is in the opposition generated between the forces that have made the predetermined circle which defines Danny's life and his effort to escape from these forces. The first of these determining forces is Danny's family background or what might be called the Irish-American culture. Farrell reveals Danny as enmeshed in an Irish character that constantly shows failures of self-discipline; that oscillates wildly in a manic-depressive cycle, rising unaccountably to the caress and dipping to the curse; that is subject to a maddeningly self-destructive piety; that is full of self-pity which easily extends itself to a total *Weltschmerz*; that is coarsely and unmitigatedly anti-intellectual. The second of these determining forces is made up of economic and class factors. The O'Neill and O'Flaherty families live under the constant pressure of economic insecurity, which is always threatening to become economic disaster. The death of Jim O'Neill, a workman who never penetrated beyond the periphery of society, is Farrell's indictment of the broken promises of American life. The poverty that forces Danny to work his way through the University of Chicago and handicaps his intellectual development is evidence of Farrell's insistence on the shaping role of economics. Out of this economic struggle comes a feeling of inferiority at failure to achieve status as measured in money and things. Over the O'Neill books there broods, then, a generally pessimistic view of life. It is fraught with intolerable difficulties. This view gives authority to Farrell's determinism as it leads us to admire Danny's escape. The pessimism is enhanced by the approaching death of Jim O'Neill, for we are made aware of the constant presence of death in all life. By the force of his relentless accumulation of detail in *Father and Son* especially, Farrell raises the pathos of degeneration and the failure of communication between the generations almost to the level of tragic vision.

The naturalism of these Danny O'Neill novels lies principally in Farrell's treatment of both the large social environment and the more intimate family group. His characters are people to whom things happen. In the Bernard Carr books (the name of the protagonist was changed from Clare to Carr in the second volume after a libel suit) the naturalism is expressed in a feeling for the incomprehensibility of life. A certain mysticism in the earlier Farrell volumes, strange as that may seem, should have prepared us for this. But its real development is in the formal conception of *The Road Between*, which has the formlessness, and therefore the mystery, of life itself. The book tries to convey a sense of the life flow with all its variation, its energy, its interruptions, its casual accident. The events are not organized into a pattern. In Bernard's stumbling growth toward self-realization as a writer, Farrell relies upon an episodic technique which draws upon the daydream or the ambiguous moral relationship in an indiscriminate succession of non-related sequences. His naturalism is expressed in the very flux of formlessness itself. And yet, he is so singlemindedly devoted to what he has seen and felt and so stubbornly intent upon shoving it all into his book, repetitious as it may be, piling it all into a mountainous mass, that a kind of miracle seems to take place. Finally, his vision leads beyond the rush of discrete detail, and what he has to say takes shape, becomes coherent, despite its apparent shapelessness. It is a miracle Farrell cannot always invoke. *My Days of Anger* and *Bernard Clare,* and the impossible *Ellen Rogers* (1941), which belongs to the south side of Chicago but not to either of these series, do not have this quality. But *Father and Son* has it, with its compassionate treatment of disintegration and growth, and *The Road Between* has it. Farrell's clumsiness and his gaucherie lead us to expect a bluntness of feeling, but they cannot quite obscure the large areas of his sensitivity in his successful books or the moving insights he is capable of. In the end one must conclude that his work is uneven because he seems to be at the mercy of a method that he cannot control, a hazardous method no more susceptible to control than life itself.

Like Farrell, Erskine Caldwell is able to make a compassionate

15912

response to his characters. It is the sympathy that one extends to the victim who is helplessly ensnared in a situation he cannot control. For one can see, among the novels that Caldwell wrote in the forties, evidence of both biological and environmental determinism. And one sees also a fascination with feckless characters whose natural state is a condition of advanced depravity. These are the marks of the naturalistic writer, but of one who does not lose sight of the possibilities in the human personality, even though it may not possess the power of will. Caldwell's essentially grim view of human experience is combined with an admiration for the humorous and stoical way in which his characters try to make adjustments to the hostile world in which they live. While his dedication to personality is often rewarding, it is not always compatible with the mechanistic view of man and nature demanded by the premises of naturalism. This incompatibility often vitiates the effectiveness of Caldwell's work. But his weakness is not simply in his failure to preserve the doctrinal purity of naturalism. It is that he makes a kind of grinning acquiescence in the antics of his miserable poor whites to whom he attaches an inherent value as isolated phenomena: the characters become for him a good in themselves, but for us they are a dubious good.

Two novels may be cited by way of illustrating these propositions. *Tragic Ground* (1944) gives us a shanty-town environment which creates the character of the people who live in it. It is the inevitable locale for a man, like the protagonist, who was born poor, will die poor, and who will not be anything but poor in between. The natural conditions of man in this milieu are idleness and hopelessness, poverty and starvation. Each of these qualities feeds on the others in a vicious, unbroken series. Even the finest folk in the world, one character says, would get mean and bad if they lived in a place like this. *The Sure Hand of God* (1947) suggests in its title the operation of divine providence, but the determining forces in this novel are social and biological. These forces bring Molly Bowser and her daughter to a life of cruel loneliness and prostitution in the most disreputable part of their town, despite every effort that the ingenious and vigorous Molly can make to escape so miserable a fate. But no escape is possible in Caldwell's world. He is apparently as pessimistic as other naturalists, his characters are low-born, his environments are desperate. Still, no useful generalization about man's lot emerges from his work; no conviction of cosmic despair justifies the naturalism.[1]

A final literary survivor from the thirties is Richard Wright, who published *Native Son* in 1940, adventitiously appearing to sum up in that book the depression decade. Robert Bone, the historian of the Negro novel in America, does feel that Wright extends his influence into the forties, although the more dynamic force shaping the Negro novel then is the war. Yet it is worth remark that the Negro novelist, whether or not we admit the category of the Negro novel, was in bondage to naturalistic fiction during the forties. Ann Petry and Willard Motley seem to have followed Wright's lead. It is not accurate to say that social protest had passed into the hands of the Negro writer. But it can fairly be said that Negro authors used naturalistic techniques to make vigorous and profoundly moving protest in this period.

Native Son has its sources clearly in the American naturalistic tradition in literature, but draws also upon Wright's experience with the Communist party and his attitude toward the urban experience of Negroes. Wright has told us how he came to communism because he thought the movement was embarked on a search for the truth about the lives of the oppressed. In an *Atlantic Monthly* essay which was later incorporated in *The God That Failed*, he writes, "Of all the developments in the Soviet Union, the way scores of backward peoples had been led to unity on a national scale was what had enthralled me." The novel utilizes Communist ideas, but they do not provide a resolution of the Negro problem, or of Bigger Thomas' individual problem, for Wright; they stand, as a consequence, on the periphery of the book. Closer to the center of what Wright tries to do in *Native Son* are certain sociological concepts which Wright may have drawn from the University of Chicago school of sociology. In two

[1] This discussion does not pretend to cover all aspects of Caldwell's work in the forties. But the quality of his contribution does not merit further consideration, to put the matter baldly. Nevertheless, for the record I should say that I have neglected his social protest, which allies him to the old liberalism, and his grotesque characterizations, which ally him to the southern gothic spirit. In addition to the books mentioned above and his war novel, his published fiction in the forties includes *Trouble in July* (1940), *Jackpot* (1940), *Georgia Boy* (1943), *A House in the Uplands* (1946), *This Very Earth* (1948), and *Place Called Estherville* (1949).

essays published in *Twice A Year*, he attempts to assess the impact of the urban experience upon a simple, folk people like the southern Negroes, showing the overwhelming difficulties they face in trying to adjust themselves to a white, urban culture in which the machine is dominant. He concludes that in the city especially the Negroes are really a colonial people who are forced to live side by side with their exploiters. As a consequence, the Negro is the victim of serious psychiatric disorders. He is subject to what Horace Cayton calls the fear-hate-fear complex. The Negro, living in a hostile environment, and a highly complex one that he has not mastered, is a creature of fear. He comes to hate a society, the white man's, which constantly attacks his personality. Quite naturally he extends his hatred to the white man. Then he realizes that he will be punished by those who are strong in that society if his emotions are discovered; he becomes again a victim of fear. This emotional cycle should help us to understand when Wright tells us that Bigger is a compound of violent, displaced Negro boys he has known: dispossessed, disinherited, the product of a dislocated society.

The novel opens with a conventional symbol for naturalistic prose, one drawn from the animal world — a rat cornered and killed in the Bigger Thomas home. This is the promise that Bigger will fulfil his destiny. And he does, when he inadvertently strangles a white girl out of fear and confusion and panic. He had always known that something was going to happen to him. So the novel runs its inevitable course: he murders again, he is caught, tried, and condemned to die. He is the helpless Negro, choking on his rage and frustration in the white man's world where his very humanity is denied. Violence is the only response possible for him in this world, and violence as part of the Negro consciousness is intrinsic to the novel. Wright himself cannot control it, and it becomes the substitute for thought and for solution of the social and psychological problems that Bigger represents. Wright seems so outraged at the affront to human dignity which he has figured forth in Bigger's plight that he finds great difficulty in assimilating his feelings for presentation within the limits of the novel. If he succeeds at all, he does so by transcending his sense of outrage, using for the purpose a strategy of total desperation. He declares as the theme of his book that life is in death. Bigger is released from the bondage of the white society only when he takes a hand in making his own fate; and he can do that only when he kills. As a killer he becomes an individual. The murders and the trial give him a personality that others are forced to recognize. In fact, they give him life.

NEW VOICES, NEGRO AND WHITE

If the heart of Wright's novel is his indignation because the Negro is not acknowledged as a member of the human race, the lesser issue is the social protest that he makes. He criticizes attitudes of white superiority, the guilt-hate complex of the whites, the tie-up between politics and justice, the economics of Negro housing in metropolitan areas, the failure of equality as Communists and democrats practice it. Other Negro novelists carry on the line of social protest in the naturalistic novel during the forties. In Ann Petry's *The Street* (1946), a tightly plotted and competently written book, black skin leads to poverty, poverty leads to confinement in an undesirable environment, and the environment or the street inevitably leads to frustration of decent life aims and then to crime. The street is the antagonist in this novel. The protest is that decent human beings are ruined by social forces they cannot come to terms with. Willard Motley's *Knock on Any Door* (1947), in which the characters are white, incidentally, voices its protest in all the stereotypes of naturalism. With plodding doggedness, Motley documents the overpowering influence of a slum environment on his hero who ends, predictably and at long last, in the electric chair. The odor of sensationalism is faintly in the air as Motley dredges up the various amusements of the lumpen proletariat when they while away the hours of their vicious idleness. Motley has discovered that since men are the victims of a bad society, we ought to have a good society. It is not fair to say that this kind of novel reveals the bankruptcy of naturalism, but since Motley invents no new thing and casts no new light, one must conclude that naturalism is in serious trouble.

Since Ralph Ellison published *Invisible Man*, his first novel, in 1952, he falls outside the scheme of this book. But he merits a brief comment because his novel reveals the fate of naturalism in the hands not only of the Negro novelist but of writers in general. Ellison feels as intensely about race as Wright does and in fact wrote short stories during the forties much in the Wright manner. His novel has certain deterministic qualities, as it has serious social and political meanings. But the significant fact is that Ellison revolts against both naturalism and social protest. He himself says that his protagonist moves from purpose to passion to perception. I take it that the perception at the end is the protagonist's need for withdrawal to explore the self-knowledge that has come to him and to determine, by his own will, what course he shall take in the world. Furthermore, the novel uses folk materials, symbolism, patterns of black and white drawn from Western mythology. In this novel the philosophy of naturalism has yielded to an acceptance of the possibility of a willed quest for identity; and the manner of naturalism has yielded to the tradition of Joyce and Kafka.

Ellison, refusing to write the protest novel and centering upon the possibilities for the emergent self, has come upon sounder and richer ground. What it is, James Baldwin has explained in the conclusion to an essay on the Negro social novel. "But our humanity is our burden, our life, we need not battle for it; we need only do what is infinitely more difficult, that is, accept it. The failure of the protest novel lies in its rejection of life, the human being, the denial of his beauty, dread, power, in its insistence that it is his categorization alone which is real and which cannot be transcended." Ellison is not quite free of the racial we-they feeling, but he is nevertheless struggling toward a realization of the humanity of his central character.

The Negro novelist had no monopoly on naturalism during the forties, of course, nor on social protest either. A writer like Ira Wolfert comes out of the thirties (a survivor who had no literary life in that time), out of a liberal-leftist orientation, to write *Tucker's People* (1943); he makes his protest against the business civilization in an urban novel almost as sordid as those of Ann Petry and Motley, in a novel, like Wright's *Native Son*, on familiar terms with Marxism. Then a novelist like Harriette Arnow writes a naturalistic novel with a rural setting, innocent of protest if not of economics. And Nelson Algren publishes three volumes in the forties by which we must finally judge the fate and quality of naturalism as it belongs to this decade.

Tucker's People has no beginning and no real ending, as Wolfert himself tells us. It is not, then, an aesthetic whole, but a slice of life, cut arbitrarily out of unceasing flow. The texture of the particular kind of life that Wolfert fastens upon can be explained by using the techniques of psychoanalysis to show the meaning of environment on character in a business society. Raymond Williams has remarked in *Culture and Society* that the one vital lesson the nineteenth century had to learn was "that the basic economic organization could not be separated and excluded from its moral and intellectual concerns," a statement that can be used to describe what Wolfert is trying to do in this novel. Wolfert seems to find the economic aspect of society basically determining, an uncompromising position that Williams would not accept. The characters in the novel all learn from experience, as they grow up, the need to fight in any way with any weapons for economic survival and then for economic power. Business virtually creates the environment. It cultivates the acquisitive instinct. Money is the goal of life for everyone. Business becomes, then, predatory and businessmen become cannibalistic. Having established these conditions, Wolfert finds it an easy matter to point out the inevitable corruption of each character caught in the essentially empty and futile pursuit of life-destroying goals. The indictment of the business ethic is most tellingly seen in the identification of legal and illegal business enterprises, which, Wolfert shows, operate on the same premises and toward the same end. In this novel Wolfert finds that no liberating act of love is possible to redeem his characters or justify an entire society dominated by business.

Hunter's Horn (1949), by Harriette Arnow, is a very different naturalistic novel, for it dramatizes the trap in the rhythm of life. The determinism of this novel is largely biological, a determinism that rests on the cycle of birth and death, so that events seem "laid out and foreordained, like rows in a cornfield waiting for their seed," as Nunn Ballew thinks at the end. The play of chance is neatly combined with biological determinism when, finally, in this story of the obsessive pursuit of a fox, the hounds, by accident coursing on the far side of the river, run the fox to earth, primarily because she is big with pups. Yet the consummation of Ballew's dearest wish — catching the fox with his hounds — does not resolve the novel. We are left with unsolved problems, as perennial as the changing seasons. In success and in failure we must confront the immutable and unchanging round of life, a rhythm that releases us only to death.

This story, which is reminiscent of Elizabeth Madox Roberts' *The Time of Man*, encompasses the whole life of a southern valley, filled with characters as authentic as the moonshine they occasionally brew. In this rural setting one is made persistently aware of the necessity to accumulate sufficient food for the winter, of the way a crop will burn when the sun is too hot — of how man stands always at the mercy of natural forces. Yet this novel is not harsh or rebellious at man's plight, for it has transcended anger at what might happen to man in the calm conviction that man is a part of nature after all, and must move with its movement. Nunn Ballew thinks sometimes that he has brought himself all the bad luck in his life, principally because he has sacrificed everything to his compulsion to pursue the fox. As it happens, his obsession with the fox brings him inadvertently to the brink of prosperity and ties him at the same time to the world of nature. The fox is in nature as the mountain in *The Naked and the Dead* is a fact of nature, and both fox and mountain represent human bondage to nature, the facts about nature that men cannot escape.

And so the trap in the rhythm of life that catches the pregnant fox catches Nunn Ballew's daughter, since all creatures are subject to the same biological law. An intelligent girl who is restless in the confining life of the valley, she yearns for escape. She tells herself she will never be caught in marriage and children, to grow old and snaggle-toothed. But her yearnings are frustrated, and she gives herself to a man she knows only casually. She conceives. Later her father casts her out of his house. Both are dismayed by this action, and both are helpless to heal the breach. The girl cannot resist the stern certitude of biological law, and the father cannot face the consequences of that law. Harriette Arnow does not rail against the broken promise of the girl's life. She accepts the girl's fate with a largeness of spirit that, enabling her to accept the universe, lends a sense of sweet peace to this book.

NELSON ALGREN: NATURALISM AS THE BEAT OF THE IRON HEART

The quiet lyricism of Harriette Arnow's novel is altogether appropriate, but the poetic tone of Nelson Algren's prose, describing the degradation of man in the filth of the city slums, is at first blush puzzling. Algren is a novelist who has embraced the conditions of naturalism — its determinism (within limits) of social environment and heredity, its preoccupation with the people of the lower depths, its pessimism about the nature of man and about man's fate in a hostile world. Algren's prose, however, while it may often be sentimental and soft about the edges, is not harsh and ungainly, as naturalistic prose has traditionally been in this country. The poetic quality of his writing comes in part from the impressionistic way in which he sees reality. He has an acutely developed feeling for mood, and he chooses his details in an artful, sometimes artificial, way to give us the atmosphere of half-light in which his characters live. He carefully sets before us the dirty Kleenex or the pavement-colored cap as details that speak to our senses in such a way as to convey his meaning. The quality of his prose comes, then, not wholly from the tradition of naturalism (although it reminds one of Frank Norris') but from Algren's conviction that his writing depends more upon feeling than upon intellect. In a *Paris Review* interview, he said, "I depend more on the stomach" than Saul Bellow; "I always think of writing as a *physical* thing." The physical quality in his writing — it is significant that he works out in a gym preparatory to writing — emphasizes the belly-head distinction which he himself makes. His allegiance is to the feelings. He is indifferent to ideas, even uncomfortable with them.

The importance which Algren gives to his feelings might be a justification for calling him a romantic. At least the appeal to the emotions in the poetic character of the prose gives him a marginal kinship with romanticism. At the end of the eighteenth century, coincidental with the early manifestations of romanticism, there appeared on the scene the man of feeling, who developed the notion of benevolence. I suggest that what I have labeled Algren's romanticism on the basis of the style of his writing is related to the compassion in the nature of his sensibility. He is the twentieth-century romantic man of feeling, inexplicably caught in the city slums. He pushes his characters on to their inevitable destruction — virtually no one wins in Algren's world — and is true in this way to his naturalistic premises. But he gives them yearnings for love or pride in themselves as separate and identifiable individuals — yearnings that reveal a tender concern for them as human beings. They are not animal-like creatures doomed to progressive deterioration. What looks like an awkward incongruity between style and matter is seen to be an organic relationship.

Algren's reliance on feeling explains a good deal about his attitude toward social reform. A writer so suspicious of the intellect as Algren could never come into a meaningful relationship with a body of idea. The Marxist influence upon his work, which is apparent in the epigraphs he selected for his first novel, published in 1935, does not lead to the novel of ideas or to an analysis of society. Not that Algren is content with the state of American society. He despises, as he has said, its marriage to gadgetry. He resents its structure and its value assumptions. He lives among the people underneath and has a feeling for them, and so he writes, not out of indignation, but, as he says, out of "a kind of *irritability* that these people on top should be contented, so absolutely unaware of these other people, and so sure that their values are the right ones. I mean, there's a certain satisfaction in recording the people underneath, whose values are as sound as theirs, and a lot funnier, and a lot truer in a way. There's a certain over-all satisfaction in kind of scooping up a shovelful of these people and dumping them in somebody's parlor." The writer's job is to accuse, to play the wasp, Algren insists, and he does so by attacking what he calls the bluebird version of America. Algren's criticism of American life is not in any sense ideological. It is a compound of resentment and perversity, of feelings; it is a conviction that the respectable classes ought to have their noses rubbed in the poverty and degradation of American life as an antidote to their self-satisfaction; it is a conviction that the poor are just as good as the rich, and more fun to boot; it is sheer sentimental sympathy for the underdog.

I should not want to accuse Algren of mindlessness, but certainly one finds in him indifference to the intellect. When he began to write he revealed a leftist orientation, but he seems to have drifted away from the radical tradition. The fact is that he was never solidly rooted in the left, and his social criticism has always been as impressionistic as his style. The Marxism in Algren's work has never been more than surface deep, in my view, and he peeled off that surface in the course of the forties. If he is at the end of the forties closer to the Symbolists than to the Marxists, this is only an indication that his style, which has remained steadily the same throughout his career, has triumphed over his fitful flirtation with ideas. It seems to me that no *essential* change has taken place in Algren from beginning to end.

When Algren was on the staff of the *Daily Illini* in college, he reports, "[I] used to go down to the city jails and wait around for something to happen. It was a good time in my life." The jail burned itself into Algren's imagination, and he has never left it. He is the poet of the jail and the whorehouse; he has made a close study of the cockroach, the drunkard, and the pimp, the garbage in the street and the spittle on the chin. He has a truly cloacal vision of the American experience. In his world dead-end streets always end in blank walls where his unheroic heroes, unattached and usually unemployed, come to their end. The heroes do not want to be unattached or unheroic. They yearn for love, and sometimes fleetingly find it. They yearn for the large, savagely virile gesture — they want to assert themselves by fighting back — and sometimes they almost achieve it. They yearn for a redemption from guilt, for a clean conscience. Strangely, love and heroism and conscience are not completely dead in Algren's world. They are just impossible. The heroes must die.

Somebody in Boots (1935) does not belong in the forties, but it is useful to look briefly at Algren's first novel, since, as I say, he has changed so little over the years. Clearly a product of the depression, the book is dedicated to the homeless boys of America. That's the tip-off. Here, Algren, in Marxist-angled social criticism, displays an unreasoning hatred for the respectable, property-owning classes in America, but unfortunately nothing of what he says has relevance in his story. In this inability to integrate such criticism and the themes of his novel one may find a reason for Algren's surrender of the techniques of frontal attack on social issues. The hero of this book comes out of the lumpen proletariat. A typical Algren character, formed by his environment and his parentage, his inheritance is his fate. He is not an admirable young man. He is, in fact, a lout, but he wants and needs love and a secure place where he belongs. He seeks love and security in the home, but his home goes to pieces: his father is in jail and his sister has turned whore. In Chicago he finds a girl, a hay-bagger (one who picks up drunks and rolls them, lower on the scale than a prostitute. In these matters Algren is as knowledgeable as anyone writing in America), and they live together in their mutual need for love. But their liaison is doomed. The dream of love ends with venereal disease.

The protagonist is a picaresque figure, and the events in which he figures are hardly plotted, but seem to slide together into an undifferentiated mass. They all leave the same gray taste in the mouth — an endless multiplication of the same thing, movement without progress. As in later novels, Algren has no patience here with plot. This novel seems to have been rewritten and published in 1956 as *A Walk on the Wild Side*. The only significant difference between the two seems to be the elimination of Marxist coloration. What *Somebody in Boots* shows, then, is the frustration of the quest for love, the unheroic hero who comes to a blank end in a hostile world, and a typically plotless story. The same themes and subject matter will appear with consistent regularity in Algren's later fiction. And the treatment he accords them will be about the same. He has written, perhaps, better books than *Somebody in Boots*, but not very different books. Algren has complained that there is no tradition for the writer in America, as there is in France, for example. It may be this lack of tradition, or more accurately Algren's failure to discern the tradition, that accounts for a failure of development in Algren as a writer.

Never Come Morning (1942) begins with a quotation from Whitman in which the poet identifies himself with convicts and prostitutes; he cannot deny them, for otherwise he would deny himself. Algren's tender concern in this book, as in others, is with the same class, but unlike Whitman, who identified himself with everyone, only with that class. The respectable Anglo-Saxon, white, Protestant American does not figure in Algren's books, does not merit his compassion. Whitman's all-inclusive vision of democratic America is not Algren's. Whitman serves Algren only to remind us that the underground man also exists and, existing, struggles with his fate as a human being.

If Algren's characters appear only half-human, it is because their lives have been stunted and foreshortened by their environment. Fireball Kodadek in this novel is like a cretin. A brutal, knife-wielding character, he is wasting away from tuberculosis;

he closes in during the rape scene smelling of canned heat and Sen-Sen. In that scene, a gang shag, all of Algren's young men show uncontrolled bestiality. The rape forces the girl into prostitution. She is not a decent and generous girl; she is selfish and indolent; but she is not a degraded and utterly promiscuous girl either. In part because of her character but mostly through circumstances, she is forced into a life in which she is always open to a new wound as a human being. In the fetid air of her "house" she endures a ceaseless boredom without light of any kind — the light of day, the light of love, or the light of intelligence or decency. She has been hunted and trapped, as the other prostitutes were, by the police and by the system, by her fallible nature and by society.

The people who appear half-human and live in a half-lit world never have a chance. The motto behind the police captain's desk is "I have only myself to blame for my fall." Even Bruno Lefty Bicek, the hero, can enjoy the irony of this, and Algren, demonstrating the inevitability of crime as he shows us the police lineup, punches home the irony. Lefty himself, who murdered an anonymous Greek during the rape, lives with the sure knowledge of his own doom, as most Algren characters do. When the police captain arrests him for the murder, Lefty says, "Knew I'd never get t' be twenty-one anyhow."

Yet neither love nor conscience is dead in Algren's characters. They are not all Darwinian creatures of appetite, blindly struggling for survival. After Lefty's girl is raped, he suffers from a sense of guilt because he knows that he has killed her "in his heart." He still loves her. And she still loves him, even though she sees him clearly as a "duped hoodlum who had kicked her into the gutter and let her lie because others might laugh if he helped her up." Lefty's guilt leads him to yearn for punishment in the obscure hope that he will be cleansed. Algren is insisting, in the teeth of his naturalism, that the remnants of some ethical order still stir in Lefty's not quite dead conscience. Then, sustained by their love, Lefty and his girl make a plan to break out of the whorehouse and to free themselves. In carrying it out, Lefty wins in a fight with Kodadek and others, but especially triumphing over Kodadek's knife which has always terrorized him, and he thinks he has found himself. He takes the girl away, feeling that "Everything was going to be all right after all." He wins a professional fight, an epic struggle of dirty tactics, and has the money to free his girl and the promise of a career before him. Redemption and love seem in his grasp. It is, of course, at this moment that he is arrested.

Algren does not swerve from the logic of his characters or his situation in this novel, but he is insisting that nothing can kill the aspiration for a more meaningful life than it is possible for his people to attain. And he is insisting most of all upon the survival of love, not as the romantic passion that men die for but as the only source of warmth in the lives of the hopeless. Lefty and his girl strive for whatever profit for the self or whatever balm lies in mutual interdependence. Their modest hope is for nothing more than comfort. Outside the naturalistic novel, in other kinds of fiction in the forties, love in the modern world is no more than this. The imagination of the writer, no matter how it conceives reality, quails before the ugly, hostile face of the world and turns to love as a refuge.

In the largest sense, the failure of love in Algren's world is a consequence of the necessity for failure imposed by his view of experience. From another perspective, however, the failure of love is the failure of the love code as a competing mode of action. Lefty is in quest of a more meaningful life than he sees available to him in the street, but he cannot escape the street, and what it offers becomes the ordering principle in his life. Because there is nothing else. He dreams of glory in the ring or on the ball field, dreams which are substitutes for the boredom he endures or which are compensations for the lack of status which constantly humiliates him. The dreams are never realized, but the reality is the street and the gang on the street. His code of behavior is shaped by these. If piety is to be defined as the action appropriate to a given orientation, then the pieties of the gang which determine ritual behavior constitute the code. In the rape scene, where courage, honor, nobility, selflessness might have been regarded as part of the love code that would impel Lefty to rescue his girl from the gang, the code of the street dictates that a boy must share his piece with the others. This aspect of the code provides Lefty with a rationalization for his cowardice. It also reveals how feeble a force the chivalric love code is on the streets of Chicago in the twentieth century. As Lefty plays it straight and regular with the boys in regard to the girl, so he does when he is caught by the police: he keeps silent, refusing to implicate others more guilty than he.

This novel is episodic and only fitfully plotted. Algren seems to have only enough narrative material for a short story. The long section on the whorehouse and the section on the police line-up, which have only a tangential relevance to the main line of the story, suggest that Algren's real aim is to give the quality of life in the world he deals with. I have the feeling that he is more concerned with forcing upon his reader a recognition of the depths to which men can sink and the dank horrors of the society they make than he is in solving his aesthetic problems. It is a society of police venality and brutality, of dope addicts and drunkards, of hookers and pimps. It is shaped by violence, crime, and sin. It makes inevitable the spiritual and physical death of those who live in it. Algren takes a kind of satisfaction in telling us that this is the way it really is.

Algren's collection of short stories, *The Neon Wilderness* (1947), has a great deal in common with his novels, of course. In fact, several of the stories, expanded or otherwise altered, become parts of the various novels. The mood of the stories in this volume is the same as that in the longer prose. His people move through a shadowy, half-lit world. It always seems to be raining in Chicago. The city sounds in the background are obtrusive and always dreary or frightening: the grinding noise of the El, the shrill police siren, the juke box always playing the blues. Algren uses these details in a freely impressionistic manner to create a climate of discordance and garish unrest. His characters come from the same world as those in the novels and proceed to the same fate. It is worth remarking that a few, never the heroes, survive. They are the most venal or the coldest, the most parasitical. In *Never Come Morning* this is one Catfoot who risks nothing, an expert at not getting caught. In these stories fight managers, brothel keepers, crooked cops are among those few who win. Yet not all cops are crooked and heartless, and Algren gives us one captain who advises the criminals he deals with to commit suicide. This is not indifference but a suppressed compassion which the captain cannot permit himself to release.

What the stories reveal that had not appeared in the early novels is Algren's humor. The ironies of the longer prose were always undilutedly bitter. The irony in some of these stories is at least bitter-sweet, as in the little account of how prayer exorcises a devil but makes a drunkard out of a little boy. The class hatred of *Somebody in Boots,* which is directed toward the haves in American society, is here transferred in the stories about the war to the officers; but Algren regards the war as ludicrous. The characteristic humor is violent and incongruous. In a story like "Kingdom City to Cairo," Algren uses his humor to make a wildly irresponsible protest against respectability. He clearly smacks his lips over this account of a minister who is having an affair with his brother's wife and running a brothel on the side. The same extravagance marks the humor of those episodes dealing with the people underneath. "Poor Man's Pennies," which was incorporated in *The Man With The Golden Arm* and is the promise of a further development of Algren's humorous vein in that generally grim novel, tells of the abortive holdup of a department store. It is a saga of organized stumbling by born incompetents toward a palpably impossible end. Algren's humor is not quiet or subtle. It is as broad and loud as a small riot.

The Man With The Golden Arm (1949) is the high point in Algren's career thus far. In speaking about it, Algren has said that he planned to write a war novel, but that the *Golden Arm* came out instead. He switched because he felt compelled to write about the environment in which he was living, which happened to be in Chicago near Division Street. The war experience, on the other hand, had slipped away. The environment is one that Algren has always, in a curious sense, cherished. He feels himself attached to Chicago and seems to believe that his roots as an artist are there. He seems to feel, further, that he has an obligation to record the city. He has written, of course, an essay, *Chicago: City on the Make,* but it is an imaginative record that he feels compelled to keep. As the city sustains him as a writer, so, in some reciprocal sense, he conceives it as his mission to reveal her.

Originally *The Man With The Golden Arm* dealt with a card dealer. The agent to whom Algren sent it suggested that it needed something more. Using the material on dope was an afterthought, Algren says, which came to him when he met some people who were taking dope. It is not surprising, under these circumstances, that Algren should say he did not plot the *Golden Arm*; he speaks of the novel as "very creaky as far as plot goes, it's more of a cowboy-and-Indian thing, a cops-and-robbers thing." Asked if he could relate the novel to an idea, Algren replied no, he just had an over-all feeling and no particular theory about what he was doing. These statements bear out what is apparent about all of Algren's work: that he is not primarily interested in either plot or idea.

We are left with feeling, and a case could be made for the proposition that the most telling success of the novel is the way Algren conveys the special quality of its feeling. He begins at once with a section called "Rumors of Evening," which is set in the police station in a leaden twilight. The artful, sometimes arty, manipulation of darkness and light, which often blur into a symbolic half-light, is a recurrent device by which Algren mirrors the despair and poverty of his characters. So effectively does he create his mood out of shadow and night wind and rain that we are prepared to agree with Sophie when she tells us that "God has forgotten us all." The mood, despite Algren's aggressive intention to force the respectable classes to pay attention to the dispossessed, is that of quiet elegy. The color of life in the city that he captures is in the loneliness of its streets, the hardness of its pavements, the sad depravity of its crime, the muted sounds of its despair rising from underground. The novel is a genre picture, done with the same loving attention to accuracy and detail that one finds in a painting of this kind, and with the same intimate knowledge of the subject. It is the feeling for the texture of urban experience that stands out in this novel and gives it its importance.

In discussing the *Golden Arm*, Blanche Gelfant has said, ". . . we cannot aggregate sociological factors to an explanation of Skid Row." It is a truth that Algren has seized, or at least it is a truth for one who knows himself more a singer than an explainer. The failure of love in the slums is more fittingly treated by the elegist than by the sociologist. Frankie Machine is married to Sophie, but he loves Molly Novotny, a hustler and a stripper. Sophie will not let Frankie go. She holds him through a guilt feeling which she nurtures in him, because he was drunk and driving in the accident that has crippled her. She punishes him because she has loved him too much. Before the accident she had never been able fully to possess him; she had been forced to come to him; she had wanted him and not he her. Love does not flourish under these conditions, and Sophie, a pathologically selfish woman who is the victim of self-induced imprisonment in her wheel chair, eventually goes mad. The love between Frankie and Molly is the tactic of the false dawn that Algren employs — the apparent escape to light will end in the darkness of death. In this love affair, which again has about it the desperate pursuit of the commonplaces of comfort, Molly satisfies her maternal instincts, caring for Frankie and helping him rid himself of dope addiction. But her love does not save Frankie. He goes back on the needle. He kills the drug peddler. Then, on the run and with no money for a fix, he commits suicide.

The guilt Frankie feels because of Sophie's accusations drives him back to dope, after he has shaken the habit. Or at least it is one reason he goes back. Frankie is a moral coward; his life is full of uncertainties and inadequacies. He has searched for the meaning of his life, he has searched for himself in the hypodermic needle. What Algren has done more poignantly with Frankie than with any other character is to bestow upon him, not will, but personality: the capacity for love and guilt, a dim awareness of the possibility of discovering identity. As Algren is compassionate with all his characters — compassionate to a fault, since he extends his sympathy to the meanest among them who do not justify it — so he is most compassionate with Frankie. As if to underline the love-guilt-identity complex that he is working with, Algren gives us Police Captain Bednar, old Record Head, who is intimate with all varieties of crime and criminal. Bednar begins to feel the weight of guilt bearing him down. Someone says to him, "We are all members of one another." And another says, "Everybody is a habitual at heart." The meaning of these sentences preys upon his mind. He feels uncertain of his own innocence. He feels the need for absolution. He comes to realize that he has loved no man and that he has been cut off from men. He feels finally that he has betrayed men. Frankie had hoped to find himself in the hypo; Bednar had searched for himself in the record book. Neither succeeds.

Algren's Frankie knows that if he cannot find his identity, and if he does not have a place, then he is nothing. An old man in jail early in the book wants to be remembered as the watchman on the old Wabash Railroad. If somebody could only remember him in this function, he would be placed; then he would have a claim on his own being. It is specifically said that Drunkie John is nothing because he had never discovered who he was. But Blind Pig, in the pay of the drug peddler, in all his loathesome filth of body and soul, has yet that remnant of human pride in being himself that attaches him to mankind.

What I have been dealing with thus far in the discussion of *The Man With The Golden Arm* arises, principally I think, out of Algren's feeling. The naturalism and the social criticism in the novel arise out of Algren's ideology. The first intimations of naturalism occur in some reflections on how one lands in jail so often. "That was the way things were because that was how things had always been. Which was why they could never be any different. Neither God, war, nor the ward super work any deep change on West Division Street." In jail a cockroach falls helplessly into the water bucket. Frankie feels a kinship with it: he too leaps and falls between walls he cannot scale. And indeed his helplessness before circumstances he cannot control is illustrated in the main line of the story. He rids himself of the monkey on his back, the drug habit. But his return to the habit is inevitable, and his complete destruction follows inexorably.

The social criticism in the novel is an indictment of the American way of life. That way goes back to the Protestant ethic. It is the bourgeois way that has given us the massive consumer-economy in which every effort is bent toward increasing the ownership and consumption of things. In Algren's view, our society has identified virtue and ownership. Or the identification has been made for us by the advertising man. Those who have not lived up to advertising's conception of America are guilty of the special American guilt of owning nothing. The disinherited are un-American. Algren is not willing to accept this standard in defining the American. He is not willing to withhold humanity from those who are without purchasing power. The wrecks and the bums are also human. It is his assertion that we must grant humanity to all.

Algren's naturalism and his social attitudes are predictable. They both conform to established formulas. His naturalism, to be sure, is enlivened by the knowledgeable use of drug addiction, which makes it easy for the novel to fulfil the deterministic pattern. The social comments are full of the reckless and perverse negativism that has led Algren to prefer the unwashed to the rest of the population, largely because they are unwashed. What gives Algren his distinction is that he is a naturalist who cares about style and who is linguistically adventuresome and aware, if not always successful. His distinction is that he has a great reservoir of sympathy which he extends, sometimes indiscriminately, to all the unfortunates in his nightmare world. What distinguishes him is the way he blends his naturalism. He blends its determinism with a sympathy for his people that nevertheless cannot deter him from sending them to their miserable fates. And he blends a determinism which should rob them of will with an assertion of will — the will to love, the will to penance, the will to find the self — which testifies finally to their humanity.

CHAPTER FOUR

FICTION AND THE LIBERAL REASSESSMENT

THE DAY OF THE LOCUST FOR THE LIBERAL SPIRIT

The Negro writers of the naturalistic novel in the forties expressed their sense of outrage at the plight of the Negro in a straightforward and uncomplicated way. But for other writers in the forties, social-protest fiction had lost its momentum as its basis in the left — a left ranging from liberalism to communism — had broken up. The dramatic and numbing factor in that break-up was the German-Russian pact of August 22, 1939. That date, says Granville Hicks, marks the decline of social criticism in the novel. If any date will serve, that one will do well enough.

The total left was in a state of shell shock during much of the forties, a state reflected in fiction. As Marxism and the Communist party faded from the American intellectual scene, proletarian fiction virtually disappeared. Liberalism went into a steep decline. The tragedy of the liberal mind, which had been so alert to the rise of reactionary totalitarianism in the thirties, was its failure to cope with fascism in the forties. I do not mean merely that liberal writers failed to turn the dramatic conflict between democracy and fascism into vital fiction. I mean that the liberal imagination retreated before the power of mythical thought which the totalitarian ideologies mobilized. Ernst Cassirer points out what a threat this mythicism was to rational analysis, calling it the most alarming feature of modern political thinking. And Albert Guérard speaks of mankind's yearning for obscurantism, which is given form and direction by dictators and theologians, and which heralds the new age of darkness. In this twilight zone, the old-fashioned liberal writer barely survived, sustaining a precarious life with the clichés of the thirties.

In this world of the left, robbed of meaningful movement, the only significant development was the emergence of what I shall call the new liberalism. It was a chastened, modified liberalism, the product of a mind and consciousness strong and honest enough to struggle out of the trauma into which events had plunged it. Its vision was not straightforward and uncomplicated but ambiguous and tortured, for it now recognized limitations and problems it had not heeded at an earlier time. Its achievement, in my opinion, was the optimum achievement possible for liberalism in the forties. It will serve as the climax in this chapter in which I shall deal with three manifestations in fiction of the left: communism, the old liberalism, and the new liberalism.

THE COLLAPSE OF MARXISM

Richard Crossman, the editor of *The God That Failed*, points out that all the contributors to the volume have this in common, that they chose communism out of despair over Western values. In a disintegrating society, they thirsted for faith. The contributions to the volume record their failure to find that faith and document the disengagement from communism that these European and American writers underwent in the forties. If they, and others, had observed Russian communism honestly, hindsight now reveals to us, their loyalties would not have been so freely given. The bitter truth about Russia during the thirties was always available, but it took time for it to filter into the Western consciousness. Russian hypocrisy had brought about the failure of the Popular Front. The apparent ambiguity of the Russian position during the Spanish Civil War was finally revealed as total cynicism. The Moscow trials demonstrated that survival in the Kremlin power struggle was possible only to those who exploited treachery and murder. The 1939 pact was only the most dismal and decisive act in this dreary history. It was this accumulation of evidence that drove writers and intellectuals out of the party, a movement that came to its symbolic close when Howard Fast finally left it in 1956, the last writer of any stature in America whom the party could still claim up to that date. Fast stayed longer than other writers because he is an emotional and naïve person who seems honestly to have believed that the Communists were the bravest among the fighters for freedom — these are virtually his own words. When he left it, he confessed that the party had hurt him as a creative person and that it had twisted the personalities of many people in it.

Far more typical of American writers was Granville Hicks, who left the Communist party in 1939 after the pact was signed. His chief reason was that the party, in its monolithic adherence to dogma, had closed out the possibility of discussion. Its unequivocal defense of the pact as a contribution to peace and democracy was a rationalization. Criticism, or self-criticism, was impossible where men relied on faith more than intelligence. For Hicks this step was the beginning of a reappraisal that would bring him to the new liberalism. It was also a step that would introduce us to the era of the ex-Communist or the nouveau anti-Stalinist. This type, it is worth recording, becomes an object of suspicion at once, not to the conservatives, but to those who had been intellectual anti-Stalinists before the pact. Why trust people like Cowley and Hicks now, asked James T. Farrell in the spring of 1940, since they were wrong once? The question presages the antagonism that all leftists were to feel in the forties, as well as the difficulties they were to suffer from self-division and internecine hostilities. Yet the former party member or sympathizer came to regard Russia and the party with a hostile eye in the forties. I do not speak of those who became professional witnesses for congressional committees, but of the serious writers and intellectuals who spoke, for example, at the Cultural and Scientific Conference for World Peace, held in March, 1949. This so-called Waldorf Conference revealed clearly at the end of the decade that the Communists had lost support and aroused the enmity of many who might have supported them ten years earlier. Mary McCarthy, Ira Wolfert, Norman Mailer, and Robert Lowell were among the writers at the conference whose questions, critical of Russia, her defenders dodged and whose statements about the suppression of freedom in Russia her defenders could not contradict.

It follows from the desertion of the Communist party by virtually every talented author it had ever enlisted in this country that the literature written from the Communist point of view in the forties would be of little consequence. Proletarian literature, even in the thirties, as a literature either of a class or of the party, had failed to make any vital or lasting connection with the American experience. It brought an undistinguished status into the forties at a time when the party, allied with liberal capitalism in the Popular Front, did not want a revolutionary literature. As early as the winter of 1939, Philip Rahv, with some justice, was doing a political autopsy on proletarian literature. As for Marxist literary criticism, it had provided no sound theoretical basis for a literature in the forties. No one in this country had successfully applied a Marxist analysis of society to literary problems or made a notable contribution to the problems of dialectical process. Marxist criticism in this decade was largely limited to two fruit-less enterprises. One was a vicious snarling at the new criticism as a fungus growth over American literature. The other was the expression of a totally unrealistic hope, in the face of the evidence, that young writers would soon be turning out great novels about the struggle for social and economic freedom.

After these dismal preliminaries, it is clearly not worth our time to linger long over the Communist party novel of the forties. The representative product is unimaginative in conception and written as though with the work-stiffened hand of the laborer un-used to the pen. It deals with the class struggle in which the pro-letarian hero is often a martyr to the cause of labor and the working class as a whole is systematically exploited by a consist-ently brutal entrepreneurial system. In such a novel the common man is generous and kind; the party members are the pure in heart. The future belongs to the workers, who do not suffer from the doubt and *Weltschmerz* that make for decadence among the rich. The party will go forward under the democratic principle of guaranteeing the rights of the miserable and the poor and in the Pauline spirit that we are all members, one of the other. The party never seeks its own ends, but it is a friend to mankind, and espe-cially to men in the union. Management is evil and management personnel corrupt. A coalition between industry and criminal forces makes violence the chief instrument on the part of manage-ment in the class struggle.[1]

---

[1] For the elements in this typical novel I have drawn on three leftist books of the forties: *The Underground Stream* (1940), by Albert Maltz; *Jake Home* (1943), by Ruth McKenney; and *The Judas Time* (1946), by Isidor Schneider.

What we are getting in such a novel is a two-dimensional world which is depthless, like a movie set. Blinded by dogma, the writer of this kind of book sees on the American scene only those aspects of reality that fit into his preconceived notion of the total reality. But when the total social reality takes a shape so radically different from that offered by the Communist writer, who rests his case upon the truth of his version of social reality, then the disparity will destroy the writer. For the rest of us, not blinded in his particular way, his credibility as a witness will vanish. Or to put the matter another way, when social reality begins to catch up with Communist demands, the basis for protest is removed. The proletarian novel loses its function, bowing to the fate common to all ad hoc literature.

The best among the Communist novelists, or at any rate the most energetic, the one with the largest reputation, was Howard Fast. Turning out a book virtually every year, he did not seem to be aware that Marxism had collapsed in the forties. It was a productivity made possible first by a consistent adherence to the assumptions and method of dialectical materialism, so that he had no need to grope about for his pattern or his ideas; and, second, by his indifference to language, which permitted him to rush from book to book without concern for the bathos of his unrestrained expression or the inaccuracy of his ear. He was aided also by what I might call the typology of communism: all the characters fit into pre-established master categories, so that each character in a book is no more than the fulfilment of a typical figure whose lineaments have been set in a mold. It is a question, of course, whether the dialectical tension of the class struggle, when incorporated into fiction, can yield a satisfying conception of human nature. The demands of the dialectic easily induce the writer to give in to the blandishments of the stereotype. Fast does not put up much of a fight in this respect. He is like other Communist writers, furthermore, in exploiting the class war in economic terms, armed conflict in revolutionary terms, and the struggle of the oppressed for freedom in social terms. But he does make one special contribution. Using the Marxist interpretation of history, he undertakes the rewriting of the American story in events or episodes stretching from the Revolution to the end of the nineteenth century. He tries, not systematically but persistently, to capture the long heritage of American radicalism, as one critic has said of him, and to make American Communists as distinctly American as French Communists are French.

This is a hazardous enterprise. Not the least of its difficulties is the application of an inflexible dogma to a democratic culture that has produced an open society dependent for its health on the possibility of variety and choice. But Fast is not one to ponder his difficulties. If Americans believe in freedom he is ready to apotheosize the struggle for freedom, especially as it is made by traditionally oppressed groups in America — the ethnic minorities. Indeed, he employs a special kind of selective vision in his rewriting of American history, for he sees only those groups or those incidents which conveniently illustrate the points he wants to make. In *The Last Frontier* (1941), for example, the minority group he chooses is the Indian. The event is the flight of a band of Cheyennes from an Oklahoma reservation where they had been arbitrarily placed by the federal government; they want to go back to their home in the Black Hills. This is a flight to freedom, and those who oppose it become the victims of moral disintegration as the price of their ethnic antagonisms. Oppression of a minority group replaces the class struggle in this novel, but in *Freedom Road* (1944) Fast is able to include, in his technique of selective vision, oppression of a minority group and the class struggle. This story tells of the growth of free Negro communities in the Reconstruction South. These communities are wrecked, ultimately, by the old southern aristocrats who wish to re-establish their power. Thus we get in one package white supremacy over the Negro and aristocrat versus working man.

And the fight for freedom is a constant, in many instances a real fight in which men have recourse to arms. For Fast believes in the glorification of revolution as a part of the American heritage. In *Freedom Road* he justifies revolutionary activity on the constitutional grounds that men are permitted, as a part of the citizen militia, to bear arms. He seems to me chiefly interested in the implications of this constitutional provision for a people's uprising. He would encourage the notion that in America men can and should fight for their rights. This revolutionary theme is most prominent in *Citizen Tom Paine* (1943). Fast conceives Paine as the first professional revolutionary the world has ever known. In this novel he treats the American Revolution as a war on two fronts: the fight against the British, and the civil war at home between the people and an aristocracy of money and family which seeks to make a counter-revolution. If Fast had been able to work into this novel an economic interpretation of the Revolution to go with his theories of class war and counter-revolution, he would have had a total Marxist explanation to set before us. It might be noted in passing that the historical record presents a considerable body of evidence to sustain the view that the professional, mercantile, planting aristocracy made the Revolution and supported it, having a great stake in it, and that the common people had a propensity for the role of summer soldier.

Fast's concern with revolutionary activity is not an abstract matter, not the disinterested play of the intellect over the American historical scene. He is always drawing the implicit parallel between the historic struggle for freedom and the same struggle in our time. He never forgets that in the Marxist view literature is a weapon. Perhaps *The Unvanquished* (1942) illustrates these points more directly than any other of his novels. It is a dull, unvarnished effort at hero worship as it draws a portrait of Washington developing into a confident military leader. It makes the point — the same point that Fast made before and continues to make — that an indomitable spirit moves men to fight for freedom. Could this novel, with its naïve picture of the father of our country who inspires respect and love, have any relation to the party slogan, Communism is good Americanism? When the 1939 pact was signed, the party hindered the American war effort in every way possible. After June 22, 1941, the date Hitler marched into Russia, the Communists in America, according to Daniel Bell, became the exemplars of patriotism. It is not farfetched, in my opinion, to regard *The Unvanquished* as a specific act of patriotic piety in the new Communist campaign to identify the party with the national tradition and the contemporary war aims of the nation.

The argument that this novel was especially timely gains some credence from the fact that Washington, the fox-hunting aristocrat, is not the typical Fast hero. Paine and John Peter Altgeld, men of the people, are more useful to Fast's pattern. Because it is the people who are good — the working man, the dirt farmer, the labor leader — and all others who are bad. This is the simplistic conception of man and life that a propagandistic purpose forces upon the Communist novelist. It entails the sentimentalization and idealization of minority groups or oppressed workers, of whoever it is that is struggling upward toward freedom. It involves the distortion of American history, which must be seen without depth and nuance, as character is seen. If it serves Fast's purpose, as it does in one novel, then Thaddeus Stevens must be put forward as a gold-plated hero, with no questions asked about the motives and nature of his Reconstruction policy. It argues that the good society will produce the good man, and is content that it has made a total explanation of human nature and society both. In short, Fast reveals the failure of the American Communist party novel. One must grant him his generous feeling for the underdog and the crude energy he sometimes shows in handling bald narrative. But the inadequacies of Marxism in accounting for the vagaries, for the significance, of human experience as revealed in history or in individual lives are all too apparent in his work.

The epitaph on the Communist novel in our period is *Barbary Shore* (1951), by Norman Mailer. It lays communism to rest as a meaningful cultural phenomenon and as a way to personal salvation. It records the failure of the social revolutionary in modern society, the victim of nameless terrors and alienation, who cannot make a vital relationship between his ideas and the society he lives in. And it is Mailer's own last essay of the political novel before he undertakes the exploration of the life of instinct in *The Deer Park*, which is to lead him to Hipsterism. *Barbary Shore* is not a Communist novel in the usual sense, as Fast's books are, but it is clearly a product of a close and sympathetic study of Marx. Unfortunately, the tedious and abstract political analysis in the book is what cripples it irreparably, Mailer being unable to bring his sophisticated grasp of political ideas into a living relationship with his characters. These ideas are simply not worked out in the action of the novel.

The action takes place in a Kafka-like ambience in which the protagonist is not sure who he is or where he is from. The action also has Kafka's strange quality of unreality, in which relationships begin and shift according to some scheme outside the realm of rationality. Perhaps it is this strange murkiness which led Norman Podhoretz to see the book as an allegory. Its real subject, he has said, is the effect on modern life of the failure of the Russian Revolution. Some of the characters represent the modern consciousness, being sick and perverted. Another character represents the narcissism that comes of trying to live outside of politics. Another is the organization man. And the revolutionary stands for vision and dedication. While this is a provocative reading of the book, I feel it does not sufficiently emphasize the deep pessimism that Mailer breathes into every page. The aimlessness and the violence of the modern world are so pervasive that there is little hope the revolutionary can reclaim it. The politics of disintegration is so far advanced and the possibility of a third world war so imminent that the revolutionary is virtually immobilized. At the Waldorf Conference Mailer had said that he thought both Russia and the United States were moving toward state capitalism and that the people of both countries were caught in a mechanism that would produce war. A plague on both your houses, he said in effect; what we have is a stand-off of mutual guilt. *Barbary Shore* seems written out of the conviction that the props have been pulled out from under radicalism, which now has, to change the figure, nowhere to turn in the world. It is the desperate homelessness of the revolutionary in a meaningless society, victimized by the sadistic inquisitional activities of a semiliterate, that the book in the end impresses upon the reader. As Mailer fled from ideology, from revolution, to Hipsterism, so in the fifties other young writers turned their backs upon, never even considered, communism. Marxism was dead in the literary world.

TRADITIONAL LIBERALISM

In the world of philosophy, of social thought and religion, liberalism was not quite dead and would not lie down. The successive shocks to Marxism had an effect upon liberalism, despite the difference in these two points of view, since the entire left suffered from a carelessly flung, all-encompassing indictment of guilt by association. Yet unrepentant liberals of various kinds persisted in affirming their faith in a creed which so many others were regarding kindly as an anachronism and at worst as a deadly menace. These liberals seemed able to agree on the essentials of liberalism, despite the differences in their disciplines and intellectual origins.

Julius Bixler defined the liberal as "man as a free being making his decisions in accordance with reason," and in emphasizing the living person as the starting point for liberalism, the idea of freedom, and the reliance upon reason, Bixler enunciated the touchstones of liberalism commonly accepted. For Horace Kallen, Mill's essay on liberty "vindicates reason as the method and form of freedom." For William A. Orton liberalism is a vindication of personality despite the encroachments of a mechanically conceived universe and a collectively conceived society, or the assertion of self against impersonal science and the impersonal state. For Morris R. Cohen, liberalism is an attitude, not a set of dogmas. Its aim is to "liberate the energies of human nature by the free and fearless use of reason." It believes in toleration, self-control, process, in the life of open possibility. All the men I have cited published books in the forties, setting forth these amazingly homogeneous views — amazing in the light of the commonly expressed opinion that liberalism means all things to all men. The views are amazing also in that their authors had the temerity to publish them at all when liberalism was in such bad odor.

The great danger to liberalism, Cohen had said, was the centralization of power — government power, economic power, military power — and the triumph of absolutistic ideas or faiths. The spontaneous life of the individual in the community is possible only when state control is held to a minimum. The smashing blow to liberalism in the forties was the threat to individual freedom, which constitutes a threat to individual identity. In the social-political aggrandizement of man's freedom we find the rationale for the writer's assertion of the compelling importance of individual human identity.

The decline of liberalism began with the outbreak of the second war in Europe, when President Roosevelt announced a policy of expedience which called for the abandonment of social service legislation. The federal government then embarked, not in a systematic way, to be sure, but inevitably just the same, on a decade-long course of curbing individual liberty and tampering with individual belief. The Alien Registration Act was passed in 1940, the first peacetime sedition law in America since 1798. Drastically restricting freedom of speech, this act contained the infamous guilt by association clause. The Selective Service Act, passed in the same year, was the first peacetime compulsory military service law in the history of the country. The civil liberties of a minority group were harshly assaulted when early in the war Japanese-Americans were evacuated from the West Coast. Near the close of the war the House of Representatives granted the Un-American Activities Committee permanent status. In *The Decline of American Liberalism* Arthur Ekirch claims that, in the postwar period, fear and suspicion of Russia and the atomic arms race made the United States into a garrison state using police state methods. The judgment seems extreme, yet the government did commit itself to a federal loyalty program and the Congress passed the McCarran Internal Security Act, both measures designed to catch spies and destined to harass innocent government employees in all grades. The anti-Communist hysteria that possessed the nation after the war found its most insidious expression in the doctrine of guilt by association and its most cynical exponent in Senator McCarthy. The emergence of the senator brought this period of liberal decline to its properly painful climax.

The total effect of these legislative and administrative acts was to pose a conflict between national security and individual liberty. The government subjected the traditional rights of the individual to a steady attrition in the name of security, until the power to inquire into and pass judgment on the beliefs and associations of citizens passed from judicial to administrative agencies. This shift marked a departure from traditional constitutional procedures in the United States. The result was to identify loyalty to one's country with orthodoxy of belief. The consequence, says John Lord O'Brian, was the establishment of preventive measures applicable to the field of ideas. The urgency to guarantee the national security overbore the need to guarantee individual freedoms. Fear settled upon large segments of the citizenry; silence followed; and dissent seemed almost dead. In this climate the liberal spirit suffocated, needing to breathe the air of freedom for life and to move among various possibilities for the exercise of its will.

The quest for economic security likewise threatened individual liberty. The social legislation of the federal government, desirable in so many ways, nevertheless encouraged the growth of a centralized state. The liberal was caught in the dilemma of wanting the social welfare that a strong state would bring but deploring the strength of the state that would obliterate the individual. The growth of the corporation in an industrialized and interdependent society also promised economic security to those who fitted into the corporate structure. But such people, the faceless organization men, stood to lose their freedom and their identity. The liberal's faith in progress and science as avenues which would liberate the individual had brought him to the bleak possibility that these avenues would instead eliminate the individual.

The assault on liberalism, made in social-political and economic areas, continued in the realm of ideas with the rise of the modern counter-reformation. The spokesmen for this latter movement, drawn from the new orthodoxy in religion and neo-conservatism in social thought, declared the bankruptcy of the liberal tradition. It was this tradition, they said, that had brought down upon Western man his tragic fate. In their view the liberal analysis of history, the liberal conception of man's nature, the liberal view of society, the liberal estimate of Russia had all been wrong. We had been brought to the brink of disaster by the foolish optimism and the haphazard planning of the liberals. The rise of totalitarianism, the subsequent war, the collapse of value, and the disintegration of society were the fruits of liberalism. As early as 1939, when he published *The Idea of a Christian Society*, T. S. Eliot, recording how deeply shaken and thoroughly humiliated he had been by the Munich crisis, saw the events of those years as casting doubt upon the validity of an entire civilization. It was, he said, an essentially negative civilization, which he excoriated in these terms:

By destroying traditional social habits of the people, by dissolving their natural collective consciousness into individual constituents, by licensing the opinions of the most foolish, by substituting instructon for education, by encouraging cleverness rather than wisdom, the upstart rather than the qualified, by fostering a notion of *getting on* to which the alternative is a hopeless apathy, Liberalism can prepare the way for that which is its own negation: the artificial, mechanised or brutalised control which is a desperate remedy for its chaos.

Eliot declared that "The attitudes and beliefs of Liberalism are destined to disappear, are already disappearing." He proposed in place of liberalism a Christian society.

The neo-conservative quarrel with liberalism I shall examine at length later on. For present purposes it is enough to say that liberalism offered in its traditional form no sense of vitality and excitement to the writer seeking in it a point of view or a set of assumptions, and that during the forties liberalism seemed outdated if not indeed downright dangerous and dishonest. The fiction based on the old liberalism has about it thus a nostalgic air, as if yearning for a happier time in the past. It is quaint in its insistence upon the inviolability of attitudes that have come in its own time under the closest kind of critical scrutiny; and when it is not quaint, it is absolutely fatuous in clinging to its unexamined principles. It does not seem fully to belong in its time, although the events of its time, paradoxically, would seem ideally to demand a liberal response. It is the liberal or the leftist writer abroad who made in fiction the enduring answer to totalitarianism. Ignazio Silone, for instance, is a heroic figure in his insistence on the kind of political life that will keep the writer free and in his enduring posture of sturdy dissent. He has brought his ideas, living and dramatic, into his fiction in a way that no American novelist has been able to do; no American has utilized the body of liberal democratic principles the way Silone has utilized his blend of social, Christian ideas. These principles have rarely been fused in America into the kind of political novel that Irving Howe defines: one in which representations of human experience and feeling and relationships are brought together with an idea of society which penetrates the lives and consciousness of the characters and makes them fully alive to political ideas and loyalties.

Yet Americans in the forties did write a species of the political-social novel, in all awareness of the opportunity and even the need to do so from a liberal platform. Fascism abroad and the possibility of dictatorship at home presented opportunities for the novelist that he took but could not fully realize. The same was true of the perennial problem of race and religion, where the liberal novels of the forties remained the prisoners of cliché and stereotype. Other novelists saw in the points of tension between security and freedom, between mass security and individual identity, fruitful subjects for fiction. In a more general way, writers hoped, by assuming a liberal posture, to capture the immediate, surface character of their society, and some of them, aiming beyond this, wished to grasp the very texture and the inner essence of that society. The fundamental reality of man and society, of man in society, is what they sought, but the truth is that in most cases they fell short. One important reason for the discrepancy between their reach and their grasp was the inadequacy of the old liberalism.

The novelists of the old liberalism go a long way on sincerity and good intentions, but their literary techniques are often crude, as those of the naturalists are, because they do not seem to respect their craft. They conceive literature as related quite directly to society in the simple sense that literary truth is based upon social fact, as Meyer Levin has put it in *Citizens*. If one uses what he calls experiences of reality — actual events — as literary materials, one will in all likelihood avoid false conclusions. Levin, and others too, thus seem to surrender part of their prerogatives as writers, since artists working at the height of their powers create their own reality and derive their conclusions, if they are indeed interested in conclusions, from that imagined reality and not from historical reality. The old liberals tend to see another simple relationship between literature and society. It is the rhetorical, or persuasive, function of literature that they cherish. They regard literature, then, as a weapon in the fight for social change. Their position encourages a reportorial attitude in literature, which is satisfied with the recording of the proper facts with the proper emphasis — facts recorded in such a way, that is, that the desired social action ought to take place. Their attitude toward language and point of view and the tactics of plot — toward all those intrinsically literary qualities of prose fiction — tends to be utilitarian where it is not contemptuous. They are innocent of concern over the aesthetics of the novel.

Upton Sinclair is a fine example of the old-fashioned liberal, clinging to the old liberal tenets as a dependable mine-horse clings to his path. In 1940, with *World's End*, Sinclair began publishing the Lanny Budd novels, carrying his hero from his birth before the first World War through the stupendous events of the 1940's. The books are assembled in a somehow way, Sinclair using primitive novelistic devices that suit his purposes. The techniques are really those of the documentary, but one that has surrendered its objectivity. Sinclair's redactions of history can be read as primers of unregenerate ante-World War I liberalism. The ghost of muckrakerdom — a vigorous, indefatigable ghost — has wandered into the forties to tell us that wars are the product of the evil machinations of the munitions makers, or that finance capitalism tends toward a strangling monopoly, or that the profit motive will not distinguish between good and evil, democracy or totalitarianism. Whatever the merits of these contentions, Sinclair himself is not interested in thinking deeply about them and certainly not in re-thinking them. He is not writing the novel of ideas. He is, in the sentimental way the forties found no longer acceptable, calling us to the ramparts to fight off social injustice. But Sinclair's easy explanations and his unexamined principles are not convincing to an age of doubt that attributes its predicament to the failure of those principles.

Joseph Freeman, who comes out of a Communist background (he left the party in 1939, he says) instead of the Socialist back-ground of Sinclair, reveals himself nevertheless as an old-fashioned liberal in his long, prolix novel, *Never Call Retreat* (1943). His protagonist is precisely a man of such conviction, one of those attractive Old World academicians who represent the finest devel-opment of the generous spirit and the cultivated mind of Euro-pean liberalism. The most notable aspect of the novel and perhaps its only achievement is the sense of Europe it conveys, especially a sense of the delightful, conversational, leisurely world of Vienna *Gemütlichkeit* which fascism has irrevocably destroyed. Freeman's professor watches his world crumble away. But not passively. He plays the historic role of the liberal, who was among the first to see and to warn of the dangers of fascism. He does not turn to the Communists to help him save this old order, for though he is in-volved with them he is never one of them. He regards the Soviet Union with a mixture of hope and scepticism, but his own liberal principles are more important to him. He believes in the idea of progress. He gives the doctrine of evolution an optimistic inter-pretation, adopting a social Darwinism that sees man embarked on an inevitably melioristic course. He believes that the dignity of man will not only survive Nazi brutality but will defeat it. The difficulty with the professor is not alone with his nostalgia. It is not so much that he seems to be living in the past as it is that he dwells in no real world at all. His convictions seem to exist in a vacuum and have no relationship to any world we can recognize.

In *The Moon Is Down* (1942), John Steinbeck also wrote about the Nazis. Curiously, this book failed to exploit the political re-

sources of the old liberalism in order to make a clear-cut condemnation, on ideological grounds, of German fascism. But Steinbeck's
subsequent novels, *Cannery Row* (1945) and *The Wayward Bus*
(1947), are built on accepted propositions of the old liberalism:
the failure in integrity, morality, and vitality of the middle class;
the shallowness and hypocrisy of the business or success ethic. The
happy bums of Cannery Row and the scientist of its marine labora-
tory represent two ideals that are superior to the values of respectability as embodied in the ulcer-ridden, trussed-up, decent citizens
of the community. And the independent, sexually potent bus
driver of the second novel is superior to Mr. Pritchard, its business-
man. In the folklore of liberalism, one must give unqualified admiration to the disengaged rationalism represented by the scientist
and to the careless abandon of the propertyless life represented
by the bohemians in the Monterey bush. Yet it seems to me a
narrowly limited view of human experience to attribute the genuine life-drive exclusively to heroes of the kind presented in these
novels. Furthermore, they are characters so typical and generalized
that if they fail to state some great truth with conviction, then
they fail in all. The weakness of these novels more than suggests
that the creative fire, insofar as he had it, went out in Steinbeck
during the forties. The passion which produced his intense relationship to the tensions of the thirties was generated in part by
the society of that decade; it was unable to feed productively on
the changed social reality of the forties. Steinbeck lost his subject
when the depression ended and the war began. He has not as yet
found another.

Still another proponent of old-fashioned liberalism in the forties
is Meyer Levin. His *Citizens* (1940) reveals him as a fair-minded
man of good will who protests social injustice, is outraged at the
follies of routine politics and the evil of monopoly capitalism. He
harbors the traditional leftist hostility toward the police as a symbol for oppressive authority. Since his novel is based on the 1937
Memorial Day clash between police and pickets at Republic Steel
in the Chicago-Hammond area, he has ample opportunity to advance his theory that the police are the victims of an historical
indoctrination that began before the Haymarket affair: all trou-
blemakers in industry are Reds who want to kill the cops and take
over the plants. Fed on such fear, the police are really the victims

of their tradition. Since they are more the instruments of that tradition than the creatures of their own will, they help to pose the principal dilemma of the novel. Levin's thesis is that the citizens of a democracy must come to see their problems and take responsibility for solving them. But the liberal, like the police officer, is not his own man. Levin shows him as the victim and not the master of his own society, a society in which he is not free to make the choices that principle dictates. Trapped between the rejection of communism and the rejection of industrial capitalism, the liberal finds himself in a society which offers him no choice even if he were free to make one. Responsible human action is of course impossible where man is denied choice among alternatives. Thus it is apparent that Levin has failed his liberal by bringing him to an ideological impasse. The author naïvely assumed the possibility of solution to the problems he posed without having sternly and closely examined the possibilities for responsible individual action in the society he was writing about.

BUDD SCHULBERG: THE POPULAR VOICE OF THE OLD LIBERALISM

The confusion that marks old-fashioned liberalism appears in Budd Schulberg as the failure of commitment. In one of the early pages of *The Disenchanted* (1950) he says of two characters, "Children of depression, guided by hearsay knowledge of Marx and Freud, they were always having to sum things up and fit them neatly into cubby holes." He might have said it of himself. For Schulberg is a child of the thirties who never outgrew his childhood. It is unfortunate that he is in the anomalous position of a young writer carrying worn intellectual baggage into a new time. It is worse that he clings to these old, familiar bags in a perplexed and indecisive way. He was in and out of the Communist party, and agonizingly uncertain whether his loyalty was to former friends in the party or to the House Un-American Activities Committee. He was the upper-middle-class Marxist, the radical bourgeois. Faced with such competing values, he has been unable to make decisive choices. The crippling consequence for Schulberg as a writer has been the failure to commit himself.

The dimensions of that failure are clear when we examine the substance of his fiction, which also reveals, of course, his liberal predilections. He is the literary chronicler of the American entertainment world: Hollywood, radio and television, boxing engross his attention. In such milieus it is easy to pose the obvious conflict between success and decent behavior. In Schulberg's treatment of this conflict, the spokesmen for decency are invariably ineffectual. They fail because they are strangers in the carnivorous jungle of American society. An acceptable reason, since it gives us a routine liberal criticism of that society. They also fail because, more significantly, they cannot fully turn their backs upon the gaudy jewels in that jungle. Al Manheim in *What Makes Sammy Run?* (1941), for example, speaks contemptuously of the movies that fall into the Golden Rut of Hollywood despite the immense social and aesthetic potential that motion pictures have. He is a stranger in Hollywood who yearns to belong if only he could make "good" movies there. Or Eddie Lewis, the press agent in *The Harder They Fall* (1947), is aware of every dirty maneuver in the fight game. He yearns for the past when a fight was a contest between two skilled athletes who fought as a matter of honor. He is a stranger in the world of a criminal entrepreneur, but he stays in that world despite disgust with himself. The popular arts, where money is both the energizing and corrupting force, seem to demand a compromise with integrity which makes for crippling self-division. Romantic and sentimental about the movies or the fights, ambivalent about the accessibility of easy money, Schulberg's characters cannot make clean-cut choices. They cannot renounce one world or the other, but must have a little of each: Hollywood, but honest movies; the fight game, but clean fights. Characters who cannot choose do not have to pay. Where there is no moral commitment there is no sense of its cost.

The stereotypes of liberalism appear also in Schulberg's portraits of women. His girls are sophisticated, intellectually and sexually emancipated, competent, respectable, cool, tough-fibered. They are the product of the leftist notion that a girl should be equally at home in a cocktail lounge, on the picket line, in field or factory, and in bed. These girls — they appear in all his novels — have the best of two worlds: they are not frustrated spinsters or mannish homosexuals in the world of affairs nor are they humdrum matrons restive at home with husband and children. They do not have to give up a career for love, or vice versa. They have a chance at everything, because Schulberg has not the courage to make choices or the wit to see that choices are necessary.

It is the freedom of bohemianism, which liberalism appropriated, that Schulberg thinks he cherishes. But such freedom cannot be reconciled with the respectability and discipline of the middle class. Schulberg's girls are not the synthesis he so improbably projected. They shy away from bohemianism. But they do not choose respectability; they abdicate to it. In *The Harder They Fall* the girl rejects Eddie Lewis because, to be sure, he has not the moral strength to oppose his criminal employer, but also (and this motive appears to me the more powerful) because he has not written his play and fulfilled their dream of success. This conclusion comes out of the remembered impulses of Schulberg's middle-class background, which eats away at the treacherous bohemianism. Schulberg himself is the clue to the course these girls take, running away from Hollywood only to make money from the movies, slinking home, as it were, laden with fortune and success.

Like Shep of *The Disenchanted*, Schulberg belongs "with the school of social significance." In his analysis of society he draws upon a diluted Marxism, and he searches for generalizations in his world of the popular arts that characterize the entire American scene. At the beginning of *What Makes Sammy Run?*, for example, Manheim senses that if he can understand what drives Sammy he will have an answer "to everything." And at the end of the novel, Sammy's career is seen as a "blueprint of a way of life that was paying dividends in America in the first half of the twentieth century." After Sammy's first success, bluffing his way into Hollywood with a stolen story, Manheim thinks: "It was America, all the glory and the opportunity, the push and the speed, the grinding of gears and the crap." If I read Schulberg right, his criticism of America, when it rests unequivocally on his complete disapproval of the system of rewards operative here, reveals a sound analogical insight. The American success story comes true for the amoral, aggressive man who achieves his goal at great social and moral expense. Sammy Glick and Nick Latka, the gangster of *The Harder They Fall*, are not representative Americans. Coming out of New York's East Side, they are struggling to achieve status. Their money-getting activity is not in the main stream of solid American enterprise. But their peripheral relation to typical America serves to emphasize Schulberg's conception of the actual nature of middle-class capitalism, since these men are seeking, by whatever means they can command, to come inside from the out-side, to imitate what they see all around them. They are, then, not so much imitators as perhaps caricatures of respectable and accepted American types. What they are in their barefaced greed and ruthlessness, all of America is covertly, behind the façade of the pillared investment house or the sprawling industrial plant.

Schulberg's social criticism in *What Makes Sammy Run?* includes an indictment of the slum as a determining factor in men's lives. This tactic also derives from the thirties. But the full cost of his bondage to that earlier decade is illustrated in *The Disen-chanted*, the novel based on the closing days of F. Scott Fitzger-ald's career. It arose out of a collaboration between Schulberg and Fitzgerald on a movie script. The book's real theme, as Alfred Kazin has pointed out, is "the tragedy of the gifted and charming writer who . . . at some time surrenders to despair and even embraces it as his special fate"; this is a peculiarly American theme — the betrayal of one's talent. Schulberg, however, while aware of his theme seems curiously insensitive to it. He insists on comparing Fitzgerald's twenties with the thirties. Carrying on this task as one who gives his loyalties to the later period, he fails to understand Fitzgerald's decade, a failure that grows out of his acceptance of worn-out syndromes. And so, of course, he fails to understand Fitzgerald. Joy and spontaneity, devotion to crafts-manship without sober-sided self-importance — these are alien to the solemnly social conscious Shep, the young writer in the novel. Shep sees mostly the foolish romanticism of the twenties when a careless generation, in its irresponsibility and lack of discipline, bequeathed to Shep and his generation all the problems of the depression. When Shep cuts through the memories of Manley Halliday (the Fitzgerald of the novel), he finds only a desperate gaiety in the twenties which often ended in violence or suicide. Manley had a big talent, as he says, and he misused it. The serious and callow young man of the thirties passes an unfavorable judg-ment upon him for that.

In his reminiscence of "Fitzgerald in Hollywood," originally published in 1941, Schulberg says explicitly what he was to repeat in his fiction about Fitzgerald in 1950. When the depression came, he writes, ". . . we consciously and a little belligerently turned our backs on Fitzgerald." Commenting on Fitzgerald's difficult last days in Hollywood and the unfinished novel he left, Schulberg concludes, "So Scott ends with another great waste to place beside all his other wastes." For a generation that had to build something out of the ruins, this was the worst crime of all.

In the novel Manley Halliday is not interested in the Screen Writers' Guild. He does not work to raise money for the Spanish Loyalists. He is virtually oblivious to the horror of Mussolini's Abyssinian campaign. In Schulberg's view these causes, and others like them, deserve support. The curious thing is that they should be superimposed on the story of the dark deterioration of an important American writer. But Schulberg has been preoccupied with such matters over the full range of his career, and sees no objection, apparently, to introducing them into this novel. One of the penalties of his affection for the stock in trade of conventional liberalism is the disruption of the unity of his book.

A far more serious consequence for his fiction generally is the thoughtless and habitual loyalty to unexamined liberal precepts as the instruments for an analysis of American society. Schulberg seems to have learned nothing from the challenge of events or of opposing ideas. He still has the "romantic and indignant outlook on life" that Wolcott Gibbs once remarked. The indictment may stand as a true bill against the old-fashioned liberalism that Schulberg has never escaped. His allegiance to the thirties has made him a backward-looking writer. It has undermined his position in American letters, for he is, one must conclude, the chronicler of the entertainment world who is himself not much more than an entertainer.

Irwin Shaw: The Popular Ideas of The Old Liberalism

Irwin Shaw resembles Schulberg in some significant ways. The most striking is not their shared incapacity to free themselves from the thirties but the adulteration of the liberal heritage in the work of both by the idols of respectability and success. Shaw can resist neither the deadly lure of what passes for metropolitan sophistication nor the comfortable corruption of bourgeois materialism. These forces have seriously disrupted the integrity of the value system he purports to believe in. They have given his work that patina of slickness and sentimentality which vitiates so much of it. They have been in part responsible for a literary opportunism which, to confine the matter to the forties, seized upon anti-fascism, the war, and the McCarthy era attack upon the entire left as timely subjects for books. He is, however, a more finished writer than Schulberg, and his prose is sometimes smooth instead of slick. He is generally competent in the techniques of the short story, and when not dogged by the inner contradictions of thought and impulse that I have noted, he can write a moving and effective story. He is of inestimable value, without regard for the quality of his fiction, for the close way he works with the surface of his society and gives us so much of the range of its manners. He does not penetrate to its heart, but he knows its surface tensions and the ready conversational currency it exchanges for ideas.

The preoccupations and attitudes that Shaw learned in the thirties he brought into the next decade, largely untouched except for the pacifism of *Bury The Dead*. The liberal antinaziism that showed up in the title-story of *Sailor off the Bremen and Other Stories* (1939)[2] remains a constant in his work. The liberal attack on anti-Semitism, a virus Shaw sees on the domestic scene as well as in the ideology of fascism, is almost truculently advanced in his pages. The pressures imposed by money, which Shaw felt as a result of the depression, were expressed in the forties as the multifarious demands of middle-class life. And an affinity for the general propositions of democracy, summed up perhaps in the idea of the value and dignity of man, marks every phase of his fiction.

But intertwined with this heritage from the thirties is a fascination with the color and things of middle-class America. Shaw admires the attractive people who might stroll down Fifth Avenue to Washington Square, who breakfast at the Brevoort or eat at home on the terrace at glass and wrought-iron tables. Shaw is enamored of these appurtenances of the middle-class life, which appear in his work as status symbols. When, in one of his stories, the old lady pleads with her impoverished tenants for her rent money because she needs it to buy food, we can feel a legitimate desperation at the shared poverty which makes the poor the prey of the poor. But where, in a story like "Main Currents in American Thought," the harried writer has to find the money for expensive piano lessons or party dresses, the value of these desiderata does

---

[2] Shaw subsequently published three other volumes of short stories in our period: *Welcome to the City and Other Stories* (1942), *An Act of Faith and Other Stories* (1946), and *Mixed Company* (1950).

not seem to justify the constant tension the writer must live with. Or in "Weep in Years to Come" we may accept the anti-Fascist theme, but it is difficult to escape the conclusion that the man in this story is fighting against Hitler in order to preserve no more than the highest standard of living in the world.

Shaw is more successful when he is content to write a tract for the Aspirin Age. He is as sensitive as the journalist or the hostess to the vital topic of the moment. He knows about the high cost of living, the problems of juvenile delinquency, the threat of atomic and germ warfare, the conflict of loyalties raised by friends who dare to dissent, the security neuroses of the organization man. He has ready at hand a collection of horrors to stock the modern man's nightmare, as he shows us in "The Climate of Insomnia." In his best moments he knows the miserable insignificance of men who are unable to rise to any imaginative grasp of the meaning of great events, as he shows in "The City Was in Total Darkness."

Shaw is also successful when his stories demand a straightforward and obvious treatment of emotions. He has no talent for the handling of ideas and no real appetite for them. In "Residents of Other Cities," a story about a pogrom in Kiev, the sixteen-year-old Jewish protagonist says, "My father was always at the side of God and he neglected life." The boy rejects his father's way when he takes a gun and kills the men who have raped his aunt and his sister. This statement and the boy's action suggest to me the activistic, antispiritual, and essentially anti-intellectual creed that is typical of Shaw. It helps to explain his addiction to violence and his joyful acceptance of the Hebraic law of an eye for an eye. The relationship in Shaw between a fierce loyalty to Jews and Jewishness and the application of violence as an instrument of justice arises from his rejection of the traditional passivity of the ghetto Jews, people of the Book, who could not and would not fight back against their oppressors, even to save their lives. Shaw seems at pains to make many of his Jewish characters basic and physically aggressive types. In this way he hopes to combat anti-Semitism, warning that the Jew will fight back against it. And he hopes, furthermore, to establish a place for the Jew in American society where active physical resistance to social ills, where recourse to violence, is a part of the cultural pattern. The Jew who shares in this pattern identifies himself as an American.

Shaw also believes that violence is forced upon good men by

their resistance to naziism. Fascism has made the kind of world in which the only possible response is to maim or to kill, to exchange brutality for brutality. Shaw does not seem to be concerned with the degeneration of character that might follow when good men resort to such brutality, although he is quick to point out the evil effects upon bad men. Again he celebrates the Jewish reply in kind to the Nazi policy of exterminating the Jews. When a German major in one of Shaw's stories confesses his guilt to a Jew and cries out, how can I wash my hands, the Jew replies, "You can cut your throat . . . and see if the blood will take the stain out." In Shaw, the way to deal with the bully, whether he lives in Germany or around the corner, is to fight him with fists or gun.

Another obvious emotion in Shaw is hatred. He is a vigorous and implacable hater. He writes about the Germans as though he were cutting them to pieces, systematically and joyfully. No reconciliation is possible, in his view, with the German mind. The Germans are obsessed with war, and already planning to try for world conquest a third time. The only good German is a dead German. While the reader may be carried along by the vigor of Shaw's emotion and even by an acquiescence in the anti-Nazi bias, which might lead for a while to a suspension of critical intelligence, it does not take long to see that Shaw's phobia against the Germans represents a race theory not unlike the one the Germans had so crudely used. The danger for the writer in relying upon the blood and the viscera instead of the mind lies in his falling into such a trap as this, to find himself supporting at one extreme what he so loudly decries at the other.

Shaw is not so primitive as to rely always upon the exploitation of undiluted, primary emotions. The athlete who takes such satisfaction in breaking up the Nazi off the Bremen may be contrasted with the athlete whose life is a long decline into stagnation from the high moment when he made his eighty-yard run. The appetitive and activistic values that Shaw often admires are in the latter case seen as unable to provide the emotional and intellectual maturity necessary for adult life. I should say in passing, however, that Shaw's notion of maturity involves a knowledge of modern painting and the theater, of politics and labor, but does not include a profound knowledge of the human heart.

In dealing with the war and the Jew, Shaw is often guilty of stopping short with the easy answer when the harder lay beyond or of finding the pleasant solution when the demands of his story make disaster imperative. I have spoken of saints and of rhetoric in connection with the war novel. Shaw's war stories, as well as his war novel, flow from a hagiographical impulse and a sense of mission. These are stories in which the camaraderie of men at arms is good to see, and everyone rejoices when the emergency operation at sea is successful or the lost plane finally comes in. They end well, in a schmaltzy blaze. And the Jew at war is also sentimentalized. Shaw sees him as a victim whom the world must rescue. And he sees the world's resentment because it must fight a war to save the Jew. But in the end, men will come together in brotherhood and mutual trust. This is the moral of "Act of Faith," when the Jewish soldier, with every reason to take his pistol home in order to fight off anti-Semites, decides instead to trust his comrades and the future, sells his pistol and provides them all with money for a leave in Paris. Here Shaw yields up his belief in violence to the kind of easy affirmation that marks him as an old-fashioned liberal. He has not developed the scepticism and the provisionalism of the new liberalism. He has not stared unblinkingly at the power of evil, but has turned his back upon its magnitude.

In addition to the four volumes of short stories that Shaw published between 1939 and 1950, he wrote two novels in the period, a form in which he is less at ease than in shorter fiction. The novels rose directly out of the experience of his time, *The Young Lions* (1948) being about the war and *The Troubled Air* (1951) dealing with the anticommunism of the postwar years. Shaw wrote a novel about the war despite the fact that in 1945 he had said he was suspicious of novels about the war. He wrote it, he has said, to make the fundamental point that the soldier must kill with a sense of sin and tragedy. It is a point that emerges, but obscurely, from the novel. He wrote it also, I suspect, in obedience to that impulse in him to make a record of what his generation believed and how it acted. The same impulse embedded in the same political context had been at work in the short stories that preceded the novel, as Shaw has made clear in speaking of the years when Americans were coming slowly to an understanding of what a growing fascism meant in Europe: "I think I was recording in my short stories what we, our age, felt then." For Shaw these motives for writing made a design for the novel in which democracy would be set against fascism, democracy representing growth of spirit culminating in the realization of one's humanity and fascism representing degeneration to total barbarism and bestiality. The structure of the novel is contained in the polarized themes. The triumph of Noah the American is in his mature recognition of the American ideal: the quiet, decent, competent, pragmatic, humane man. The complete disintegration of Christian the Nazi follows logically from the premises of fascism: the love of war and killing, the cultivation of the predatory and egotistic elements in man, the unrestrained lust, the utilization of treachery, the belief, as Shaw himself has put it, that the end justifies the means. Between them stands the liberal dilettante who wavers between the ideal of service and the opportunism of self-service. Noah's example and his death bring the liberal also to maturity. The war is a purgation when the liberal finally accepts the commitment to it that makes him a responsible human being. The chief problem of the novel lies in the logic of its structure, which demands unbroken parallel lines, one ascending in growth and one descending in disintegration. As a diagram these lines have the appeal of simplicity, which is precisely what is wrong with this conception as the foundation for a novel. Nothing of the unpredictability of human behavior and no sense of the ambiguity of human motive can be permitted to disrupt the smooth flow of these lines. This structure, and the conception of human nature and political ideologies which it assumes, satisfies the demands of rhetoric but does not satisfy any sense of the complex texture of experience.

Shaw treats the problem of the Jew in this novel by identifying Noah Ackerman with the American ideal. He brings Noah to a fulfilment of a personality pattern which, in its virility, its activism, its self-reliance, is the American type as Shaw defines it. Shaw's concern for the Jew, then, turns out to be, not a hope that the Jew might exist in the United States as a unique person with his own culture who embodies an idea of Jewishness, but a hope that the Jew will assimilate himself to the dominant culture and become like everybody else.

The sensitive and sophisticated liberal of this novel becomes the protagonist of *The Troubled Air*, under a different name still confused, still a victim of forces more decisive than any he can command. The producer and director of a radio show, the liberal is faced with a crisis when a hate sheet accuses five members of his cast of being Communists or Red sympathizers, and the agency handling the program demands that they be fired. The book may very well draw upon the activities of a newsletter called *Counterattack*, which was established in 1947 by a group of former FBI men, according to Alan Barth. Under its auspices, *Red Channels*, a formal index for the purge of leftists and dissidents in radio and television, was published in 1950. But it is not necessary to establish a specific source for this book. What Shaw wants to do is to show the havoc that stems from the witch-hunt hysteria that had possessed a large part of the articulate American public in the postwar years. He wants to dramatize the vicious character of reactionary forces as they try to eliminate from American life the possibility of dissent. He wants to show how fear eats away at the lives of men who must live in an atmosphere of universal distrust. He wants to convey his complete disillusionment with the Communists, whose treachery he makes palpable in this book. Earlier in his work Shaw had pleaded for understanding and tolerance with respect to Russia and the Communists, but this novel clearly repudiates them. This novel is different also in that its liberal is left at the end a ruined man with no more than the decency and good will he had at the beginning. Shaw had been willing before this only infrequently to admit the tangible effects of evil as real and lasting. He found no easy answer this time. But the purpose of the liberal's self-immolation is cloudy. He is certainly the victim of sobering events, but he gives no evidence that he has learned from them or that he will change his social-political orientation. As the book ends he is poised on the edge of nothing, with nothing to look forward to. To this the old liberalism had brought him.[3]

It is something, however, that at least Shaw should recognize the limitations of liberalism's faith and optimism. It is worth remarking that he had done so once before, in his short story "The

[3] Another ad hoc novel, in a related area, is *The Sure Thing* (1949), by Merle Miller. It also contains unexamined liberal assumptions. It is addressed to the problems of loyalty and security and built around a dismissal from the State Department on the grounds of Communist sympathies.

Passion of Lance Corporal Hawkins." In fact, he views sceptically in this story the entire complex of liberal ideas that stem from H. G. Wells. Doubt is cast on the idea that reason will prevail in human affairs, that man's social condition will get better and better, that socialism will be an improvement on what has preceded it. The horrors of the war and the peace, and the plight of the Jews, especially in their struggle to establish and hold Israel, seem to have brought Shaw to the beginning of a sober reassessment of his views. The title and action of this story, suggesting a connection with the passion of Christ, is perhaps Shaw's acknowledgment that men must suffer bitterly, must even die, if they are to endure the ironies of history or seek the knowledge that saves.

THE POPULAR FICTION OF THE OLD LIBERALISM

A less self-conscious form of the old liberalism is found in those social-political novels that appeared during the forties dealing with the problems of fascism and of minority racial or religious groups. By and large these novels are an outgrowth of humane convictions about democracy and equality which are nevertheless closely allied to the liberal spirit. The group dealing with the threat of fascism and dictatorship at home is, of course, in that liberal tradition which had demonstrated a sensitivity to the dangers of totalitarianism before other segments of opinion had been aware of its existence.[4] But these American novels of the forties, much as they may share in the virtue of having been right politically, came rather late and offered rather too little in the way of literary merit. The latter point may be seen in a general way if we compare them with the work of Silone or Malraux, who certainly set the standard for the anti-Fascist political novel. In a specific way a comparison to Mann's "Mario and the Magician" is illuminating. Some of the American novels discover a Fascist tactic in the leader's insistence that he is a mere instrument of the people, and that his will is in reality theirs. But no

---

[4] This discussion is based on the following novels: *Sun in Capricorn* (1942), by Hamilton Basso; *A Lion Is in the Streets* (1945), by Adria Locke Langley; *Final Score* (1944), by Warren Beck; *Tommy Gallagher's Crusade* (1939), by James T. Farrell; and *See What I Mean?* (1943), by Lewis Browne, which form a representative group. *Number One*, by John Dos Passos, and *All the King's Men*, by Robert Penn Warren, which deal with the same subject, are analyzed elsewhere.

American novel can approach the profound understanding of this phenomenon that Mann displays when he makes his Cipolla rob men of their will and yet act as the agent of those same wills, when he shows Cipolla imposing his own will and then permitting the people to impose theirs upon him, and when he makes Cipolla suffer in both cases. The satisfying philosophical and psychological understanding displayed here is something American novels do not achieve.

These novels, in addition to their effort to dramatize the corruption of the people's will, employ the other ideological and organizational techniques of international fascism. They show the development of the leader cult, for instance, or the operation of the scapegoat theory, or the alliance between criminal and political forces to achieve tyrannical power, or the use of the big lie. Such material belongs to their subject, but these novels do not succeed in imparting either novelty or vitality to these theoretical considerations of fascism. Where the novels are of interest, however, is in their application of Fascist ideas to a society peculiarly American. These books offer, to illustrate this last point, variations on the theme of class struggle as a means of achieving Fascist power. In his *Sun in Capricorn* Hamilton Basso sees his southern dictator as a product of what he calls the politics of retribution. What he means is that the South has brought upon itself its necessary abdication to dictatorship. Its class structure had penalized the poor whites for so long that they became the willing instruments of an effective demagogue because he would give them the semblance of power and destroy the decadent southern code which had held them in bondage. In an essay on "The Revolt Against the Elite," Peter Viereck points to the dangerous potential in the dissatisfactions and suspicions the lower classes entertain toward the socially prominent and the intellectuals, a resentment which, for instance, pushed people into the camp of Senator McCarthy. Other novels besides Basso's perceive and capitalize upon these class tensions in American society. Writers are aware of how such tensions drive individual men and groups of men to release their frustrations and aggressions in the Fascist attack upon the status quo; they sense how such men wish to merge their suppressed identities in a group that promises a triumph in which they can share. The support for fascism in this kind of fiction is also seen, curiously enough, as coming from the respectable element in society. The group here becomes a refuge for the victims of the status revolution, that is, for middle-class people who have been pushed out of positions of leadership and prestige by those who have risen from below in a dynamic society.

A word should be said here about Hemingway's *For Whom the Bell Tolls* (1940), although it is not essentially a political novel. Politics is a kind of overlay in this book, covering the famous code which exists unchanged as the essential inner fiber of the book. Nevertheless, Robert Jordan, who says he has no politics, is conscious of social issues to a greater degree than any Hemingway hero who preceded him, a reflection of Hemingway's own heightened consciousness of the meaning of both fascism and communism. Jordan's political sentiments, furthermore, belong to the liberal democratic tradition. He is said to believe in liberty, equality, and fraternity. He is fighting for all the poor of the world and against tyranny. It is clear that there is nothing programmatic in his position, and he says he is not interested in the planned society and he is not a Marxist. Jordan's simple, humane creed, a product of the Enlightenment and perhaps of his own western frontier background, brings him to the defense of the Spanish Republic. Hemingway does not have much to say about the Fascist attack upon that government, seeing the bestiality of all men in war, but his sympathies are clearly anti-Fascist. They are also anti-Communist, despite the apparent Russian support of the Loyalist cause. In his recognition of the cynical and hypocritical course of the Russians in Spain, Hemingway seized upon a truth that the liberal mind in the West would accept only later and more reluctantly. This early disenchantment with the Communists speaks for the shrewdness and honesty of Hemingway's political observations, an acuity that may have been possible because he had no ideological commitments to blur his vision. His loyalties are as simple as Jordan's. He is on the side that is morally right, the democratic side. When Jordan dies for that side, it is true that we have an act of individual courage, which the code demands, more than the culmination of a political tragedy. But we have also an overwhelming sense of the danger to the democratic cause, a sense of the inevitability of defeat in the face of the constant pressure of a superior force. As we look back upon it, we can see that Hemingway's book might have prepared us for the intense trials and the harsh challenges the liberal mind would face in the next decade.[5]

The representative, run-of-the-mill novels of the decade treating the problems of minority groups failed to rise above mediocrity because they failed to grasp in all its immense complexity, a real idea of society.[6] Like the anti-totalitarian novels I have just discussed, these novels fail in moral intensity, in the range of their social vision, in the grasp of the intellectual profundities of the problems they confront. If we think of Stendhal's achievement in *The Red and the Black*, for example, where one gets an almost tactile sense of the threads in the social fabric of post-Napoleonic France, we have some notion of what the social-political novel can do. The righteous indignation of the American writer in the forties who protested against the lot of the Negro hardly rivals this level of performance. The exploitation of titillating material like miscegenation or lynchings seems likewise an ill-chosen basis for a novel. Such indignation and exploitation are as feeble as the burlesque or gimmick approach to social problems in which whites are not really white but black, and gentiles who put on glasses become Jews. Not much better is the strategy of shock, which tears the veil — a well-frazzled veil by now — from middle-class respectability to reveal that nice people can be anti-Semites. Common to all these novels is a sense of shame and loss that human beings in America should be denied the dignity of their humanity, but this impulse has generated more propaganda as fiction than it has true social vision. Even when the writer gives us some understanding of the social forces at work — the economic basis for hostility toward the Negro, the influence of enlarged

[5] The only other anti-Communist novel of the decade I know that is worth mention is *The Tender Men* (1948), by Willa Gibbs. The point of this curious, but rather subtle, treatment of its problem goes beyond the Communist conspiracy to take over the country. It lies in the sensitive delineation of the treacherous ambivalence in communism: humanity and decency pulling in one direction and the demands of ideology and political tactics pulling in the other. Out of this ambivalence comes the central irony of the book.

[6] The discussion here is based upon *Focus* (1945), by Arthur Miller; *Gentleman's Agreement* (1947), by Laura Z. Hobson; *Kingsblood Royal* (1947), by Sinclair Lewis; *Strange Fruit* (1944), by Lillian Smith; *Lonely Crusade* (1947), by Chester Himes; *The Winds of Fear* (1944), by Hodding Carter; and *Albert Sears* (1947), by Millen Brand.

horizons on both Negro and white in the postwar South in dealing with race relations — we do not get a cogent and convincing
feeling for human beings involved in the deepest kind of social
tensions. The real shortcoming of such fiction, then, is its failure
to understand the interaction between character and society; in
manipulating the two, it overbears character with a predominant
and numbing interest in the social problem. Even when the writer
is aware of the need to develop his characters in terms of their
particular social crisis, he sometimes is unable to make the interaction meaningful. Chester Himes provides a noteworthy exception to this failing in *Lonely Crusade.* The psychological strains
in the protagonist of this novel, which induce frustrations and
hatred, rob him of his sexual virility and his social role as a male,
force him into the role of the eternal victim, and are the normal
and necessary outgrowths of his effort to act, not like a Negro,
but like a man. The novel is dominated by a conception of a
closed white society that the Negro must penetrate in his quest
for identity as a human being. The self is to be found in identification with the dominant white culture, in acceptance by it, as
the Jews in Irwin Shaw's fiction try to assimilate themselves with
the American people. Himes's novel is not finally successful, because he tries to move in two different directions at the same time.
His protagonist seeks this unity of black and white, but most of
the emotional energy in the book is expended to show that there
are two distinct races, and that each entertains contempt, fear,
hatred, and homicidal urges toward the other. But the novel does
illustrate an important tendency in the fiction of the forties: it is
to fasten attention upon individual man, even when he is deeply
involved in social crisis; the crisis is less important than the self.
The quest for identity becomes, for many writers in this period,
so compelling that it leads them away from political-social considerations altogether.

THE NEW LIBERALISM

The one productive avenue still open in the forties to the writer
who could not surrender his liberal cast of mind completely and
would not turn his back upon men in society was the new liberalism. It was a road that had to be built painstakingly out of the

ruins of traditional liberalism, a process of reconstruction, of borrowing and compromise that only a few were hardy enough or patient enough or honest enough to undertake.

The need for the new liberalism arose out of the betrayal of the Soviet Union and the horror of Fascist dictatorship. Men discovered that old ways of thinking and acting were not relevant in meeting the challenges issued by these two forces — challenges about the nature of man, the nature of political power, the structure of economic life. As they cast about for a new stance, one that would not force them to abdicate every belief they had cherished in order to meet these challenges, some men came to the new liberalism. Its prophet in England was George Orwell, in Italy, Silone. In America, no single commanding figure emerged, but the movement found spokesmen from the field of political history in Arthur Schlesinger, Jr., and Granville Hicks, and from the field of literature in Hicks, John Dos Passos, Mary McCarthy, and, above all, Lionel Trilling. All these people were engaged in what Schlesinger has called, in *The Vital Center*, ". . . the fundamental enterprise of re-examination and self-criticism which liberalism has undergone . . ." during the forties.

In reshaping the liberal mind, neither rationalism nor a naturalistic bias was sacrificed, but the limitations of reason were recognized. It was now understood that reason could not be counted upon to solve all problems, and that, indeed, not all problems were soluble. This recognition constituted a retreat from the naïve optimism of an earlier day. It also meant that reason could not be trusted to contrive political or economic systems which would meet all exigencies and guarantee a good life. In short it was now necessary to reject total planning. Ideology — conceived as a dogmatic intellectual construct of given propositions — fell into disrepute, and the idea of utopia as a closed and closely organized system of social beliefs came under suspicion. In place of total solutions, the new liberalism returned to the American tradition of improvisation and experimentalism, of exploration and tentative progression. It accepted the possibilities of what Karl Popper has called, in *The Open Society and Its Enemies*, piecemeal social engineering. In every sphere of human activity it narrowed its optimistic conceptions; from seeing the world as open possibility it came to see it as limitation. A deepening knowledge of man led it to view the human being as the prey of alienation and as a fallible, uncertain creature. Starting now from this dark view of man, it expected less of him than before, while urging him with tempered insistence to fight his self-division and his estrangement from society. The tough-minded sobriety of the new liberalism rejected the bleeding-heart attitudes that had moved earlier liberals to action. There was no room now for sentimentality about man, especially mass-man or the proletariat who, it was discovered, was not a particularly attractive fellow. Nor could there be any sentimentality about the dangerous potential in centralized power. The new liberalism tried to be clear-eyed in its vision and slow, almost tentative, in its commitments. It tried to be disciplined and responsible. In the forties it was the best guardian of the liberal idea in America.

John Dos Passos and the Need for Rejection

John Dos Passos' relationship to the new liberalism lies more in what he has rejected than in what he has embraced. Communism, native fascism, and centralized bureaucracy are all unacceptable to him, for he sought in the American past, during the forties, a definition of individualism that would be viable in the present. The theme of all the writing he did between 1939 and 1951, including the history and reportage as well as the novels, has been the imperative need to guarantee the survival of the individual in the modern state and to protect his personal liberties. In seizing upon this issue, he acted to meet the crisis of modern, secular man, the crisis of man and society in an age of reconstruction, as Karl Mannheim has called it. That crisis arose as the result of the breakdown, in the long view, of nineteenth-century democracy and freedom. In the more recent past it is the product of totalitarianism, with its corrupting power, its planless regulation, and its abrogation of democratic culture. It is the result, in this country, of a failure in democratic planning, represented by the New Deal, which threatened the survival of human responsibility and individualism. In the spirit of the new liberalism Dos Passos turned from the left, away from the centralized, social-service state and the planned society. In the spirit of a new Americanism he turned toward a Jeffersonian conception of individualism, seeking in the past his solutions to that crisis. His nostalgic and sometimes sentimental effort to revivify the American heritage in the twentieth century, drawing upon the Jeffersonian conception of power and equality and the mystical Transcendental faith in the people, separates him from the new liberalism; but his sense of quest for individual and political fulfilment identifies him with it.

Dos Passos' nonfiction reveals a series of disengagements from contemporary power structures and ideologies. Once close to communism, although probably never a Marxist, Dos Passos said in *Tour of Duty* in 1946 that in the past the Soviet Union had been a dream but is now an ugly reality. It has failed to build a free society; it does not permit the individual to talk back to his government; it has given absolute power to one man. Uncritical liberals, he wrote in *The Prospect Before Us*, have been the victims of their own honorific abstractions. They cannot make an honest analysis of world socialism because they are blinded to the harsh reality by a terminology they are conditioned to accept. The "curse of capitalism" in our world is, like that of socialism, "the too great concentration of power." It creates a society in which freedom is denied to many people. Dos Passos then rejected all aspects of corporate society — Marxist, Socialist, and capitalist — finding each one a mode of regimentation corrupted by the dirty itch for power.

Having surveyed the contemporary scene and found it a wasteland, Dos Passos concluded that his only recourse was to lay a claim against the American past as a source of solutions to man's problems in the present time of troubles. Investigating the past in *The Ground We Stand On* and *The Head and Heart of Thomas Jefferson*, he found that the spirit of the Commonwealth had taken root in America. It had helped to make the early heroes of American history Protestant, dissident, individualistic, rational, and unhappy with the status quo. He found that the habits of a society determine its character and destiny. He admired the Founding Fathers who, understanding human behavior, had limited the power of the governors in order to protect the liberties of the governed. All his beliefs were summed up in Jefferson, who understood that the conflict between authority and self-government is never quite resolved, but that government must protect each man's freedom of action under a system of law. These American affirmations — self-government, individual freedom, limited state power — are the means Dos Passos would use to fertilize the contemporary wasteland. More than this, the excursion into the past, like Jack Burden's in *All the King's Men* and like that of so many of the heroes of Wright Morris' novels, becomes Dos Passos' quest for his own identity.

Dos Passos' nonfiction bears a symbiotic relationship to the four novels he published in this period. The *District of Columbia* trilogy deals with three varieties of political experience. *Adventures of a Young Man* (1939), the first volume, is an examination of the relation of the individual to the Communist party; *Number One* (1943), the second, is the story of a dictator's rise in a democracy; and *The Grand Design* (1949), the last, examines the relation of the individual to the "democratic" bureaucracy. In these novels Dos Passos rejects the party, the dictator, and the centralized bureaucracy, all of them forms of concentrated power in the hands of the all-engrossing state. The individual or the people — i. e., the common man — in these novels, however, are triumphant or at least defiant. *Chosen Country* (1951) is a hymn to America as Dos Passos accepts his native land, for good or for bad, with all her inconsistencies.

The governing imaginative principle in the novels of the trilogy is the shocking disparity between appearance and reality, a view of experience eminently appropriate to the sceptical tone of these works. The appearance-reality dichotomy reveals the gap between Communist profession and performance in *Adventures of a Young Man*, between the would-be dictator's promise and what he is and does in *Number One*, between the New Deal's aspirations for the people and the way it humiliates them in *The Grand Design*.

The hero of *Adventures of a Young Man* is Glenn Spotswood, a naïve idealist who is unfitted by his liberal heritage to cope with the party or with American capitalism. Dos Passos' problem is to endow this character with will and personality in order to make him a free and responsible human being, even while accounting for many of his actions as the result of his environment and parentage. It is a problem he does not fully resolve, and his failure weakens his statement of theme in the novel, which is that the party destroys the individual as a free man aware of his own identity. One of the Communist leaders says, "We are not interested in the fates of individuals." Both Glenn and his scientist friend Paul

Graves rebel against this indifference toward man. Paul has the pragmatic, experimental, and inductive qualities of mind that mark the scientist and the democratic American. He goes to Russia in the spirit of inquiry, but leaves because there both social and scientific experimentation are frustrated by political dogma and the prevalence of terror. Glenn, who moves from the single tax to radical syndicalism, then to the party, and finally to lonely, unilateral dissent, dies in the Spanish Civil War through the treachery of the Communists. His quest for political salvation has been his education. What he learns proves fatal. The moral indignation and love of mankind that fired him do not save him. The last resort of idealism is martyrdom to an organization of power that will not tolerate decent human behavior. Yet Glenn's dedication to principle does demonstrate the authority of individual integrity.

Number One is Dos Passos' grim analysis of the native Fascist. The would-be dictator presents a public face composed of egalitarian features: spontaneous good fellowship; an economics — "Every Man a Millionaire" is his slogan — based on the communal sanctions in the Bible and on hostility to the corporations; identification with the common man. Beneath this mask Chuck Crawford is a rock-hard manipulator of men and money, an adulterer, a hypocrite, a careful politician whose spontaneity comes out of a card file. Frightening as this portrait is in the dangerous difference it reveals between appearance and reality, it is still a stereotype. Crawford simply mushrooms ineluctably under Dos Passos' hand, filling every crease in the face of the idealized version of the dictator. He has no hesitations, no moral ideas, and no moral conflicts. He moves on the straight string of violent inevitability. As a Fascist he is chilling, but as a character he is a convincing demonstration of Dos Passos' tendency to run to types.

Yet Dos Passos does create moral conflict in this novel. Tyler Spotswood, Glenn's brother, works for Chuck. He is caught between his own moral idealism and Chuck's total immorality, a conflict Dos Passos does not make particularly believable. The climax of the novel comes when Tyler must make a choice between accepting the punishment he deserves or making a dirty political deal that might lead to his exoneration. He chooses the former because his brother Glenn has exhorted him in a posthumous letter from Spain not to sell out. To save the nation and the people, Tyler knows, we must begin by saving ourselves. Tyler frees his will for a moral act whereby he destroys his life that he may gain it.

It is not clear that "the people" will profit from Tyler's act, but of Dos Passos' emotional attachment to this abstraction called "the people" there can be no doubt. Each chapter of this novel is preceded by a forechapter which begins, "When you try to find the people . . ." Like Whitman, Dos Passos finds and identifies with many different kinds of people, until he discovers that when you try to find the people you find that the people are everybody, the people are the Republic. Dos Passos believes in both the one and the many, in the individual and the mass. It is a Transcendental problem in reconciliation that Whitman also had to face. Both writers celebrate the co-equal sovereignty of the self-conscious, self-willed individual and of the mass who make the nation. Thus we can say that *Number One* is a rejection of dictatorship on moral grounds by a revitalized individual acting in the name of the people who "rise at once against the never-ending audacity of elected persons."

The Grand Design is based on a pattern of rejection-affirmation. Dos Passos turns away from the New Deal as an example of bureaucracy in the corporate state, from the Communist party once again, and from the city of Washington, the symbol of government as Leviathan. He turns toward, or back to, Jeffersonian individualism and agrarianism and the Whitmanian mystique as regards the people. It is these roots in the past which enable his characters to survive. The first extra-narrative section in the novel gives us the mood and method of Whitman: a ubiquitous consciousness, identifying with people on the farm and in Wall Street, participating with boundless compassion in their lives. The principal characters in *The Grand Design* are attached to the Department of Agriculture, among them Paul Graves, whose great objective is to save the small, family-owned farm. In *State of the Nation*, which is the source book for this novel, Dos Passos had said that the independent farmer was the balance wheel of popular self-government. In the novel, Paul tries to give flesh to the Jeffersonian dream of agrarian democracy by settling people on the land and making them independent.

The frustration of the Jeffersonian and Whitmanian ideal is the heart of Dos Passos' criticism of the New Deal. Paul discovers that the corporate state in reality humiliates people while professing to help them. It lowers their consequence. Furthermore Dos Passos claims that big government means the concentration of power in the hands of one man, although no man is good enough to be trusted with more than limited power. The book ends with the bitter charge that the President, the only one who has power, has misused his power in redesigning a world in which men's freedoms are left out. Finally, Dos Passos sees the decline of the New Deal when politics interferes with the performance of the bureaucrats and crisis pushes it from experimentalism to conservatism. The point is made in the almost vicious portraits of characters who resemble Henry Wallace, Harry Hopkins, and Jesse Jones.

In 1951 *Chosen Country* appeared, the story of the making of an American. It is the love story of Jay Pignatelli and Lulie Harrington, of John Dos Passos and the United States. The time of rejection has passed. Jay, in a position to make a conscious choice, since he is as much European as American, deliberately chooses to be an American and live in America. But not until he has made his journey of self-discovery which has led also to the discovery of America, his new-found land. It is a sober but exhilarating assessment of the American experience. The horror of war, the assassination of a radical labor leader, the judicial tragedy of what is called the Sabatini case, the bourgeois persecution of the creative mind are all here. These are the experiences that had broken the heart and pierced the faith of earlier Dos Passos heroes, and of Dos Passos himself, but here they are assimilated in the love and understanding of a country where the frustration of the present is mitigated by the "feeling of anticipation of a dazzling future," where everything is new and unformed, and where freedom's scaffolding, the institutions that are the Republic's framework, is renewed daily. American society, with all its opportunities and defects, gives the young man the freedom to find happiness. The testament to America is palpably Dos Passos' conviction, for Jay Pignatelli is Dos Passos. The shy autobiographical intimations of the Camera Eye in *U.S.A.* are superseded here by thinly veiled personal experience: the "real" experience of Harvard, the war, the Sacco-Vanzetti case, and the spiritual experience of the diffi-dent spectator, always a little alien, accepting at last his identity as an American.

Dos Passos has in this novel expressed a more buoyant con-fidence than the new liberalism, in its chastened and cautious temper, might reveal and has accepted more than it might be willing to endorse. In fact, a certain ambiguity of allegiance ap-pears in the total process of self-criticism and in the enterprise of rethinking his political position that he undertook in the forties. His rejection of old-fashioned liberalism was not a rejection of traditional liberalism. He saw his task as the restoration of Jeffer-sonian principles, as the need to save them from those in the twentieth century who had corrupted them. Dos Passos found he could not savor the historical irony that had made Jefferson the patron saint of the liberals who, in the thirties, sanctioned the growth of the corporate state. As a consequence, his attack upon those liberals and his reliance upon tradition brought him into an apparently sympathetic relationship with the reinvigorated right in American life, especially that segment of the right that found its conservatism in preserving, paradoxically, our tradition of liberalism. Yet finally I should say that Dos Passos belongs in the company of the new liberalism because he has expiated the guilt and failure of American liberalism in the two preceding decades. In the end, it can be said that he spoke up more for traditional liberalism than for tradition.

GRANVILLE HICKS AND THE PAINFUL PROCESS OF RECONSTRUCTION

Granville Hicks belongs more surely to the new liberalism. As so many ex-Communists rushed to publicize their confessions of error and so many liberals fell into confused silence, Hicks, like Dos Passos, undertook the painful task of evaluation and recon-struction: What was wrong with being a Communist? Why must one leave the party? Where does one go now? Hicks could have become a professional witness for congressional adventurers or a noisy convert to religion, like some other ex-Communists. He chose instead to shuck off his Marxist orientation toward art and to investigate for himself the relations between literature and so-ciety. He sought to find his troubled way to democratic solutions of his political problems. In *Where We Came Out*, a kind of political testament, he evolves a position he calls critical liberalism. It has all the essentials of the new liberalism.

Our interest is in how Hicks works out this position in the four novels he published in our period. He began with *The First to Awaken* (1940; written with Richard M. Bennett), a socialistic utopian novel in which Hicks denies the possibility of utopia. This paradox is easily explained. Utopia, of course, means a perfect and finished society. Hicks makes it clear that his state and his people have achieved neither condition; through the application of science, however, economic well-being and psychic health have replaced the uncertainties and exploitations of capitalism. Hicks's restraint gives him a dynamic society peopled by flawed human beings as an optimum state of being. This limited view escapes the criticism that Karl Popper levels against the Platonic notion of utopian social engineering. Popper argues that utopianism is dangerously totalitarian. As aestheticism values order and unity in art, so utopianism strives for the same qualities in society, sacrificing all other considerations to these artistic abstractions. To this criticism of the inflexibility and dictatorial character of utopian thought, Popper adds his conviction that it is irrational to believe in the complete reconstruction of society. Reacting against the Marxist blueprint, Hicks in all probability came to conclusions very like those of Popper. While the society of the year 2040 to which Hicks's protagonist awakens is clearly socialistic, a decentralized, self-sufficient regionalism guarantees some autonomy to the sections and preserves the characteristic differences of each. Hicks wants socialism, but he rejects its dogma and its power-concentration, he rejects its aspirations for totality and perfectibility. As a novel, *The First to Awaken* is far less successful than as a social document, however. It is derivative, with many echoes of Bellamy's *Looking Backward*. It is not sufficiently imaginative or ingenious in its projection of scientific achievement. It is, by its very nature, predictable.

Hicks's next book, *Only One Storm* (1942), shows obvious improvement and is, indeed, a convincing fiction because, for one thing, it is built on a sound structural pattern. The story of a small town in the Berkshires, it derives its form from the rhythm of village life. The counterpoints in this rhythm are two: the world of nature of which the villagers are always aware and the great society, or the macrocosm, where the terrifying events of 1938 and 1939 are being played out. Another structural device is the posing of a dilemma for the protagonist; he is forced to make a choice between the Communist party and the macrocosm, and the democratic politics of the microcosm, the village. We are able to watch the development of his character as he struggles to clarify his ideas and to apply his will to the resolution of his problems. Hicks himself, in his nonfiction *Small Town*, has formulated the general question of *Only One Storm* in this way: "could a person bring to a small community some benefit from the knowledge and experience he had gained in college, in an urban career, in a world of ideas beyond the small town's life?" The effectiveness of the book rests also on Hicks's intimate understanding of this problem.

In the novel, Canby Kittredge is a pragmatic hero who rejects the negative attitudes about him, refuses to join the Communist party, flees the big city, and begins to participate actively in the affairs of the small town in which he settles. By putting Canby into the politics of his town, Hicks is trying to say that active participation is a means of revitalizing the traditional democratic processes. By setting the story in a small town where personal relationships are necessarily close, he has tried to show how the impersonal element in our lives may be diminished. By having his character spurn the party of planned world revolution for the more limited activity of trying to govern a village, Hicks expresses a healthy distrust of what he himself called, in 1954, "ambitious, all-inclusive schemes for the making over of society." Canby has chosen the adjustment and accommodation necessary to the town meeting instead of the dogmatic ideology of the party line.

In the politics of the closed society, the system of ideas is more important than the people. But in the politics of democracy, the people are of primary importance. Trying to illustrate this difference, Hicks gives us a sense of the special importance of the individual. He tries to deal with virtually all the people who inhabit the village in his novel. And he tries to see them as individualized characters whose personal relationships are interwoven with their social and political activities. He does not succeed in developing each one, but he does show his characters as at once selfish and generous, mean-spirited and large-hearted, dogmatic and narrow but cautiously open to a new idea or a stranger. This kind of personalism is clearly no romanticizing of the villager. It is a considered return to the village in contrast to the revolt against it of the twenties. It is a return made possible by a newly matured view of human nature. The old liberal faith in environmentalism had led to the view that the manipulation of social institutions would guarantee an improvement in human nature. In the forties, Hicks has come to see the shortcomings of this view and makes, instead, a revisionist interpretation of human nature. He depicts the jealousy, the destructive gossip, the adultery, the incest in a small town, but he acknowledges also the sturdy independence of this man and the benevolent wisdom of that. In short, a balanced view of human nature emerges in this novel, one as aware of man's proclivity for sin and violence as it is of his potentiality for disinterested action, loyalty, love.

Only One Storm retains the optimism of the old liberalism and its sense that democracy is a great, unfinished adventure. It is a novel of affirmation then, but written in a chastened mood, the mood of the new liberalism, in which Hicks accepts American democracy and mankind for what they are, even while recognizing the weaknesses of both.

Hicks published *Behold Trouble* in 1944 and *There Was a Man in Our Town* in 1952. The first of these novels is clearly a failure and the second adds nothing to what he had said earlier. In both Hicks persists in saying that it is essential in understanding human beings that we recognize their inconsistency and irrationality. In both he remains in the small town, the latter novel especially demonstrating Hicks's hope that the village is not only a self-contained refuge from the city, as he had said in *Small Town*, but the instrument for a modified decentralization. This fiction is modest and knowledgeable. It is, like the other books, aware of the world as limitation. All the novels are a product of Hicks's struggle to reconcile his principles and aspirations with the erratic course of history and the insidious attraction of dogma. Hicks has emerged from this struggle on a plateau I have called the new liberalism. It is a position flexible, rational, tough-minded, and thoroughly American.

MARY McCARTHY AS THE SCEPTICAL NEW LIBERAL

It is also an obvious position, developed in the open air, as it were. Hicks is as transparent as a window glass; everything is visible to the observer who looks in. His ingenuous and innocent stance is likewise American. When I say that Mary McCarthy is very different from Hicks, I do not mean to suggest that she is un-American but only that the new liberalism appealed also to a writer of very different temperament and a more opaque vision. The fiction of Mary McCarthy is in the tradition of the novel of manners. She is the heartless chronicler of the fashionable middle- and upper-middle-class world, far too intelligent and too intent on maintaining her distance from it to become emotionally involved with it as Irwin Shaw does. She is likewise the chronicler of the fashionable and faddish intellectual world. She examines all with a cold honesty that is her chief merit as a satirist. That coldness has meant an indifference to commitment to political creed as much as to moral code. Such doubts as she has had as to man's social behavior have created the proper pessimistic basis for an examination of liberalism and have induced in her the sceptical spirit of the new liberalism. Her intelligent reading of Freud has convinced her that human reason must be regarded with suspicion; and in the dualism which critics have seen in her — impulse and instinct as over against mind and thoughtfulness — reason is usually overborne. Such a bias again is in tune with the spirit of the new liberalism, which reacted against what it conceived to be the exaggerations about the potential of reason. All this suggests neutralism instead of advocacy, so that it is probably most accurate to describe Mary McCarthy as a satirical critic of liberal modes of thought, whose criticisms are close kin to those made by the new liberals. Yet she has said, "I believe in a kind of libertarian socialism, a decentralized socialism." The similarity to Hicks's position is here striking; but when she adds, "I don't see any possibility of achieving it," the depth of her detached pessimism is in sharp contrast to his commitment.

Mary McCarthy's first book of fiction, a collection of short stories called *The Company She Keeps* (1942), reveals at once the sharpness of wit and the penetration of character that are to mark all her work. The penetration is made possible by an admirable intelligence and a relentless, a pitiless, insistence on seeing everything — but it is, as will be the case in her later books, without imaginative depth or emotional profundity. She seems a completely disengaged writer. This volume has in it also a scientific, unflagging curiosity about sex, much like Professor Kinsey's and little more imaginative than his. It is a curiosity that satisfies us right down to the most accurate detail of the safety pin on the panties, clinical and spectatorial as any antiseptic census-taker for a reliable sociological enterprise might be. But the most remarkable feature of these stories is that they are redolent of the thirties; they are dated. I do not refer to the way that Miss McCarthy lifts the cover from some odd corner of the depression, giving us intimations of the scramble for existence in that dreary time. I am talking about what I shall call the clash of two cultures, which is a conflict that had lost much of its meaning by the forties.

"The Man in the Brooks Brothers Shirt," "Portrait of the Intellectual as a Yale Man," and "The Genial Host" illustrate this clash. The first two deserve discussion. In "The Man in the Brooks Brothers Shirt," the business culture in America is represented by the man who wears the right clothes and entertains the conventional romantic notion about giving up "everything" for a grand passion. The bohemian-intellectual-liberal culture is represented by the woman who permits herself to have an affair with the man. The conflict is expressed largely in sexual terms and centers chiefly in the man. He feels himself pitted against a conception of freedom in sexual behavior and in intellectual attitudes that challenges his conservative tastes (which are shoddy), his respectability, his attachment to his family and his business. His initial triumph is to sleep with the woman; he does not thereby attain freedom from conventional modes of moral behavior but he does victimize her by the conventional male standards of his class. In the morning he thinks he is in love and proposes to her unlikely schemes for his liberation from the bourgeois life he leads in Cleveland. This is the most intense point of the affair, which dwindles away thereafter in the mutual loss of ardor. The man is a willing, an inevitable prisoner of his status and his conventional, confused mind. The woman's representation of the liberated personality, in the face of his money and his masculinity, is robbed of its force. In the end, when they part, each is entrenched in his prejudices. Neither way of life is shown as admirable. The two worlds remain uneasily apart. Miss McCarthy has shown no partisanship. She is as critical of passive and weak bohemian liberalism as she is of middle-class sterility.

"Portrait of the Intellectual as a Yale Man" is another version of this clash. The issue in this story involves the integrity of the liberal left position in the face of a challenge from the comfortable middle class. Bohemianism plays no part here. The acidly etched portrait of the respectable young man who sees that common sense and morality dictate allegiance to the left, but who cannot outgrow or escape his ingrained bourgeois impulses reveals rather more partisanship than Miss McCarthy ordinarily permits herself. In the corruption of this young man, who moves from the liberal weeklies to the equivalent of *Time* and grows fat in mind and body, she has traced one route that liberalism took in its decline. Her controlled contempt for the apostate is what gives the edge to the satire in this story.

I cannot leave this volume without a comment on the female character who, under different names, seems to turn up in several of the stories. She is sometimes mannered and heartless, sometimes brittle and unstable. Miss McCarthy's treatment of her is always admirably clever, but never profound. As the woman contemplates divorce or an affair, as she undergoes psychoanalysis, she is revealed as a conventional product of a certain segment of sophisticated, metropolitan society in America. She glitters with all the social and psychic maladies that beset her world. And so she stands as a criticism of that world. When Miss McCarthy wishes us to believe that this woman suffers real anguish, however, we are not convinced. Does she seek a father-figure because her real father induced insecurity by neglecting her? Does she have a sense of loss because she has no male genitalia? Does she react against the Church because her stepmother embodies all the grossest superstition of religion? Does she find an outlet in mild nymphomania? It is all too pat, a tour de force. Nothing is on trial, not middle-class society, not the liberated intellectual personality, not even womanhood itself. Yet one does feel that far down at the core of these stories lie some elementary truths about women; one does sense the deep, sex-related resentment of the woman, forced into the passive and receptive role in life, forced in her intelligent and both aggressive and sensitive way to treat with the inferior male. Unfortunately, Miss McCarthy withdraws from these glancing insights. She seems unwilling to give sufficient thought or imaginative energy to their development.

Miss McCarthy's first novel, *The Oasis* (1949) is a slight work, yet a more intellectualized and sophisticated consideration of the utopian theme than Hicks's *The First to Awaken*. Hicks reminds one, thinking of the tradition of associationism in America, of the earnest George Ripley, the moving spirit in the Brook Farm experiment, who believed, with that largeness of spirit character-istic of Transcendentalism, that it was the duty of Christian men to redeem society from all evils. Optimistically, he thought Brook Farm was the way to his goal. Miss McCarthy reminds one of Hawthorne, who viewed Brook Farm and the spirit of reformism, in *The Blithedale Romance*, with a sceptical eye, pessimistic about eradicating evil from the human heart or from society, no matter how much outward circumstances might be changed. The theme of *The Oasis* is the refractory nature of things; that is, man and external nature are too complex to submit themselves to the easy solutions proposed in the dream of utopia. It is a satire on all who commit themselves to foolish hope. It is a critique of exuber-ant liberalism. If we take into consideration the show of loyalties in "Portrait of the Intellectual," the novel becomes a reassessment of liberalism, if not a retreat from it.

In her study of the questions raised by group behavior, Miss McCarthy makes of the utopians a feckless lot. Confronted with various crises, they tend either to refurbish outworn ideologies, which at once divide them into cliques and paralyze action, or to drift into fantasy. Dedicated to saving the world, they reveal themselves as inept and impractical at surviving in it. Faced with a problem presumably within the limits of their strength and prerogatives, they funk it. They propose to live by heightened moral scruples and to act in accordance with enlightened social principles, and are astonished to discover that stubborn circum-stance permits neither. An illuminating incident occurs when sullen interlopers invade utopia's property to pick utopians' ber-ries. Spoken to, indecisively, by utopians who do not believe in or know how to assert property rights, the interlopers refuse to leave. They do depart, however, when they are threatened by a gun-bearing veteran, a singular character among the utopians. The primacy of force is not Miss McCarthy's point but the inde-cision that eats out the liberal-reformist will. It is a point made boldly, with the satirist's sword, but not subtly. The scene, like the novel as a whole, is not a success, because Miss McCarthy does not fairly explore the moral nuances of a partial commitment, of a calculatedly tentative one. She can knock away the underpinnings of orthodox liberal-leftist ideologies with a firm hand, but she does not understand either the pain or the virtue of leading the moral life in the world of ambiguity. In this most important respect, she muffs her opportunity in this novel. She falls short in other ways too, particularly as the sense of the importance of idea casts a shadow upon the book and inhibits the rounded development of the characters.

Cast a Cold Eye (1950) is a collection of fictional and autobiographical pieces. The latter, incorporated into *Memories of a Catholic Girlhood*, published in 1957, are relevant here insofar as they confirm the intelligence and the capacity for honesty and self-examination which one sees in the stories. The fiction in this volume adds nothing to the examination of the new liberalism, treating instead the manners of society and the neuroses of its more sensitive members. It freely distributes sharp comments on the sterility and tensions of upper-middle-class life. Whatever the center of her story, Miss McCarthy brings the same relentless, intricate, probing intelligence to bear. It is a technique she seems to owe to Freudian analysis, a conviction that if human action is explicable it is to be understood only through the careful accumulation of the psychic evidence that lies well buried in the human personality.

The self-criticism of the autobiographical fragments is the quality of mind in Miss McCarthy that turned her away from the rational society of *The Oasis* and turns her, in *The Groves of Academe* (1952), away from the world of liberal education and the liberal mind. Clearly belonging to the intelligentsia, she is always snapping at it, as though, in a masochistic fit of impatience, she were to turn upon herself. The strain of self-disgust that marks this last novel is apparent also in those autobiographical pieces, which prepare us for the portrait of Henry Mulcahy, the unpleasant Irish protagonist of *The Groves of Academe*. Mulcahy's Irish manners and his Irish home are sticky, unclean, revolting by antiseptic Protestant standards. Mulcahy is a clever, amoral scoundrel. Miss McCarthy seems more intent upon rubbing her own nose in the intimate, tribal details of his Irish life and character than

she is in the reader's reaction to Henry. She seems to feel the outsider's guilt at being outside the society. She has the insider's
disgust, as one of Irish descent, at a life different from the going,
acceptable standard of life. It is self-disgust.

It is that emotion which makes others possible in this mordant
satire, the least well controlled of her books. Having freed herself
from any clinging racial loyalty, she feels herself free to set upon
any groups or any beliefs that might have claimed her allegiance.
Her novel becomes a kind of fable, then, to illustrate liberal culpability and susceptibility: an attack upon humane education, the
intelligentsia, upon literature itself. It is the story of a small
progressive college — one thinks of Bard or Sarah Lawrence — with
a progressive, liberal president. It is set in a period of fear and
reaction: Alger Hiss has been convicted, spies like Fuchs and
Greenglass have been uncovered, and Senator McCarthy is abroad
in the land. Against this background, the president fires Mulcahy,
a brilliant but difficult personality who has been identified with
liberal-leftist activities, although the president had earlier spoken
out against the witch hunt in the universities. To intensify the
president's dilemma, Mulcahy circulates the story that he is a card-
carrying member of the Communist party. It thus appears that
the president has fired Mulcahy for his political beliefs and convicted himself of hypocrisy. Mulcahy is so skilful in manipulating
his colleagues and the total situation that in the end he keeps his
job and the president is forced to resign.

What might have been a grimly serious story about the ravages
of reaction, in the manner of *The Troubled Air*, becomes instead
a madcap tissue of intrigue in which justice and morality are set
aside as irrelevant. The question of whether or not Communists
should be allowed to teach in the universities is only a bugaboo of
the liberal academic mind, which takes itself too seriously. When
Henry spreads the word that he is a Communist, he has deliberately made himself in a particular image that would, he knew,
excite the sympathy and support of a particular kind of person,
many of whom would be his colleagues. Miss McCarthy is surely
commenting here upon the perversity of the liberal mind in finding the most difficult of all possible causes to champion. She is,
I am sure, amused at its impulse toward self-immolation. When
Henry tells his story to a young faculty member, he reflects,

At bottom . . . she was conventional, believing in a conventional moral order and- shocked by deviations from it into a sense of helpless guilt toward the deviator. In other words, she was a true liberal, as he had always suspected, who could not tolerate in her well-modulated heart that others should be wickeder than she, any more than she could bear that she should be richer, better born, better looking than some statistical median.

Naïvely, she acts in the liberal pattern he has guessed she would follow, "even when one would have thought that her eyes would have been opened to a darker truth about human nature than her philosophy admitted."

That quotation is the key to the novel, I believe. It does not explain, to be sure, the satire on the poetry conference or on the jargon of the academics. But it does explain the controlling temper Miss McCarthy exercises over the entire novel. She presides there, caustic, sceptical, detached, even a little unpleasant, ticking off the follies the old liberal orientation had led us into and toting up the damage its miscalculations about man and power have cost. She seems superior and indifferent to all schools of thought or political allegiances. She is a new liberal by default. While she asserts nothing except man's folly, she criticizes the old liberalism in the same way that the new liberals have done.

LIONEL TRILLING AND THE CRISIS IN OUR CULTURE

The most distinguished contribution to the new liberalism has been Lionel Trilling's *The Middle of the Journey* (1947). This novel is remarkable for the breadth of its intention and relevance to its time. In it we see the interplay of human experience and political idea which produces a penetrating and convincing analysis of the crisis of our culture. The fate of the liberal mind and the full emergence of the new liberalism are likewise to be seen here. For these reasons, I offer an extended analysis of this book.

It is the kind of novel for which Trilling's criticism would have prepared us, but the novel, curiously enough, preceded most of the relevant critical essays. These are nevertheless helpful in understanding *The Middle of the Journey*, if they are not a defense of it, and I propose to glance at them as a preamble to the discussion of the novel itself. It is a novel of ideas, the kind that Trilling defended in "The Meaning of a Literary Idea" when he argued that literature is concerned with man in society and that the very form of literature is an idea: "Whether we deal with syllogisms or poems," Trilling wrote, "we deal with dialectic — with, that is, a developing series of statements." The dialectic is the organizing principle of *The Middle of the Journey*, which treats a clash of ideologies. Four different positions may be distinguished: the Communist and the Christian, both embodied in Gifford Maxim; the fellow-traveller or leftist-liberal, represented by Arthur and Nancy Croom; the new liberal, represented by John Laskell, the protagonist. All of these are brought into skilfully arranged conflict.

If it be said that Trilling's critical principles neglect those passions of men that literature should properly treat, he rights the balance in "Manners, Morals, and the Novel." For there he says that the most effective agent of the moral imagination is the novel. We need, he says, a moral realism that will perceive the dangers in the moral life itself. We must beware the corruption produced when we impose our most generous impulses as human beings upon others. Moral realism, the product of the free play of the moral imagination, is the instrument, says Trilling, that will save us from this most ironic and tragic failure. Specifically, it is his own imagination and insight in his novel which brings this paradox home to the consciousness of his readers with the conviction of art. The Crooms and Maxim, all good people, grow passionately harsh in the interest of the other man's well-being.

Other clues as to the meaning of the novel are to be found in Trilling's two essays on Freud. In *Freud and the Crisis of Our Culture*, Trilling describes that crisis as the "progressive deterioration of accurate knowledge of the self and of the right relation between the self and the culture. . . ." This, I take it, is the real subject of the novel, the relationship between the self and the culture, which John Laskell seeks to determine as he tries to discover his own identity as well as to understand the society in which he lives. It is a problem constantly and naggingly present to the modern consciousness. Meeting it in his essay on Freud, Trilling argues that no matter how generous the culture in its intention to honor and value the self, the culture may misapprehend the nature of the self. In such a case, biology becomes a liberating force in Freud's thought, freeing us from the control of the culture by suggesting that there is some human quality beyond its reach. Somewhere in all of us is a "hard, irreducible, stubborn core of biological urgency, and biological necessity, and biological *reason*, which culture cannot reach and which reserves the right, which sooner or later it will exercise, to judge the culture and resist and revise it." Trilling is, in short, asserting the primacy of the individual or the self on the basis of what he has learned from Freud. He finds further evidence of this same primacy in the death wish. The death instinct, he concludes, is "the effort of finely tempered minds to affirm the self in an ultimate confrontation of reality."

Now literature is dedicated to the conception of the self, says Trilling, and for the past two centuries the particular concern of literature ". . . has been with the self in its standing quarrel with culture." In the closing paragraphs of an earlier essay, "Freud and Literature," Trilling outlines the conception of the self that he finds in Freud and that he obviously accepts. The death instinct and the reality principle, in which the mind embraces its own pain for some vital purpose, are the two broad Freudian conceptions that give us a view of man as a various and complex creature. Everything that man gains ". . . he pays for in more than equal coin; compromise and the compounding with defeat constitute his best way of getting through the world. His best qualities are the result of a struggle whose outcome is tragic. Yet he is a creature of love. . . ."

In his novel Trilling explores on two levels the culture in which the self, so conceived, must live: the philosophical and the political levels. Philosophically, he brings John Laskell to the end of his quest for identity through a consideration of the metaphysics of time, existence, and death; on the ethical plane, he confronts Laskell with questions of moral responsibility and distinctions between moral and political action. Politically, Trilling moves Laskell from an uncritical liberalism to a new humanistic liberalism. In defining this position as Laskell achieves it at the end of the novel, Trilling has replied to the attack of the new conservatism upon the liberal mind. He has made his answer with the self-consciousness of the liberal who has come to the end of innocence. His Freudian interpretation of man's nature undermines the simplistic optimism about man prevalent among the old liberals of the thirties, yet it denies the God-dependence and guilt-obsession to be found in many of the new conservatives.

The interaction between the self and the culture becomes apparent on the first page of *The Middle of the Journey*. Maxim and Laskell are traveling by train from New York to Connecticut. Maxim is going to "make arrangements about acquiring an existence," because as an underground worker for the Communist party he had had no individual identity. Laskell thinks poor Maxim mad, but his madness a measure of the world's sickness. Only a wildly chaotic society could rob a man of a sense of his own being. Laskell thus at once consummates in his mind the marriage of two orders of experience — that of personal identity and that of the world's condition. This new awareness of man as an individual stubbornly holding himself apart from society but nevertheless enmeshed in it illustrates again that major shift in vision for the social novelists of the forties. Faith in society is not all in all for them.

Now Laskell himself, like Maxim, must also find a new identity. He had been committed to the hopeful and progressive aspects of modern life, but as the result of a long illness he begins to find his own changing self more interesting than social problems. While sick, he has a love affair with death. Trilling, borrowing the Freudian death instinct, uses it to bring Laskell, paradoxically, to that ultimate confrontation of reality. His illness is a symbolic crisis marking the middle of the journey of life when men stray into the dark forest and must seek again the right path, as Dante says in the opening lines of *The Divine Comedy*. The change that comes over Laskell as a consequence of his illness readies him for the repudiation of the old liberalism.

Laskell is nursed by Miss Debry and Miss Paine. The former represents life on its simplest biological level. But Laskell, still engaged by death and unprepared to discover the self, is not interested in her. In the Freudian context of the novel, she would be the life-affirming force that liberates the self from the culture. Miss Paine *is* pain — the travail attendant upon the passage from life to death to new life. She impresses upon the new, emerging selfhood of Laskell the unavoidable harshness of a reality where pain and death are imminent. She has seriously jarred his easy allegiance to the hopeful and progressive aspects of life. Furthermore, she impresses upon Laskell the need for pattern and discipline in life.

Part of the change in Laskell's conception of his selfhood is his recognition of a need for the ordering forces in life, a recognition that contributes to the developing alienation between him and the Crooms. Arthur and Nancy Croom (the leftist-liberals) profess to have no patience with formalized and traditional modes of action, for they are concerned with the welfare of man and not, presumably, with the life-style of individual man. Yet Laskell discovers in the Crooms certain felt needs for the ritualistic and traditional that respectable liberals do not have. The picnic that Nancy arranges, for instance, is the unconscious satisfaction of such a need: she demands that it be an old-fashioned, stylized occasion.

The Crooms also reveal to Laskell certain contradictions in liberal thinking. Nancy admires Duck Caldwell, the Croom's handyman, as a kind of native American proletarian. But when Duck is revealed as viciously evil and empty-minded, it is seen that Nancy is the victim of a genuinely sentimental preconception about the working class. Nancy is a pacifist, but she approves the war in Spain because there, she says, people are fighting for something. And when Maxim, in order to establish a public identity, publishes an article in which he takes a religious view of *Billy Budd*, the Crooms choose to believe that he is crazy. Then they insist on a leftist interpretation of the article after all, Nancy seeing an analogy between the convicted Billy and the commissars of the Moscow trials, for the latter are made to say the equivalent of "God bless Captain Vere." The conformity of the commissars to the Stalinist line is acceptable and just, but the conformity of Maxim to the Christian line is madness. Thus Trilling dissects the dogmatism of one sort of liberalism and reveals its rejection of variety and tolerance.

The liberal mind represented by the Crooms suffers in general from the inability to face unpleasant facts like evil or death. Laskell discovers that the liberal deludes himself; more than this, he is guilty of a basic miscalculation about the nature of man and the world he lives in. It comes to Laskell that there is in Nancy "the desire to refuse knowledge of the evil and hardness of the world. . . ." It is a crucial recognition for Laskell, because it leads to the conflicts with the Crooms which create much of the dramatic interest of the novel. It leads also to that reassessment and modification of liberalism which brings Laskell at the close of the novel to the end of innocence.

That end is on the far side of the wood of error, beyond that uncritical liberalism which Laskell and the Crooms had accepted. In thinking his way out of the wood, Laskell is forced to consider two philosophical questions. The first has to do with time. Laskell begins to sense that the future and present are one and that one could not look for the fulfilment of one's present desires in the future unless one remained a child. For children, especially of the middle class, the future is always brighter than the present. Laskell finds Marxism unacceptable in part because he sees the hollowness of the metaphysics of expectation and in part because he discovers that the premise of expectation commits Marxism literally to a childish conception of man. His every impulse throughout the novel is to seek out a mature and responsible mode of behavior. He is the man Ernst Cassirer speaks of who develops the power of self-knowledge that he may combat the power of myth, in this case specifically the myth of the Marxist state. He is more interested in the question of identity than in the ideology of politics.

The second question is ethical. It involves the problem of individual responsibility for one's acts, which is the question of innocence and guilt and the problem of moral judgment. Laskell knows that Marxism denies the possibility of individual guilt by attributing wrong human action to the impersonal operation of historical forces. Trilling has no difficulty in showing that the Crooms cannot accept the determinism of environment and history while they also speak about personal immorality and responsible human agents. Nancy, for example, is caught in this dilemma when she regards Duck as both guilty of causing his child's death and merely a product of his environment. Another variety of ethical confusion is the readiness to make political and moral truth identical. In Arthur Croom's eyes, when Maxim breaks with the party he commits a moral wrong. Laskell too feels as though Maxim has been guilty of personal treachery. This emotion, characteristic of the political and moral history of the forties, Trilling finds understandable but deplorable, for it is based on the apotheosis of the party. Individual identity is swallowed up in this worship of the political group. Laskell's insistence on the inviolability of the self permits him to triumph over the threat posed by the myth of the state.

The Crooms pose that threat. Maxim is even more dangerous, for he poses a double-edged threat to Laskell — in the beginning the myth of the Communist state, and later the myth of Christianity. When Maxim was a member of the party, he exercised a tremendous moral authority over his friends, which derived from his commitment to the future and from his belief in the infallibility of his political ideas. He imposed a sense of guilt upon those of his friends who were not equally committed. Laskell was the victim of the pressure of Maxim's personality and beliefs as a Communist, but he never succumbed to this force.

When Maxim reverses "in mid-course the journey of his life" (the phrase comes from Whittaker Chambers, who bears a striking resemblance to Maxim) and becomes a Christian, he finds Laskell more vulnerable to attack than before. The power of Maxim's religious ideas has a great effect upon Laskell, because he himself is in the middle of a journey. Maxim and Laskell do not, of course, follow the same path. Maxim displays the same dogmatism as a religious man that he had shown as a revolutionary. And he is as ready to identify with religion as an institution as he was before to identify with the party. This is why his effort to reassert his own individuality is ultimately a failure. In Trilling's view, I think, it is not possible to realize one's individuality within the rigid framework of an institution. Maxim takes a self-defeating course.

Laskell is slow to see the danger to himself in Maxim's switch in loyalties. But when Maxim argues that good and evil, pity and cruelty, live side by side in the hearts of each of us, even in the hearts of those on our side, Laskell feels that this view of human nature, so much more accurate than Nancy's view of Duck, for example, is profoundly right. Then Maxim launches a brutal attack upon Laskell, based on his Pauline convictions that we are all members of each other and that each of us must share the guilt of all men. The upshot of this harassment is to reveal to Laskell entanglements of human destinies he had not before been conscious of.

Laskell and his kind will be eliminated, says Maxim, and will not appear again "until the Crooms and I have won and established ourselves against the anarchy of the world." The Crooms will preach the law for the masses: rights and the freedom from blame. Maxim will preach the law for the leaders: duties and nothing but blame. Social revolution, or the myth of the state, and religious affirmation, or the myth of Christianity, will combine to make the new world and to destroy Laskell. And Laskell suspects what Maxim believes — that when these two forces get to quarreling, the final victory will lie with the ex-Communists.

What is Laskell to do in the face of the spiritual dogmatism and moral fanaticism of Maxim, the headlong devotion to liberal shibboleths of the Crooms? He must continue his quest for the self. Trilling's strategy is to make Laskell's position desperate, because Laskell must test whether or not the self alone can survive in modern society. Maxim's attack on Laskell is part of this testing process. Laskell fights back because his identity is at stake. His final position is that we cannot have absolute freedom from responsibility and that absolute responsibility cannot be imagined. Mature humanity must be "at once responsible and conditioned." Maxim regards this statement as an evasion, possible to Laskell because he is moving securely in an atmosphere of love. And indeed love has been the saving agent in Laskell's struggle to find out who he is. Knowing who you are depends on releasing your capacity for love, since man is a creature of love and love is a self-affirming force. So it is that when Laskell had come upon Emily Caldwell bathing nude in the river, he had taken her on the bank. He had come to see, before this event, that Emily had a kind of biological dignity, the dignity of a womanly woman. This sexual act is the full affirmation of life and selfhood; it is the final rejection of the death wish for Laskell. At the same time and as a natural consequence, the lovemaking involves Laskell in tragic responsibility, because it sanctions his pseudo-parental relationship to Emily's daughter. It is his exercise of this authority that in part accounts for her death.

At the end Laskell has won a full sense of his selfhood, but he has uncovered also a sense of the terrible complexity and unpredictability of events and persons. He understands the moment-to-moment dangers of the humanistic middle position he strives to

maintain. Even when Laskell refuses to acquiesce in his own ex-
tinction under Maxim's merciless pounding, he is threatened with
defeat. For the dilemma of any liberal is that when he fights for
survival the very act of fighting endangers his position. The triumph of Laskell as a new kind of liberal is in recognizing and
understanding the hostility and variety of man and circumstance,
and in coping with them unaided by forces outside himself.

It should now be clear how much is suggested in the title of the
novel. The middle of the journey comes to Laskell (he is thirty-
three years old; Dante was thirty-five) when he undergoes the
Freudian passage from life to death to a new life in which he
finds the true nature of his self and of his beliefs. He does not
choose to define his self in terms of the purblind optimism of the
Crooms or of the obsession with guilt, responsibility, and evil of
Maxim, but he modifies and takes from both positions. His
beliefs, as well, represent a mid-point between the leftist liberalism
of the Crooms and the fanatic Christianity of Maxim. It is inescapable, I think, that the title suggests finally the dialectical
form of the novel.

The dramatic conflict in this novel is in its structure, and its
structure is determined by its ideas. The fusion of idea and movement is a fine example of obedience to an organic principle. Trilling, I am quite sure, used the dialectic self-consciously. Near the
close of the book, Laskell and the Crooms ask themselves why so
many disagreements had arisen among them. Laskell wants to say,
"Because we are parts of history, elements in the dialectic." And
indeed one can see that the Crooms, the hopeful liberal-leftists,
are thesis; Maxim, the guilt-ridden Christian, is antithesis; and
Laskell himself is synthesis. Laskell is synthesis because he occupies a mid-point between the polar positions of the Crooms and
Maxim, and he is synthesis because, as Maxim recognizes, Laskell's
type will emerge after the Crooms and the Maxims have had their
way in the world. But Laskell is synthesis not merely as compromise between the two extremes. He is something different from
them and beyond them. He is the enlightened new liberal who
has shed his shallow and oversimplified conception of man, society, and the utopian future. He has shed his innocence.

The new conservatism, which Maxim could well represent, has
called into question the necessity and validity of the liberal mind.

And to be sure, Trilling has shown that the liberalism that flowered in the thirties was delusive, inconsistent, easily and foolishly optimistic. Laskell's liberalism has been purged in the hard alembic of disillusionment and honest self-analysis. It is flexible, tolerant, rational, self-dependent, essentially humane. It retains, of course, the ambiguity implicit in a position of poised balance between self-assured and certain commitments. But it avoids the limiting schematization of the new conservatism. It is the new liberalism, which is finally what *The Middle of the Journey* gives us.

A CRITIQUE OF THE NEW LIBERALISM

The law of the conservation of energy and matter tells us that nothing ever really disappears. It would be folly to predict, then, that the uncritical liberalism which sustained writers like Irwin Shaw and Budd Schulberg is, after the forties, forever dead. A safer guess is that such fiction as finds its premises and derives its spirit from that liberalism will for a long time meet a hostile reception, if it is accorded anything but indifference, among critical readers. In part, this way of regarding the fiction of the old liberalism is a matter of fashion, since the new criticism has taught the reader to look for aesthetic and cultural values not present in this fiction. In part, the hostility will rest on the failure to suspend disbelief; the faith and optimism demanded by such fiction will not be freely yielded except by the most naïve reader. This is not merely a matter of our aesthetic sensibilities having been turned in other directions by a dominant new criticism. It is that the total of our experience in the haunted world of war and totalitarianism, in the strait-jacket world of corporate entities, attacks the essential credibility of the old liberal imagination.

The task of the new liberal has been modification and reconstruction. He has had to conserve what he could of the great liberal heritage which has animated our culture since the Enlightenment. He has had also to mute its excesses, to adapt himself to a world never envisioned by Jefferson or Paine. He must timidly strive for values without making the errors of his old liberal predecessors. He must accept the past and recognize the value of community without sliding into the conservative camp. He cannot escape the defect of his virtues. He is flexible and supple of mind; he is capable of fine discriminations. But practicing his virtues, he finds himself in a no man's land where the opportunity for vacillation is immense. The imagination and the psychology of the new liberal must quiver in a perpetual state of tentativeness, for there is no firm resting place for the eternally uncommitted mind. One consequence of the effort to maintain such unbearable equilibrium is that the new liberal tends to slide toward the center, where he meets the reasonable neo-conservative, coming from the opposite direction. This is not a vital center, for here differences of conviction and technique begin to disappear. Out of such a failure to maintain ideational polarity arises an intellectual blandness which robs American life of the excitement of conflict. Such conflict, such ideational tension is often the matrix whence springs the fruitful and creative energies of society. Much of the responsibility for the loss of tension and polarity is the new liberal's, since he has compromised his position by taking over conservative ideas in an effort to keep his position alive. Some of the conservatives must share the culpability in this matter also. But wherever we place the blame, the consequence is a net loss for the entire society. The quality of our fiction in the forties reflects this loss.

CHAPTER FIVE

THE
CONSERVATIVE
IMAGINATION

NEO-CONSERVATISM AND THE IDEA VACUUM

The new liberalism, rising unsteadily from the ashes of a discredited faith, can hardly be regarded as the single, vital impulse in the thought and fiction of the forties. But it may be seen as one of the alternatives to the old liberalism that writers in the period had discovered. The passing of the old liberalism created an idea vacuum, and into the empty space flowed this modified liberal view of man and experience. It was not unchallenged in that space, for neo-conservatism, another alternative, also moved into the vacuum. The period, it is clear, had no substantive unity. It was the playground for various points of view.

Actually, of course, the formulation of this neo-conservative philosophy in America belonged to the 1950's. Intimations of its coming during the forties, however, were apparent even to the casual eye. More obvious was the presence of a conservative fiction in this decade. But it was a ficiton that drew its suppositions from the past, from the well of tradition and not from the contemporary scene. Such fiction was in a sense, then, a source of the neo-conservative philosophy, rather than the opposite being true; and we have an example of how the literary imagination (paradoxically, the unchained conservative imagination, freed in a period of flux) leaps ahead of systematic thought, sums it up, and projects it into the life stream of the nation's experience before economics or religion or history is aware of the nation's need or readiness. In the fifties, the work of people like Russell

Kirk, Peter Viereck, and Clinton Rossiter is a codification of what the conservative fiction of the forties had already in large measure expressed. The usefulness of the new conservative philosophy for present purposes, then, is that the framed and defined doctrine offers a direct road to the conservative fiction that preceded it. A review of neo-conservative principles and of the conditions that nurtured them will help to explain the intellectual history of the forties as well as the conservative fiction of the time.

I have already pointed out that as early as 1939 T. S. Eliot had announced that liberalism was destined to disappear. In 1950 Allen Tate said liberalism as a philosophy is "pretty well washed up." We have seen what happened to liberalism in the years between those dates, when the world lived in a condition of perpetual crisis. In America, perpetual crisis encouraged those who put national security above civil liberties and dissent; it encouraged the growth of a military elite, indeed, of a power elite. The pressure of crisis discouraged many liberals, who sank to silence or disaffected from a creed that had lost touch with the masses, that had been proved wrong and inadequate. The fear of communism contributed heavily to the atmosphere of crisis, but the carefully nurtured fear of liberalism discredited that once dominant philosophy among people on virtually every level in our society. Communism and liberalism were linked into one object of hatred and suspicion. In *Witness* Whittaker Chambers aimed his accusations at communism and at the "great socialist revolution, which, in the name of liberalism," had been taking place in this country. The heart of the Alger Hiss case, he wrote, was the revolution made by these liberals. As these statements from Chambers suggest, the fear of communism was tied to the rejection of liberal leadership. And when the liberals were identified with the Communists, and the Communists were identified with sin, the discrediting of liberalism could hardly go further. The neo-conservative intellectual stepped into the gap thus created.

The conservative had a double task: he had to attack liberalism and to define his own position. The attack came out of a conviction, in Reinhold Niebuhr's case, that democracy needed a more compelling justification and a more realistic vindication than the liberal culture has given it. Conservatives generally agreed that the liberal view of history, society, and man had been overly optimistic and dangerously mistaken. The definition of what might be called the consensus conservative position took into account these errors. The secularism of the liberal must give way to a reverence for God and a conviction that society must rest upon religion and morality. The egalitarianism of the liberal must give way to a belief in an hierarchical class structure and to faith in the stewardship of an elite; liberty is more important than equality. The liberal's appetite for change and experiment, derived from his historic allegiance to science and faith in reason, must be supplanted by a mystical and pious affirmation of the viability of tradition; change, if accepted at all, must be slow and must take into consideration the necessity for continuity and the integrity of the community. For tradition, continuity, and community are the constituents of the organic view of society, which guarantees the stability necessary to conservatism. That liberal trust in reason, and the abstract speculation to which it leads, must be looked upon with suspicion. The liberal view of man and events is supplanted, finally, by the hard view of man; Chambers summed it up when he said "I came to feel that the problem of evil was the central problem of human life," which was another way of saying that he believed in original sin.

In its reliance upon prescription and prejudice, much of the conservative philosophy in America seemed to come from Edmund Burke. His view of man as a "mixed mass of human imperfections and infirmities" appealed to those who felt themselves betrayed by the liberal promise or those who have never been able to take that promise seriously. Burke provided a model for the insistence upon the viability of tradition. He argued cogently for the necessity of continuity in human affairs. Society, he had said, is a contract between those who are living, those who are dead, and those who are to be born. He pointed to the dangers inherent in abstract principles applied without reference to circumstances and relations. He saw the need to subordinate the private judgment to an authority outside of and beyond the self.

In America it was time for a revitalization of the Burkean position and for a resurgence of Christian ideas. It was time for a revisionist historiography that would emphasize the conservative character of the American tradition. Fiction was a part of this turn toward conservatism, but, I repeat, it did not find its sources in the contemporary scene. The vital connection between conservatism and fiction during the forties was not established in politics. Either the conservative fiction writer shared the general disenchantment with current politics or he found too little genuinely conservative political leadership and action to attract his attention. James Gould Cozzens, who is surely a first-rate conservative writer, treats the politics of the period only incidentally in his novels. But the general Burkean tone of his social philosophy, as we shall see, is unmistakable.

Nor was there a vital connection in religion. Cozzens again may serve as an example. In his novels he emphasizes the institutional characteristics of religion and largely ignores the hard interpretation of doctrinal matters being made by theologians of his own time. Nevertheless, his attitudes on religion and politics are sufficiently clear to justify the claim that he feeds neo-conservatism rather than feeding upon it.

In general it can be said that the fiction of the decade revealed no significant return to religion, although the *Partisan Review*, in a symposium held in 1950 on "Religion and the Intellectuals," remarked that the revival of religion had been most noticeable in the literary world in the forties. Even so, the contributors to the discussion did not find religion or religious ideas in American fiction, wherever they might have found them. And with good reason. No religious writer appeared in America of the same ability and dedication as Graham Greene or Evelyn Waugh, whatever genuine religious sentiment one might find in their fiction. America in the forties could offer only passing obeisance to themes of sin and guilt, some concern with the institutional aspects of religion, and only one writer of promise — J. F. Powers — who was translating into fiction the mystery of the religious sensibility.

A greater vitality in the relationship between conservatism and fiction may be seen in the South, where the conservative spirit flourished before it was rediscovered by the rest of the country. Southern writers feed neo-conservatism in the way Cozzens does. Their history is revisionist, and they draw upon the southern temper that grew out of the southern past. It was a temper fired in part by certain practitioners of the new criticism, which certainly took a role in the creation of the Southern Renaissance and which directed some literary energies into conservative channels. When

John Crowe Ransom spoke of the natural affiliation that binds together the gentleman, the religious man, and the artist, a composite figure whose manners are aristocratic, whose religion is ritualistic, and whose art is traditional, he was drawing the portrait of the artist who ought, ideally, to come out of the South. Perhaps neither Faulkner nor Robert Penn Warren fits this description. The ideal may not have been realized, but it provided a model for conservatism in southern fiction that was not ignored. The ideal was, in fact, pursued to the enrichment of our literature.

JAMES GOULD COZZENS: THE PENNSYLVANIA VOICE OF AGGRESSIVE ARISTOCRACY

Cozzens came into the forties as the most neglected major talent in American letters. The novels he wrote in that decade confirmed the judgment about his talent, but they had little effect upon his reputation: he was neglected. He had published his first novel in 1924. It was not until 1957, when he published his twelfth, *By Love Possessed*, that he really made an impact upon the American literary scene. Some notice, to be sure, had been taken of him prior to this. Bernard De Voto had scolded coterie critics and academicians in his usual ill-natured way as early as 1949 for the conspiracy of neglect apparently aimed at Cozzens; *Guard of Honor* had won the Pulitzer Prize for 1948; and one of the book clubs had selected three of his novels for distribution before it chose *By Love Possessed*. Nevertheless, Cozzens remained virtually undiscovered and un-discussed until the publication of that novel. It brought a flood of essays and reviews and proved the occasion for evaluations of his total work. In 1959 Frederick Bracher capped the Cozzens boom with a book-length study of the novels.

Critics regarded Cozzens as an old-fashioned novelist, but they were generally puzzled about finding a place for him in the contemporary scene. Of course, he does have a place. Like Robert Penn Warren, Cozzens is a conservative, although his conservatism differs from Warren's, a difference more of tone than substance. Cozzens' place may be defined by attaching him to the native American literary tradition to which he belongs. In the nineteenth century this tradition is represented by the James Fenimore Cooper of *The American Democrat* and the novels of the Littlepage trilogy, by the Henry Adams of *Democracy*; in the twentieth century it is carried forward in the work of Edith Wharton, Willa Cather, and Ellen Glasgow. Two traditions combine in this line of descent. One is that of the novel of manners, which led a precarious life beside the romance in American fiction until the end of the nineteenth century; the other is that aristocratic-conservative tradition as naturally concerned with manners as it was with the disturbing tensions in democratic life, with the changes wrought by industrialization and immigration.

While Cozzens' allegiances and similarities to the diffident critics of expanding nineteenth-century democracy and to many of his own contemporaries of the Southern Renaissance help to define his place, they do not altogether explain his importance. In the world of the forties, he was one of the major conservative figures in fiction, and the one who advanced most determinedly and aggressively the conservative position. It was a world in which the social distance between the classes was shrinking and the new phenomenon of an equitable distribution of income was working toward egalitarianism. In a world thus grown bland and tasteless in its social uniformity and dull in its intellectual concentration on the safety of the center, Cozzens took a stance. He made an effort to polarize American life by himself occupying one of the poles. He made an effort to introduce bite and character and meaningful opposition into a climate of opinion that offered about as much challenge as the senescent-coddling climate of southern California. Against the intellectual liberalism that survived into the forties, he posed a vigorous anti-intellectual conservatism; against the synthetic avantgardism of some of the new fiction of this decade, he posed the conservative, old-fashioned Jane Austen-George Eliot kind of novel. For his pains he was ignored. But he serves the function of other conservative voices of his time, nonetheless, for he is surely a part of that complex of forces that contributed to the process of re-evaluation in literature, in politics, in the world of ideas generally. He gave the liberal mind the variety and opposition that it had always claimed was vital to the health of democratic art and politics, and the liberal mind rewarded him by minimizing his accomplishments.

What Cozzens has achieved, few if any of the other novelists of the forties could match. Cozzens has found a position and made a commitment. Bracher is reluctant to admit that Cozzens is a committed man, rightfully fearing the limitations imposed on a writer by an ideology; he prefers to see Cozzens as a spectator rather than as a partisan. I should agree about the dangers of an ideology, but I should insist on Cozzens' commitment. In the well-fragmented world that everyone now recognizes as a cliché of contemporary intellectual history, Cozzens wrote from the security and stability of an aristocratic conservatism to which, apparently, he was born. Yet, from the outset, he displayed a disturbingly obsessive attachment to that conservatism, an insecurity in his security that is rich in paradox. The explanation for such disquiet, I would like to suggest, may be related to the status revolution, a concept which has been used to interpret American politics and history: the emergence or decline of status groups becomes a key to the understanding of various movements of reform and dissidence. Cozzens, who is descended from an American Tory family that fled the country at the time of the Revolution, gives evidence of feeling that middle-class, liberal America has pushed him aside. Like Kirby Allbee in Saul Bellow's *The Victim*, Cozzens feels his rightful place has been usurped in American life by others who have neither the claim nor the qualifications that he has. It is as a consequence of this alienation that he has adopted the position of the wilfully bigoted spirit which Irving Howe detects: he becomes the *aggressive* white American Protestant. In *The New American Right*, Daniel Bell points out that the liberals dominated the intellectual and publishing community, even through the forties, which suggests a reason for Cozzens' neglect and a cause of the alienation he felt. And Richard Hofstadter, in the same volume, argues that the long tenure in power of the liberals had aroused a sense of victimization and powerlessness among their opponents. The churlishness of Cozzens' conservatism and the occasionally gratuitous attacks on liberalism in his novels may be explained by the status revolution, which for most of his life, ironically, relegated Cozzens, the well-rooted American, to a minority position: he is the victim, the authentic voice of America, who is virtually silenced and whose channels of communication with the people are virtually closed off.

Yet in a sense history has vindicated him and the conservative spirit has caught up with him. He went his own stubborn way until America began to find that his path was hers. Not that he would stoop to direct her steps. He is a novelist, and for a novelist to attempt to instruct his readers, he said in a letter written in 1934, is impertinent. The shift from a period of dominant liberalism to a time at least hospitable to the rise of the new conservatism took place without his help. When it did take place, his voice was heard, and heard to be singing the words to the prevailing tune. This is why *By Love Possessed* caused a sizable stir.

In 1949, when T. S. Eliot set down his *Notes Toward the Definition of Culture*, he outlined the conservative complex that one may uncover as the hard substratum of Cozzens' fictional world. Eliot postulated the necessity for religion and for an elite class in an hierarchical, stratified society. The elite would be the consumers, bearers, and transmitters of culture and would assume a greater responsibility in government and society than any other group. The elite would preserve, communicate, live by standards of behavior: they would, in short, have manners. Cozzens seems to have known and felt the conservative propositions in Eliot's statement long before Eliot framed them. I suppose one could say that Cozzens is an instinctive conservative, but saying it, one would have to admire the thoroughness of the instinct. Because Cozzens' world view also includes much that Burke, and his modern American followers, might have taught: the pessimistic view of man that is inherent in Christianity, the organic view of society, the respect for history that a belief in tradition dictates, an attitude of simultaneous distrust and respect for reason, and an abnegation of the self in the face of duty and authority. It includes much that John Dewey (only in appearance a strange contributor to conservatism) might have taught: a pragmatic and activistic approach to life, which subordinates abstractions or theories, even the Christian theory of predestination and the operation of divine providence. Like the American Puritan who struggles with the same dilemma, Cozzens ultimately elevates the purposeful human will over God's providential plan, over the intractable nature of things. This view includes much that the Stoics might have taught: the limits of that human will, despite its determination to act; the sense of resignation in the face of what God and things might impose; the determination to endure despite all inducements to surrender. All these strains are to be detected in Cozzens — Christian orthodoxy, classical conservatism, ancient Stoicism, and modern pragmatism. His is an eclectic conservatism. All of its elements are in the fiction that we are about to examine.

The novels of Cozzens' apprenticeship anticipate the themes and methods of his maturity. He begins almost at once to explore the need to endure, and the conflicts between passion and reason, principle and reality. He investigates the fictional possibilities in Christian dogma. He introduces an active masculine girl who raises the wholly intriguing question of his attitude toward women. He "works up" material for a novel, a method that will in time bring down on him unfavorable judgments. The first novel of that maturity, *The Last Adam* (1933), exemplifies so much that is typical of Cozzens' thought and art that I beg leave to pause long enough to draw out some illuminating generalizations, even though it does fall outside our period.

A need for order dominates Cozzens' principle of construction in *The Last Adam*, and in every novel that follows. With the exception of *Ask Me Tomorrow*, Cozzens' novels cover a short, rigidly delimited period of time, as though he would press the very hours into a schematized pattern that could somehow reduce the chaos of life. It is as a by-product of this practice that Cozzens achieves a kind of intensity of effect, since he characteristically concentrates a great deal of varied action in a short period. That action is arranged, to to speak, on a horizontal plane. Imagine a long straightaway, like a running track, dotted irregularly with hurdles of varying heights. The hurdles are problems or difficulties that the protagonist must get over in one way or another as he traverses the course. If that should prove impossible, he must at least get around them. The highest and most awkward hurdles generally occur toward the end of the track. This analogy for the structure and movement of a Cozzens novel represents in good part his view of life: man must meet and conquer obstacle after obstacle in his effort to attain and establish some sense of meaningful existence. But the persistence of such a pattern in his novels, the succession of protagonists overcoming the succession of obstacles, suggests a mechanical quality in Cozzens' method. His work seems too neatly planned. The formless raw material of life offers too little resistance to his organizing skill. He maintains a too complete mastery of the tension between art and life. Cozzens has, in sum, no rage for order, only a reasonable need for it.

The protagonist in *The Last Adam* is a physician. Novels about a clergyman, an author, a judge turned soldier, and two about lawyers will follow. One thinks of Sinclair Lewis covering American business, medicine, and religion; or, as Stanley Edgar Hyman suggests, of Balzac's *Human Comedy*: perhaps Cozzens is writing a Professional Comedy. Cozzens' concentration upon professional men has a twofold purpose. First, they are the leaders of the community in whom the power and prestige center. As a class these patricians represent for Cozzens what is best in America. Furthermore, bearing the responsibilities of leadership and service in their communities, they must make the command decisions; they are subjected to the moral tensions inherent in the stewardship role they have assumed. Second, as professional men they move in spheres of order that define them and define life, spheres which set reasonable and discernible limits, sanctioned by institutions and authority, to men's actions. Here again is Cozzens' need for order, which he feels as a necessary defense against the destructive romantic or liberal spirit.

The Last Adam is laid in a small Connecticut community, and two other novels among those that have appeared subsequently are set in a region that suggests the Delaware Valley, or even more specifically, the Bucks County area. More than a decade after the revolt from the village movement in American letters, Cozzens is seen in this book to be the chronicler of the small town, returning, if you will, to the village, in a characteristically perverse gesture. It is my feeling that Cozzens' view of society as a whole, or one might say his idea of society, is reflected in this choice of the small town as setting. For Cozzens, the conception of the organic society, to which he subscribes, has its reality in the small community where social interactions are visible and predictable. All the lines of power, authority, influence are defined, as are the roles of every economic, racial, religious, and class group. The small community is an organism that Cozzens can apprehend. Furthermore, his mind seems to turn away from any larger unit. The politics of his imagination does not comprehend, cannot take in, the great city, the nation, the world. True, *Men and Brethren* is set in New York City, but Cozzens gives us no sense of the city. The action of that novel is for the most part confined to a vicarage which is isolated, like an island, in the city. *Guard of Honor* puts in the place of the small town an air force base, which is perhaps even more satisfying to Cozzens' need for order and more obviously organic than the small town. Indeed, Cozzens said in a letter to his English publisher that he regarded the air force as something more than an organization, as, quite explicitly, an organism.

Cozzens' preoccupation with the small town in these older, settled regions of the country is a reflection, furthermore, of his interest in a community where the weight of history is palpable — palpable in the eighteenth-century houses that still stand, in the old families that are still at the top of the social hierarchy whence they manage the affairs of the town. Cozzens needs a sense of place and a sense of tradition to keep him going in an America that has, so to speak, betrayed him by changing so completely and rejecting the old ways and the past. He needs a sense of place which he knows securely is his own and from which he may thus shut out the intruder.

The Last Adam has two female characters with marked masculine traits who are like the other women in Cozzens' novels whom he regards with approval. The ideal female in Cozzens, as a composite portrait reveals, is an active, competent, rawboned woman who always looks like a man. She is an excellent horsewoman, swimmer, or tennis player, often being better at these sports than the men around her. She shows the same crisp efficiency in managing these men as she does in handling her car or her fate. Cozzens seems to accept only those women who resemble men, except for the accident of their genitalia. Women as women he neither likes nor understands.

Women, when they act like women, are a troublesome nuisance: unstable and unethical. The males in the novels often reflect that the motives and feelings of these women have a merely hysterical origin. It is natural for such women to use any means to an end that they desire. Really, they need to be dominated. Francis Ellery in *Ask Me Tomorrow* is typically condescending about women, who inhabit some "fantastic female world of the emotions" and who never manage a quite adult habit of thought. Yet they are a commodity, a precious property trained to play a specific role in an ordered society. Again, in *Ask Me Tomorrow* Francis comes to see that as a penniless writer he cannot marry his girl, who, carefully brought up and educated, is an investment. The man who marries her has to be able to take care of that investment.

Cozzens' treatment of women confirms a view of him as representative of the well-to-do American Anglo-Saxon. The white Protestant male in this country is traditionally baffled and angered by women. He regards them as inferior in mind and morals. His attitude is dictated as much by suspicion and fear of women as it is by failure to understand them. And by failure to penetrate imaginatively to any real comprehension of the meaning of either sex or love, Cozzens shares in these views. As he has no rage for order, he surely has no rage for sex, that is, no grasp of the profoundly disturbing and liberating power in the act of love, no knowledge that love may be the most important power in the lives of men and women. We must conclude that Cozzens shares in the well-known American sex hostility and inhibition. When, indeed, Cozzens does deal with sex, I detect a locker-room bawdiness and even nastiness which I believe is designed to cover up virility ill at ease. What he hopes will pass for open and healthy sexuality here and there in his novels too often seems to be the smirking of the superior male taking his pleasure. When Marx claimed, in the *Manifesto*, that "The bourgeois sees in his wife a mere instrument of production," he must have based his observation on men who held the same upper-middle-class values that Cozzens holds.

The protagonist of *The Last Adam* is the descendant of an aristocratic family in whom a full-blooded vitality surges unchecked by age or position. He is the embodiment of Cozzens' belief in an essential life-spirit that demands active participation in all the possibilities life offers. As an aristocrat, Dr. Bull despises outsiders like Catholics and Jews, and wishes to secure the integrity of the home place and the social hierarchy there. He has a sense of his duty and perseveres in meeting its demands. As a proponent of the conviction that life must be fully lived, he is given to active problem-solving and is impatient with abstract theory. As a sinner, he accepts the doctrine of original sin and despises the sentimental yearning toward human perfectibility. He is the conservative alive — pragmatic, responsible, aristocratic. Cozzens' succeeding novels will offer men like him in these ways at least, men insistent on living life but recognizing its social and institutional limitations.

The Last Adam thus prepares us for the novels Cozzens wrote in the forties. It does not include that Hegelian tendency in Cozzens to give the institution priority over the individual, nor does it have the infallible protagonist who seems to have escaped Adam's Fall: these are matters of prime interest that may be seen in *Men and Brethren*, which he published in 1936. Unfortunately, his next novel, the autobiographical *Ask Me Tomorrow* (1940), suffers from a diminution of intensity. Its subjects are the moral life and the life of the creative imagination, areas of sufficiently ample and exciting dimension. But Cozzens does not succeed in making the moral choices intensely crucial or the engagement in the life of art profoundly stirring.

The protagonist in the novel is Francis Ellery, a young writer who goes to Europe in the twenties. He finds it a largely destructive experience. Ellery looks down his nose at the little, jabbering, dirty Europeans with their strutting airs, and he condescends to Europe itself. I believe his feeling is based not so much on Anglo-Saxon prejudice as it is upon disquiet with himself. For one of the major tensions in his life is made by the conflict between the lure of the rich expatriates in Europe and his sense of devotion to his craft. Insofar as Europeans are involved in this portrait of the idle rich, Cozzens has given us a variant of that Jamesian theme in which Europe is viewed as a corrupting force. Ellery is drawn to the purposeless hedonism, the mindlessness and lechery of the people he meets; their wealth and leisure delude him. He is robbed of his creative energies. But Cozzens draws back from the final consequence of Ellery's errors in judgment and treachery to his art. The destruction Fitzgerald wrought upon Dick Diver, corrupted by much the same forces in *Tender Is the Night*, has no parallel in this novel.

The tragedy of waste, exemplified in Diver and in Fitzgerald too for that matter, might have been one way for Cozzens to approach the problem of the artist. But he does not take it. He has no talent for tragedy, of course, and no predilection toward it. His fear of sentimentality, I would guess, sometimes becomes a fear of sentiment, and thus he disqualifies himself for painting the portrait, in the necessary passionate tones, of the frustrated and unfulfilled artist. Or perhaps Cozzens has a kind of guilty contempt for writers (what are you, a mere scribbler? the ghost of Hawthorne's ancestors might have said) and cannot concern himself deeply with the failure of even a writer of his own creation. Whatever the reasons, Cozzens' Ellery is disappointing as the writer manqué. Ellery's failure is one of commitment: he will not face his task as writer or make the necessary sacrifices for it; he takes a job rather than write and starve. Yet he cannot give up writing: ". . . like most writers, he had begun to write before he had the judgment to see the almost hopeless difficulties; and by the time he was old enough for judgment to begin to develop, it was too late, he liked to write." There is too little of this sort of perception. Cozzens' failure in this novel is, like Ellery's, one of commitment, for committed to a writer as protagonist, he refuses to give us in meaningful dimension the writer's peculiar problems and character.

When Cozzens turns to a consideration of Ellery's devotion to his duty, the novel is more successful, evidence to my mind that Cozzens feels more at home with manners and morals than he does with art and aesthetics. The conflict between the life of wealth and leisure and the life of art is never so real as the conflict between the moral responsibility of duty and the pleasurable satisfaction of the self. In episode after episode Ellery shirks his duty, and, being sensitive and perceptive, he knows it. His failures lead finally to a sobering recognition of responsibility. Bringing Ellery thus to maturity, Cozzens has readied him for an ironic observation: that once a man gets what he thinks he wants he is unhappy in the possession of it. Ellery must face Cozzens' conviction that a worm lies at the core of the apple of life. The only possible triumph for the man who has achieved maturity is to go on bearing the weight of his duty, dealing with intractable events and people, accepting the evil that men do. The difficulty here is that the heady burden of these mature reflections about life is too much for the frailty of the vehicle Cozzens has provided. Cozzens' wisdom lies in knowing how bad things can be, but his weakness, as here, is that too often he involves his character in situations that are only trivial and not very bad at all.

Pessimistic and severe as his reflections about life are, they do not lead to hopeless surrender but to that Stoic acceptance and endurance which Cozzens seems to see as the best possible expectation of man. It is this minimal expectation which rules out tragedy. And it rules out with equal effectiveness, granting its assumptions, utopianism or liberalism. Cozzens cannot refrain from explicit attack upon these social views, which stand in opposition to his own. I feel that while his conservatism is justified insofar as it emerges from the context of episode in his novel, his hostility to the left is almost gratuitous. Thus there occurs in *Ask Me Tomorrow* a passage in which Ellery thinks of Trotsky,

. . . of the tailor's body like a dwarf in its Cossack's greatcoat, of the hope and fear, the love and hate, behind the screwed-up Jewish comedian's face, brooding (in ever deadlier personal peril as, his great services forgotten, enemies in his party worked to pull him down) on the havocs and ecstacies of the Soviet apocalypse — the Byzantine treachery, the torture chambers, the spies in the wall, the concealed revolvers, the monster parades, the waving red flags, the broken furniture and the frozen plumbing. Like scenes from *Gulliver's Travels*, all day and all night a double column serried past the mummy of Lenin; and in the factories the moron mechanics sang as they ruined the new machines; and in the fields the peasants like Nebuchadnezzar ate grass; and in crowded halls a thousand commissars shouted speeches; and in a thousand frowsy committee rooms the illiterate architects of the future scratched for lice and made mistakes in arithmetic as they tinkered with their millenium.

This is Cozzens' answer to the happy platitudes of the left about man and reform.

When he was at work on *The Just and the Unjust* (1942), Cozzens was preoccupied still with this spirit of liberalism. He told an interviewer in 1940 that the novel was to be called "The Summer Soldier," and would be, in a sense, a refutation of Tom Paine's position that a man should give up everything for an ideal. Cozzens approved of the summer soldier, and thought a man might do well to spend most of the year attending to his own business instead of fighting for some abstract cause. "The idealists, the intellectuals, haven't done any too well by the world," he told Robert Van Gelder. His book was to be about a choice between an ideal and a practical, selfish consideration. And, indeed, the theme of the novel is that man must come to terms with life as it is around him — imperfect, unexpectedly disastrous, as it may be. Accept what seems unacceptable, endure what seems unendurable, and go on to meet your problems, for this is the best of all possible worlds, since it is the only possible world.

In such a view, obviously, enterprises for reform are wasted efforts and the status quo is a condition of reasonable and practical justice. When Abner Coates, the protagonist in this novel, shilly-shallies around with his little moral problem — what sacrifice of my integrity is involved in accepting the Republican nomination for district attorney? — his superior turns on him and says that not liking the way things are run is kid stuff. Who says they would be better if they were run your way, he asks. "Why you say so! That's what the dopes, the Communists and so on, all the boys who never grew up, say." Cozzens is more inhospitable to change than even the classical conservatives like Burke or one of Burke's modern followers like Clinton Rossiter. Cozzens not only defends the status quo against attack, but he is eager to assert his approval of its essential character. He accepts the fact, for example, that the pursuit of wealth ought to be the dominant activity in this society; men are to be measured by a monetary standard. In *Ask Me Tomorrow* he had said that the poor, whatever their virtues, were not capable of mastering their environment; in *The Just and the Unjust* possession of money is equated with worth of character or, negatively, drudgery and economic insecurity are the consequences of too little will and intelligence. Cozzens' sociology seems in direct line of descent from certain distortions in the Puritan doctrine of the calling whereby wealth, piety, and character were all bound together, and from Fisher Ames's complacent phrase about the wise, the good, and the opulent.

In his sociology generally, Cozzens tries to strike a balance between the forces of individual will and of intractable circumstance, but he leans toward the former. He is always willing to recognize the important part played by environment and event which are beyond the control of the individual yet determine to a great extent what he is and does. And he recognizes as well the workings of divine providence. But his larger allegiance is to character and will. It is his special virtue that he contrives situations which all but overwhelm his people, but which they must somehow accept and learn to live with. At least, the good people bear up. The weak are borne down.

The discussion of this balance brings us now to the problems at the heart of the novel. One of them involves the murder trial which Abner Coates, as assistant district attorney, is helping to prosecute. The defendants in the trial are clearly guilty and deserve a verdict leading to the death sentence. The jury inexplicably finds them guilty only of second-degree murder, for which the maximum penalty is twenty years. This obdurate and completely unexpected action by the jury testifies to the limitless possibilities for the frustration of the human will and the limitations of human beings. Yet one must make accommodation for these weaknesses and summon resolution to bear them.

The miscarriage of justice which Cozzens deliberately perpetrates in this novel strikes at the validity of any absolute conception of justice that fallible human beings might entertain. The distinction between what is just and what unjust is not visible to all men at all times, but is dependent on ability to judge and the point of view from which judgment is made. Malleable as justice may be, the law which dispenses it is nevertheless a fortress. Abner's father, a retired judge, tells his son that a life devoted to the law is a good life. There will be errors and disappointments. "But they don't matter much. It's the stronghold of what reason men ever get around to using." The hard recognition of the limitations of reason and of man's institutions is a logical consequence of the recognition of human shortcomings generally and of the futility of any absolutes promulgated by human beings. Will and intelligence, fortified by the order provided in the structure of the law, must be balanced against irrationality and chance if chaos is to be staved off.

Another problem at the heart of the novel is Abner's relation to the local boss of the Republican party. Abner is asked to run for district attorney. Nomination and subsequent election to the post will give Abner sufficient income to get married. Something

a good deal less than a passionate man, he is nevertheless represented as wanting to get married. Yet the political boss seems
to Abner's fastidious eye a shady figure who will demand a man's
soul in exchange for office. Abner thus faces a conflict between principle and expediency, between theory and practice, between the
ideal and the selfish consideration. Cozzens finds overriding reasons for forcing Abner to accept the practical and expedient and
to lay aside his scruples about principles. Yet it must be said that
he explicitly condemns the merely expedient means, no matter
how good the end. Cozzens himself would not wish to accept the
merely expedient, but he and his characters are forced close to
it when they defend the status quo or find it necessary to adjust
themselves to the way things are.

In Cozzens' view, I am sure, Abner is thus brought to a recognition of the realities of life. In the knowledge and acceptance of
such realities lies the meaning of maturity for Cozzens. The mature, older man is always more admired in his novels than the
young man. The characters of this novel are a good deal bemused
by Abner's stubborn, apparently groundless scrupulosity. Age is
preferable to youth, as experience is to the lack of it. Wisdom will
be found with the aged and experienced if it is to be found anywhere. These are Cozzen's settled convictions, and they are illustrated in this novel and the two that follow by what I might
call the patristic principle. Cozzens is as pious about the fathers
as Cotton Mather was. By their example they show us the way.
By their exertions they have created that which is good, which
we must continue. It is our heritage to benefit by their wisdom.
They give us continuity and solidarity. In *The Just and the Unjust*, Philander Coates, Abner's father, is a stable center in his
son's life. A sagacious and understanding man, he gently attends
Abner's ripening. His friends of about his own generation, the
two judges in the novel, are also wise men. Cozzens' piety, I fear,
blinds him, in drawing these portraits, to the universal weaknesses
that are indispensable to his view of human nature. He has fallen
victim to one of the errors of the conservatives that E. V. Walter
has remarked: they tend to think "as if they believe that aristocracy has been immaculately conceived."

Actually, the goodness of man, any man, is not a view Cozzens
consciously holds. Old Philander believes the spring of human

action is self-interest. Noble and disinterested acts are impulsive, never deliberate, he says. Even Abner is forced to see that one has to take the practical view that a man will lie in his own behalf. The jurors are a corporate example of human obtuseness. The principal attorney for the defense is flashy and opportunistic in his conduct of the case, and will do anything to win, even though he is convinced that his clients are guilty. The evidence for original sin in this novel is decisive.

In this hazardous world where reason is often helpless, principle must be compromised, and man is a selfish liar, how is one to conduct himself? The answer to this question that Cozzens proposes for the very unheroic Abner is heroic in its simplicity. It includes honesty about yourself and self-discipline. It includes facing the fact that life is often unpleasant. Most of all, it demands that life be met, day by day, and lived. The good life for Abner, who is a plodding, not brilliant young man, lies in devotion to duty in his small town, in the assumption of the responsibility that is his by virtue of profession and birth. To ask of him no more than this is still to ask the impossible. But precisely that is what is expected of him.

The Just and the Unjust is a researched novel; Cozzens spent a good deal of time in the Doylestown, Pennsylvania, courthouse listening to lawyer-talk, and he read in the law by way of preparing to write this novel. For Cozzens the law is a continuing interest; it is for him as much the stronghold of reason and order as it is for Philander Coates. Dwight MacDonald has criticized Cozzens for substituting the pragmatic, objective spirit of the law for the emotions of real life and for the thought of real philosophy. Against these comments Cozzens would set the destructive role of the emotions and the failure of the intellectuals to solve man's problems or even to relate their thought to what he would regard as the real problems. *Guard of Honor* (1948) testifies to his conviction that the realities of experience are best apprehended by the mode of thought characteristic of the legal mind; this novel shows that a dogmatic formulation of experience is disastrous where the practice of the art of the possible is successful. Some of Cozzens' critics have objected that he could hold his position because he did write researched novels and was a spectator of life, uninvolved in daily tensions and securely isolated in his Lambertsville farmhouse. Cozzens' reaffirmation of his position comes, however, in a lived novel. Even if the protagonist of *Guard of Honor* is a former judge, the book must rest in part on Cozzens' own experience as a major in the air force — and so must be a confirmation by life, in Cozzens' eyes, of a conservative version of the pragmatic view.

Marjorie Grene has called attention to the innate conservatism of orthodox pragmatism. Cozzens, who would surely reject the spirit in which John Dewey offered his ideas, shows especially in *Guard of Honor* to what extent he would accept the substance. He would agree with Dewey that the moral and social qualities of conduct are identical with each other; that conduct is molded by environment; that intelligent conduct takes into consideration the possibilities and necessities of the social situation; that human behavior must be discussed with reference to its social context, not with reference to abstract principles, because men do not act on principle; that an idea is valid if it is instrumental in the reorganization of a given environment; that rigid moral codes do not work because there are too many exigencies to which they do not apply. Out of these ethical conceptions, brought in this novel to the ripest perfection Cozzens had yet achieved, he has created a realism that recognizes the dynamics of society but paradoxically defends the status quo. He has written a story in which he traps man in a blank determinism but nevertheless demands that man exercise his will. In this pragmatism he finds the sanction for the art of the possible, which suggests a sliding relativism, but he insists also upon moral means to moral ends. The paradoxes and the contradictions have produced a tension which makes *Guard of Honor* the best novel Cozzens has thus far written, and one of the few memorable novels to come out of the second World War.

In this novel Cozzens has expertly arranged a series of events that grow out of the problems in Negro-white relations at an air force training base in the South. He is intent on bringing home the folly of reform and the necessary survival and dominance of his complex organism, the base, which provides the institutional stability in his story. The festering question of segregated treatment for Negro personnel at the base commanded by General Beal is raised at the beginning of the book when Benny Carricker, a superb pilot and a primitive roughneck, slugs a Negro flier and hospitalizes him. Shortly thereafter a Negro journalist, accredited by Washington, gains admission to the post, is ejected, and protests to Washington. Lieutenant Edsell, a defender of Negro rights, makes this incident even more explosive by quarreling with his fellow officers about the treatment accorded the journalist. Furthermore, General Nichols appears on the scene from the Pentagon to award a medal to the very flier whom Carricker has hospitalized, because Washington has decided to publicize the announced antisegregation policy in the air force. Actually, since Beal has not honored this policy, disaffected Negro officers on the post are on the verge of mutiny when Nichols arrives.

General Beal is not competent to meet these problems, but he is fortunate in having as his air inspector Colonel Ross, a judge in civilian life, who can deal with them. Ross is a mature, wise man, the father-figure of judgment and authority in this novel. In dealing with the Negro problem he understands that military policy must take into account the beliefs and customs of the people in the southern town adjacent to the base if smooth relations with the civilian world are to be maintained. He understands also that sentiment or ideals merely becloud issues. He knows, for example, that in principle a man's color should not influence a case in court, but that in fact a white man, imperfect as he is, has a better chance than a black man in the kind of society in which we live. Things are as they are, and this is what men must face, not things as we would have them. Caught between the town and the prejudice of the white officers on the base on the one hand and Nichols' mission and air force policy on the other, Ross counsels and executes a skilful series of compromises. Carricker is placed in arrest and later is persuaded to apologize. A semiprivate presentation of the medal by Nichols is arranged. The dissident Negroes are outmaneuvered. The virtue of Ross's means is that they work, that is, they keep things going, they protect his chief, Beal, and they leave things essentially as they are. In staving off change, Ross gives the appearance of motion where actually there is none. The dynamics of society are denied.

Lieutenant Edsell, who does wish to change things, fails. Cozzens relates his failure to his character in two ways. Being impulsive, Edsell supports what amounts to revolutionary change by blitzkrieg tactics. He cannot understand the complexity of social change, and consequently its tortoise-like pace, in institutional life. He is therefore frustrated, failing, as he does, to fit means to end. He illustrates Cozzens' settled conviction that change does not really lead to progress. A more fundamental fault in Edsell, however, is a kind of psychic derangement to which Cozzens attributes his reformist zeal. Edsell is the frustrated outsider, a sorehead, and because of this condition he would destroy the social fabric. Reform, in Cozzens' world, is always in the hands of the immature or the ill-born or the neurotic. Such people want to smash things, but Cozzens wants to preserve them. As does Colonel Ross. Edsell would never learn what Ross knows — that imperfect men make imperfect institutions which we should maintain as well as we can since they are the best we can expect.

Ross also knows that we must work within the realm of the possible or we work in vain. Much of the novel is given over to defining the limits of the possible and to reconciling the moral idea with the way things are. As an apostle of prudence and the sagacious long-term view, Ross does not make impossible demands upon men or circumstances. He tolerates the inefficient Colonel Mowbray, another of Beal's aides, because he knows that ideal means are not always available. Ross knows that there is a sacrifice in efficiency in using Mowbray as a means. What Cozzens does not altogether honestly face in this portion of the novel is that there is a sacrifice in principle, too, since the means color, in this case taint, the end. It is Mowbray who makes the mistake which results in the death of several paratroopers. Everyone covers up for him, and he is not made to pay for what he has done. Cozzens seems to say it is better to accept such mishaps than it is to make the futile effort to find the ideal man for every post.

Captain Nathaniel Hicks gives us another view of the role of the moral idea. In thinking about the war and his place in the army, he finds no reason to take into account moral principle. He is not interested in "any feelings about the merits of the contest," for these did not matter once the war had begun. The only important question now is to beat or be beaten. Cozzens reveals a belief in activism that we have seen before. Man must do what it is possible for him to do. Despite the senselessness of life and the weakness of human beings, man must get on with his immediate business.

As Cozzens is given to hedging abstract principle, if not disregarding it, he generally discredits abstract reason. It is not the instrument whereby man can accommodate himself to circumstances or impose his will upon them. One of the characters in this novel is a mathematical genius. In his profession, the quality of a man's work is the demonstrable quality of his mind. He naïvely extends this relationship between ability and result to all of life, and holds the unsophisticated view that people get only what is coming to them. It is a logical and straightforward approach which Cozzens is pleased to reward with untoward misery. Experience is too crazily complicated and life too much directed by chance to permit of successful interpretation on the one-dimensional level of logic alone. John Dewey himself is suspicious of reason when its product cannot be checked in experience.

It is General Nichols, the most formidable figure in the novel, who best understands the limits of the possible. He follows an activist course with clarity of purpose and the greatest awareness of possibilities, imposing his point where he must. His mind and heart are free; he is completely objective and committed to nothing. He has rid himself of all fable, all myth, all illusion about men and circumstances and even himself. He has an air of perfect detachment. He never expects too much. Armed thus with godlike equipment, Nichols influences events at the post and makes a fair assessment of Beal's leadership ability in order to advise the Pentagon about future, more important, assignments for Beal. Like Ross, Nichols knows he cannot find the perfect man. And indeed Beal is far from perfect. He cannot solve all his problems. But then some are insoluble. Nichols tells him no one expects him to do the impossible, not even Washington, where the art of the possible is so well understood.

Abner Coates, in *The Just and the Unjust*, is asked to do the impossible, but there is no significant difference between the doctrine of that novel and the injunction in *Guard of Honor* to limit oneself to the possible. What Cozzens means in both is that it is well-nigh impossible to carry on the day-to-day activities of life, given all the determining forces outside ourselves and the refractory nature of men and events, but impossible or not, we must carry on. It is the supremacy of the will over all else that in both novels provides the kind of quietly courageous answer that, tentative as it is, Cozzens keeps offering.

In *Guard of Honor* Cozzens is at some pains to make clear the harsh necessity most of us are under to submit to experience, for he wishes to demonstrate this bondage in order to make all the more impressively grim the human effort to impose meaning and purpose on experience, that is, to embark upon meaningful action. Cozzens begins, on an early page, by speculating on how all the breaks can go against a man. It is only chance, perhaps, that one man is a major general at forty and another is ready to blow his brains out. A few pages later Captain Hicks suddenly catches sight of himself, a magazine editor in uniform, talking to a fighter pilot. Neither he nor the pilot would have chosen his circumstances. "Here was nothing they had elected to do and then did. This was done to them. The dark forces gathered, not by any means at random or reasonlessly, but according to a plan in the nature of things, like the forces of a storm. . . . When the tempest reached its hurricane violence, . . . you make the best of its million freaks." We see Hicks as both proponent and victim of the proposition that conduct is influenced, if not determined, by environment. His allegiance to a moral code of sexual behavior is made clear, he believes in love and devotion and continence in marriage, and yet he commits adultery with a decent, appealing WAC lieutenant. It is almost against their mutual wills that they thus act, as if the circumstances of their particular time and place had simply taken charge. The obstacles to directed and deliberate human action thus sketched out, Cozzens comes, near the end of the novel, to the positive statement on activism that links this book to virtually every other he has written since *The Last Adam*. "A man must stand up and do the best he can with what there is. If the thing he labored to uncover now seemed in danger of stultifying him, could a rational being find nothing to do? If mind failed you, seeing no pattern; and heart failed you, seeing no point, the stout, stubborn will must be up and doing. A pattern should be found; a point should be imposed."

In most respects *Guard of Honor* does better what Cozzens had done before and was to do again in *By Love Possessed*. The unity characteristic of his novels is attained here by squeezing all the events into a weekend and by localizing the action on the base. These limits make possible a concentration in time and place of dramatic events. Within these stringent limits, he sets out to capture the immensity and complexity of the air force as an institution, and he succeeds. Always the master of detail — he is in love with facts — Cozzens gives us in depth the multivarious forms of life contained and organized by the spirit and ordinance of the base. It is a completed, going organism which Cozzens accepts and cherishes. It is a hierarchical organism, carefully structured to reflect the possession and use of power and respectful of the integrity and precisely limited authority of each of the parts. It goes without saying that he would not wish to change it. If it is a coercive organicism (which E. V. Walter says is a fault of conservative institutionalism) that deprives the individual of autonomy, Cozzens would merely point to the dangers of undisciplined individualism. If he be charged with being content to describe the what, the fact, but unwilling to go on to the why, to an investigation of those forces which made the war on which the base is dependent, he would confess, I suppose, his antispeculative bent and call attention to the difficulty of knowing what is beyond the range of the eye. If it is said that age always comes off better than youth, Cozzens could only say, yes, it does. But I think there is no answer to the fact that General Nichols and Colonel Ross, the two elderly men whom Cozzens admires, seem to share a kind of prelapsarian virtue, not innocence, with the oldsters of *The Just and the Unjust*.

By the time he wrote *By Love Possessed* (1957), he had become aware of the need to round out his gentleman-leader. I do not wish to discuss this book at length, and there is no need, since hardly anything in it is new. But among the few points I should like to make is one about the protagonist. Arthur Winner, Jr., is a kind, gentle, wise, moderate, thoughtful man, a leader at the bar and a vestryman in his church, but he has also put horns on his best friend, he has failed as a parent, and he is about to commit a felony. Winner, the protagonist as embodiment of original sin, is, on the score of his culpability, more persuasive and impressive than earlier Cozzens figures. And not only because he so fully participates in human imperfectibility. He is the embodiment, despite his heavy burden of guilt and failure, of the life-lived doctrine. He knows what Cozzens emphasizes everywhere: a man must go on in life, carrying his burden, with no guarantee that he will ever be able to put it down. The critics hostile to Cozzens have claimed that he does not solve the problems he creates; that everything gets said, but nothing gets done; that he dissipates the potential for tragedy. These objections are valid, but, if I may flaunt the intentional fallacy, they are irrelevant in view of Cozzens' intention. Most of what he has written goes to deny the possibility of solving the really important problems or of resolving the really tragic situations. What he intends to tell us is that we must endure in the face of what we cannot escape or sometimes even understand. It is our duty, our commitment to life, that we live in a state of painful suspension and dwell in a climate of permanent irresolution. Paul Tillich has said, "The act of accepting meaninglessness is in itself a meaningful act." The need for such acceptance is Cozzens' finest perception.

If Cozzens is in fact destined never to penetrate the reaches of great art, it is because art is dependent ultimately upon imagination and emotion. "In art," Frank O'Connor says, "knowledge can reach us only through our emotions." Cozzens is deficient in both. He offers a counsel of courage and endurance good enough for our tired time, and valuable in any time, but his hedged allegiance to reason and his appetite for fact tie him securely to the ground. He is a writer who says all he knows, and who expects that to be enough. Everything is spread before the reader — all of it so apparent that one critic complained it was difficult to find anything to write about in Cozzens' work. No ultimate mystery, never to be plumbed, throws its shadow upon his world. The great writer says more than he knows. Cozzens would be impatient with the notion of the inexplicable in life. Those deepest and most profound insights about the dimensions of human experience, those insights that rise from the far recesses of the consciousness of the great writer, are simply not in Cozzens.

THE TRUE RELIGION AND CONSERVATISM

The tone of much modern fiction is religious, if we include in such a designation a concern with Christian ethics, the serious investigation of sin and guilt as thematic considerations, the search for a relation of love between man and man, the pursuit of self-knowledge and spiritual fulfillment in the agony of man's confessed inadequacies. These matters belong to a traditional view of life, which of course religion supports and colors. They appear, then, in the fiction of those writers who are allied to the conservative tradition, whether these writers are specifically religious or not, that is, even when such writers have not made an open commitment to Christianity. With this pervasive religious tone, one that appears even in the work of the new liberals sometimes, I am not concerned here. Many writers have availed themselves of this religious aura and have carried on a vigorous flirtation with religion that they have never permitted to reach the marrying stage. This tentative indulgence in religion has consistently balked at the free acknowledgment, at the open assertion, of the reality of God. This religious tone, this occasional use of the religious vision or insight, is too scattered and elusive a phenomenon, in my opinion, for discussion here. I shall remark it, have indeed already remarked it, in passing, as I deal with the writers in whose novels it may be detected.

My interest here is in the religious novelist as such, the one who has declared himself; it is in the relation of his work to the conservative stream of American fiction in the forties. Let me say at once that I rule out of discussion the work of people like Lloyd Douglas, the popular writers whose treatment of religion in literature is of a piece with the factitious revival of religion in the forties and fifties in a phenomenon like the community church. But once the popular writer is ruled out, very little remains. No serious writer appears to explore in fiction the world of Protestantism or Judaism. Only two Catholic novelists seem worthy of mention,[1] and they are marginal figures, since Harry Sylvester's importance is largely symptomatic and J. F. Powers' position was not yet established by the end of the forties. Clearly, something in American life prevents the development of a religious fiction. None exists in our past, none of the direct and committed kind that I am talking about. None emerged in the forties, despite the most hospitable conditions — the questioning and fear of science,

[1] In addition to Robert Bowen, that is, whom I have discussed in the chapter on the fiction of the war, and Caroline Gordon, to be discussed shortly, who became a Catholic writer only at the end of the period.

the failure of secular liberalism, the renewed interest in theology, the offensive of conservatism in general — since the Puritan era.

Harry Sylvester provides partial answers, at least with respect to a Catholic fiction, to this enigma of the malnourished and paralyzed religious writer. Before he left the Church, he had investigated with vigorous acerbity the obstacles to Catholic fiction. At bottom, they rest, in his opinion, on the Jansenist heritage of American Catholicism that comes by way of the Irish Church. He affirms here a widespread feeling that so far as there is intellectual and aesthetic sterility in the Church in America, it is the result of Irish domination. In *Moon Gaffney* (1947), one of Sylvester's characters attributes some serious faults of American Catholicism to Jansenism. It is responsible for the oppressive idea that sex is filthy and that chastity is more important than charity or love. The consequence of such religiocentrism, Sylvester says in his controversial talk, "Problems of the Catholic Writer," is to provide an atmosphere wholly uncongenial to the arts, one that wilfully balks at the thoughtful exploration of the human condition. In this country, Sylvester continues, Catholicism discourages and sneers at creative writing, identifies good writing only with good propaganda for the Church, and regards any serious treatment of evil in creative writing as an occasion of sin. He laments the absence of any tradition here comparable to that which has produced Georges Bernanos (after whom he tried to model himself) and François Mauriac in France and Graham Greene in England.

The problem, then, is not with Catholicism itself. Sylvester has said that he was emotionally and intellectually committed to the Church and felt it to be the "highest and best authenticated" way of life and belief for him. His own fiction catches something of the genuine Catholic piety and of the sensed dedication to the life of the religious spirit. He subjects his characters to the dark night of the soul, testing the depth and strength of their spiritual resources. He accepts, more than this, he affirms, the reality of the devil. He glories in the experience of grace. He regards despair as the worst of man's sins, but he shows that it is washed away when men submit themselves to the test of obedience or find peace through the violent purgation of their sins. He recognizes the saved, who may be priest or labor union leader, as unselfish, courageous, and wise. They are committed to the Pauline doctrine of love and responsibility: we are all part of one another in Christ. His principal characters all stumble toward self-knowledge, losing their lives in order to find them. Their triumph is the discovery and accession of spirit. In all these ways Sylvester is a traditional Catholic novelist, although he shows little or no feeling for the enduring stability and continuity of the Church itself, as, for example, Willa Cather does in *Death Comes for the Archbishop*.

It is not surprising, then, that two of the three novels written while Sylvester was still in the Church are admittedly anticlerical.[2] Sylvester sees the conflict between dogma and piety (he accepted these) and the bigoted attitudes among priests and lay Catholics; but he is unable to transmute the tensions generated in that conflict into convincing art forms. He cannot transcend that conflict because he remains too much a prisoner of the religious provincialism, of the very Jansenism, that he condemns. His books tremble with a sense of disquiet at his own boldness in dealing with sin or un-Christian priests. But this Jansenism also forces him into tortured analyses of chastity, concern with nymphomania, in short, into a preoccupation with sex. Another problem Sylvester tries to meet is how to combine questions of social conflict with the inner realm of the spirit. He does not join these two areas of experience because he is unable to reconcile his traditional Catholic frame of reference with his impulse toward social reform. Trilling and Cozzens, secularizing the spiritual issues, have succeeded where Sylvester has failed.

How much his failure may be traced to his faith or how much to his shortcomings as an artist — his writing is plodding, his thinking confused — one need not determine. His value is not inherent in his work. As I have said, he is symptomatic. He reveals the difficulties of the religious writer, although they are not insuperable difficulties. He illustrates the inward turning tendency of fiction in the forties, even while it remains aware of the social world. In the one volume J. F. Powers published in this period, *Prince of Darkness and Other Stories* (1947), he shows how a Catholic writer may succeed where Sylvester failed. These stories, caught up in the same tensions that Sylvester recognized, work

[2] These two are *Dearly Beloved* (1942) and *Moon Gaffney*. Sylvester also published in the forties *Dayspring* (1945); *All Your Idols* (1948), a volume of short stories; and *A Golden Girl* (1950).

their way to convincing resolution. Powers it not a victim of Jansenism. He has shed or never had crude prejudices about the superiority of Catholic morality and the sinfulness of Protestants, prejudices which mar Sylvester's work. Powers achieves the kind of objectivity in examining his subjects that permits him to focus the cold glow of irony on the false priest and that enables him to carry us willingly into the constricted heart of spiritual crisis. Powers exercises aesthetic control: he has disciplined his mind and imagination and his language.

Powers' real subject is spiritual victory and defeat, the difficulties of spiritual vision. For him the reality of a Christian profession is demonstrated in the act. The more difficult the act, the more assured may we be of the Christian virtue that impels us to it. In "The Trouble" Powers fuses his concern for the Negro with his dedication to charity and mercy. He makes this vital connection by submitting the life of the spirit to its ultimate test: can the member of a despised and oppressed race, under conditions of intolerable personal loss, live in obedience to virtue and forego vengeance? Clearly, the affirmative answer that Powers gives is not easily won, since it is given with knowledge of the cost in the love of a man for his wife and the identification of a man with his race. To forgive and to refrain from killing is to reject the Hebraic law and to live humbly in the spirit. Sometimes Powers' characters, preoccupied with the necessity for inner discipline and the intricate turnings of soul-searching, seem to be moral athletes as introverted if not as haunted as the Puritans.

But he is saved from taking himself too seriously by a talent for discrimination and balance. It is this which makes his portraits of the false priest possible, gives him the opportunity to display his fine capacity for irony, and rescues him from a lugubrious and sticky immersion in the coils of morality. Those stories which are critical of the priest are not so much anticlerical as they are a recognition of human fallibility when men are gauged by the exacting standards of Christianity. What makes these stories effective is that Powers' characters are not self-conscious about their sins or shortcomings or do not recognize them at all. They do not live in the self-recriminatory hell of Graham Greene's defaulting Catholics but in a bland ignorance of their inhumane or dishonest lives that somehow increases the enormity of their failure as Christians. "The Lord's Day" is a mordant study of such a priest. Done with impeccable objectivity, it chronicles the systematic humiliation of a group of nuns by the Father, who is such an insensitive boor that he does not know he is violating the souls of his charges. "The Forks" shows the difference between the substance and the manner of Christianity. It contrasts the Monsignor to the young curate. The former loves his big car the way he would a woman and has a secure knowledge about table settings. The latter is deeply engaged in discovering the spiritual implications of money gifts that appear to be bribes for silent acquiescence in social wrongs. But the "Prince of Darkness" makes the point most effectively. Here the priest is not bad but feckless. His sins are those of omission rather than of commission. He is less evil than the devil but more despicable. He has no genuine spiritual life, no real learning, no compassion, no dedication to the Christian way. He is a glutton. He is meanly ambitious. But the Church does not reward his ambition. Without appearing to know or see anything about him, it sees everything and condemns him to the life of an assistant, a curate, who may safely pursue his hobby of photography in his darkroom. The Church is vindicated in its wisdom. It is seen to be stronger than its weakest link and to possess the vision which penetrates the darkroom without appearing to have eyes. All this Powers accomplishes in a loosely made story that yet moves toward its inevitable end, reached by way of devastating understatement.

The secular stories, so to speak, do not abandon ethical considerations, but a specifically Christian framework is hardly obtrusive. Powers' stories about Negroes are invariably loaded with moral overtones that may be heard beyond the controlled conduct of the story. Notable among these is "He Don't Plant Cotton," which depicts a contest of wills between Negro musicians and whites. The whites want the satisfaction of seeing the Negroes act in the stereotyped role that confirms white superiority over the Negro. The Negroes resist the delineations of the stereotype and refuse to acquiesce in their own sentimentalization. By asserting their will, they make a legitimate claim to human dignity, a claim they persist in although it costs them their jobs in a time when jobs are scarce and it is winter. This story, incidentally, contains a treatment of Negro music that is to be compared with

Eudora Welty's "Powerhouse." The music made by Powers' Negroes is the food for their will and the lines that mark out their
being; it is the world that the gross, flesh-bound whites cannot
enter, the world where matter flows into immaterial but sustaining sound. Powers' subtle achievement is that he gives moral dimensions to such a world.

Powers shows his versatility in a story like "Jamsie," which
concerns the morality of aesthetics as against that morality of
religion and society which shapes the foundation for so many other
stories. Powers gives new life to an old theme in this story of a
boy's initiation into evil. Here the boy is made aware of two
definitions of evil by two art forms — cheap, juvenile books and
classics such as stories about Lancelot and Gulliver. Art is made
to instruct life when the boy is forced to accept, in his own experience with his idol who has taken a bribe, the hard version
of morality, the hard definition of good and evil that the classics
presented to him. Convincing definitions of morality and reality
emerge from art.

SOUTHERN CONSERVATISM

No region of the country is so hospitable to a conservative view of
life as the South. And perhaps no region has been as deliberately
self-conscious about its identity and so quick and persistent in
asserting its unique quality. For these reasons, the South offers
the best available argument for a regional discussion of American
culture. It is an argument that must be respected at least to this
extent: one must recognize at once the broad homogeneity of the
literature coming from the South, seeing as a whole all that com-
prises the southern literary renaissance. I am fully aware of
these compelling reasons for regarding the southern fictional
contribution in the forties as a totality. Yet I wish to make a distinction between that fiction which rises from the heart of the
southern conservative tradition and that which, while indubitably southern in provenance and quality, does not claim the essence
of its existence from an intimate relationship with the whole of
that tradition. The latter kind of fiction — that written by Truman
Capote will serve as an example — feeds upon particular aspects
of the southern sensibility, emphasizing these to the exclusion of
others. I shall treat this fiction in the next chapter. Here I am

concerned only with that fiction which stands in living relationship to the total culture of the South.

To define that culture is to assert its conservative nature. Those who have sought the meaning of the southern temper or of southern identity, sympathetic writers like C. Vann Woodward or Robert B. Heilman, to name but two, have been in general agreement about it. In the South the past lives in the present, and it is this intense awareness of its history that gives the South the continuity of its heritage. What the South must live with, wants to live with, from the past is the bone-deep knowledge of defeat, from which it has never recovered; is the experience of poverty and stagnation in a country that was otherwise rich and progressing; is the sense of guilt over slavery, which gave it a profound and universal knowledge of evil; is the sense of social, economic, and political frustration that the rest of the Union forced upon it. It cherishes from the past what it knew then, clinging to anachronisms like the patriarchal family or a code of honor, and resisting change in every area of life. So it accepts a given social order. So it accepts, demands indeed, a dedication to place, for this fixes a man in time and in geography. This relatedness of the individual on all the levels of his being — to a family, to a social group, to a geographical location — leads to the southern need for totality. Totality or wholeness is a recognition of the organic order that encompasses all life, a providential order which includes man in society and man in nature. Firmly fixed in time and space, the southerner has at hand all the stable virtues that tradition and continuity can offer. Fully conscious that the tradition includes poverty, defeat, guilt, and frustration, he embraces as his own the tragedy of life. Out of the blighted promise, out of the collapsed dream that was the southern legend, the southern writers have made, says Allen Tate, a universal myth of the human condition.

WILLIAM FAULKNER: SOUTHERN ARCHETYPE

That universal myth finds its fullest expression in William Faulkner, whose work is rooted in the history and mores of the South and written in the conservative spirit dominant there. A full treatment of Faulkner's universality, which must involve the total body of his work, is beyond the scope of the present volume. But a discussion of Faulkner — since he is one of the initiators of the Southern Renaissance and its chief caretaker — as the archetype of the conservative imagination in the South is a necessary and appropriate introduction to the writers I shall treat subsequently in this section. It might be argued that Faulkner is too awkwardly big a writer to be pigeonholed in any way that the convenience of literary history might dictate. And I should agree. Yet no serious distortion of the meaning of Faulkner's fiction, I trust, will result from a consideration of it designed primarily to show how the southern imagination as a whole worked during the forties.

In that decade Faulkner published *The Hamlet* (1940), *Go Down, Moses* (1942), *Intruder in the Dust* (1948), *Knight's Gambit* (1949), and *The Collected Short Stories* (1950). These titles, with the exception of the last, which contains materials published at earlier dates, will serve as the basis of my comments on Faulkner.

In the beginning of time, there was the wilderness in the South. It stands behind the history of the South and behind its land and its men. In Faulkner's writings the wilderness is the starting point in the epic of man and the South, representing pristine, Edenic nature where dwelt human beings as pure as their world. The wilderness land belonged to no white man, and perhaps not even to the Indians who roamed it so long before the white man came. It has a quality of permanent inviolability. It cannot be passed down in ownership from generation to generation, then. The white man is at best a seeker in the land, establishing his possession of it in a kind of spiritual kinship; at worst, he is a usurper. At best, he has the virtues of the creatures who dwell naturally in the wilderness and draw their character from it. Old Ben, the bear, has these virtues: endurance, courage, and pride. Old Ben stands for liberty. He is the epitome of wild life, with a seeming immortality. Sam Fathers, who is part Indian, has these virtues; he is a natural man in a natural world. A creature of Eden, he dies with the passing of Eden. And Isaac McCaslin, by shedding all attachment to his white society, by being reborn in the wilderness, approaches the purity that is necessary if one is to merit the uninhibited companionship of nature. Faulkner accepts the view that the simplicity of paradise, which is the condition of man in the wilderness, is superior to the idea of civilization.

But it is inevitable that man fall from grace and that the wilderness pass away. These events are in the nature of things and in the web of history. Ike McCaslin accepts the fatality that dictates the death of the bear at the hands of the white man. This death is the symbolic destruction of Eden, for the white man must live in the world. What Ike accepts is the burden of being a human being. The essence of being human is the progress from innocence to knowledge. What Ike learns is the guilt of the South and the guilt of his own family in the transition from the wilderness to the plantation. Both the land and the Negro are sinned against in the inexorable course of events in the South. Ike, coming to see this, must seek redemption for the sins of his fathers, who bequeath him a legacy of guilt and sin that goes with the land he is to inherit. He believes himself and the entire South to be under a curse. The Civil War and its aftermath are parts of that curse. But his quest for personal redemption cannot be allowed to separate Ike from his people, that is, from the southerners who have given him his identity. He comes to an acceptance of them as he had to an acceptance of man's fall. Faulkner brings him to a point of such deep knowledge that when he is an old man, still hunting, he can afford the high and selfless innocence of a young boy. This man has learned from life what he must know of his own impotence and fragility. He is the mature human being who accepts the imperatives of endurance despite all limitations — his own, those of mankind generally, those of the South. In his unorthodox orthodoxy, in his epitomization of the total southern myth, he is the man who will appear often in the fiction of the conservative southern imagination.

The principal guilt that haunts Ike, and all southerners, is the wrong done the Negro. In treating the relations between the races, a subject on which Faulkner had much to say in the books published during the forties, this guilt of the white man appears as the old curse of the fathers. This guilt is in the miscegenation in the South that makes the white wrong the Negro, even when love and remorse enter in. It is in the haughty ancestral pride, based on wrong and shame, which makes the white assert a superiority over the Negro, although no superiority of virtue and talent can be demonstrated. It is in failing to recognize the dignity of man in the Negro, because he must be made to act like a nigger in order to preserve the myth of superiority which is a part of the unhappy heritage of evil from the past. The guilt of the white man is that lynching is a human shame and not a racial outrage, as the Negro recognizes. This guilt only a few whites are able to perceive, those who are somehow outside the community or take themselves outside: Ike McCaslin, as we have seen; Charles Mallison, a sixteen-year-old boy; Miss Habersham, a seventy-year-old spinster — eccentrics, children, old women, who pay less attention to fact than to probability.

But those who are, in a sense, outside the community are also inside. As Ike comes to accept his destiny and his guilt as fashioned by white southerners, young Charles Mallison comes to learn that he must be one with his people even though he may move counter to their impulse and their desire in the way he helps a Negro. Faulkner thus reveals the paradox in the nature of the relationship between the white community and the Negro, the paradox whereby the Negro's rights must be protected even as he is forced to maintain his subordinate position in the social hierarchy.

The paradox of the Negro's position is that he is both man and slave or descendant of slaves, and the paradox of the white man's position is that he is both master or the descendant of masters and fallible human being. The slave wishes to assert his rights as a member of the community of man, as Lucas Beauchamp does wherever he appears. But he is always aware that any triumph he wins must always be contained within the framework of the racial hierarchy. Lucas may get his wife back from Zack Edmonds' house because he is strong in body and strong in his determination to behave like a man, but his victory is tempered by his own judgment that the black man wins, finally, only by white sufferance. The psychological strength of the Negro in these encounters derives in part from the white man's sense of guilt, which weakens the latter's resistance to the Negro. Or from the white man's failing faith in the efficacy and rightness of his own institutions or his merely habitual observance of them. Something of this laxity accounts for the victory of Tomey's Turl in winning Tennie as wife over the opposition of his white masters. It is only when the Negro makes up his mind to pay for his deeds with his life, assuming complete and final responsibility for his own acts, that he is freed from the whites.

In all the intricacies of this relationship between the races that Faulkner perceives, the theme of white guilt and Negro endurance is constant. Yet equally constant is the view that finally it is the white man in the South who must resolve the tensions of this relationship. The sociology of the South, as it appears in Faulkner's fiction, is one fully aware that the South preserves its ancestral guilt by insisting on keeping the Negro in his place. But the overly rhetorical *Intruder in the Dust* contains several passages in which it is said that the South, not the federal government, must set the Negro free. The South in this case is an entity made up of white men who have the power to give the Negro his rights, and the day is coming when the gift will be made. The guilt will not thereby be washed away. But if the South abolishes injustice, without help from laws made in the North, then the South may expiate its own guilt and endure its own suffering, in the immemorial pattern of men enduring everywhere. Faulkner's assumptions are not those of the white supremacist, but they do largely deny genuine political and social power to the Negro in winning his way to equality in the South. And in arguing against federal interference in the South — and some passages in *Intruder in the Dust* seem to be pure argument — Faulkner threatens the country with division at a time when division may be fatal to the life of the nation, a position that well reflects the myopia of a tradition-bound and provincial mind not unaware so much as unconcerned with the vast world outside the American South.

This sense of tradition is Faulkner's strength as it is, sometimes, his weakness. It gives him that idea of the community and that feeling for place which are elements in his fiction as inevitable as his deep preoccupation with the history of the South. That mutual sense of responsibility that the races have toward each other arises out of a feeling of shared community in which both races have deep roots. The community, the place, gives identity to those who dwell in it and who are recognized as products made in it over the generations. This is why Faulkner is often so careful to trace the family background of his characters, even when they are of secondary importance, as Houston is, for example, in *The Hamlet*. And it is why he brings Houston back to Frenchman's Bend, for the community becomes or is his fate and he must meet his fate by this return. In the same way Mrs. Harriss, in "Knight's Gambit," fulfils her destiny. She is so firmly attached to her place that, although she wanders through the capitals of the world, she is impervious to any influence they may exert. She preserves unchanged a self that emerged in Mississippi when she was still a child and Gavin Stevens fell in love with her. And it is this unchanged person, now the widow of a New Orleans gangster and the mother of two grown children, whom Gavin marries. On the negative side, Flem Snopes wins to his cold-blooded mastery of Frenchman's Bend in *The Hamlet* in part because he is outside the community and never recognizes any communal responsibility. He is always depicted as alone; even when in a crowd, he stands outside the circle of men. In his rapaciousness he violates the community because he does not belong to it.

In this traditional view of experience, the integrity of the family is of equal importance with attachment to community and place. Here again Flem fails in order to succeed. He violates the imperatives of kinship in refusing to come to the aid of Mink Snopes, a cousin, when Mink is on trial for the murder of Houston. In the eyes of the townspeople, this is an incredible failure even for Flem. Faulkner, it is safe to say, regards it as inhuman. Familial love and attachment and responsibility transcend any other kind of obligation — to abstractions like justice or to collective intangibles like the community. Faulkner is fond of making the point ironically, showing family loyalty operative even in the case of individuals least likely to deserve the offering of love: the ruffian Vinson Gowrie, whose one-armed father grieves for him, and the murderer Sam Beauchamp, whose grandmother sees him properly buried. Or Faulkner makes the point symbolically. The hearth is the center of the home and the symbol of the family. A fire burns in it continuously, its warmth and its constancy standing for human coherence and solidarity.

Like the Southern Agrarians, Faulkner has found a ready exemplar of a traditional way of life in the folk. A large part of *The Hamlet* is devoted to the depiction of a folk community pursuing its principal activities, in particular its economic life. Economic activity reveals, on one level, the shrewd and laconic character of the countryman when he engages in a trade. On another level, it shows him victimized by the great bucolic gamble, the horse-trade or the myth of buried treasure. Faulkner views economic activity as a game in which the playing itself is more important than the profit made, as character is always more important than money. Herein is the important difference between Ratliff and Flem Snopes, for the former understands the rules of the game but Flem understands only money. The rules include an ultimate compassion as they dictate ultimate limits beyond which the pursuit of profit cannot carry. Ratliff and even the Texas horse-trader know these things, but Flem does not. Finally, the folk element in Faulkner reveals the boisterous humor of the rural South which is often created out of a compound of violence in nature and gullibility in the peasant.

Bound to history and the institutions of the past, engrossed in the preservation of what was good in the past, Faulkner has naturally turned a hostile gaze upon modern times. The attack on the modern ethos in the books of the forties strikes first at the business civilization, a modern way of life as against the traditional pastoral or agricultural way. Faulkner regards that civilization as dehumanized, impersonal, non-productive, and unprincipled. All these adjectives can be applied to Flem, who is the prototype of such a civilization. Without conscience, this type-figure of business with the calculating-machine mind ruthlessly devours Frenchman's Bend, never seeming to savor what he eats.

The buried-treasure fever (with its roots in folklore, incidentally), which Flem so carefully induces, may be seen as a degeneration of the pristine hunting ideal: man's energies are dedicated to a get-rich-quick scheme which yields money without any genuine productive effort. Faulkner's use of buried treasure is thus another facet of his criticism of the modern ethos. The harm that may eventuate from asserting the primacy of money values is revealed especially in the threatened collapse of the Lucas Beauchamp household, when Molly determines to divorce Lucas because he has gone mad with money fever. She regards the money he hunts as the curse of God that will put out the fire in the hearth by which the home and the family exist.

In other ways the home is threatened by modernity. Faulkner sees the home as a place to live in, and thinks it untenable when it is filled with gadgets. His critique in this instance is part of a larger protest against mechanization in general. He clearly prefers the comfortable house of the widower-owner who stayed at home, sitting on his front gallery in his homemade rocking chair and reading the Latin poets, to the house it became with its humming dynamos and pumps when it passed into the hands of Harriss, in "Knight's Gambit." For the old house reflects the life of an old southern squire and the new one the life of a twentieth-century bootlegger. In farming, mechanization is a violation of the land; Lucas has never allowed a tractor on his farm or permitted an airplane to dust his crops. This notion that the machine rapes the land is reminiscent of Steinbeck's view in *The Grapes of Wrath*. But where sentimentality colors Steinbeck's resistance to the machine, Faulkner does not permit his veneration of the past to blind him to its faults, and he sees that its agricultural methods were not superior to those of the present. At the same time he knows that the machine comes at a high price. Craftsmanship, the understanding and use of good tools, is necessarily sacrificed to the machine, as Lucas shows, and so are the dignity and worth of labor.

The essentially conservative impulse in Faulkner, which runs broadly through his work in the forties, is the kind of conservatism that would preserve the good of the past and acknowledge and pay for its evils. The patterns of guilt and expiation which this position imposes might be expected to produce a religious orientation of the sort that Caroline Gordon comes to. But despite Faulkner's conviction, shared by Miss Gordon, that modern life has brought spiritual impoverishment, he has avoided a formal commitment to Christianity, remaining ambiguously on its periphery, as Robert Penn Warren does. This conservative position also binds Faulkner to time, imposing on him the necessity to trace the history of the South in order to search out both the good and the guilt. That imaginative historical enterprise has given us in fiction the perspectives on the past that other writers have simply assumed or only sketched. But Faulkner has taken us from the southern wilderness, inhabited by Indians, to the plantation days, through the Civil War and postwar periods to the modern planter with his sharecroppers. Yoknapatawpha County is a microcosm that stands for the South and the southerner. When he is at his best, Faulkner makes it stand for man and the world.

CAROLINE GORDON: THE LOGIC OF CONSERVATISM

In 1953 Caroline Gordon remarked that a trend toward orthodoxy in religion was apparent among fiction writers as it was in the world at large. It was a trend she approved, for she saw a perennially valid universe of discourse within Christianity. "I believe that it could be shown," she said in the same essay, "that in the nineteenth century and in our own century as well the fiction writer's imagination often operates within the pattern of Christian symbolism rather than in the patterns of contemporary thought." It is no more surprising that in her quest for the universal myth she should have come to Catholicism than that she should have found, before her conversion, the touchstones of her being in the southern past. She is not, in the forties, a Catholic writer. But the entire, combined force of her need — for order, for tradition, for piety, for absolution and grace, for a shaping world view that would take the place of the shapeless chaos of the world — forced her inevitably and logically toward the Roman Church; and at the end of the decade, in 1951 to be precise, she published her first overtly Catholic novel. She had made the open commitment augured in all her predispositions. The wonder is that writers like Faulkner and Warren, who, for the same reasons, seemed to press toward the same end, had not yet entered the Church a decade later.

Before the Church there were the South and the past. The elegiac tone Caroline Gordon adopted toward the past derived from her conviction that a total conception of life, life as good, stable, and continuous, had disappeared or been destroyed. A pervasive sense of cultural loss flows through her work. The fragmented lives of her characters are a reflection of this destruction of a whole and coherent cultural pattern that might define life. No force appears in the secular world to act as anchor for man, since neither the cosmopolitanism of urban culture nor the intellectualism that flourishes there provides a satisfactory center for human existence. Nor is the world of nature in itself sufficient. The urgent pessimism of her fiction is the result of her conviction that man's hope and his fate are equally blasted.

These conservative themes she treats in her books in the manner of the new fiction. If this mixture of the old and the new seems a paradox, let us compound it by saying that the new fiction in her case means largely a turning back to models who had that same dedication to the craft of writing that is apparent in her own work. One is aware especially of the influence of James and Flaubert, two culture heroes of the modern literary sensibility. Less often one notices the manner of Joyce. In her use of classical myth, however, she is reminiscent of him and, clearly fashionable in the forties, making the effort to find in the past the archetypes of action and character which are forever applicable and illuminating. As her practice in the novels links her to the new fiction, so does her critical writing, where she reveals a self-conscious concern with all the questions of prose strategy. One such question, which illustrates her critical tendencies and at the same time has an important bearing on her fiction, is raised in the "Preface" to *The House of Fiction* (the title is from James) which she edited with Allen Tate. There the statement is made that the single important principle of imaginative reality distinguishing prose fiction since Flaubert is "the *intense dramatic activity* of everything in the story. . . ." This admiration for what she calls dramatic structure, which renders everything in the story active, appears, ironically, in the criticism of a fiction writer who frequently falls short in precisely this respect.

Miss Gordon had published four books of fiction before the forties opened. The first of her novels I am concerned with is *Green Centuries* (1941). It is an historical novel, laid in the old Watauga section of Tennessee in the time of Daniel Boone; its main subject is the push to the West. One is struck at once with Miss Gordon's treatment of American history. The loving attention she lavishes upon the detail of life in the past suggests that engagement with history is an act of piety, an act, for her, redolent of nostalgia. Such a mood suggests the romanticizing and sentimentalization of the past, but nothing could be further from the case. For she is subjecting to hard examination the great myth of the West. The myth has it that progress, freedom, growth, democracy, and much more were all made possible by American expansion into the West. In our folklore and our fiction, in our cultural history from Frederick Jackson Turner's thesis on the frontier to Henry Nash Smith's analysis in *Virgin Land*, this myth of the West exercises a powerful hold over the American mind and imagination. In *Green Centuries* Miss Gordon's evaluation of this myth becomes a part of the conservative revisionism applied to our heritage. It is a re-evaluation in which she will be joined by others, most notably by Warren.

The drive to the West in *Green Centuries* is undertaken by a rootless, wandering pioneer, forced to flee Carolina for his part in the Regulator movement. The cost of his westering is in the consequences of change: not only the destruction of a traditional pattern of life but the death of his children and his wife, the collapse of ordered domesticity, the loss of love. He loses, in short, everything that symbolizes a stable life and a stable society. He sacrifices everything to his wild desire to go West and take up land. He pits himself against the wilderness, for it is his need to subdue nature, since as a civilized white man he cannot be at one with it. The Indian may create a right relationship to the world of nature in forest and marsh, but for the white man the wilderness is the antagonist. He needs the world of ordered nature in the settlement in order to establish the necessary organic relationship between society and the natural world. These assumptions explain Miss Gordon's sympathetic treatment of the Indian, who has established a kind of society which is indigenous to the wilderness. The ritual behavior of that society is right; the erratic behavior of the restless white can end only in loss.

Historical fiction of such density is rewarding in its concern with the proper place and viability of contrasting cultural patterns. *The Women on the Porch* (1944), Miss Gordon's next novel, is somewhat disappointing in the commonplace quality of its conception. According to Willard Thorp, the germ of the novel was a performance of Gluck's *Orpheo* which Miss Gordon heard in Paris. The opera version of the Orpheus and Eurydice myth forms the basis of the novel. On this framework Miss Gordon has placed two themes. One is the death of the South and the other is the spiritual corruption inherent in the metropolis.

We are given three variations on the first theme. The authentic southern woman is dead. Either she lives in the past, which she cannot make vital in the present, like the grandmother; or she suffers the frustration of her love and must therefore endure the emptiness of life unfulfilled. The three women on the porch all reveal to Catherine Chapman, who comes home to the South, the sad decay of life forces there. The second variation is the synthetic southerner, a blot on the land. One character thinks to re-create the traditional way of life in the South (among other means, by erecting an imitation of Mount Vernon designed by a homosexual architect from New York) by imposing upon it the tastes and values of a money culture. She is thus an alien in the land who represents a corruption of the genuine agrarian tradition. Finally, even the character who gives himself completely to the agrarian way cannot resuscitate it. All the people in the novel are haunted by a pervasive sense of guilt and by memories of failure.

The corrupt metropolis, from which Catherine Chapman has fled when her marriage has collapsed, is no better than the dessicated South. In New York, one learns to regard adultery lightly, and one enters upon it out of boredom. The city is a vast collection of uprooted souls who have lost the direction of their lives. Catherine's husband specifically is a man — a professor, incidentally — who belongs nowhere. He is a typical male character in Miss Gordon's fiction, a sterile intellectual, a man who fails his woman.

These two themes are combined to give us Miss Gordon's view of the modern dilemma: in the face of crumbling cultures everywhere, men are unable to find a refuge where they might pursue a valuable and lasting experience. Catherine returns to her husband because she has no choice that will bring her back to life. The pessimism of the novel is alleviated only by the implication that some solution to man's dilemma must be sought in areas beyond those to which modern man has thus far entrusted his fate.

The Forest of the South (1945), a collection of short stories, may be seen, at least in part, as a kind of supplement to *The Women on the Porch*. If, in the novel, the South appears to cling to an identity which now turns only a stricken face to the light, those short stories dealing with the despoiling of the South explain why. If the novel presents us with the failure of the intellectual, some of the short stories point to the advantages of a primitive, nonintellectual, and natural way of life. The theme of the despoiled South forms an indispensable part of the post-Civil War southern mythos; its counterpart is the guilt of the Yankee. Miss Gordon brings depths of emotion, of hatred and resentment, into play in treating this latter theme which tax all her considerable capacities for realism. But such emotional intensity is not well spent on the naïve polarization of good southerner and bad Yankee. Especially in the attribution of evil to the northerners does Miss Gordon seem to lose perspective. She bestows upon them the sins of materialism, which belong to an industrial-acquisitive society, although it is difficult to believe that insensitivity and cupidity are at home exclusively in the North, or anywhere else, for that matter.

The stories about nature concern Aleck Maury, a figure Miss Gordon has treated lovingly in earlier work. These stories are immensely knowledgeable about hunting and fishing lore. They are intimate with the mystique of the out-of-doors. The questions they raise at once are these: are the rituals of fishing, especially, and of hunting an end in themselves? are they an escape from the world of adult responsibility? are they an effort to come into a right relation with nature? In Hemingway's "Big Two-Hearted River," which reveals the same kind of deep involvement with ritual behavior, the compelling motive for the intense concentration brought to the details of fishing lies in the need for therapy; the protagonist is a disturbed personality. But in Miss Gordon's stories the world of outdoor sport is not a cure for neurosis. On one level she seems satisfied with that world, simply for the open pleasures it gives. On another, she finds that peace and a kind of self-fulfillment are the legitimate fruits of man's absorption in nature. What these stories seem most emphatically to say is that hunting and fishing are the pastimes of a primitive or a leisure society. Both these qualities belonged to the plantation South. In cherishing the kind of society, rooted in the past, in which such pastimes flourished, Miss Gordon implicitly rejects another kind of society — a more complex, sophisticated, urban, intellectual kind. She has said elsewhere that life hardly seems worth living anywhere but in the country. These stories go to demonstrate her unfaltering feeling that man must not be cut off from the world of nature.

The stories also carry forward the pessimism of the novel that preceded them. Two of the most effective of a rather mediocre lot are "The Brilliant Leaves" and "All Love the Spring." The leaves of the first story symbolize the paradox of the fall, that season whose promise of glory must end in death. In the story the promise of life which is contained in the consummation of love is blasted in cowardice and death. In the second story, a masterpiece of indirection, the theme is the way life is blighted when a too heavy burden of responsibility is imposed on one. In these stories we see that the failure of love, which always conveys in Miss Gordon's fiction a deep sense of loss, may result from the inadequacies of human beings as much as from the crumbling of cultures.

The Negro plays a curiously limited role in Miss Gordon's fiction, a conspicuous omission in the work of a southern writer; but some of the short stories are devoted to him. She sees embodied in the Negro the violence of life and the lust of man. An introduction to all evil is thus made through the Negro. He is useful also because he thrusts upon us the problem of differentness and so provides a foil by which white identity may be established.

The most satisfying volume that Miss Gordon has published, among those considered here, is *The Strange Children* (1951). It is a novel of richer texture than those that came earlier, one in which she gives full play to the substantial body of ideas demanded by the conflict she poses: the life of religious faith and the pursuit of regeneration versus intellectualism and cosmopolitanism. Her style, hitherto at its best when it depended most on the straightforward use of short sentences and Anglo-Saxon words, takes on a richer quality here, commensurate with her material; it becomes a more flexible and resourceful instrument. Her manipulation of the point of view in this novel is especially worthy of remark. In this respect *The Strange Children* reminds us of Henry James's *What Maisie Knew*, as the story is told through the eyes of a child who sees more than she can understand. But since the child's name is Lucy, which means light, as one of the other characters tells her, she has a compensatory vision, being able to see what others cannot see; that is, the innocence of her perception makes visible that which is not apparent to tired, less sensitive adult eyes. The irony that adoption of this point of view affords Miss Gordon enriches the book throughout. The strange children of the title are the adults in the book. Insecure and misled, they wander like befuddled children in the maze of life. And in a scene in which they play at charades — a scene in which the point of view yields up its most finely wrought gratifications — the adults act like children; they are especially childlike as they reveal the unrestrained pursuit of appetitive satisfaction without regard for moral law or the canons of good taste.

The genuine concern of an adult in a Catholic novel must be the search for grace. Miss Gordon gives this role to Kevin Reardon, who has been converted to Catholicism and has seen a vision. The reader can see that Reardon is designed to show the meaning of the daily pursuit of religious experience; that his dedication to the care of the soul is supposed to give him a degree of warmth and a range of imaginative understanding that the other characters cannot match; that his suffering, chiefly on the score of a wife who is both unfaithful and mad, should constitute the kind of spiritual immolation that intensifies his quest for regeneration. He stands for the true religion, but unfortunately this is more apparent in the intention than in the performance. Miss Gordon simply does not demonstrate to us the life-giving force of religion in the man she selects to stand as its witness.

Nevertheless, his is the true religion, and it is set over against two false religions. One of these is represented by the McDonough family, who are Holy Rollers. In acknowledging the real presence of God and Jesus in the daily conduct of their lives, these people impress Lucy at least with the genuine character of their piety. When Mr. McDonough reverts to snake-handling at a Bush Arbor meeting in the hope of curing a sick boy, we are made to understand how primitive superstition and atavistic, non-Christian practices vitiate the religious commitment of these people. The other false belief is the intellectualism of Lucy's parents, the Lewises. Their interest in religion is as passive observers of its spectacle or as objective manipulators of its ideas. They speak of religion in a learned and disinterested way; they have no direct experience of it. They are, in fact, removed from the world of experience. Lucy notices that they always talk about books, mostly in a critical way, and that they never say what a thing is, but always what it is like. Aleck Maury, who is Mrs. Lewis' father, finds the family boring because they are cut off from the real world as he knows it, the world of nature. As they are spectators of religion, so they are spectators in the South. They had torn up their roots there. Now returned, they do not plant them anew. Stephen Lewis is writing a coldly objective book on the Civil War, which might appeal to the mind but cannot speak to the spirit.

The allegiance of the Lewises *is* to the mind and to the cosmopolitanism of the house of intellect. In Miss Gordon's view, blending perfectly her convictions as a southerner and a Catholic, the Lewises suffer from the curse of the abstract and the immobility of the objective stance. The intellectualism to which they are dedicated is the enemy of faith, a threat to piety, and an insurmountable obstacle to the commitment of the soul.

Uncle Tubby, a visitor in the Lewis' home, is like them. He and Stephen are both born under the sign of Scorpio, the sign of death unless a man is reborn. Both men commit sins that betray the spirit of grace. Tubby is an adulterer and runs off with Reardon's wife. Steve is an intellectual. At the end, Steve recalls the sign of Scorpio and realizes he must live in the house of death unless he is reborn. But he knows he has resisted rebirth. He groans aloud, the man of knowledge, empty of faith. And thus Miss Gordon makes her case for the pressing need for religion to counteract the decadence of Western man, a plight which she constantly underlines by viewing it, stark and unmodified, in the light of a child's holistic morality.

While I find this the most readable of Miss Gordon's novels — her dialogue is brighter and her touch generally lighter than hitherto — I feel that *The Strange Children* is not wholly successful. It suffers from a failing apparent in all her work: she seems to lack a kind of dramatic nerve. That is, she cannot rise to the controlled passion, to the directed frenzy that will channel her action into the revelation of its essential meaning. She does not seem to have the calculated abandon necessary to create the grand effect. She muffs or muffles her big scenes. It is not that she strives for deliberate understatement. It is that she fails precisely at that point which she is at most pains to emphasize in her criticism — the need to make everything intensely dramatic. At the crucial moment she tends to be static instead of fluid and to turn away, before the task is finished, from her large-sized climactic actions.

ANDREW LYTLE AND PETER TAYLOR: CONSERVATIVE FICTION IN TENNESSEE

Andrew Lytle has indisputable credentials as a southern conservative. He was associated with the Southern Agrarians and contributed to their manifesto, *I'll Take My Stand*. He has had a close relationship with the writers of the Fugitive group, has served a literary and critical discipleship under John Crowe Ransom, and is the editor of the *Sewanee Review*. He is a native of Tennessee and has lived and taught in the South for many years. A novelist and short-story writer, Lytle published two novels in the forties that deserve consideration here as contributions to southern conservatism.

At the Moon's Inn (1941) is an historical novel dealing with the Spanish expedition to Florida led by Hernando de Soto. The book bears many thematic similarities to Caroline Gordon's *Green Centuries*, but surpasses it, I believe, in the fluency of its style and in the dramatic intensity of its treatment. Its problem is the clash of two ways of life and two faiths: the Indian way and the Spanish way, the pagan code and belief and the Christian faith. The resolution of the problem is in the implicit triumph of the Indian over the Spaniard. The meaning of the Christian defeat for the ethos of the South is that here in Florida is one beginning point for the guilt of the white man in America. He is a sinning intruder in pristine nature where he is unable to maintain his faith whole; he is a would-be conqueror bent on subduing and humiliating the natives who rightfully belong there. The themes of white guilt and the corruption of nature that Faulkner worked out in *Go Down, Moses* are thus seen to be here also, in different dress and with different emphasis, to be sure, but similar enough to confirm the unity of the southern point of view.

What is the failure of the Spaniards as Christians? Their mission to Florida has an apparent Christian motivation: they have come to bring the true faith to the savages. And they have come as professing Catholics who are careful to observe the rituals of their faith even in the wilderness. Lytle never permits us to forget what their religious faith is; he calls them Christians, especially when they are opposed in one way or another to the savages. Their real motives, however, are greed for gold or the fulfilment of a vision of conquest as an expression of personal ambition. The Christian-savage opposition, then, is pregnant with irony, since the Christian acts with savage ferocity in trying to achieve his un-Christian goal. In a crucial scene de Soto explicitly rejects the Christian way, despite the warning of his priest, in order to follow a course that he deems will advance his conquest. Lytle's point, I take it, is that the integrity of the Christian faith crumbles under the imperatives of greed and ambition. The reward that follows upon de Soto's choice is an inglorious death for the leader in the wilderness and spiritual sloth for his men, who have lost the sense of an ordered life in an ordered universe that religion and ritual can bestow.

Failing in their relation to the supernatural world of Christianity, the Spaniards also fail in their relation to the natural world. The New World is an Eden, but the white Catholic, who has already fallen, must of necessity be a stranger in this paradise. The New World as undefiled nature is the natural habitat of the red savage; but the Christian is not a natural man and cannot immerse himself in nature. His entire course through the book is, in fact, a violation of nature.

The Indian, on the other hand, maintains the integrity of his faith throughout the novel. He lives by the ethic it dictates. He respects the vows he takes; he acknowledges his tribal responsibilities. The perseverance of his dedication to the death of the Spaniards and the immense, stoical courage with which he faces his own death are possible because the Indian remains an undivided man. He is at one with his faith and at one with his environment. He belongs in the nature of the New World.

The southern conservative would say that the white man is in nature but must transcend it; that his life may be wholly realized only when he maintains a living relationship to a traditional faith. In this book, Lytle's Spaniards fail in these respects, and the failure is an expression of the same pessimism that we saw in the novels of Caroline Gordon: from the beginning, the traditional well of life was poisoned in the South by the guilt of the white man. That same burden of guilt and the same pessimism are felt in *A Name for Evil* (1947), the second of the novels that Lytle published in this decade. This novel is a ghost story, reminiscent of "The Turn of the Screw" in its evocation of an intangible evil and of Poe's "The Telltale Heart" in its use of a mad narrator. This madness is induced by the pressures attendant upon an effort to re-create an order of life from the past. The material symbol of such a life is the beautiful old plantation house and garden that the narrator and his wife buy and set about restoring. But the narrator gets more with his house than he bargained for:

he gets the ghost of the former owner. The charm and grace of the house represent what was good in the past. The ghost represents what was evil. The ghost belongs to a family that removed to the West in order to take up land. The narrator knows that to yearn for the West is to yearn for death. The ghost stands for an aristocratic and patriarchal way of life. But this way had led him to an egomania that destroyed his slaves, his property, and his family — his many wives and his children. The narrator is heir to the evil this man had done in life. He is haunted by that evil, by that heritage of failure, which is the evil of the South. Not only haunted, but driven mad. At the end of the novel his madness leads to the death of his wife and their unborn child. *A Name for Evil* is Lytle's parable for the South where, if man tries to reclaim his total past, he may well destroy himself.

A younger man than Lytle, Peter Taylor is more a product of the new criticism than a peer of those who made it. His work divides neatly between the manner and techniques of the new fiction and the substantive bias of the conservative imagination. While it would be possible to consider him with southern writers of the new fiction in the next chapter, I think he may appropriately appear here, after Miss Gordon and Lytle, whom he resembles very closely. He serves to remind us of the close relationships between these two kinds of fiction and the relationship they bear to the new criticism. He suggests how arbitrary divisions must come into play in the constructs of literary history, since writers do not always fall conveniently under the rubrics critics prepare for them.

Taylor was born in Tennessee and trained under John Crowe Ransom, whom he followed from Vanderbilt to Kenyon College. His first volume, *A Long Fourth and Other Stories* (1948), had the blessing of Robert Penn Warren, who wrote the "Introduction" for it. These bare facts suggest at once Taylor's general orientation. The stories in this book reveal him as an objective and disinterested craftsman, sensitive to the interior lives of his characters, capable of subtle nuances in which much is hinted — about evil, for example — but little directly revealed. Much in his method clearly derives from Henry James. His theme in many of these stories is the disintegration of traditional life in the South.

This has also been Miss Gordon's theme, and Taylor shows much of the same pessimism that marks her treatment of a crumbling culture. In Taylor the break-up of the family is symptomatic of this disintegration. The old southern way is also victimized by an invasion of modernism: modern morals or lack of morals; modern social ideas, in the form of intellectualism or radicalism or cosmopolitanism; even modern buildings. Taylor recognizes the inevitability of change, but he coolly observes that change without direction or purpose is worse than meaningless. His stories assail the idea of disorder, for order is necessary if life is to have definition. But he sees in the South no one who can or will resist the invasion of modernism or channel change into an orderly path that would provide continuity with the past. Instead, he gives us ineffectual representatives of the old way like the sentimental widower in "The Scoutmaster" or sterile people disoriented by northern influences like those of "A Long Fourth," the most impressive story in this collection.

A Woman of Means (1950) is also Jamesian in its method and conception. It is a short novel, skilfully told from the point of view of a young boy and carefully controlled everywhere in its disciplined and delicately written pages. It is not specifically a southern novel — its setting is St. Louis — but its theme is very close to Taylor's principal concern in his short stories. He seems to be saying here that any value system that rests upon money, that derives its sense of order and stability from the possession of money, will destroy those who live by it. No explicit contrast to the traditional southern way of life is made in this novel, nor is one even hinted, but one still feels the unspoken presence of some alternative to the corruption induced by wealth and the sense of failure induced by the lack of it. The young boy who tells this story is in search of a stable existence and in flight from a life where it has been denied him in every way. Motherless, moving from city to city with his father, he has lacked a sense of place and a sense of belonging. He needs psychological, familial, and economic security, and when his father marries a wealthy woman, he seems to have found it in the loving home of his stepmother. And yet he is still haunted by a feeling of insecurity and the dread that his new life is ephemeral. His nightmares materialize. Money is responsible for the corruption of his stepsisters and

destroys their love for the boy's father. The father's money failure
leads to the break-up of the marriage. Divorce, in fact, is made
easier because the stepmother possesses money. Money creates tensions in human relations at every point of contact. The problems
of the novel are framed in an economic and moral context that
is peculiarly modern, revolving around business success and divorce. They are modern, particularly, in contrast to the values
of another, departed order in which human relationships were
conducted in obedience to established moral ideas of responsibility and authority. This implicit contrast makes Taylor here, as
in his first volume, an elegist, a critic of the pointless or destructive new way and a mourner for the old that has not survived.

ROBERT PENN WARREN: THE CONSERVATIVE QUEST FOR IDENTITY

The conservative southern imagination may be best summed up,
for the 1940's, in the work of Robert Penn Warren. He belongs
to this period, as Faulkner does not. But, like Faulkner, he is a
writer of such considerable achievement that he cannot be totally
contained within a formula. Or perhaps it would be better to say
that Warren reveals, better than any other writer except Faulkner, the potentials for a universal interpretation of experience
that lie in southern conservatism.

The particularities of Warren's revisionist and conservative
position may be framed in a dialectic of affirmations and repudi-
ations. Such a formulation may ignore the spontaneity of Warren's mind, but it will have the advantage of setting before us
the naked girders in the structure of his thought. To begin, then,
he rejects the heritage of eighteenth-century Enlightenment. He
finds its optimistic view of human nature shallow and its faith in
reason and abstract principle misplaced; most of all he fears its
untrammeled individualism, which leads to the autonomy and
thus to the heresy of the self, by which he means a destructive
overconfidence in the capacities of the self-isolating individual,
cut off from society and God. He accepts a more complicated and
darker view of man, whose good is always susceptible to corruption. He is suspicious of reason and impatient with abstractions,
since he brings to bear on life an ironic and sceptical vision which
abhors dogmatic decisions and makes a virtue of provisional resolutions. While he regards the realization of the self or of human

identity as the highest, final goal of man, he believes this realization can be achieved only by reference to authority beyond the self. He rejects the heritage of nineteenth-century science, which is responsible for our God-abandoned world of today and which has bred the variety and multiplicity that contribute so heavily to the disintegration of society and of individual consciousness. He accepts an unorthodox orthodoxy which rests on the validity of religious myth and religious metaphor; out of the Christian conception of the communion of men will come unity to replace the present fragmentation. He rejects the industrialism and the metropolitanism of the twentieth century because they too stifle the human personality. And they cut man off from the fructifying past. He affirms the enduring value of the past, of its tradition and its myth, in establishing the continuity of human identity in the present and for the future. He rejects the romantic, "democratic" conception of the West as the land of golden opportunity, settled by Frederick Jackson Turner's individualistic and independent frontiersmen. This myth of America he inverts, and he sees the West as a region of license and as an escape from responsibility. The West is the world of nature. While man is in and of nature, as Warren recognizes, man must nevertheless separate himself from nature if he is to achieve the discipline commensurate with his humanity. For Warren, in short, Jeffersonian liberalism, Darwinian science, and American industry comprise an unholy trinity that has spread its infection throughout the modern world, fragmenting our universe, inducing a chaos of beliefs, destroying the possibility for stable society, and threatening the existence of the human personality itself. He is at war with all these forces.

THE BACKGROUND AND SOURCES OF WARREN'S FICTION

He did not suddenly declare war in 1939, when he published his first novel. He had committed himself to this war when, under the influence of the Fugitive group, he was writing his life of John Brown in 1928, as Louise Cowan tells us. He had carried on the unremitting struggle later as one of the Southern Agrarians — as a contributor to their manifesto, *I'll Take My Stand*, and as an editor of the *Southern Review*. The Agrarians had looked to Edmund Burke for direction, a thinker who was one of the ancestors of Warren's mind. The group was convinced, like T. S. Eliot, that Western man had suffered a cultural break-down. It aimed, consequently, at cultural integration, trying to embody in traditional modes of thought and action a concrete way of life. The southern way the Agrarians sought to establish, or really to re-establish, included a class society as an instrument of stability, religion as an instrument of order, the rejection of abstract rights, a sense of mutual obligation on the part of all members of society. Warren shared many of these ideas.

Warren's religious attitudes were early shaped by John Crowe Ransom's *God Without Thunder*. An unorthodox defense of orthodoxy, that book expresses its religious convictions in mythic and poetic terms, avoiding commitment to established religion or formulated dogma. The religious spirit, Ransom says, is always the tragic spirit. Now Warren's novels are lit by a rich play of religious metaphor and extensive use of Christian conceptions like redemption; and the tragic sense that hovers over his work and the ready acceptance of evil in it — cosmic, human, and natural evil — indicate firm agreement with Ransom's dedication to the myth of religion. At a later period Warren seems to have been influenced by the "hard" spirit in the Christian realism of Paul Tillich and Reinhold Niebuhr. Indeed, the latter's book, *The Children of Light and the Children of Darkness*, seems of immediate relevance to Warren's work. The children of darkness, says Niebuhr, are those moral cynics who know no law beyond their own will and interest. The children of light are those who believe that self-interest should be brought under the discipline of a higher law, a more universal law. Niebuhr refers, I take it, to the law of God, and this Warren has not accepted. But the description of the children of light applies with uncanny accuracy to those characters in Warren's fiction who find their sanctions somewhere outside themselves. And likewise the children of darkness describes those who are the victims of what Warren calls the heresy of the self. Warren's position is thus analogous to that of the young postwar writers in England as G. S. Fraser reveals it. They yearn toward religious orthodoxy, but they cannot bring themselves to make an outward act of faith and acceptance.

It was Warren's southern orientation that brought him as a novelist to historical revisionism before the historians themselves had fully embarked on this course. What the historians came to through research, he came to through vision. All, historians and novelist alike, sought the meaning of the past in order to establish a conception of identity. Warren's goal in all his fiction is to know man, to free him from whatever forces would crush and distort him. In the spirit of revisionism, Warren rejected the frontier myth and repudiated the West as the home of hope because he wished to give man back his past so that man might claim his self. In Warren the man on the frontier, rootless, mother-less, fatherless, without a past, is a lost soul. Man must return to the mother, the father, and the home place — this is the archetypal pattern of return — if he is to claim his identity.

Warren also regards industrial capitalism as a threat to the realization of the self. Just as the Industrial Revolution brought home to Marx the realization that now only a cash nexus existed among men, that capitalism had imposed a new, impersonal character on human relationships, so Warren, viewing American economic life from the opposite pole, paradoxically comes to the same conclusion. He knows that industrialism and mechanization threaten the agrarian and patrician identities that have tradi-tionally been at home in America, indeed threaten all identities.

If the conditions for ego identity in Warren are reactions against modern industrial society and against the American myth of the West, if the conditions are patterns of return to parental sources of security and life and acceptance of tradition, what then is the process of individuation, to use a Jungian term, in Warren's fiction? The process is dialectical for Warren, as it is for Jung, whose description of the emergence of the individual personality tallies to a remarkable degree with the struggles for the self that dominate Warren's novels. In fact, Warren's fictional characters aim at precisely what all men, Jung says, must aim at: ". . . everyone's ultimate aim and strongest desire lie in de-veloping the fullness of human existence that is called person-ality," and *one must learn to know oneself in order to know who one is.* For Jung, the psychological process of individuation con-sists in the play, the conflict, of the consciousness and the un-conscious, of the reason of the former and the chaotic life of the latter; there is collaboration between them as well as conflict, and out of both comes the individual. Individuation is a centralizing process, during which a new center for the personality develops. That center is the self. As one reads Warren, it is this sense of process and the insistent quest for self-discovery that one perceives at the heart of his novels. His great conflicts are carried on within the individual souls of his people, who darkly struggle with the disparate elements of their characters to find and make their ultimate identities, to shuck off mask after mask and come to the quintessential self. It is their deepest need, as it is, I suspect, Warren's and Jung's, to fall back on a realized self in a world that seems engaged in a gigantic conspiracy to eliminate the self.

WARREN AS HIS OWN CRITIC

The terms that Jung uses to describe the nature of the self are consciousness and the unconscious. Warren's term is self-division or sometimes, in a somewhat larger sense, the doubleness of life. For Jung, writing on "The Spiritual Problem of Modern Man" in the thirties, man faces alone, without the help of traditional creeds, the problem of his subjective processes. Warren, writing in the following decades, turns man in upon himself in order to find fulfillment beyond the self. These two differences — in terms and in the nature of self-independence — can be easily illustrated. In his little book on *Segregation*, significantly subtitled *The Inner Conflict in the South*, Warren concludes by saying that the segregation problem in the South is the problem of irremediable self-division, which angers men because they cannot find identity. In his poem, *Brother to Dragons*, he says that fulfilment of the self is possible only in the recognition of the common lot of mankind, "And the death of the self is the beginning of selfhood." Man must find himself outside himself in the community of men, which is, I take it, a conception of secularized brotherhood.

Both Warren's criticism — and he is a critic of high seriousness and brilliant perceptions — and his poetry reveal from first to last an abiding preoccupation with the problem of identity; his explicit treatment of that problem, especially in the criticism, lays bare many of the assumptions of his fiction and provides a guide to the intelligent reading of his novels. Indeed, the whole range of ideas, attitudes, and method in his novels is so accurately reflected in his criticism that he is his own best critic. With respect to the problem of identity, he says that good fiction must give us "the stimulation of a powerful image of human nature trying to fulfill itself." The method of finding the personality, as in Jung, is in a process of living whereby mutually competing versions of life and being confront each other, and the personality is created out of the antimony. Warren has expressed these ideas about Katherine Anne Porter's Miranda in describing the terms of her "dialectic of living." But his most complete non-fictional statement on identity is in an essay called "Knowledge and the Image of Man." Here he argues that man's right to knowledge is indispensable to his right to define himself. This view of personality is a heritage of the emphasis of Christianity upon the value of every soul in the sight of God. When man has an image of himself, he discovers separateness. That discovery leads him to knowledge of the pain of isolation and self-criticism. With this recognition of the tragedy of life, man can return to a communion with other men and nature, having accepted love and law, that is, having achieved moral awareness which now makes his redemption possible.

Communion and redemption are Christian terms always present to Warren's mind. Although he is not an orthodox believer, redemption is nevertheless necessary and appropriate to Warren's world view. In *Brother to Dragons*, Lucy Jefferson tells her brother that his was a noble dream, but there is a nobler:

> It will be nobler because more difficult and cold
> In the face of the old cost of the human redemption,
> And knowledge of that cost is, in itself, a kind of redemption.

Earlier in his career, Warren was able to use in a purely secular sense an argument for community of interest between owner and sharecropper which assumes, I believe, that the integrity of the human communion is a good. The two conceptions come together in his discussion of Conrad's *Nostromo*. Warren admires the sense of human community in Conrad, whose characteristic story, he says, is the relation of man to the human communion. The story of awakening and redemption engages Conrad most deeply: the story of those who sin against human solidarity and then save themselves. That redemption must be earned, and continually re-earned, through a man's identification with the general human condition. But since contamination is implicit in the human condition, as Warren says in an essay on Faulkner, it is through love that man must cleanse himself if he is to achieve redemption. As a critic, Warren, clearly, is very close to the orthodox Christian view. His fiction, from the beginning, is concerned with Christian themes, especially love and redemption, which are the avenues to the self.

From the beginning, like Conrad and like the "hard" theologians, Warren has feared reason, because it can deny life; and he has cherished illusions, because they may provide man with the truth. In the twentieth century we have lived in a world dominated by reason, as he sees it, and hostile, consequently, to Christian ideas. Warren's writing is a work of reconstruction, as I have said, because he strives to impose order and stability upon a world which is suffering from moral confusion induced by unmitigated rationalism. The chief cause of our present disorder is nineteenth-century science, the most destructive offspring of reason, which poses for Warren now the same difficulty that it posed for Matthew Arnold in the last century: the ethical and epistemological implications of science are at war with the religious and/or humanistic impulses in man and seek to destroy those impulses. Warren's most succinct statement of our general plight is made in his discussion of Faulkner. The modern world, he writes, "does suffer from a lack of discipline, of sanctions, of community of values, of a sense of a mission. It is a world in which self-interest, workableness, success, provide the standards. It is a world which is the victim of abstraction and of mechanism. . . . "

It is a world that has pushed Warren into the past where he seeks answers that will sustain him as he lives in the present. Since the central task of the writer is always self-definition, the past exists for Warren as a storehouse from which he can draw some sense of who he is. As southerner, especially, he lives in a present that has been exposed in a particular way to shock, to a clash of values brought on by rapid industrialization and by the growing self-consciousness of the Negro. The consequent dislocations have forced him as a southerner to seek a redefinition of life. Warren tells us this in a *Paris Review* interview. In the introduction to *A Southern Harvest* he reveals that any effort at such redefinition would involve, for him, a consideration of American history and myth. Since men also define themselves in time, the past is valuable in providing the line of continuity to us and through us. In these ways Warren constructs the traditionalist's rationale for reverence toward history and at the same time explains the need for a past and for an interpretation of the past that will support a life-giving myth. The uses of the past in Warren's fiction, it may be concluded, go beyond an attraction to historical setting and historical event; Warren is searching for a meaning for life which he feels can be found only by placing man in time and history.

As Warren's fiction is dependent upon the ordering of the past, so it is dependent upon the ordering of nature. And, as always, his criticism mirrors his fictional practice, and his analyses of other writers' work reveal the preoccupations and predilections of his own creative life as a novelist. When he says that Hemingway's characters sink into nature, he is describing what happens to some of his own. In Hemingway the famous code is the discipline that helps to impose order on nature. Only when man thus exerts his will can he assert his selfhood. In Warren's fiction, idea takes the place of code. Idea is the formulation of a conception which transcends the naturalistic level of human experience; it is therefore different from nature. Man's hope for realizing his humanity rests on maintaining a resolved tension between idea and nature.

The clearest nonfictional exposition of this complex relationship is found in Warren's commentary on Stein's remark in *Lord Jim*: "In the destructive element immerse." Conrad means, Warren asserts, that man must justify himself by an idea; he must find moral significance and order. For man is, in one sense, a creature of nature, "an animal of black egotism and savage impulses." So man might live only on the naturalistic level. But there is a "supernatural" level, the world of idea or dream. Man is not born to swim in the dream, but he can try. Man's fate and his triumph, if his humanity is not to be frustrated, are to recognize the necessity of the idea. What Warren sees in Conrad (and in Eudora Welty, too, as he shows in another essay) is that wisdom lies in recognizing and resolving the constant oppositions imposed by the human condition: idea to nature, justice to material interests, innocence to experience, individuality to communion. The dialectical process he so acutely observes in these writers is precisely what underlies the themes and structure of his own fiction.

THE FICTION

Night Rider (1939), Warren's first novel, is a book in which his mind outspeeds his imagination and he knows better than he does. The major problems of the novel are two: how a man may become the victim of events, contingencies, when he does not know who he is, and how the quest for social justice can lead to injustice. These two problems pose a series of relationships between the private and the public world, between politics and identity, between the community and the self. In the history of the novel in America during the twentieth century, this book must occupy a pivotal position, precisely because it does combine the examination of social problems with concern for the nature of selfhood. It represents a turning away from social realism and proletarian fiction, as Warren himself has recognized. In the *Paris Review* interview Warren has said that he was aware of the shadow that the events and the fiction of the thirties cast on his own book; in one sense, then, *Night Rider* is a novel about "social justice." But, Warren continued, he was trying to find a different and deeper point than those his contemporaries in fiction were looking for. This modification of social realism by introducing a treatment of the tensions between private and public realms of being is not only the beginning of a characteristic novelistic method for Warren, but it marks, virtually at the opening of a new decade, the introduction of a distinguishing feature in the fiction of that decade.

The central social irony of the book emerges from the imperatives of a situation in which independent tobacco-growers seek a just price for their crop from the tobacco companies. The action, based upon the tobacco war of 1905 to 1908 in Kentucky, begins with the establishment of the Association of Growers of Dark Fired Tobacco, organized by men of probity for the purpose of wrenching justice from those companies. Pursuing this end, the leaders discover the necessity for a growing intensity in the coercive methods they use; they discover they cannot control their membership; they discover that inevitably the fight for justice leads to a degradation of the goal — to destruction of property, to usurpation of civil law and order, to murder. Later in the book, the Free Farmers' Brotherhood of Protection and Control is organized as a terroristic group which Warren endows with strongly fascistic characteristics like militarism and blind obedience. The irony involved in this unleashed social momentum is double: the necessity to win the struggle with the companies overshadows the ideals of justice that originally motivated the farmers; and the resort to violence and civil disorder, which means the sacrifice of those ideals, does not lead to victory but to defeat, a defeat in which nothing, not even honor, is salvaged.

The tobacco war, then, is the public scene against which the private destiny of the characters is worked out. It is Warren's practice to give the reader a firmly conceived sense of the exciting historical events and movements that swirl about his characters. These are not merely *mise en scène*; they are formative in the life of the characters; and Warren wishes us to feel a vital connection between characters and society. Warren in this respect is comparable to Stendhal, who involved his characters in political intrigue for the throne of France or in the massive confusions of the Battle of Waterloo, insisting upon the impact of these public events upon them, but viewing the public event primarily as it contributed to the meaning of the self. Balzac, on the other hand, was at least as interested in an analysis of society for its own sake as he was in his characters, and saw them as more definitely the product of their society than Warren does. Warren, of course, understands that social forces may mold character and dictate human action, but he establishes a tension between the individual and society in a relationship that permits character to jerk free and transcend events in the search for its own meaning.

In the contrasting fates of Percy Munn, the protagonist in *Night Rider*, and Captain Todd we can see these tensions worked out. At the beginning of the novel, Munn is caught up in the movement of a crowd on a train, as people come into Bardsville for an organizational meeting of tobacco-growers. Munn feels this pressure, both human and inhuman (because in the mass no one person is responsible), and resents it. We see Munn at once, then, as a character who has chosen and yet not chosen his fate. He has chosen to come to the meeting, but he is subjected to pressure outside himself and pushed further in participating than he might have anticipated. He yields up a kind of reluctant but free commitment, and at the same time his action is determined by the pressure of the crowd and of friends. The play between free will and determinism in Munn is an early example of Warren's characteristic dialectic. And the failure of Munn's will signalizes his failure to achieve full identity. Captain Todd, involved also in the growers' association, enjoys a sense of his own identity that is drawn from an inner certitude that Munn does not possess. Todd's scepticism and relative solipsism — he has no confidence in things and events — help him to understand who he is. At a critical point he withdraws from the association, because it is taking a course he cannot approve. He knows his own mind because he knows his self. Munn, not knowing who he is, remains in the group and is destroyed.

Munn, wishing to be free and to be himself, constantly turns to others and to the organization for some definition. When he is told that he has been made a member of the board of the association, he involuntarily says no. Later, even when the association had claimed "the inner substance of his being which was peculiarly himself," he reflects on his initial refusal, but he does not understand it. Warren's tactic is to depict Munn often as an uncomprehending man, unable to analyze the experience he undergoes because he has not established essential criteria with reference to the self. In this instance, I believe that Warren is simply asserting that Munn will fail in self-knowledge if he is dependent upon the association for it, since that organization, and any other, will sap a man's powers of individuation.

Munn cannot find himself in other people, either. He goes hopefully to his wife for an explanation of who he is, but she cannot help him. When he makes his first speech for the association he is filled with despair, because he recognizes that his words have not come from a man who has found himself or from a man who fully understands the common tie of humanity. In Warren's scheme of things, the activated sense of communion is possible only as a final transcendence made on the basis of a realized self. In still another abortive attempt to define himself, Munn has an affair with a young woman. He sees her at one point standing "as though she could sink at will into the deep and complete satisfaction of her own being." But possessing her does not give him the sense of identity that she has. Munn's last desperate effort to find himself through others comes in his design to kill Senator Tolliver, the man who has betrayed the association and in so doing violated the human community. He thinks that if he could kill Tolliver he would not be nothing. But when he reaches the senator he can do nothing. He is immobilized. At this point soldiers track him down and kill him. He dies because he never knew who he was.

He had tried to learn about himself throughout the novel, as he had been aware of others' identities. But he had been overpowered by failures of his own judgment and by the tide of event. His relations with Buck Trevelyan capsulize his fate. He has successfully and altruistically defended Buck against a murder charge, but he comes to feel that Buck is guilty. Later, when Buck tries to blackmail a member of the Free Farmers' Brotherhood of Protection and Control, the fascistlike organization that grows out of the association, the brotherhood decides to kill Buck. It falls to Munn to fire the shot. Here Warren has made the now obvious point about human fallibility, and about how evil comes out of good, as blackmail and now murder come out of Munn's disinterested defense of Buck. We are made to see the danger inherent in good intentions. Before Munn shoots Buck, he tears off the mask he is wearing so that Buck will know who kills him. Munn has been brought to murder, but, pathetically, he wishes to commit the murder in his own person, so to speak, to identify himself. He takes off the mask as if he wishes to find himself in the open air, a free man committing an act of his own will. The measure of his failure comes toward the end of the book when he knows that the "seed of the future in himself, the live germ," had gone out of him. Man, he realizes, is what he is in the act, and not what he says he is or conceives himself to be. And Munn's act was murder willed by a group.

Near the end, Warren brings Willie Proudfit into the novel and permits Willie to tell Munn the story of his life. Willie's excursion into the past is designed to reveal the past as a deposit containing the secret of identity. For the past defines a man, and we come to know Willie as he knows himself. Furthermore, Willie, who had gone West and lived among Indians, had now come back to the homeland: he is the native returned, acting in obedience to one of the archetypal patterns that Maud Bodkin remarks. Aesthetically, Willie is in the novel to reveal how identity is realized in contrast to Munn's descent to nothingness. But since there are no parallels between Willie and Munn as there are between Captain Todd and Munn, the introduction of Willie seems to me merely Warren's device to assert certain of his conservative convictions — and to assert, perhaps too insistently, his interest in the process of definition of the self.

As Irene Hendry has said, Munn is the divided man who turns to the objective world of action and organization and there loses his subjective existence. Warren tells his story relentlessly and at times mechanically, pursuing Munn's disintegration as thoroughly as Dreiser did Hurstwood's. The melodramatic, the consistently underplayed scenes that are never fully convincing, the abrupt introduction about halfway through the novel of Munn's two dark angels, Professor Ball and his son-in-law, are the faults of a beginning novelist whose imaginative and technical resources are not equal to his themes. These are the themes, however, of Warren's mature work, running from Burke's admonition that reformers forget man's nature to Jung's process of individuation, and here they are all opened for exploratory investigation.

At Heaven's Gate (1943) is not altogether successful either, although it is not a falling off, as so many second novels seem to be. Warren deals with the disintegration of character in both novels, and feels it necessary, for this reason, to maintain considerable distance from his people in order not to become auctorially involved. The consequence in both novels is a certain remoteness in the *reader's* relation to the characters as well. The reader is aware of a chilled air in these books, which is the proper if inhospitable atmosphere for the author's brisk, almost clinical efficiency in the matter of destruction. Subsequent novels do not suffer from this inadequacy; they are saved by a hard-won redemption or by a philosophical density which engages the characters and the readers.

This is not to claim that Warren fails to achieve a certain measure of philosophical complexity in *At Heaven's Gate*. He has said that he was deep in Dante when he wrote the novel and that the Seventh Circle of Hell, with some liberty of interpretation, provided "the basic scheme and metaphor for the whole novel. All of the main characters are violators of nature." In Canto XI of the "Inferno" we are told that this violence may have three objects: God, oneself, one's neighbor. In the succeeding cantos devoted to this circle, specific kinds of violators are named: the usurer, the suicide, the spendthrift, the sexual aberrant. In Warren's novel, Bogan Murdock is the usurer; Slim Sarrett the homosexual; Sue Murdock, with self-destructive tendencies, the potential suicide; Jerry Calhoun the violator of family bonds and the spirit of familial piety; Ashby Wynham, in the beginning, is violent against God; Private Porsum, through most of the book, does violence to his neighbors. The book may be seen, then, as variations on this Dantean theme.

Or it may be seen as a series of misadventures with the self in which the characters try to find themselves in each other, as Percy Munn tries to find himself in his wife and in other people; and in which they put on, figuratively, one or another mask to hide or distort their identity. Sue Murdock, perhaps the most desperate character in the book, plays the part of the respectable debutante as Jerry's betrothed; she wears the mask of bohemianism, as Slim's creature; she wears the mask of lover with Jerry and with Jason Sweetwater. Jerry, the farm-boy who became an All-American back, wears with gnawing discomfort the mask of college man; with equal discomfort, he wears the mask of Sue's lover; with equal inappropriateness, he wears the mask of banker and broker. Slim, the homosexual, is the most sophisticated mask-wearer. He is the virile boxer; he is the poet in a garret whose mother, touchingly, was a whore; he is the perceptive critic of Shakespeare. Bogan Murdock wears the mask of quiet power and omniscience. Underneath, he is nothing. These characters, then, appear to be one thing, but turn out to be something quite different, like Slim. Or they are people who have lost the notion of who they are and later find it with tragic consequences, like Private Porsum. Or they never find it, and in the end must die, like Sue, or face bewilderment and impotence, like Jerry.

Perhaps the chief irony in this novel is that a character like Slim should give us in positive terms the theme of the novel, that the bone-deep truth should be in a man who is a liar, a poseur, a murderer. It is he who knows the mystery of personality — that people must discover themselves. It is he who claims such discovery for himself because he is a poet: "Poetry is a [superior] technique for achieving self-knowledge." Warren's dialectic is obviously at work when out of Slim's factitious and melodramatic story of his own life comes his valid statement of the need for the tragic sense and the knowledge of isolation and discipline. Out of this same manufactured story comes his sound view that, "The man who has not fulfilled his nature is the man who needs sympathy." When Slim writes his paper on Shakespeare for a graduate course, he says that the theme of all tragedy is the necessity for self-knowledge. The tragic flaw in Shakespeare's heroes is a defect in self-knowledge. Again the dialectic is at work, and the irony too, when Slim confronts Bogan in the struggle for ascendance over Sue. Slim has been feeding his obsession with power by manipulating Sue. Yet he says Bogan is guilty of "the special disease of our time, the abstract passion for power, a vanity springing from an awareness of the emptiness and un-reality of the self which can only attempt to become real and human by the oppression of people who manage to retain some shreds of reality and humanity." In the "Introduction" to the Modern Library edition of *All the King's Men*, Warren, com-paring Bogan to Willie Stark, says quite explicitly that Bogan was supposed to embody the dessicating abstraction of power and "to try to fulfill vicariously his natural emptiness by exercising power over those around him. . . . "

Warren arranges the fate of his characters in such a way as to illuminate and embroider his ideas. The lineaments of power apparent in Bogan are actually a façade; he is revealed as an empty coward. Sue, driven by perversity and desperation, comes to live as if she were out of time. For Warren, life is meaningless when men are removed from the stream of time that bears their personal histories. Because men are defined by the past, they must maintain in the present a sense of continuity with the past, for this continuity makes the future possible. Jerry's fate is related to this general proposition. His sin has been a terrible failure of piety, for he denies his family and his history. He faces the truth about himself late in the book: men are the sum of their heredity and experience in the past, and they must fashion their lives to accommodate that totality.

Jason Sweetwater seems to have discarded piety altogether; he embodies, not the neglect of ancestors we see in Jerry, but the positive rejection. In the pursuit of the self, Jason casts off his lying, sentimental father. He goes into his father's church on weekdays, as a boy, as a "kind of avowal of self, a compensation for, a repudiation of, the not-self which he was when he sat there on Sunday. . . . " Jason learns some hard lessons in his quest. He knows for instance that "A man could not believe in himself unless he believed in something else." For Jason, apparently, this "something else" was not his father's religion but the cause of labor. It seems to me that Warren is not clear about how Jason's beliefs enable him to fix so securely his image of himself, but Warren is clear in the formulation of the proposition that man can know himself only by transcending himself. Jason knows that a man must pay for what he gets, and so he will have to pay for being in love with Sue: always, "you paid . . . with a chunk right out of your soul. . . . " He is no "God-damned Liberal" to feel you can get something for nothing. The payment demanded of him is marriage to Sue, who will bear his child. He will not violate his own conception of what he is in order to pay, since Sue sees in him a father-image and a father-substitute which she both wants and repudiates. He will not assume this role.

The comment about the liberal that I have quoted above is Warren's most succinct and provocative statement on the political-social scene of the thirties. With it, he separates Jason at once from the proletarian heroes of social realism and he repudiates the easy hope of liberal reform. With it, he shows both the connection his novel has with the fiction and the times that immediately precede it and the difference between his work and that of others who wrote about labor organizers. And with it, he reveals again how attractive the world of affairs is to him, how, indeed, he wishes to bring his conceptions of self and society into the open and not to trust in cloistered virtues. Behind this novel lies the world of labor unrest and strike-breaking, the world of high finance and political maneuver. The prototype for Bogan Murdock is supposed to be Luke Lea, onetime United States senator from Tennessee who served a term in jail for his part in the $17,000,000 failure of the Asheville Central Bank and Trust Co. The prototype for Private Porsum seems, in some ways, to have been Sergeant York, a hero of the first World War.

I feel that in this novel Warren fails to resolve all the problems that he raises, just as he fails to dispose satisfactorily of all the characters. A cryptic quality pervades the book, qualifying and sometimes even crippling Warren's commitments and his conclusions. But the novel clearly points to his major work, and the conceptions which are here rehearsed are being readied for a grander performance.

In *All the King's Men* (1946), Warren emerges from apprenticeship and brings his many characteristic themes together in one of the most distinguished novels of the period. Politics is the framework for his story, and amid the thrust and surge of the public scene where a great, virtually omnipotent political boss takes and wields his power Warren weaves his complex of beliefs. The end of man is to know, he demonstrates. What man seeks is the knowledge of good and evil, and the knowledge of truth, and out of these, self-knowledge. But man's way is hard, not simply because truth is elusive, but because it has different shapes for different men, who are all the victims of the modern world and of their own self-division. Man's way is hard because he must come to the painful recognition of what he is as man, which takes him apart from and enables him to transcend nature. Since man exists in time, however, he has history, and history may help him to find the truth and to understand the world. The past may reclaim for a man the present and give him a world he can understand and live in. The past may give a man his father and his mother, and giving them, it may release him to live in the world and understand himself.

If these are the themes to be discovered in the novel, we are prepared to consider sympathetically Warren's contention that Huey Long did nothing more than suggest Willie Stark. Yet I suspect that Warren's comment was prompted by tactical considerations: he wished to give the authority of his own voice to the repudiation of a purely political reading of his novel. A sound enough purpose. But the social scene, Warren and his *Sewanee Review* champions notwithstanding, has the largest kind of meaning for this novel. I do not speak of the class tensions that are present and exploited by Willie in the conflicts between aristocracy and rednecks. Nor even of Jack Burden's treason to his own class at Burden's Landing when he allies himself with Willie, the cocklebur candidate whose economic policies are a threat and an affront to the well-born and the well-to-do. (Although Jack's dilemma, the conflict in social and political loyalties, is instructive, because the resolution of such a dilemma is a step on the road toward self-knowledge. . . .) What I am saying is that the social-political scene, aside from its intrinsic value for movement and interest in the novel, is the indispensable background for working out the view of man's character and destiny that Warren wishes to set before us. All the ideas in the novel, then, are in a sense socially oriented, for they have their reality, not as abstractions which emerge as valid for Warren or Jack, but as strands in the fabric of social interaction. The obvious should not be over-looked: men in life are political creatures, living in society among other men and by institutions created by men and according to moral standards conceived by men and preserved for their use as a social heritage; and it is equally obvious that the actions and beliefs of such men are the raw materials of fiction. *All the King's Men*, to be sure, is not the story of a dictator. But that story, like the story of Jack's social dilemma, takes its place in the novel to say something about the nature of man, about man and human history, about man's morality, so that what Warren finally achieves is an integrated view of man *and* the world he lives in.

The totality of that view can be formulated in terms of the Hegelian dialectic. Men are good, like Adam Stanton, Hugh Miller, the Scholarly Attorney, or Lucy Stark; these characters may stand for thesis. And men are totally bad (depraved would not be an inaccurate term here), like Tiny Duffy and Byram White; these characters are the antithesis. And men are mixed, like Willie Stark and Judge Irwin, and finally Jack Burden himself; they are the synthesis. Everyone in the first two groups, with one possible exception, is incomplete. In the last group Willie, with the potentials of indivisibility within his grasp, gives way to a fatal yearning for absolute good, in violation of his intrinsic character and beliefs. Judge Irwin dies to preserve the successful synthesis as he had lived by it. Jack, alone of the last group, survives to embody the final understanding and acceptance of this position, this acceptance of good and evil, this burden of an optimum condition of life which is at best only a set of provisional resolutions.

Adam Stanton makes the fullest statement of the thesis. He is a brilliant surgeon and the son of a former governor. He wants to do good. But he is appalled by the world when it does not conform to his picture of what it ought to be. Since for him all politics is dirty, he holds aloof out of a spirit of moral fastidiousness that is absolute. The structure of his moral ideas, while it is simple, is nonetheless appropriate to the rational and scientific mind. Morality, for him, is as orderly, straightforward, and predictable as physical laws. Because he cannot stay aloof and because he cannot, in his simple-minded morality, cope with the evil in the world, he consummates his life in violence, which is usually the end of uncompromising principle and undeviating rationalism (a lesson Warren might have learned from the French Revolution as Burke did). Faced with the charge that he was made director of Willie's hospital because Willie is sleeping with his sister, Adam's only possible response is murder. He kills Willie in the capital and is in turn shot down. They were doomed to destroy each other, Warren says, because they were two halves of each other: Adam the man of idea and Willie the man of fact.

Hugh Miller, Willie's attorney general, also takes a straight-line view of morality. He believes that if a man is guilty of malfeasance in public office, such a man should be prosecuted and condemned. When Willie saves Byram White, who is certainly guilty, Hugh resigns. Willie saves Byram because he has to use the Byrams of this world and because he cannot permit the opposition to use Byram, i.e., to bring his administration into bad odor by revealing Byram's corruption. Willie has to stay in power in order to bring his conception of good to his people and his state. He is acting in accordance with a moral idea, but it has not the rigidity of Hugh's absolutism. Hugh has the satisfaction of intact principles, but he surrenders the public arena in which he might display them. Willie is still in power fighting to bring into effect his vision of good despite the evil that surrounds it.

The Scholarly Attorney, Ellis Burden, is another good man who, unable to cope with the evil of the world, withdraws from it. When he discovers that he is not Jack's father, he leaves his wife. He becomes a religious fanatic and undergoes a perpetual debasement of the self, losing his individuality in the lives of others. His position is ultimately life-denying and cowardly, resting as it does on the failure of the world to conform to his subjective notion of reality.

Lucy Stark disturbs a little the schematization here established, for if she is incomplete in her attachment to the simple verities, she is nevertheless close to irreproachability. She and Miller represent two varieties of simplistic morality; hers is a naïve, stubborn, biblical, folk honesty which has all the strength, and some of the limitations, of Hebraism. She tells Willie that if he protects Byram White she will leave him, and she is as good as her word. When her son promiscuously fathers a child, she takes it unquestioningly, exchanging her love for its innocence. When her son is seriously injured, she rejoins her husband, understanding that the great crises of parenthood, the crises of life and death, supersede differences in moral evaluations. Before her adherence to a given code, an adherence where the cost in pain and responsibility is always hers and no one else's, loyalty to Willie's realistic, ambiguous morality must blush.

The characters who are evil are nothing, as Percy Munn was nothing. Willie says of Byram White that he is a thing, less than a man. He has no inner essence, but is, in his being, what Willie tells him to be. The same is true of Tiny Duffy, who, as Willie's campaign manager during the first gubernatorial campaign, was a part of the double-cross that victimized Willie. After Willie breaks the Harrison organization to which Tiny had belonged, he permits Tiny to join him. He makes Tiny his creature so that Tiny's success is a measure of Willie's. Tiny is the complete politician, the very stereotype of the pig in the trough; as Willie's other self, Tiny provides an outlet for Willie's self-contempt. It is Tiny who, frustrated in the pursuit of that graft which is natural to his species, sets Adam on Willie. The irony is that a man who is nothing should kill the man who gives him substance and animates him. But I must say, parenthetically, that Tiny is not alone in this, for like the death of the Swede in "The Blue Hotel," many people must share that responsibility.

Among them, Willie himself. Warren is not altogether fair to Willie when he describes him, in the "Introduction" to *All the King's Men*, as "the politician [who] rises to power because of the faculty of fulfilling vicariously the secret needs of others, and in the process . . . discovers his own emptiness." What Willie so fatally discovers is the lure of the absolute. All through the novel, from the time of his great drunk during his first campaign to the moment when he decides to build his hospital, Willie lives with the stern knowledge that good must come out of evil, and the evil it comes out of is man, who is conceived in sin and born in corruption and passes from the stink of the didie to the stench of the shroud (for Willie, it must never be forgotten, went to a Presbyterian Sunday school). Willie knows that men cannot go into the world without getting the dirt of the world upon them or the poison of it under their skin. He knows that the government of his state is made up half of slaves and half of sons of bitches. But he tells the mobs, who listen raptly, your will is my strength, your need is my justice, and he is not at all sure that this is demagoguery. Warren gives us in Willie a brooding, thoughtful man of destiny with a sense of the mystery of life. He is a man who, as he sat studying law, felt growing inside himself, painfully and imperceptibly, his own world. Out of his reflection comes a conception of good and an understanding of how at least limited good can be imposed on people. And of how means, even evil means, must be adapted to good ends. Knowing all these things, Willie inexplicably sets them aside. He decides to build a hospital that shall be a memorial to purity and a justification for his political chicanery. It is his expiation. It is the sacrifice he offers to placate the stern Hebraic God whom he cannot, after all, escape. This inconsistency — the knowledge that good comes out of evil but the refusal to let Duffy (who is certainly evil) negotiate the usual crooked deal in the construction of the hospital — leads to Willie's death. Warren has said that Willie was corrupted by power, even power exercised against corruption. The statement is true enough. But it seems to me also to be the case that Willie could not live with the truth he had discerned. He could not accept finally the mixed nature of man and things.

Judge Irwin, in many ways Willie's most formidable political opponent, is the living demonstration of Willie's theories about the nature of man and ethics. His aristocratic appearance of unimpeachable probity does not deter Willie from ordering Jack to get something on the judge, because there is always something. Jack finds it. Irwin had once taken a bribe when he was broke. When Jack tries to use this knowledge to force the judge to call

off a political offensive against Willie, the judge commits suicide.
He does not swerve from his principles when confronted with an
impossible situation. He does not use the fact that he is Jack's
father to persuade Jack to call off the attack. He had been a good
judge and he had done good. But he knew, like a Russian that
Warren may have had in mind, that you have to break eggs to
make an omelette. He had been a strong man and he had broken
plenty. He had cuckolded his friend and betrayed his own wife.
He had taken a bribe and driven a man to suicide. Warren's point
is that good and evil are intertwined, but it must be pointed out
that there is no necessary connection in the judge's case between
the good he does and the evil. Irwin is simply an illustration of the
proposition that, in the nature of things, man achieves good
despite himself.

The only completely successful synthesis is achieved by Jack
Burden. It is not simply that he survives, but that he is reborn,
as Norton Girault has so cogently argued. Or that, to use Joseph
Frank's formulation, Jack transcends the good and evil of reality
to reach a dualism which caps his moral evolution. Jack succeeds
in reconciling good and evil because his synthesis is on a grand
scale: he brings together history and time, knowledge and self-
knowledge, apparent truth and real truth. His synthesis is his
maturation as it is Warren's resolution of the problems raised
by the novel.

Jack is the narrator of the novel, and very close to the beginning
he gets at its ironic center. "The end of man is knowledge," he
observes, "but there is one thing he can't know. He can't know
whether knowledge will save him or kill him. He will be killed,
all right, but he can't know whether he is killed because of the
knowledge which he has got or because of the knowledge which
he hasn't got and which if he had it, would save him . . . the
end of man is to know." Jack's struggle is to know himself, but in
order to do this he must work out a means of knowing and he
must understand the past. In college he believes in Idealism,
which holds that if you did not know a thing or recognize it, it
did not exist. He persists in this epistemological subjectivism well
into the novel. If you think you are sorry, then you are, he tells
Anne Stanton, and that's an end to it. He will discover that objective truth exists, and when it is uncovered, he will know with

finality whether he is sorry or not. When he discovers the truth about his father, that makes a real difference in how he thinks and feels. Warren is concerned to show that part of the maturation of Jack is the shucking off of this Idealism, which is the heresy of the self and which cripples the human capacity to deal with reality.

As a student of history, Jack makes two extensive excursions into the past. The first, a failure, is a doctoral dissertation which convinces Jack that if the human race never remembered anything it would be happy. He will revise this judgment when he comes to understand the meaning of his materials. These are the adultery and expiation of Cass Mastern during the Civil War. And the meaning is that the world is one, and to be in the world is to be evil, for evil is a function of living. What is seen in the story of Cass is seen and reinforced in Jack's story.

The second investigation into the past is the one that reveals Judge Irwin as a bribe-taker and Governor Stanton, the judge's friend, as an accessory to the crime. It is successful in the sense that Jack finds what Willie has asked him to find. It is successful because it yields Jack a father and a mother. When the judge kills himself, Jack's mother, a woman he has despised, tells him that Irwin was his real father. Jack has, then, in one blow, found his father and killed him. These are the fruits of the pursuit of truth. Later, his mother summons Jack to Burden's Landing. This much-married lady tells him she is leaving her present husband because she knows now that she always loved the judge. When she does this, she gives Jack back the past, ". . . which I had before felt was tainted and horrible. I could accept the past now because I could accept her and be at peace with her and with myself." In killing his father, accepting and loving his mother, Jack is liberated. He is freed for love and marriage to Anne; together they may go forth into the convulsion of the world, shed of their innocence, like Adam and Eve walking hand in hand out of Milton's paradise.

For the past and the future are forever tied together, and "we can keep the past only by having a future." Self-trust gives us the confidence to live in the future; having such confidence, we need not live in the past. Warren wants his characters to take account of the past but not to be bound to it. This attitude toward the past, linked to Jack's growth toward self-knowledge, is illustrated in the episode at Burden's Landing when Jack undresses Anne in his room but fails to sleep with her. He fears to destroy the meaning of the idyllic summer that they have had; in fact, he is afraid for their total past as companions. Such a need for the past exists for the immature man who does not understand himself and does not know where he is going. The sentimental view of the past paralyzes action. And not knowing who he is, he does not know how to act. The deepest meaning of this episode lies in the paralysis it reveals. But another meaning may be discerned as Jack rationalizes his behavior, hiding from his own identity. With Anne lying on his bed, he suddenly says, we can't, it isn't right. His explanation for his failure is that he was noble. But if he had slept with Anne, they would probably have been married, and then she would not have become Willie's mistress later on. My nobility, he says, had as dire a consequence as Cass Mastern's sin. I suspect that Warren wants us to see the irony here as a valid manifestation of the ambiguous relationship of good and evil and at the same time to see Jack's rationalization for what it is.

The maturation process in Jack consists in large part in his learning to accept and absorb such ironies in which apparent evil comes out of apparent good, to accept the notion that the discovery of the truth is more often than not calamitous. Early in the novel, in a conversation with Anne, he is confident about grasping the plain truth, as he talks about why Ellis Burden, his putative father, left his mother. In the event, it turns out that Jack did not know the reason or have the truth at all. The truth about Jack's father, when it is discovered, leads to the death of his father, as I have already said. Pursuing the truth about Judge Irwin, Jack reveals to Adam and Anne that their father had helped Irwin to take the bribe. Later, when Jack asks Anne why she is sleeping with Willie, she says because she loves him and because there was no reason not to once she had heard about her father. The truth has destroyed an image of moral integrity by which Anne had lived. Jack thinks, I only told her the truth, and from this truth has come this sin, this adultery.

Hard-boiled Jack Burden, armed with a mucker-pose, finds it excruciatingly painful to deal with the complexities he has uncovered. He throws up a series of defenses, all of them escapes from the self-knowledge that will ultimately be forced upon him, or obstacles to it. These are the ways, Girault says, in which he resists being reborn. These are the Great Sleep, the Great Twitch, and the flight to the West. Jack's response to crisis is withdrawal — when, for instance, he loses his job; or flight — when he learns that Anne is sleeping with Willie. But he always returns, to consciousness or to home. The Great Sleep is an induced and deliberate failure of consciousness which makes it impossible to continue pursuit of the truth; it may be a withdrawal to the womb out of an inability to face life. When he runs away to California, he discovers the Great Twitch, which is, I take it, a philosophy of nihilism, a belief in a purely mechanistic view of man and nature. He thinks for a while that he has uncovered knowledge which will give him power, but he soon surrenders this empty belief as he had surrendered Idealism. In the West responsibility is meaningless and life is an illusion. Jack is momentarily soothed and believes he can return home with a defense adequate to his need. He is to learn that he must return home, there to find the truth that will release him to a life of responsible action.

The maturation process in Jack includes also his rejection of a role as alter ego. The masks that hide the self in *At Heaven's Gate* are transmuted into a technique of alter egos in this novel, whereby a personality is complemented or completed by another personality. As in the earlier novels, so too here, Warren makes the point that self-definition cannot be achieved through another person. Cass Mastern knows this. It is part of Willie's failure that both Tiny and Adam represent elements in his personality — irreconcilable elements. Near the end of the novel, Jack finds himself in a position to be like Duffy in order to kill Duffy. Such action would be the perfect revenge for Duffy's having unleashed Adam against Willie. By this time, however, Jack is strong enough to resist this kind of complement to his selfhood.

The synthesis Jack makes is reflected in the structure of the novel. If all things are in time, and time is a continuum, then it is necessary to peel back layer after layer of experience in any individual life to reveal how an event came to pass and why it had precisely the impact it had. It is necessary to move deeper and deeper into the past, exploring contingent lives, if time makes all things one. If one theme of the novel is that man must possess and believe in his history in order to live in the present and look forward to the future, then there must be constant movement in time in the novel. There is such movement, and the manipulation of time levels becomes an informing device both structurally and thematically. The scheme of the book therefore reinforces the theme; the structure is carefully adapted to the end. Despite the time shifts, the first chapter begins at what is essentially the beginning — Burden's Landing where Jack comes from and Mason City where Willie comes from — and in neat circularity it suggests and contains the ending, which is the death of the Boss and Adam and Judge Irwin, and the consequent freeing of Jack. Furthermore, abandoning straight chronology permits Warren to show the irregular and abrupt stages of self-revelation in Jack Burden, as any given episode leads him into the past.

This novel is Warren's finest work to date. No writer in our time except Faulkner has given us a book that speaks so eloquently with a conservative voice; no writer has so well anatomized the modern world, showing it to be the product of history expressed in those social terms we call politics.

In 1947 Warren collected his short stories in a volume called *The Circus in the Attic and Other Stories*. My feeling is that the stories do not, on the whole, succeed. When they are not discursive and loose in structure, like the title story, they are too neatly packaged, like "The Patented Gate and the Mean Hamburger." The humor and the irony are sometimes so obvious that it is difficult to understand why Warren should have wanted to preserve such work; I have in mind especially "A Christian Education" and "Confession of Brother Grimes."

The most authentic note Warren strikes in this volume is that of reminiscence, because looking backward gives scope to his piety and opportunity to assess the growing-up process. These characteristics make meaningful such stories as "When the Light Gets Green" and "Blackberry Winter." The second story treats the maturation theme as a series of disorientations from the lovely green world of nature and the secure, isolated world of the farm. "When you are a boy . . . you want to stand there in the green twilight until you feel your very feet sinking into and clutching the earth like roots and your body breathing slow through its pores like the leaves. . . ." But one cannot retain the innocence of boyhood. The stranger, who does not grow into the ground, brings the meaningless viciousness of the urban world to the boy. The dead cow in the river and the old veteran of Forrest's cavalry bring home the horror of nature and life to the boy. Even the familiar and gentle Dellie, now irascible and mean in her illness, shows the unhappy reality that lies under the surface of human life; and her usually spotless yard, now littered with filth brought out by the flooding creek, signalizes the destructiveness of nature. Not everyone can survive the knowledge of good and evil and the wrenching away from nature. The boy in this story does. But the men in stories like "Goodwood Comes Back" and "The Patented Gate" cannot do it; they thus reveal themselves as only half-men.

"The Circus in the Attic," the title story, is another approach to the dualism of life, an examination of the relation between the world of illusion and the world of reality as it bears on the discovery of truth. Warren seems to be showing that what is important is what men choose to live by. In so doing they make an enduring truth, and it makes no difference whether or not it is a verifiable truth. The counsels of imperfection and tentativeness contained in this story, like the use of time as a continuity which helps to create a truth that never was, are typical of the Warren syndrome, even as the indecisive conduct of the story is an aberration from the disciplined form he so often provides.

World Enough and Time (1950), the novel which followed *All the King's Men*, is a considerable falling off from the level of excellence achieved by that latter book. Warren has become here a victim of his own manner. The New Critic in him has throttled the novelist. The New Critic knows that the novelist must not moralize. He knows the novelist must give aesthetic form and imaginative meaning to moral ideas. Warren has learned the lesson so well that, one feels, he has overburdened *World Enough and Time* with ironic complexities; he has pressed too hard with his characteristic dialectic. He is so intent upon the doubleness of life that the reader cannot always tell when he must laugh, for this part is farce, or when he must weep, for this part is tragedy.

Perhaps these judgments are too harsh. For the novel does give us at least Warren's most protracted effort simultaneously to separate and unite conceptions of the world or reality and of idea or idealism. It does give us his fullest account of the world of non-human nature as the quagmire of the spirit.

In dealing with the reality-idea dichotomy, Warren creates a protagonist whose idea of reality is private. Even though this man's idea encompasses justice and honor, the man fails. The external world intrudes upon his reality to frustrate him, but his ultimate failure is in the realization that private, subjective judgment must always be false. The assertion of that judgment, without reference to any scheme of transcendent value, is the heresy of the self. The dichotomy thus posed lends itself in the novel to the theme which Warren calls the doubleness of life. The complexity of this work may be judged by suggesting that the following three meanings, at a minimum, may be attached to that phrase: obviously, to begin with, the world and idea as antithesis; the dualism of man, which includes both the good and evil in man and his life-urge and his death-urge; the confusion between appearance and reality, whereby friend is really foe and the seemingly guilty are really innocent.

This same dichotomy is the basis of "To His Coy Mistress," the poem by Andrew Marvell that provides Warren with his title. In the poem, reality or the world is more highly regarded than an impossible ideal — of courtly love, in this instance. Warren's predilection for the dialectic complicates his resolution of these opposites. While he is no champion of the expediency and opportunism of the world, neither is he ready to accept the ideal as subjectively conceived. Warren believes that the validity of the ideal is conditioned by the adjustment of the ideal to the terms imposed upon it by the world. Poor, deluded Jeremiah Beaumont, the protagonist in this novel, is the victim of the painful farce enacted here precisely because he does not understand the necessary interplay of idea and reality. He tries to live only by the idea.

But since the world is present always to man, we must now ask what its meanings are in the novel. First, the world is palpable in the novel as history and social force. The story is based on a famous murder trial which took place in Kentucky in the 1820's when the parties of Relief and anti-Relief were in conflict. Warren's principal source is the "Confessions of Jereboam O. Beauchamp." The world is also embodied in Wilkie Barron, Jeremiah's friend, who betrays him. "For what was Wilkie's face but the mask of all the world?" Wilkie is the essence of the world, utterly at home in it in his malignancy and diabolism, in his skill at manipulation and duplicity, in his unbroken series of successes. Yet Wilkie kills himself finally because he realizes that man must be something in himself; man cannot live by the world alone. And the world is at war with the idea. Jeremiah thinks he must live by an idea of honor. To reclaim honor he must kill Cassius, who had seduced Rachel Jordan before her marriage to Jeremiah. But Jeremiah is lulled by the comfort of the world and bemused by the contradictions in it between private and public justice.

Jeremiah cannot live in the world. He cannot reconcile his own ideals and impulses to the demands of the world. It is necessary for him, then, to create both his own world and a self that will fit into it. The tragic quality of the novel is in the picture of a man who is unfulfilled and incomplete because he perversely cuts himself off from other men, from society. Jeremiah's failure is in dedication to the pure idea in a world which cannot tolerate the pure idea, only diluted and compromised ideas with which men must learn to live. Jeremiah is thus like Adam Stanton and must fail like Adam, as all men fail who do not achieve the synthesis which is the consequence of the logic and movement of Warren's dialectic.

Responding to the need for self-definition, Jeremiah must search out the situation that excludes worldly interest. By finding and performing the completely gratuitous and disinterested act, he will discover the self. In pursuit of this purity he marries Rachel, a wronged woman, and kills Fort, her seducer and his benefactor. It must be added here that he performs these acts in obedience to another need beside the one to reject or flaunt the world. He is the victim of compulsive self-immolation; he is the victim of victims. Against reason and principle, he rushes to the aid of the helpless and the wronged. This irrational and sentimental streak in him, first apparent in his childhood reaction to the picture of the burning martyr, prevents him from ever achieving selfhood. In these aspects of his character, as in his preoccupation with the idea, Jeremiah is a fool, and Warren, for this reason, must deny him maturation.

Yet Warren forces Jeremiah constantly to seek selfhood. Jere-

miah wants to know and live by the truth within him. At one
point, about to confess the murder to the lawyers who defend him,
he is poised "on the brink of myself . . . for the moment when
a man falls into himself, into the past which is himself . . . ,"
but he cannot confess. Not until it comes home to him that he
has acted for honor, but all has come to a bitter end in degradation, is he ready to confess. Not until the end, when he realizes
that his crime was in trying to isolate the idea from the world
and to live by it, when he recognizes that he has isolated himself,
is he ready to confess. Even then he knows he cannot seek redemption. All that remains for him is to suffer.

Nature, as we have seen, is as gross as the world. Jeremiah's
response to nature is represented to us in a childhood experience,
as his self-sacrificial tendency is explained by the martyred maid
in the fire. Swimming in the Kentucky River, he watches a keel-
boat approach and pass and listens to the music coming from it.
Later, on the river himself, escaping from prison, he remembers
this event. The two times merge for him. He is sucked into the
river and the darkness, and he feels at peace. It is the same peace
that he felt when he lived at his ease with Rachel on his estate —
an animal peace that does not know the voice of moral duty. Warren is here suggesting Jeremiah's desire to bury himself in the
world of non-human nature and to identify with it, as an alternative to the more difficult human course of separating oneself from
nature. The peace Jeremiah experiences on the river he feels again
when he flees west to the incredible domain of La Grand' Bosse. It
arises from a surrender of the moral will — the essential and human quality which distinguishes us as human beings — to sloth
and filth, to the degradation of the appetitive life. Clearly, Warren
does not accept the myth of the West as innocence. The West is
raw, non-human nature that pulls man down to its own bestial
level.

In addition to his treatment of the world and nature, Warren
plays persistently in this novel with an idea of drama. He makes
Jeremiah conceive of his life as a drama, and he has Rachel also
see parts of her experience as drama. By using this device, he
succeeds again in setting off action and idea from the world. At
the beginning of the book Jeremiah says he has prepared an "ambiguous drama which seemed both to affirm and to deny life, to

affirm and to deny humanity." Such a drama is necessary if one is to live "against the ruck of the world." Jeremiah's was to be a tragedy of blood, but the actors sometimes turned it into bloody farce. For the characters, the idea of drama is refuge; for Warren it is a technique for gaining aesthetic distance. Twice-removed from his characters — who are in the drama within the story — Warren can manage the detachment necessary for irony. Rachel can say that she is acting in a charade which becomes the essence of truth and her only reality, and Warren, divorced so to speak from any responsibility for her position, can speak about her plight from the reference point of a more solid-seeming world. But when the drama ends in a pratfall, when the suicide pact of Rachel and Jeremiah ends only in miserable vomiting, one wonders if we have Jeremiah's ambiguities or Warren's — if Warren did not, after all, get too close to his material?

Which brings me back to the point at which I began talking of this novel. It seems often to be a literary exercise for Warren, who stands outside calculating the number of devices he can work into it and the way to apply them. Sometimes he miscalculates. It occurs to me to ask, is this a great joke Warren has perpetrated on us, giving us this apparently serious inquiry into the mixed nature of man and the dark nature of reality in a contrived vehicle that he himself does not believe in? Maybe not. But my final judgment is that Warren did not master his materials. Its people and its plot cannot carry the weight of speculation imposed upon them. Here the intricate play of moral nuance is dull and confusing, not illuminating. It is, finally, a pretentious book.

Band of Angels (1955) is beyond the limits of the present study. But a word about it will serve, perhaps, to suggest some of the problems that Warren must face as a novelist. The book reveals a further development of Warren's penchant for the melodramatic and the bizarre. Melodrama does not yet threaten to become an end in itself in his novels, but it may come to overwhelm or obscure for the reader the more serious aspects of Warren's work. The style of this novel is resourceful and elaborate; the danger is that a further elaboration of this style will make the writing fancy and bookish, as some critics think it is now. *Band of Angels* deals again with the question of identity. The series of masks for his characters that Warren has worked out in treating the quest for the self is more labored and more deliberately schematized than anything he has done before. Such treatment raises the possibility that Warren may be substituting ingenuity for originality. It suggests that he has reached the intellectual limits of this question of identity. Once again his characters try to feed on each other to find themselves; once again they are alienated from the father or from the past. One feels that the repetitions in Warren's work derive from intellectual commitments that have imposed a bondage upon his imagination.

The final question raised by Warren's work concerns the lure of orthodox religion. Critics may and do read his novels as religious statement and find in them religious conceptions like paradise and innocence, communion and guilt. In *Band of Angels* religion is not rejected; it is simply not accepted. One wonders, given Warren's over-all allegiance to conservatism, if he will resist that religious conversion which seems to be the logical end dictated by the convictions that now guide his writing. What restrains him, I suppose, is the importance he attaches to the tensions inherent in a sceptical and provisional attitude. This conflict within the conservative mind between orthodoxy and scepticism makes for the most fascinating kind of speculation Warren affords us.

A CRITIQUE OF CONSERVATISM

Neo-conservatism was not, during the forties, a running tide in the life of the nation, except in the South. It had no popular roots, and it controlled no significant political power. It created no *school* of fiction, despite the appearance of conservative writers. It created no school in any of the other arts. It had to combat the same centripetal force in American culture that in the forties was attacking the possibility of manning any position located far from the center. Perhaps the principal service that the neo-conservative revolt rendered to the intellectual life of the country was corrective, challenging the weaknesses in the once unchallenged liberalism and forcing it to make modifications. But this service was potentially self-destructive, since by this process all cats could come to look gray. Actually, sufficient difference of opinion did exist to generate critical discussion of the neo-conservative position. In a paper presented to the Modern Language Association in

1950, Harry Levin made a sharp attack on the notion that tradition must be our guide in literature and criticism, pointing out that there are a good many American traditions, among them the traditions of experiment, exploration, examination, progression, and even subversion. These are not the traditions the traditionalists are interested in. Or in a smashing attack on conservatism, E. V. Walter makes the same point about religion. The conservatives, he says, rely upon religion. But what kind? Surely not the religion of the Church Fathers who defended the Christian conscience against the state and not the tradition of radical religion in ante-Nicene Christianity. This sampling from two critics is perhaps sufficient to demonstrate the obvious: the neo-conservatives were by no means invulnerable. Yet the important point about neo-conservatism is that in a time that seemed to demand the tragic view of life and a serious concern with the life of the spirit, it appeared to provide a definition of human experience emphasizing the tragic and the introspective. Unfortunately, it seemed to claim that it alone was concerned with these matters, all other approaches to life having ignored them. Be that as it may, neo-conservatism put its mark upon the time. No one can yet say how lasting an impression it made and is still making, but one might safely guess not as great as rationalism on the eighteenth century or Transcendentalism on romantic America. It will not entirely pass away; the conservative spirit never has. But it will be obedient to the same law in American cultural history as these other modes of thought. They went out of fashion, passed from dominance, leaving more or less of their spirit and substance in our mixed heritage.

CHAPTER SIX

THE NEW
FICTION

THE NEW FICTION DEFINED: THE TRIUMPH OF ART

In the forties certain novels and short stories began to appear that
critics presently identified as the "new fiction." The term is far
from satisfactory, but since nothing better offers and since it has
gained a certain currency, I shall use it. One difficulty with it is
that it does not designate a fiction that is genuinely new in any
significant way. No innovations of technique and no original ideas
appear in the new fiction. What newness it has lies in what it
emphasized and what it rejected rather than in what it originated:
in concentrating its attention upon certain thematic considerations, in rejecting social-political or philosophical ideas as the
legitimate subject matter of fiction, in emphasizing the crafts-
manship of writing. Another difficulty is that the term does not
apply simply to one kind of fiction. It embraces the psychological
novel and the novel of manners, as written by Jean Stafford, for
example; the desperate nihilism of Paul Bowles; the gothic decadence of Truman Capote. What unity it has as a meaningful
category is not found in any monopoly of region or generation, for
the new fiction appears in North and South, is written in the forties by writers old and young. Yet the new fiction *is* different, despite the variety within its own boundaries, from anything else
written in the decade. And its difference will help us, in a positive
way, to see what, essentially, it is.

The task of defining this difference is complicated by the similarity of the new fiction to other kinds of fiction written in the
forties. It is not an isolated phenomenon in its time. It shares with
the new liberalism and the conservative imagination a conviction

that the end of innocence has come to America. Lines of sympathetic understanding run from it to the conservative imagination; they both have a high regard for myth, tradition, a code of behavior, aesthetic form. They have a mutual ally in the new critics. Caroline Gordon and Robert Penn Warren, as critics and fiction writers, are at one with the new fiction in many respects. But they, and the new liberals too, are always conscious of an idea of society in their work and are attached to a particular idea. The new fiction is generally innocent of any such idea. Its writers want to create a pure fiction, apolitical and asocial. In this desire lies one aspect of its separateness. Since, in my judgment, no fiction is without some connection with the society in which it is created, the safe generalization about the new fiction is that it is without loyalties to any order of society and without hope for a different or better order than the one it sees. This is a second part of its separateness from both the liberal and the conservative imagination. It has no allegiance to a particular social structure. Yet in regarding society as a subject for satire or a reason for nihilistic despair, it reveals its dependence upon a social order, or disorder — the given social situation which it tends to view with contempt, or horror, or indifference. It tends to be solipsistic, but not because it regards the pursuit of the self as a sustaining quest for meaning in life, as Warren does, for example. On the contrary, the new fiction confronts the irreducible self negatively, fantastically, pessimistically.

This same ambiguity of difference within similarities extends into a consideration of the origins of the new fiction. It may be explained as having a social origin, as being a negative reaction on the part of writers in the forties to a world of such bleak confusion and hopelessness that they have had no choice but to reject it. The difficulty is that so many other writers rejected the world they lived in during the forties. The differentness of the new fiction is that it turned its back more firmly, more studiedly, more finally upon the Western world of experience and idea than others did. Yet such an observation applies more to the work of Paul Bowles than it does to that of Jean Stafford. Her novels suggest that the origins of the new fiction may be found in literary history and that it may be defined in terms of its literary progenitors. She is an authentic daughter of Henry James. To Miss Stafford the new fiction means a combination of the psychological novel and the novel of manners in work wrought with careful attention to the craft of writing, fiction in the tradition not only of James but of Edith Wharton too. The new fiction generally, to leave Miss Stafford, found in Flaubert and Joyce other masters of technique, from whom it learned the lessons of point of view, novelistic structure and dramatic action, stream of consciousness. It found in the work of Hawthorne and Melville models for the symbolic rendering of experience. Beyond technique, that work revealed the sharklike, ubiquitous evil that the writers of the new fiction found peculiarly appropriate to their time. The new fiction had available, finally, the work of Kafka, the haunted mind from Central Europe, who domesticated the alienated personality in the twentieth-century nightmare. To be sure, the new fiction shares this literary ancestry with other kinds of fiction, especially that of the conservative imagination. But these influences, regarded in their totality, play such an intense and decisive role in the new fiction as to differentiate it from all other contemporary work.

Perhaps the most ambiguous problem related to the genesis of the new fiction is presented by the new criticism. Grant, for a moment, a certain homogeneity to a body of work called the new criticism which in the forties began to turn its attention from poetry to the aesthetics of fiction. Set aside the question, did the new criticism actually shape some fiction written in the forties? (It probably did.) The important point, I believe, is that many of the ideas and preoccupations of the new criticism are suggestive in formulating the general character of the new fiction. For instance, the new fiction may be regarded as pure fiction in that it is a work of the imagination and not journalism, polemic, sociology, politics, psychology, theology, ethics, or philosophy, and it is not to be read as any of these. The new critics insist that, as an art form, fiction is totally dependent upon technique, which is everything. Technique is the way the materials of art are apprehended and organized. It includes the style of the writing, which is the agent the writer uses to grasp reality and to deform it, as Ortega y Gasset puts it, making a representation or image of life that will move us. Technique, then, removes art from life or dehumanizes art; technique creates aesthetic distance and makes it possible for the writer to exclude from his work the sincerity or spontaneity that, says Ransom, might dilute the quality of art as ceremony. These generalizations describe much of the new fiction written in the forties.

The new fiction, to continue this formulation, tends to reject its own contemporary world, as I have indicated; it is inward-turning and backward-turning. As it records the inner experience, the psychic life, of its characters, it finds opportunity to use the stream of consciousness method, although it does not, curiously, use it as widely as one would expect. This method, encouraging intense subjectivity as the writer fastens upon a single character, raises the question of point of view for the writer. The new fiction has learned from James, and from Percy Lubbock who so faithfully explained James's method, the virtues of a controlled point of view or the uses of the central intelligence in fiction. This single consciousness can serve a dual purpose as it unifies the story; it can reveal itself, and it can report all the events of the action that it has knowledge of.

The backward-turning tendency of the new fiction appears in its penchant for myth. In the dim past men figured forth stories of the great experiences of human life as they relate to man in society and to man in the cosmos. These stories are metaphors for archetypal experiences. Richard Chase points to such experiences as birth, initiation into life, friendship, marriage, war, death. Myth, he says, " . . . gives significance to these crises of life by an emotive appeal to the past, to the traditions of the culture, or to the superhuman powers of heroes." The inherent attraction of myth for writers lies in the seal of universality it places upon men involved in certain spiritual or natural crises and in the figurative way it treats them. This figurative or metaphorical mode of communication predisposes a writer toward the use of symbols, devices which enable him to expand his meaning. The new fiction began to appear at a time when scholarship was reawakening to the possibilities of symbolism, myth, ritual, and religion, and when the work of Ernst Cassirer and Susanne Langer was revealing the many implications of this field of study. The positive impulse toward myth and symbol, in contrast to the negative rejection of the world, might well lie in the excitement generated by this new key to art as well as to philosophy.

The shape of the new fiction thus emerges in this abstract way, a shape attached to no name or no book. It is the generalized shape of a body of work that appeared in the forties. It may be characterized, in summary, like this: Technique is all, or virtually all; the craft of fiction is always in the forefront of the writer's consciousness. It is, then, a pure fiction, for it is art removed from life. It does not concern itself with an idea of society. It is subjective; it concerns itself with the inner man. It conveys its meanings often by symbols, occasionally through the use of myth. This is the fiction to which we now turn our attention.

THE NEW FICTION AND THE GOTHIC SPIRIT

One kind of new fiction draws heavily upon the gothic imagination. It is a kind especially at home in the South during the forties, breathing and thriving on the foul air of decadence it knows is rising from the historical and spiritual ruins there. This place and this time — the forties and the succeeding decade — seem particularly hospitable to the gothic. But gothicism is not the exclusive property of the South in our time or in an earlier one; and it does not belong exclusively to the new fiction. It is a way of apprehending experience that served, during the forties, in other areas as well and has served almost from the beginning of the American career in the imagination.

Fascinated with such devices as talking pictures and mechanical monsters, the early gothic revealed something juvenile in the American imagination. But presently, what seemed to have started in the sheer delight and curiosity of investigating the outré finds itself staring into an abyss of real horror, discovered, stumbled upon, inadvertently or unconsciously as it were. The gothic writer is like the gifted child, left alone to model what he will from the mud of the Nile; he creates out of the pure innocence of his impulse the image of those hideous prehistoric creatures who, before man ever appeared on the earth, might first have crawled out of the Nilotic slime. Such images rise from deep in his childish soul, escaping without conscious volition into the fingers that shaped the dream or the memory of that filth from which man might have sprung. In the intimacy with which the child lives with terror, in his innocence, and in his lack of restraint or knowledge of convention lay the truth of the horror he thus glimpsed. Such a version of the juvenile applies to the American gothic writer, who begins with the obvious and the melodramatic. But the truth is there beneath the monstrous trappings: the secret necrophilia made public, the necessity for flight confessed, the sadism no longer contained, the horror of real life recognized. To perceive this truth of the gothic vision, one must strike through the mask to discover that all men are victims or cripples. The mask not so much hides as symbolizes the essential flaw. So that the picture on the wall, the mansion with the broken columns, the metal robot stands for something, is the physical object that expands into a meaningful abstraction.

The gothic has a symbolic content, then, that links it to the new fiction. Even if it begins in the unconscious, a symbolic representation of reality may rise to the level of art. Then it becomes a self-conscious way of distorting reality. And this suggests that the rage for the gothic in the forties was the product of a preference for art over life. The truths of life that men could see in their daily experience were too harsh to assimilate, to have to confront face to face and to live with. The artist did not then decide to escape into fantasy, fantasy being so unreliable it might prove worse than the world. But he might have decided it is better to filter these truths through an art form and so come at them, when it is necessary to do so at all, at one remove. In this way art becomes a wall between men and the horror of life, a horror which we cannot take straight, so to speak. It is a wall which shuts us off from the real horror, but encloses a synthetic horror, a kind which has the truth in it that we do not have to pay for. The synthetic truth or synthetic decadence or synthetic horror takes the sting out of reality. Thus the purposes of art as ceremony are served. Thus art is dehumanized. The gothic is linked to the new fiction in its dedication to this doctrine of the dehumanization of art.

The writers I wish to consider now all make use of the gothic spirit. But I do not mean to suggest that to label them as gothic writers is to have explained them. Such a label will tell us a great deal about Truman Capote and Paul Bowles, somewhat less about Carson McCullers; it might prove slightly misleading with respect to Eudora Welty. Nevertheless, these figures represent one expression of the new fiction that is perhaps best characterized as gothic. This spirit they all have in common, and consequently I have grouped them together. Since the gothic led so full a life in the South during the forties, I shall consider first the three southern writers — Capote, Mrs. McCullers, and Miss Welty — and then discuss Paul Bowles.

TRUMAN CAPOTE AND THE TWISTED SELF

No one reveals more clearly, or more obviously, the uses of the gothic than Truman Capote. His work has no bearing at all upon the smiling aspects of American life. It has no relation to the area of public or ordinary experience; Capote has said he has no convictions, in an orthodox sense, about religion or politics. The world of his fiction is a world of terror, defeat, and loneliness in which children who are not childlike grope through a nightmarish reality. Everyone in this world is a cripple, a physical or emotional or mental defective. Everywhere is the thick air of the supernatural or the occult, in which the characters drown. But Capote's people do not will their own destruction. They yearn for fulfilment in love. They wish to open the channels of the spirit and flow toward each other in heartfelt communion. They wish to banish loneliness and discover in love their own identities. The gothic interpretation of experience is not an expression of Capote's appetite for sensationalism (although there is a taint of this) or a reaction of blank revulsion against the world. The gothic vision is a symbol of his conviction that both society and man frustrate the quest for the self. In this sense the gothic becomes, in Capote's hands, a variation on the pervasive theme of fiction in the forties: the inward-turning search for the dimensions of the self.

This quest — or is it more accurate to say the failure of this quest? — is the subject of Capote's first novel, *Other Voices, Other Rooms* (1948). The protagonist is Joel Harrison Knox, the child of divorced parents. He has been given his mother's family name, but his mother has died as the story opens, and he goes to find his father, a man named Sansom. The boy, then, does not know who he is — does not know what his name is or who his father is, although he does know that he is descended from a Civil War general. The story takes place at Skully's Landing, a decayed plantation near Noon City, a stagnant little town in the South.

The prose is fanciful, often gossamer-light; the manner is self-conscious and arty; the book has a contrived air.

Note, for example, the treatment of that not altogether novel subject, southern decadence. Skully's Landing is the mysterious bourne where Joel will make his quest. Capote has no difficulty in endowing it with decay and mystery. Part of it has been destroyed by fire; the columns in the front are broken; the garden in the rear is a jungle. One is tempted to make a game out of reading this evidence of ruin as symbol, but I shall confine myself to two comments. All the evidence attests to the collapse of a civilization, that of the ante-bellum South, that has been replaced by nothing else. The past exists only as a memory of faded grandeur or as a reproach to the present; surely the past has no vital connection with the present. As a result, the decadence here described is isolated, existing for its own sake. In addition to this generalized meaning, the broken columns are a metaphor integral to the meaning of the novel. They stand, I suppose, for the smashed psyche of all the characters trapped in Skully's Landing, but especially for Joel's, whose childhood innocence might have been likened to the columns in their wholeness and purity. Both his childhood and his innocence are to crumble at the end of the book.

Decay as a reproach is seen in the contrast between Joel and his forefather the general. The southern ideal of military honor and chivalric conduct represented by this dead worthy is a way of life that an epicene youth like Joel cannot possibly sustain. The ideal is doomed in the degeneration of the family. The decay motif as the haunted voice of the past, immobilizing and deadening men, is seen in Drownin' Pond, once the site of a brilliant resort. Here the old Negro who lingers on hears voices of the past, and the only life is in death.

The mystery of the house is conveyed with equal deliberation. Joel arrives there at night in a wagon driven by an ancient Negro. He is asleep, in the grip of a dream demon. This initial impression of the place that Capote gives us, filled with images of darkness and fright, of somnolence and nightmare, is carried forward by the abnormal behavior of the people in the house: the "black mass" of the Negro servants, the fleeting appearance in the window of the unaccounted-for woman, the failure of his father to appear at all.

In this setting, so inauspicious for his tasks, Joel must find his father, establish his own identity, grow from childhood to manhood, and uncover a love that will sustain him in his enterprises. The quest for the father ends in the discovery that Sansom is a helpless paralytic who is condemned to a perpetual semicoma from which he can escape neither to sleep nor to full consciousness. Joel can expect neither love nor protection from his father, since these cannot flow from a paralyzed source that is neither dead nor alive. His effort to claim his masculinity is frustrated by a tomboy, Idabel, and by his own nature. He looks to Idabel for love in a normal groping toward a heterosexual relationship, but she repulses him, refusing to give him an opportunity to exercise his incipient maleness. She denies him love and denies his function as a male. Worse, she arrogates to herself the male role when he abdicates it. Confronted with a snake as they are crossing a stream, he freezes with the old primal fear, but she seizes a Civil War sword he is carrying and dispatches the creature. All this blocks off his normal development as a male and conditions his growth toward homosexuality. In his search for love he does not know enough even to call upon God for help. The Negro girl's belief in spirits does not help him, nor can she. The only one who asks for his love is the carnival freak, the midget Miss Wisteria, but he cannot answer to her need. Blocked at every exit into a relationship that might fulfil him, he retreats to the dream world of the self, which is the other room where all quests are satisfied and he can find admiration, his father, love. The dream world is sterile, having only Joel's incapacities to feed upon. All alternatives exhausted, Joel turns to Cousin Randolph and homosexuality. His growth from childhood to manhood is a development to an accepted perversion which was, from the beginning, latent within him.

Randolph is a transvestite who seeks love, like so many other characters in the novel. The loneliness which drives him to corrupt Joel works also in the Negro girl, in Wisteria, in Joel too, of course. In Randolph's case, it is a loneliness ultimately laid to a woman, as it is a woman who gives him a justification for his homosexuality. The female who captures and subjugates the male will eventually eat him up. The only escape is into homosexuality, and the female closes this door too by running off with the man Randolph loves. In his alcoholic retreat at Skully's Landing, Randolph thinks of himself as dead. Joel sees him as a zero. Randolph himself prefers a blurred vision of reality, as he sees it in a distorting mirror, to the reality of experience. It is his world that Joel leaves his boyhood to enter. He is trapped as the bird he finds in his room the first morning is trapped and smashed. It is Randolph who establishes his identity for him.

The themes of this novel may be the authentic concerns of a serious writer. The search for identity, the portraits of loneliness, the ambiguity of reality as reflected in the distorting mirror, the cost of human imperfection, the meaning of a decadent culture — these constitute an impressive array of thematic material. Capote has made an impressive integration of these various matters. But for me, at least, the book exists more as a detached art object than as a felt, imaginative experience. Its emotional life is not genuine, as its themes are. It is a real question whether Capote has given us a meaningful view of the universal disorder that madly throbs in the human id. His themes demand profound reflection and tragic resolution; we get close but eccentric observation and a hothouse horror that arouses no emotion stronger than pity.

The same weaknesses are apparent in the short stories in *A Tree of Night* (1949), where the characters go down to similar dark defeats, evoking pity and sometimes terror. One feels the presence of Poe everywhere in this volume, in the ubiquitous threat of death and in the easy familiarity with madness, in the exploitation of the abnormal, in the calculated striving for effect. If Capote is not always as convincing as Poe in his exploration of the underside of the maimed human personality, his occasional successes are sometimes startlingly reminiscent of the master's work. In a story like "Shut a Final Door" Capote uses the same situation that occurs in "William Wilson." The protagonist is dogged by an opposing self who is the moral arbiter in his career of deception and cruelty. This other self, Capote suggests, will destroy Walter Ranney, as the second William Wilson destroys the first. Capote seems less interested in the morality of his story than he does in the manipulation of the occult means of communication between the two selves. And perhaps he is most interested in the phenomenon of the divided self; it is failure to know the parts of the self and to integrate them that leads to destruction. Capote uses the same theme in an impressive story called "Miriam," dealing with an elderly widow of that name who meets a little girl of the same name — or believes that she meets such a little girl, for the child seems to us to be a hallucination. The child and the woman are alike: unchildlike, inscrutable, alone, selfishly self-dependent. When the woman feels herself possessed by the child, to whom she has lost her identity, she has not reverted to childhood but has uncovered the hidden and hitherto unacknowledged self. The shock of discovery, made too late, reduces her to madness. The impoverishment of the spirit and the diminution of the self, as in the story about the girl who sells her dreams; ignorance about the self or failures in self-knowledge, as in the stories discussed — these are consistent themes in the short fiction. But the psychological and moral truths of his observations seem to be of less importance to Capote than the implications for disintegration in the situations that he has imagined.

Children figure in several of these stories. The tree of night, in the story of that name, is the symbol of childhood horror which, in an atavistic way, overwhelms a nineteen-year-old girl. She surrenders her will to the irresistible forces of evil and undergoes a symbolic burial; she has died under the weight of implacable terror. In Capote's fiction the abnormal person or the freak always exercises an ambivalent pressure upon others. He frightens them off as, perversely and against their will, he attracts them, an attraction sometimes associated with sexual excitement. In other stories children dream of release from their miserable lives in the golden world of Hollywood. The irony of these is that only children of distorted personality and vision could see that tawdry place as a symbol of beauty and fame. Over all the stories of children hovers the unhealthy aura of twisted psychic energies or misdirected powers of the will. In Capote's fiction, the dark world of the child is the world that man never escapes.

Capote's predilection for total defeat is somewhat diluted in *The Grass Harp* (1951), a parable of innocence and evil. In this short novel Capote shows his otherworldly characters accepting the world of reality, and in accepting, passing from innocence to knowledge. While innocence is defeated, to be sure, the characters who undergo the initiation into evil emerge as stronger in their maturity than they were before.

The conflict in this novel is between innocence and the independence of one's being on one side and the forces of acquisitiveness, respectability, and law and order on the other. The innocents are misfits — the gentle, impractical people: an elderly spinster, a little boy, an antisocial young man, a wise old judge. They take refuge in a chinaberry tree to protect themselves and their private vision from the external world. For they are all committed to the idea that all private worlds are good and must be kept inviolate. But the spinster comes to understand that the demands of love must sometimes supersede the integrity of one's dreams. She recognizes that the world is evil, but she knows too that even the evil people in it need love. She understands that people must be able to speak freely to each other, but she realizes that such communication must take place in the real world. Such wisdom, coming after her vigorous protest, is a measure of her ripened maturity, and it is what fastens the fable to the ordinary world of experience. So innocence makes its stand and wins its partial victory.

Capote's problem in this book has been to draw attention to the claims of innocence and love and yet not to isolate the innocent and the lover from the main stream of life. Capote is firm in placing a high value on the fey spirit and the eccentric, but he tempers that kind of judgment with a recognition of the hard facts of reality. His is not an ultimate kind of romantic rebellion, and his restraint is what saves this little book from sentimentality. The tone is idyllic, poetic, otherworldly, whimsical. The style is light and fantastic, created out of the color of the sky and the flight of butterflies and the whispering of the grass. It is attuned to its subject. Capote seems to have solved his problem by keeping a firm hand on the dialectics of his theme and by fusing theme and style. *The Grass Harp* is a modest success. In its concern with love and the individual personality, it is typical of Capote's work. But the gothic element in his other work has been transmuted here into mellowed fantasy.

Capote's authentic gothic mode is carried forward in *The House of Breath* (1950), by William Goyen, the first novel of a promising talent who belongs really to the fifties. Goyen's gothic treatment of homosexuality, of southern degeneration, of futile lives embarked on futile flight from scenes dead to love — all this promises continuity to the kind of fiction Capote has written. Goyen has the characteristic southern talent for the evocation of place, and he commands the typical techniques of the new fiction: the Joycean stream of consciousness, the poetic prose, the addiction to symbols. The pessimism in this novel is set against a romantic conception of the unity of all things. Out of this sense of a universal relationship, which is reminiscent of Whitman, comes an urge toward life, expressed in the breath metaphors that appear constantly in the novel. The tension created by this ambivalence results not in a sense of resolution but of sterility, which is induced by the pervasive homosexuality of the novel.

CARSON McCULLERS AND THE FAILURE OF DIALOGUE

In an essay on "The Understanding of Fiction," John Crowe Ransom argues that fiction brings us into a primitive world of spontaneous and natural affections. He opposes the primitive to the intellectual and sentiment to idea. Since an art work must touch the heart, the substance of fiction should be drawn from feeling and not mind. Such a theory becomes at once a justification of the poetic vision as a means of apprehending experience. It gives sanction to a writer's commerce in a fabulous rather than in a literal truth. Out of these rich implications, such a theory makes a beginning in the description of Carson McCullers' work. She is governed by the aesthetics of the primitive. This means that her overview is essentially antirealistic. She has cut herself off from the world of ordinary experience and ordinary human beings who might entertain ordinary ideas. Her people are bizarre, freakish, lonely, hermaphroditic. This aesthetic dictates an intense concentration on man's most urgent emotional needs: a communion of dialogue and love. For her, further, the truth of the fable is the truth of the heart. It is not concerned with abstractions about the structure of society or with ideological conflicts in the contemporary world. She has banished these sociological and intellectual matters from her fiction, narrowing its range, perhaps to its detriment, in favor of memory and mood, and above all, feeling. This aesthetic demands a poetic prose and a style which, in Mrs. McCullers' case, often appears childlike. Her prose has a deliberately jerky rhythm and uneven pace, creating a movement which is designed to give the impression of simplicity. Toward that same goal of simplicity, she is occasionally monotonous in tonal qualities and repetitious, again deliberately and to good effect. Her extravagant use of color and sensuous descriptions of food are further evidences of her immersion in the world of the senses.

The purpose of her aesthetic lies in the artist's need to communicate his vision, a need that Mrs. McCullers says she feels intensely. "The function of the artist," she has written, "is to execute his own indigenous vision, and having done that, to keep faith with this vision." If to keep faith is to pursue consistently a single theme, then she has succeeded. For everywhere in her fiction she works at variations on the theme of moral isolation. It is the paradoxes of loneliness and love that impel her characters to a wretched abandonment of hope and leave them to feed on the pain of frustrated communion. She is fascinated by the loneliness of individuals in a world full of individuals. She is possessed by the unceasing failures in the consummation of love, because the lover is always rejected by the beloved, who would himself be a lover, and the lover thus goes on dying, into infinity, his spiritual death.

Capote's characters, seeking the self within the self, follow a twisted path to an abysmal zero at a dead end. Mrs. McCullers' maimed half-people hope to make themselves whole by entering into a fructifying human relationship. She understands the need of the individual to define himself by something outside himself. This is the motive force behind her play on the dialogue of love. The desolation of her characters, and her own pessimism, lie in the failure to achieve the kind of communion that Martin Buber has described, the meeting of *ich und du*, joined in a mystical reciprocity. "What do we expect when we are in despair and yet go to a man?" asks Buber. "Surely a presence by means of which we are told that nevertheless there is meaning." When there is genuine dialogue, then there is genuine community, which "is the being no longer side by side but *with* one another of a multitude of persons. And this multitude, though it also moves towards one goal, yet experiences everywhere a turning to, a dynamic facing of, the other, a flowing from *I* to *Thou*." In genuine dialogue, men, or men and women, establish a living mutual relation. In monologue disguised as dialogue, each speaks with himself "in strangely tortuous and circuitous ways and yet imagines [he has] escaped the torment of being thrown back on [his] own resources." Lovers often engage in such monologue, enjoying their own glorious souls. Mrs. McCullers' implicit hope is that lovers, all men and women, might flow toward each other as the imperatives of Buber's mystical insight bids them do. But the visible assumptions of her theory of love doom them to inevitable failure and condemn them to eternal loneliness. Their fate is to be at the end what they were at the beginning — half-people.

But it must also be said that the failure of dialogue lies in the carefully selected characters Mrs. McCullers permits to engage in it. She has stacked the deck to guarantee ruptured communion and fruitless love by choosing people whose need, to be sure, is demonstrable but whose capacities are crippled. It is her gothic imagination that dictates this narrowly specialized range of character. It is the gothic principle that drives her to a consideration of the outsider: the adolescent who has no place and no sex, the deaf mute, the beloved hunchback, the bisexual adult, or the maternal male. These bizarre characters, alienated from society and the self, dramatize the problem of their ambiguous sex in a life that is curiously desexualized. Mrs. McCullers has said that flight in itself interests her. The remark has meaning not in images of terror from which her characters flee, for this is not the pattern of her fiction. It is flight from normative behavior; it is the frantic flight of the divided soul between the poles of male and female in the prison of the self that interests her. It is her gothic vision that denies a final resting place to this tortured soul, for no resolution of its dilemma is possible.

Although Mrs. McCullers published *The Heart Is a Lonely Hunter* (1940) at an unbelievably early and presumably impressionable age, the novel is indubitably all her own. Yet it displays certain qualities of earlier writers, even if it does not derive from them. The general ambience of tone and feeling in the novel reminds one of Sherwood Anderson. The grotesques of Mrs. McCullers' southern town want to find out why, want to burst out of their shells in the same yearning way that the people of Anderson's Ohio town show. In listing the writers she admires, Mrs. McCullers does not include Anderson, but she does mention, among others, Dostoevski, Proust, Joyce, and Faulkner. All, including Anderson, are present in this novel, but sitting quietly in the far background. They help to define the gothic tones and the new fiction bias of the book. Dostoevski's dark vision and fictional nerve — the determination to push irrevocably to the ultimate conclusion what he has set in train — are what one sees, in a generalized way, in this novel and in others written by Mrs. McCullers. The concern with the inner life, using it as a way of defining external experience, is here as it is in Joyce and Proust. As for Faulkner: he stands in the same relation to the contemporary southern gothic that, in Hemingway's opinion, Huck Finn occupies in relation to all subsequent American literature — the fount from which flows everything good.

But in its statement and treatment of theme the novel is still her own. Here she bares the loneliness of each sentient human being whose need is to create an image of wisdom and receptivity which receives and resolves one's problems, providing release and fulfilment. And here, with magisterial firmness, she condemns her characters to failure. The image they create out of their need has the same need they suffer from. They have wilfully obscured the fallibility of the image. They have stubbornly embarked upon a monologue in the mistaken notion that they have established the reciprocity necessary for dialogue. They are self-deluded in the conversation each holds with himself. And the dimensions of this failure of dialogue are in the collapse of the inner self and the frustration of the social being. Mrs. McCullers does not, in a kind of warmth generated by a barroom milieu, permit her characters to live by the illusions they create. Honesty, not harshness I think, triumphs over warmth when she strips the illusion to reveal its essential nothingness.

The principal characters in *The Heart Is a Lonely Hunter* are arranged in a circle which revolves around Singer, a deaf mute, who occupies the center. Mick Kelly, an adolescent girl,

Jake Blount, an itinerant workman, Dr. Benedict Mady Copeland, a Negro physician, and Biff Brannon, the proprietor of the New York Café, constitute the circle. But Singer is also in orbit, in a separate and transcendent circle, around another deaf mute named Antonapoulos. All the others unburden themselves to Singer, each one creating in Singer the particular response he needs. "Each man described the mute as he wished him to be." And Singer does the same with Antonapoulos. Singer's physical disabilities stand, of course, in an obviously ironical relation to his name and to his role. Since he cannot communicate by voice, or refuses to, his dependents are in effect talking to themselves. Since he is silent, they assume he is malleable; his state suggests a plasticity that lends itself to anyone's shaping hand. He has an air of calm patience and intelligence; his presence conveys a sense of brooding peace. Everyone regards him as sympathetically receptive, and Blount says of him that he is one of those who know.

It has been claimed that Singer has a God-like function in the novel, but I prefer to see him as the figure of the Virgin Mother and the Son. He has none of the terrible majesty of God, but he does represent for the others that all-embracing, comforting, maternal force that Henry Adams descried in the Virgin of Chartres. He is also the type of the Savior: it is no accident that the text of an incidental Sunday school lesson in the novel is "All men seek for Thee." All men seek understanding and compassion, and above all communion, which gives everything. If Singer is conceived as hermaphroditic, incorporating in one body the male and female principles, then in him is the potential for universal balm. But, of course, he is not really engaged by the others and has very little to offer them. His emotional life centers on Antonapoulos, whom he loves. His intellectual life is meager; he cultivates it with one mystery story and one movie each week. The intrinsic value of Singer for the others is thus small. It is true he is perceptive enough to see that all have something they hate and something they love. But this observation is coldly made to Antonapoulos and not to any of them. They do not exist for him, either intellectually or emotionally, in any consequential way. Yet he is at the center of their lives. He is, although they do not yet know it, the false Virgin and the false Son.

The further irony about Singer, and the bitter one that the

others must eventually face, is that he is as dependent upon Antonapoulos as they are upon him. When the deaf mutes part for the day, Singer puts his hand on his friend's arm and looks for a moment into his face. These gestures are the token of his hope that communication had been established and that somehow he has reached out and touched another human being with love and understanding. His need is the same as the one he satisfies for the others, and as great as theirs. And that need is vested in a bad man. For Antonapoulos, inscrutable and bland, had never received or recognized the communiques so urgently issued by Singer; being insane, he is unable to understand anything, and presently he is placed in an institution. There he dies. When Singer learns of his death, he falls into the despair of the true lover. He rejects the company of other mutes, since no substitute will do. He commits suicide. In the transcendent circle, then, is the mad Greek, upon whom all in the novel are ultimately dependent. But what is the Greek if not a symbol for vacuity, for nothing? He cannot communicate, and he cannot love. He can neither give nor receive. He is the reduction to the abysmal zero of the human hope for communion.

Man's need for illusion derives from the frustration of human love and intercourse. And this frustration, in turn, derives from the crippled nature of man. If each of his dependents has something he loves and something he hates, as Singer had said, then each is torn by these warring forces within him. This observation is particularly applicable to Blount and Copeland. Blount loves the ideal of social justice and the commonalty of men, and he hates the inequities of capitalism and the failure of the indifferent workers to rebel against them. As his social ideals are so far from realization, he is always angry. He works for a carnival and lives in the aura of violence in the carnival world that answers to the pent-up violence in himself. Only Singer can give him peace. But this peace is illusory. It does not help him to understand the *why* of human beings and institutions. It does not open the channels of communication between him and Dr. Copeland, even though he is essentially sympathetic to Copeland's views, one of the most ironic failures of dialogue in the novel. It does not prevent him from engaging in what begins as a race riot at the carnival, which at first he had tried to prevent. The fight becomes a free-for-all, when it is every man for himself. Blount is a participant in this symbol for the collapse into anarchy of his social ideal. The surrender to violence and the failure of communication are the measures of Blount's defeat.

Dr. Copeland loves his people and hates their oppressors. A theoretical Marxist, his strong, true purpose is to win justice and dignity for the Negro and to abolish an exploitative capitalism. His disease is fanaticism, and the motive force in him is an "angry, restless love." Like Blount, he fails to penetrate the indifference and ignorance of insensitive men; they do not understand that he has discovered what is good for them. He cannot communicate the purpose to them. He cannot even mold his family to his purpose. On the rock of this human impenetrability, this stubborn intransigence of man, he destroys his family and himself. Singer cannot save him from the fruits of his own fanaticism, which destroys the very love it would engender and makes impossible the communion in brotherhood that it envisages.

Biff Brannon is not so much divided between love and hate as he is between male and female. His task is to heal the division or reconcile the parts and make himself whole. He is not as dependent upon Singer as the others, and so is able to see that Blount and Mick have created in Singer a sort of homemade god. In a way he yearns for Mick's allegiance, feeling for her an uneasy, maternal love. After the death of his wife he becomes more and more feminine, developing qualities that identify him with his wife. Like Singer, he becomes the unitary expression of both the male and female principles. This development is linked to the speculative turn of mind he displays. He is a secular seeker, trying to learn the why of men and women, of life and death. When he relies on the deduction and observation of the scientific method and regards himself as an apostle of cold reason in his dealings with people, he cannot achieve understanding. But when he unites male logic and female intuition in his hermaphroditic soul, he emerges, as at the end of the book, in the most favorable position of any of the characters. He combines defeat and hope, he is at once the past and the future, he is suspended between radiance and darkness, between irony and faith. Insofar as he knits up his troubled soul — and he is not entirely successful, bearing a burden of guilt at the love he feels for Mick — he represents the best possible confrontation of life that Mrs. McCullers here imagines. If we take his solution literally, it is not, obviously, an avenue open to many people.

The most sensitive treatment of character, and the most successful, is saved for Mick Kelly, the adolescent girl in the novel. She is like all the others in her isolation and in her failure to communicate love, in her case a generalized love for people. Full of dreams and aspirations that will not be realized, she feels herself different from others. She is independent of spirit and rejects God. She yearns for she knows not what. She is forced in upon herself, but she cannot achieve an inner peace. In a word, she is the typical adolescent struggling blindly toward maturity, unaware that the pain of alienation she now endures is the proper preparation for later life. Her refuge in her loneliness is her inner room, where she may create her own world. But the unalterable condition of adolescence is insecurity, and it manifests itself in Mick in the terrible self-consciousness and the trembling uncertainties that overtake her. Stifled like the other characters, she must in addition undergo the painful process of growth. It is growth toward sex awareness, which has its culmination when the boy next door takes her. This event does not altogether end a certain ambiguity about Mick's sex, for she has seemed, in the course of the book, to resist the role of woman toward which she is destined. The adolescent girl, in Mrs. McCullers' fiction, has the problem not only of sex awareness but of sex determination. It is not the responsibility of womanhood that she reluctantly must take up but the decision to be a woman at all that she must make. She is, then, sexless, hovering between the two sexes, this girl with a boy's name. In Brannon and in Singer, the sexes seem to achieve a beneficent union. In Mick they make for a chaotic confusion.

The bedding of Mick is a determination of this sex ambiguity more redolent of surrender than of glory. And this is characteristic of the fate Mrs. McCullers has arranged for her. Afraid and alone as she is during much of the book, she nevertheless waits with intense excitement upon the infinite possibilities of life. Then she is more or less compelled to take a job at Woolworth's. All her hopes are dashed. She feels trapped and cheated. She can no longer get into her inside room. Her potentiality in music will be dissipated in this numbing descent into the humdrum. Release from the anguish of adolescence, in Mrs. McCullers' view, brings one into nothing better than the stifling world of adulthood. No measured sense of responsibility comes to Mick because she now earns money necessary for the household. She is angry all the time with a bafflement at life's blasted promise.

A peripheral matter in this novel is the way in which Mrs. McCullers treats social problems. She has said the novel is an ironic parable of fascism. The comment makes sense only if we assume that the economics of capitalism and the racial practices of the South suggest to her the barbarism of fascism. But these matters are hardly at the heart of the novel. It is true that Mrs. McCullers reveals a cold realism in portraying the diseases of her society. But she makes no overt social protest. Her reformers offer no reasonable solutions, and indeed cannot agree on any solution. It may be that she was attracted to this material because she felt still a kind of bondage to the thirties. The relevant use of it in the novel, I think, is to confirm her pessimism by depicting social arrangements as cruelly unsatisfactory. But it is her people in whom she is chiefly interested, not society. Isolation is of the soul, not of the small southern town. The failure of love is the failure of communion, not of labor unions or Negro-white relations.

Nevertheless, the troubled quality of life in that southern town provides a kind of anchor to the reality of this world for *The Heart Is a Lonely Hunter*. The novel elicits a warmth of response from us partly because its psychological problems are placed in a familiar social context. The same cannot be said for *Reflections in a Golden Eye* (1941). Its scene is an army post in the South, but Mrs. McCullers makes no attempt to render it in depth. Neither soldiers nor army life is the subject of this novel. The book is virtually cut off from the external world of recognizable social reality. It creates its own bizarre climate. Barometer readings by its critics are likely to be more subjective than scientific, for like unusual wind and weather anywhere — the kamseen in the Sahara or the föhn in the Tyrol — the kind that blows through this novel is unsettling and ambiguous.

It does seem clear, however, that Mrs. McCullers is pursuing a theme that she began to explore in her first novel. Human beings, she seems to say, are not whole. As half-people, their deficiencies prevent them from realizing their humanity; their course in life is errant, unpredictable, painful. This theme of human inadequacy is illustrated by the six characters in *Reflections in a Golden Eye*. They divide evenly into two groups. One is made up of Leonora Penderton, Major Morris Langdon, and Ellgee Williams. These people live in nature, enjoying (in the literal sense) life at the creature level. They illustrate the healthy principle of natural animality. For the first two especially the appetitive life — food, drink, sex, and sport, all of them equally attractive — is all-encompassing. They are insensitive and unintelligent. They are incapable of asking any questions about life. The other group is made up of Captain Weldon Penderton, Alison Langdon, and Anacleto, a Filipino houseboy. These people are cut off entirely from the world of nature. They represent the sensitive feminine principle of culture, that is, the cultivation of the mind and the arts. They are full of self-doubts and adept at self-torture. The two groups, even though they are moored to their separate spheres of being, destroy each other. No one succeeds in making himself whole, in borrowing from the other group what is lacking in his own personality.

The simplest characters are Leonora Penderton and Major Langdon. Leonora understands, in a purely intuitive way, the nature of the flesh, but this is all she understands. She enjoys her adulterous affair with Langdon in an untroubled way. Since her own hubsand does not understand the demands of the flesh, she has sought satisfaction for them elsewhere, moving toward Langdon in much the same way that water moves downhill. Leonora is at one with her stallion, Firebird, and like him, she is a magnificent creature of nature. But she is too stupid to comprehend or to be affected by the horrible events that take place around her. These include, besides her own adultery, self-mutilation, death, and murder, carried on in an atmosphere heavy with homosexuality and sadism. Her paramour, Langdon, is a little more sentient. After his wife has a breakdown and dies, largely because of his faithlessness, the animal juices seem to run out of him, and he even comes to a vague disquietude about life, which he is helpless as a baby to cope with.

Ellgee Williams, a soldier on the post, is more complicated in his simplicity. With a face like that of a Gauguin primitive, he is a man who feels but does not think. But he feels obscurely and unself-consciously. He is a kind of Pan who lies naked under the sun in the woods, or, still naked, rides about on a horse. This apparent animal innocence, this equiniphilia, is artificial. His attitude toward nature and horses is an outlet for a repressed sexuality induced by a fundamentalist father who had insisted upon the utter evil of any relationship with women. When, early in the novel, he catches sight of Leonora in the nude, his deeply buried normal sex instincts begin to stir. He is, of course, drawn to her because she is, like him, so much a creature of nature. Although he creeps into her bedroom at night to watch her sleep, and sometimes touches her hair or nightgown, he never assaults her. She is bringing him to that troubled state which is the prelude to the knowledge of flesh and sin in which man shall know woman. This is the human state, but Williams never achieves it. Captain Penderton kills him in Leonora's bedroom.

The murder is the inevitable outcome of a love-hate relationship that Penderton has with Williams. Penderton is apparently bisexual, with more than latent homosexual tendencies, but he has the active powers of neither sex. This accounts for his failure as a husband. His tainted masculinity accounts for his cowardice, especially in the face of her adultery, which he knows about but refuses to face. All this makes the instinct toward death more powerful in him than the instinct toward life. Williams represents for him, in a way he cannot understand, an approach to life through nature, where Williams is at home and he is an alien. Leonora's horse represents nature, too. Penderton cannot understand the horse or establish rapport with it any more than he can fathom Williams. As he hates the horse, so he comes to hate Williams. He is conscious of Williams as a man in nature, but not as one in the community of human beings. He cannot communicate with him in that strange, other realm. He cannot make himself whole through Williams. His only recourse is to destroy Williams in a gesture which is essentially a denial of nature. For Williams and Leonora together — and they would eventually have come together — would represent the ripe outpouring of primitive sexual energies in which Penderton would drown. But the deed kills him. After the shooting, he seems to go to pieces like a broken and dissipated monk. The object of his emotional life, of his love and his hate, is dead. And so he is reduced to nothing.

Alison Langdon and Anacleto, her houseboy, are unhealthy, cloistered people. Anacleto is a eunuch, a half-person because he is sexless. Alison is a sickly woman overborne by the sin of her husband and the loss of a child. Cut off from the vital sources of life — from love, from motherhood, and from nature — she has neither the will nor the strength to survive. In a fit of depression she mutilates herself, a physical act which is symbolic of her psychic mutilation. She moves steadily toward a destruction, eventually going mad and dying, which is virtually self-induced.

These two agree that the reflections in the immense golden eye of the green peacock are tiny and grotesque. The prevailing tone of the novel derives from this image given back by the bird's eye. The image describes the uneasy and remote relations of the people to each other. It describes the atmosphere through which these people move, so often filled with cold yellow light or blunt splashes of yellow. Mrs. McCullers even makes an attempt to justify the grotesque, insofar as it may be equated with the aberrant. Penderton argues that if human fulfilment is obtained even in an abnormal way, it is good as long as it brings happiness; moral judgments about such means are irrelevant. But the book is not really a defense of the deviant any more than it is an attack upon the heavy-handed, army-shaped moral standards of so essentially conventional a man as Major Langdon. Mrs. McCullers takes a few false steps toward such rhetorical goals out of a sense of rebellion against conventional morality or taboos which could block the natural movement of the personality toward fruition. But her real theme seems to be the impossibility of such fruition, given inherently incomplete human beings.

The Member of the Wedding (1946) takes us from the obsessed and fevered world of *Reflections* to the warmer and more understandable world of the adolescent, where the pursuit of love and human communion is as real as the southern kitchen in which much of the action takes place. The reality of this novel displaces the gothic character of the first two, and in doing so makes it necessary for Mrs. McCullers to skirt carefully around a sentimentalization of her material. She avoids this danger, happily, but she does lay herself open to the charge of repetition. The Frankie Addams of this novel is the Mike Kelly of *The Heart Is a Lonely Hunter*. The themes are those of the first book: that human beings wish to ameliorate their loneliness by joining themselves, one to another, in meaningful relationship, and that the pains of adolescence are succeeded by a growing recognition of the limits of selfhood and the inevitability of aloneness. As the book marks no advance for Mrs. McCullers in thematic considerations, so it is similar to earlier work in method. The emphasis is on the interior life of her protagonist. The substance of the novel is conveyed in an investigation of feeling — the poignance of adolescence offering so rich an opportunity — offered with an artist's eye to color and a heightened sensitivity to mood. The particular movement in the novel may be charted in this way: Frankie suffers from insecurity and a sense of loss at the beginning; she is then the victim of a self-generated fantasy about belonging; finally, at the end, her effort at joining is frustrated and she resolves her disappointment.

Frankie, who again bears a masculine name as a sign of the not-yet-determined sex of the adolescent girl, is at the beginning a member of nothing at all, the juvenile outsider alienated from her peers and her elders. The world seems separate from herself. Then she determines to join her brother's wedding and become a *we* person instead of remaining an *I* person. She is motivated by the search for love and security that will banish fear. The fear is a compound of the ineffable sadness of growing up, of the melancholy of a summer afternoon, of an undefined sense of guilt, all rendered with a skill that captures the evanescent moment and the inarticulate yearning. The love is the girl's wish to be accepted as a part of the magnetic chain of humanity, and it is the love of man for woman which Frankie does not yet understand. It is her innocence which permits her to think she can join her brother's wedding. It is this innocence the drunken soldier assaults when he tries to seduce her. It is this innocence that Berenice, the Negro cook, quietly dissolves as she instructs Frankie in the meaning of love. Out of all these episodes comes a knowledge of sex, but she has not yet undergone a decisive initiation into sexual love. The limitations of the novel are in its focus on the child's self-centered world in which the macrocosm plays no part. The contribution of the novel is to state once more the universal need for human dialogue.

In 1951 *The Ballad of the Sad Café* appeared, a volume containing the title story, six shorter stories, and the three novels. The subjects of the short stories are music (Mrs. McCullers went to New York from her home in Columbus, Georgia, to study music; Mick Kelly wishes to go away to study music), the imaginative experiences of the inner life, and the problems of love. The characters are the inevitable children or the equally omnipresent grotesques. One story, "A Tree. A Rock. A Cloud.," deserves comment, because here Mrs. McCullers works out a hierarchy of love and reveals how thoroughly she has engrossed herself in this subject. An old man who has suffered the pathos of loneliness and lost love undertakes a scientific study of love, making his life a pilgrimage toward understanding it. His conclusion is that men should begin by loving a tree, a rock, a cloud, and at last, a woman. Love is the kelson of creation by which everything in the cosmos is united, the insentient thing of nature and the aspiration of the soul. Out of the life of love comes a transcendent understanding. This mystical and monistic idealism, so suggestive of Whitman, is the happiest view of love Mrs. McCullers gives us, although this conviction that love is all comes to us from a broken man.

"The Ballad of the Sad Café" offers, in partial contrast, the theory that lover and beloved are different. The beloved, who may be the most outlandish sort of person, is merely the stimulus for love. The lover determines the value and quality of the love. Everyone wants to be a lover and not a beloved, as everyone wants to be a subject and not an object. The beloved hates the lover, but the lover will accept any relationship with the beloved. This doctrine is explicitly stated in "The Ballad," which is written to illustrate it. It is a doctrine which makes inevitable the futility of love and denies the possibility of communion. It condemns man to spiritual isolation.

The story begins on this note of isolation, speaking of the dreary town, "lonesome, sad, and like a place that is far off and estranged from all other places in the world." It is an appropriate setting for the strange tale of three lover-beloved relationships, all in the pattern described. Marvin Macy loves Miss Amelia. Miss Amelia loves Cousin Lymon. Cousin Lymon loves Marvin. None of these people is lovable. Marvin is a fearless, cruel man. He is a Satan: there is evil in him, and he never sweats, even in August. Miss Amelia is a dark, firmly muscled, cross-eyed woman who stands six feet two. Cousin Lymon is a hunchback from nowhere. Love reforms Marvin, but when he is rebuffed by Amelia, he is enraged. He leaves town, becomes a criminal, and goes to the penitentiary. The lover scorned by the beloved is ruined. Then Cousin Lymon arrives in town, claiming kinship with Miss Amelia. She takes him in. She is a hard woman who had never before offered anybody a meal or a drink. But they drink together, and it is whisky that can warm the soul and reveal the message hidden there: Miss Amelia's soul was warmed, and the message was a message of love. The new Amelia and Cousin Lymon, who had an instinct "to establish immediate and vital contact between himself and all things in the world," open a café, where it is observed that Amelia has changed for the better. Being in love, she is not so quick to cheat; she lavishes gifts and attention upon Cousin Lymon. He takes but does not give.

Then Marvin Macy returns to town. Cousin Lymon is immediately drawn to him, although he treats Lymon with cruel indifference. Amelia suffers helplessly. Then Cousin Lymon brings Marvin home to live with him and Amelia. She can do nothing. "Once you have lived with another, it is a great torture to have to live alone . . . it is better to take in your mortal enemy than face the terror of living alone." But the intolerable situation cannot last. On Ground Hog Day, when a bloody hawk is circling overhead, Amelia and Marvin fight. Just when she has the fight won, Cousin Lymon leaps upon her back. At this act, her will to win is lost, and Marvin beats her. She is broken by the perfidy of her beloved. Marvin and Cousin Lymon steal many of her things, destroy her property, try to poison her, and then leave town together. She boards up her premises and goes into seclusion. The town is as lonely as it was at the beginning. One might as well go down and listen to the chain gang sing. There, twelve men, white and black, "who are together," make music that seems to swell out of the earth and the sky. Here, where freedom is denied, men live harmoniously together in community.

Mrs. McCullers explains the ballad as she goes along. The magic potion, the desolation of the place, the portents of disaster, the criminal character have all given it the air of mystery and the aura of simplicity — not at all factitious — upon which the idea of a ballad may draw. The bitter ironies of love in the three parallel relationships reveal once again the desexualized treatment Mrs. McCullers characteristically gives to love. It is twice-fruitless in that it is always frustrated and always barren. Free men, at least, are alone and ultimately without love. This is the persistent and universal gothic horror that transcends the choice of the hump-backed dwarf as a love object or of a leaning, deserted-looking, boarded-up house as the site of the sad café.

Out of the still and twisted world in which her imagination dwells, Mrs. McCullers has drawn some truths that come home to all men. She has illuminated the possibilities for loneliness and the capacities for deviant behavior that mark the human lot. But there is a troubling sense of something wanting in what she does. The world of the adolescent child is, after all, only a promise of life to come in adulthood. The crazy, private world of her freakish and tortured adults is on the periphery of our experience, even if a significantly disturbing one. It is a narrow corner of human existence that she has chosen to exploit in her fiction. Her view of man's fate, therefore, adds little, in the largest sense, to the dimensions of our understanding. The gothic view of life has conjured up the terror of life but has not weighed the consequences of that terror. Mrs. McCullers knows something of the conditions under which life must be carried on, but she has gone beyond this to examine how men might endure under these conditions. There is no room in her work for the *consequences* of human action; there is no sense of the continuity of life. She has succeeded perhaps too well in creating an art form that is cut off from life. It is a form cut off from society, from morality, from religion, from ideas, from concern with man's burden or with man's hope. It is a special art form, and its special quality makes it symptomatic of the phenomena we have always with us — a disturbed psyche and a disturbed time.

EUDORA WELTY AND THE TRIUMPH OF THE IMAGINATION

The similarities between Eudora Welty and Carson McCullers are many. Eudora Welty is also on familiar terms with gothic abnormality, although not as deeply possessed by it. She uses her characters — *her* deaf mutes or mad, decadent aristocrats — out of the same preoccupation with the themes of isolation, love and separateness, communication. Like Mrs. McCullers, she constantly probes the problem of identity or of separateness which leads to isolation, while at the same time she forces upon her characters a recognition of the demands of love which can be fulfilled only through communication. The tensions established by this movement from pole to pole, from separateness to love, are the staples of her work. Like Mrs. McCullers, she shares in the southern tradition of the neo-conservatives, but her attitude toward the shape of southern society is, at best, passive. A defined social scheme is there in her work; it is a given. But it is hardly at the center of her concern as an artist. That center is occupied by an absorption with the mystery of personality.

Clearly, Miss Welty is a southern writer of the new fiction. Indeed, independent of literary coterie and scornful of literary fashion as she may be, she stands at the head of the southern gothic stream of the new fiction in the forties. Her work is a summation of all that it represents and a major contribution to American literature of the twentieth century. Merely in quantitative terms she made, between 1941 and 1949, a very respectable contribution toward an *oeuvre*, publishing five volumes of fiction. Furthermore, she has been the pioneer in the new fiction. The history of literature in the forties must show that she, above all writers of fiction, made the sharpest break with the prevailing modes in fiction and made it before any other writer. Men as different as Robert Penn Warren and Walter Van Tilburg Clark wrote as transitional figures at the beginning of their fictional careers, unable to free themselves in the forties of some attitudes they had from the thirties, attitudes which, to be sure, they would sharply modify or drop in time. Miss Welty, however, broke clean, hardly seemed to be aware of the literary issues of the thirties, struck out on her original line, and initiated thereby a new school of fiction.

Her achievement was possible because Miss Welty is so intensely dedicated to the power and mystery of the imagination in the creation of prose fiction. This commitment as writer to the ineluctable, the vagrant, but perhaps the more profound aspects of the human personality has made her stories apparently formless:

she confesses herself, indeed, unsympathetic to the systematic analysis of stories and will not promise symmetrical development in
her own. It is this commitment that causes her to regard reason,
as a writer's instrument, with deep suspicion, for a writer's choices
are only incidentally reasonable; they are impelled by feeling, by
art, and only last (if at all) by reason. Perhaps the best explanation of the writing process that Miss Welty herself makes is this:
". . . that subject, method, form, style, all wait upon — indeed
hang upon — a sort of double thunderclap at the author's ears:
the break of the living world upon what is stirring inside the mind,
and the answering impulse that in a moment of high consciousness fuses impact and image and fires them off together." This
passage, which occurs at the close of an essay entitled "How I
Write," brings to mind Coleridge's ideas on the imagination. Miss
Welty has already made a distinction between the imagination
and analysis which is comparable to that of Coleridge between
the imagination and the understanding. But a more specific similarity is to be found in her intense concentration upon the fusing
function that welds external and internal experience. For Coleridge has claimed that the creative activity of man is to be seen
in the work of the imagination, which fuses insights of reason
with the sense impressions yielded up by the understanding. The
imagination, says Coleridge, is "that reconciling and mediatory
power, which incorporating the reason in images of the sense, and
organizing (as it were) the flux of the senses by the permanence
and self-circling energies of the reason, gives birth to a system of
symbols, harmonious in themselves, and consubstantial with the
truths of which they are the conductors."

The usefulness of Coleridge in discussing Miss Welty may be
further seen in her attitude toward place. She is, she says, touched
off by place, which opens a door in the mind. Place stirs an emotion in her out of which will issue, after mysterious transmutations,
a particular fictional work. In "Some Notes on River Country,"
she writes, "I have never seen, in this small section of old Mississippi River country and its little chain of lost towns between
Vicksburg and Natchez, anything so mundane as ghosts, but I
have felt many times there a sense of place as powerful as if it
were visible and walking and could touch me." For her, the reality
of place quite naturally gives rise to the intangible sense of place;

and it is this which nourishes Miss Welty, which accounts even for a certain piety about place. The images born of absorption in place become the harmonious system of symbols, the imaginative truth, that may be discerned in her stories.

Other critical conceptions are at play in Miss Welty's mode of interpreting experience, each of them testifying, again, to the primacy of the imagination. For example, in a letter to the *New Yorker* rebuking Edmund Wilson, she defends her own militant regionalism on the ground that the imagination must be free to create in its own way, and so must be free of cosmopolitan aesthetic standards. And when she condemns moralizing stories as flat-surfaced and speaks out for the mystery of allurement that every good story has, one sees that she will make imaginative demands upon herself as she will upon her reader. The beauty of a story, she claims, is often in its reticences, in what the author holds back, because beauty springs from deviation and from desire not to comply but to act inevitably. Or when she condemns patterns in stories as Poe has written of patterns, one sees her instinctive withdrawal from the rational and mechanical faculties in the creation of fiction.

In the practice of fiction, in the exercise of her imagination, Miss Welty, as one would expect of a southern regionalist, lives in close proximity to the past. Like other southern writers, her constant effort is to repossess the past. She wishes it to be meaningful for the contemporary experiences of her characters. She uses it to help them account for themselves and to help us account for them. It is the past of the South that interests her most, the past, perhaps, of the Natchez Trace country, but her treatment is not confined to history in any ordinary sense. One is more aware of the bright color of myth and legend in her treatment of the past than of the presence of drab fact. She is herself, in fact, as one of her critics has suggested, a legend-maker; and when she gets beyond the confines of the South, she is quite willing to enter the realm of world myth. Her utilization of myth, another dimension of her preoccupation with the past, arises from a conviction that mythic patterns are deeply ingrained in the human consciousness and possess therefore a perennial relevance.

In the practice of fiction, further, she has worked out various techniques. One method that accommodates her liking for reticence and indirection is what I shall call the technique of simultaneity by which she seems to split time into two parts, which she makes to co-exist. By virtue of this device she often gives us a report from more than one consciousness about the same event at the same time. But it is seen, of course, from different points of view. As a consequence, Miss Welty is able to introduce into her stories various versions of reality, the various and different versions entertained by different characters. Another practice that contributes to her subtlety is to see reality as public or private, one kind set against the other, reality taking on in these cases two faces. And finally Miss Welty believes in what may be called the doctrine of the moment. A photograph, she has said, imprisons a moment in time and by so doing steals, in a sense, its soul or spirit. Such theft is the purpose of nearly everything we do: " . . . certainly in the arts, painting and writing, we steal spirits and souls if we can. . . ." What this doctrine demands of her is a search for the significant moment of realized human experience which, once found, yields up its rich meaning.

Miss Welty published two volumes of short stories in the forties, *A Curtain of Green* in 1941 and *The Wide Net* in 1943. Since she manages her short fiction with a particular skill and flair, I propose to begin the discussion of her work with these volumes, using the stories to illustrate various important facets of her practice of fiction.

Five of the first six stories in Eudora Welty's first volume deal with abnormal characters. Lily Daw is feeble-minded; the petrified man is an exhibit in a freak show; the Morgans are deaf and dumb; Keela, with a traveling circus, eats live chickens; the narrator in "Why I Live at the P. O." is at least eccentric if she is not suffering from dementia praecox, as Katherine Anne Porter seems to believe. At first blush it appears that we are to have a gallery of horrors, and certainly the impression is inescapable that Miss Welty, in this early stage of her career at least, was fascinated by the macabre and the freakish. She is, in this respect, like other southern writers of gothic fiction. But she is different in a significant way, because the abnormal characters do not exist as symbols of southern decadence in her stories, and neither personal nor social decay is her theme. In fact, a comic spirit informs three of these stories. It is a comedy quite different from the superiority that Erskine Caldwell, say, evinces toward his rural degenerates. It is a comedy that does not exploit the abnormal but, as it were, absorbs it. Feeble-minded Lily, in "Lily Daw and the Three Ladies" for example, comes off very well. Despite the efforts of the officious but conscientious ladies of the town to exercise their stewardship over Lily and protect her — she is a maturing girl — Lily has responded to her own needs and her own rhythm and given in to a traveling xylophone-player. The ladies, who were packing Lily off to an institution, prove surprisingly flexible and resourceful when they discover Lily's commitment, and pack her off, instead, into marriage. In the other two stories the comedy has a sharper bite, but again not at the expense of the abnormal character. Even when she does not invoke the comic spirit, Miss Welty manages to avoid lugubrious decay and still use the abnormal. Stories like "The Key" and "Keela, the Outcast Indian Maiden," two of these five, have the trappings of the outré but the quite legitimate themes of communication and guilt. The point is that the center of interest in Miss Welty's stories is not in any psychological or physical deviation. She uses her freaks and eccentrics much as she uses her regionalism: they are the specifics from which she launches herself toward those generalized conceptions that have universal meaning and appeal.

It is that same effort at the apprehension of universality that may very well account for Miss Welty's use of myth, although she has always loved folk tales, fairy tales, and old legends for their own sake, as Katherine Anne Porter tells us. Critics of her work, sometimes showing more zeal than judgment, have found evidence of various myths in the stories and in the novels, too, for that matter. The Proserpina descent into Hell, the rising of the Phoenix, the story of guilt and the Ancient Mariner, the apples of mythology, the Zeus-Danaë-Leda myth, the Perseus and Ulysses myths have all been identified in her fiction. I think it is clear that Miss Welty uses myth, but she is not inclined to take over whole any single myth. Since she tends to work by indirection, she might be expected to give out hints rather than fully completed analogues. Her practice in the short stories shows her relying on association and allusion more than on direct borrowing. In a story like "Keela," I believe that Miss Welty felt the suggestive power of the old legend about how an unexpiated guilt haunts a man. Her story derives tone and meaning from the memory it evokes of that ancient mariner whose experience, in its broadest sense, is so dreadfully open to all of us. Again, old Phoenix, the ancient Negro woman in "A Worn Path" (in *A Curtain of Green*), rises periodically like the mythical bird of old. She makes her pilgrimage of love to get the medicine that keeps her grandson alive. The endurance, the devotion, the self-sacrifice that the old woman displays take on increased size when referred, in the reader's mind, to that ancient story about the bird and the cyclic drive toward life. Miss Welty, I daresay, is content to juxtapose the two Phoenixes and permit them to nourish each other in the reader's imagination. The eternal truths the old woman has absorbed — the need to endure and the sacred force of the life-drive — are reinforced by the shadowy presence, somewhere behind her, of the ancient Phoenix that has always symbolized the same need and force for man. Despite the fact that Miss Welty is obviously conscious of the mythic tradition as she writes, the reader must guard against the temptation — a temptation that she herself is responsible for —to find a schematic rendering of mythic materials in her stories. It is the spirit or the idea of some myths that she calls upon to lend authority, weight, or timelessness to some of her stories.

Here and there in Miss Welty's fiction one finds characters, created out of her own resources, who may stand as minor deities in the pantheon of her imagination. They take shape as river gods or field gods, like the young man in "At the Landing" (*The Wide Net*) or the overseer in *Delta Wedding*. They are kin to the creatures of ancient myth or kissing-cousins to the men and women of legend and folk tale indigenous to the American frontier. They testify to the myth-making impulse in Miss Welty. And they reinforce her attachment to the past.

The past is also history, and history is used in Miss Welty's work as an imaginative record of those who have lived in the past. "A Still Moment" (*The Wide Net*) is an impressive example of her treatment of historical personages. They are Lorenzo Dow, the obsessed evangelist; James Murrell, the archcriminal of the Natchez Trace; and James Audubon, the naturalist. These three come together at a live-oak tree in the forest. There they see a snowy white heron. Each reacts to the beautiful bird. Then Audubon shoots it. The men go their separate ways, each one significantly changed. For the shooting of the bird is the climax of the story, the act that works the change. Before that act, each man had been the victim of a monomaniacal passion. Each had an inadequate and partial vision of experience, although unaware of its shortcomings. The bird, a symbol of the beauty of nature, momentarily dissolves each monomania and brings each man to an unsolicited and damaged self-consciousness. The historical characters thus take shape under Miss Welty's hand as embodiments of various value structures.

In the early portions of the story, each man is driven by a different passion. Dow, who would save all souls, is a man who had tried to see by God's signs the accumulated radiance of saved souls, but he had not succeeded. He had not trusted God to free him from danger, but had relied on his own strength and argument. His channels to God are clogged. Murrell is evil, and identifies himself as the Devil. As a consequence, he is blind to the glorious mystery of being in general. Really, he is akin to Dow, and at one point he "stood beside him like a brother seeking light." Audubon is obsessed with remembering and grasping everything. He does not want anything to be lost.

When the heron appears, Dow thinks God's love has become visible. Murrell can see "only whiteness ensconced in darkness," because his vision is clouded by his desperate past and by his evil plans for the slave rebellion, made in vanity and pride. Audubon sees the heron as no more than a natural phenomenon. But presently, as the heron begins to act upon them, each man's vision grows less painful and his burden less heavy:

What each of them had wanted was simply *all*. To save all souls, to destroy all men, to see and to record all life that filled this world — all, all — but now a single frail yearning seemed to go out of the three of them for a moment and to stretch toward this one snowy, shy bird in the marshes. It was as if three whirlwinds had drawn together at some center, to find there feeding in peace a snowy heron. Its own slow spiral of flight could take it away in its own time, but for a little it held them still, it laid quiet over them, and they stood for a moment unburdened. . . .

The bird acts as a catalytic agent on the passions of the men, and they fall into uncertainty. Murrell and Audubon both become sharply aware of their shortcomings, especially in self-knowledge.

Miss Welty says of Audubon, "But if it was his identity that he wished to discover, or if it was what a man had to seize beyond that, the way for him was by endless examination. . . ."

Once the heron is dead, the men feel they have taken the pride out of each other. Audubon realizes that he has been unable really to possess the heron, for he had to kill the thing he loved in order to utilize it; he had to take it out of the world of nature in order to subject it to the kind of examination that science demands. He is forced to recognize the limitations of his mode of life and, in accordance with the demands of science, of his way of seeing only the outward aspect of things. Murrell hides in the cane to prey on the innocent traveler because his faith was in innocence but "his knowledge was of ruin." Lorenzo realizes that he will never know God and will never be able to explain to God about Time and Separateness, since God would not want to listen to him. Thus the empiricism of science, the dominion of evil, and the mystical certainties of religious faith are all found wanting. Each of these men stumbles before the weakness inherent in his way of seeing, before his monomania, before the mystery of self-knowledge. History, to return to the point at which this analysis began, becomes a reservoir for Miss Welty of life attitudes. She chooses in this story to show and examine three, embodied in three historical personages. History is thus lifted to a moral level, where values are attached to these people. The past is possessed, not as episode, but as ethical alternatives. The past is possessed, also, as alternative ways of seeing, of grasping experience. In these ways, Miss Welty makes history meaningful in her fiction. Or perhaps the other emphasis is more desirable: absorbing history into her fiction, she makes her stories more meaningful as they are richer in texture and resources.

"A Still Moment" reveals more about the nature of Miss Welty's fiction than simply the way in which she uses history, for the alternatives she poses may be looked upon as alternative versions of reality. Many of her stories turn on this juxtaposition of various versions of reality. The force of this tactic is twofold. It reveals the limitations of human consciousness and opens up the possibilities for the existence of two simultaneously recognized and ongoing versions of reality. And it shows the necessity to reconcile public and private conceptions of reality. "Clytie" (from *A Curtain of Green*) will illustrate the workings of this tactic.

Clytie is an old woman who wishes to establish some communion with the world in love and sympathy. She gazes into the faces of those about her, trying to judge their capacity to give love. But she cannot reach anyone. When she sees her own face reflected in a rain barrel, looking pained, ugly, old, wild, she knows that her face could never attract the face for which she yearns. She drowns herself. Clytie has created in her inner world a view of herself that does not correspond to the reality that she presents to the external world. In this latter world of reality, Clytie had never known what she was. She tries to reach the outside world by searching for love, but people are repelled by what they see on the surface of her face. She tries to reach it from her house, which the rest of her decayed family keeps locked, with the blinds drawn: she is always secretly opening a window. Like Hawthorne, who tried to open a figurative window to the world, she seeks to establish some contact with reality that will rescue her from her isolation. Unable to eradicate or even to mitigate the irreconcilable differences between the two worlds, she commits suicide.

What Eudora Welty achieves by using differing versions of reality is a sense of the richness of life, of always greater possibilities; of the confusion of life, introduced by the presentation of alternatives; of the limitations of human beings, who are unable to comprehend more than one reality or unable to reconcile two if they are dimly perceived. But she does not insist upon the superiority of any one kind of reality — public or private, external or internal. She does not always force her characters to come to terms with public and external reality as the price of survival. The character who can survive successfully in two worlds need not sacrifice either one. Her story, "A Memory" (*A Curtain of Green*), deals with the problem of existing simultaneously in two different spheres of experience. It begins with a girl, lying on a beach, who thinks about the boy she is in love with. She has never spoken to this boy. She has observed him from afar; once she brushed by him. Her memories of him and their meaning to her thus constitute an order of experience largely created within her self. She has generated a self-created idea of the world, as it were. The gesture she uses, of placing her hand over her eyes, indicates her wish and perhaps her need to impose a frame upon experience, and so organize and limit it in accordance with her desires.

As she dwells in the world of idea created out of her own being, so she dwells simultaneously in the world of sun and beach where she now lies. There she observes a gross family cavorting with meaningless violence on the sand and in the water. Foolish, shameless, insensitive, these people constitute a realm of experience quite different from that of her secret world. The girl's world is polarized: the harshness of experience and nature is on one side and the innocence of the dream is on the other. But it does not necessarily follow that these polar worlds will clash. Both the dream of the boy and the view of the metallic people on the beach are ideas of reality and both must be dealt with. The girl, whose psyche shrinks from the people, knows that her experience on the beach must nevertheless become a part of her relationship to the boy, of her love for him. "I could imagine the boy I loved walking into a classroom, where I would watch him with this hour on the beach accompanying my recovered dream and added to my love." The final effort of the girl is to merge the two versions of reality. The merging tactic is not a matter of choice but of necessity if the dream of love is to be protected. The secret world is a better world, but it needs the other; by virtue of absorbing experience from the public world, the secret world may win enduring validity.

Characters who entertain or are exposed to two different versions of reality, a public and a private, will of course live much in isolation. Miss Welty's exploration of isolation as a theme goes beyond the exploitation of an interest in psychological eccentricity or illness, although it is clear that characters like the Morgans in "The Key," Lily Daw, and the boy in "First Love" are cut off from the common world of experience by their special disabilities. Miss Welty is also concerned with the problem of communication, for she sees in the failure of understanding among people the failure of self-realization. Clytie is an example in point here, since her effort to break out of her isolation is frustrated by her inability to communicate with the people in her town. Perhaps the most meaningful context in which the theme of isolation appears is in those stories where apparently normal characters are cut off from the essential life forces; either they are spectators of life or they are lost souls. In *A Curtain of Green* the figure of the traveling salesman apparently presented itself to Miss Welty's imagination as an embodiment of this alienated fate. The salesman in "The Hitch-Hikers" observes life going on all about him—people go to parties, women seek him out and love him, a man commits murder — but he seems unable to participate; the theme of isolation opens, in this story, a view of the helplessness of human life where mystery and many possibilities make experience so various and contradictory that man cannot grasp its meaning. In "Death of a Traveling Salesman" the protagonist is literally lost in a country he knows well. He takes shelter with a simple, quiet, proud country couple who are soon to have a baby. He comes slowly to an awareness of how complete their lives are, defined by a sense of their own dignity and by their love. He sees how lonely and barren his own is. The realization that he is cut off from the elementary life processes overwhelms him and, weakened by illness, he dies as he walks away from their cabin.

It is an index to Miss Welty's attitude toward society that in the two stories which seem to reflect some interest in social problems, the same theme of isolation should be at work. It would be unfair to claim that she views society as centrifugal, flinging its individual members into isolation, but not unfair to suggest that she sees society as inhuman and heedless. Poverty, bitter need, unemployment account for the isolation in "The Whistle" and "Flowers for Marjorie," also from *A Curtain of Green*. The first of these is of interest because the implacable forces of nature and society have combined to benumb as well as isolate its miserable tenant farmers. Yet they possess just enough energy to lay claim to their humanity by rebelling against the iron-bound fate that compasses them about. Against the determinism of economic forces they pose their own determination to maintain a connection with life.

Self-imposed isolation as a refuge from the real world of experience is a variation on this theme in Miss Welty's work. The title story of *A Curtain of Green* concerns Mrs. Larkin whose husband had been killed before her eyes by a tree that had fallen in a storm. She finds it possible to go on, after this accident, only by absorbing herself totally in her garden, where she grows things in random profusion as if to compensate with the life of plants for the life she has lost. She seems to want the garden to overflow "as if she consciously ventured forever a little farther, a little deeper, into her life in the garden." It is a curtain of green shutting out the everyday reality in which her husband was killed. But the curtain is rent by memory of his death, so incredible to her because her love for him, she had thought, was keeping him safe. Neither her substitution of plant life for human life nor her desperately imposed isolation is a successful tactic in her effort to survive. She finds herself, at the climax of the story, on the point of braining her Negro gardener with a hoe. This is Mrs. Larkin's response to her own helplessness in the face of accident, unaccountability, the inscrutability of all life and death. It is her confession that she cannot shut out the reality in which her husband was killed by living only in that other reality of her garden. As she raises the hoe, the rain comes, interrupting her action and dissolving her curtain of green. A sense of loneliness and loss sweeps over her, and she falls fainting to the ground. In this story, the real world is more desirable than the dream world, and isolation is no compensation for life in the real world.

The vitality of human beings, the intense claims of the life force — these are always present to the mind of the reader of Miss Welty's fiction. She does not beweep innocence lost in the chaos of experience. On the contrary, it is experience which accounts for the mystery of personality, a mystery which, at its most profound depths, leads us to the secret of life itself. One senses many of these things in her character sketch, "Ida M'Toy," which is reprinted in the *Accent Anthology*. Ida, who used to be a midwife and now sells secondhand clothes, has spent her years in delivering the child and clothing the man. She is on intimate terms with the fundamentals of life and so expresses in her being something of its mystery. Ida is a self-conscious character, aware of her own dignity and status. But Lily Daw, to return to her, all unconsciously yearns toward life, as represented by sexual intercourse and marriage, and turns away from the living death of an institution, where the three ladies originally want to send her. The same contrast between the living and the living dead may be seen in "A Visit of Charity" (*A Curtain of Green*) in which a Campfire girl pays a visit to two old ladies who do live in an institution. We have already seen the operation of this life-force in "Death of a Traveling Salesman," where imminent birth is placed over against death. In "Livvie" (*The Wide Net*) Miss Welty shows us youth and love as natural forces displacing age and being freed from it by death. The inevitability of the events in this story is achieved by a method of narration which conveys the impression, somehow, that what happens is as natural as the rhythm of events in the non-human world of nature.

As Livvie shows the inevitable working of natural forces in a variation of the January-May wedding pattern, "At the Landing," (*The Wide Net*) shows what happens when the forces of nature, these same life forces, are unleashed upon a character who cannot accommodate herself to them. Jenny is a girl who has lived in forced isolation. Her grandfather has so stifled her will that she would be obedient to anyone, as she is obedient to him. She never performs any act for herself: "It might seem that nothing began in her own heart." Then her grandfather dies. She goes out into the world where she encounters Billy Floyd, a kind of river god. He draws her into the wonder and mystery of love and of personality.

She walked in the woods and around the graves in it, and knew about love, how it would have a different story in the world if it could lose the moral knowledge of a mystery that is in the other heart. Nothing in Floyd frightened her that drew her near, but at once she had the knowledge come to her that a fragile mystery was in everyone and in herself, since there it was in Floyd, and that whatever she did, she would be bound to ride over and hurt, and the secrecy of life was the terror of it.

He does not love her. He saves her life in a flood, and then he violates her, taking her as though it were an act of nature, or of a god. He leaves her, but she lives as though in a dream of love, bemused by these mysteries. To banish them — to discover the secret of love and separateness and the meaning of individual being and to discover wisdom — she goes in quest of him. She goes to the river, among the rough fishermen. They tell her Floyd is on the river. They put her in a hut. Then one by one they come and take her.

The fate that overtakes Jenny rightfully comes to one who has hoped for too much: she has yearned for the happy, mutual consummation of love in a little cottage, a sentimental dream. It is a fate that comes to one who is released into the world too suddenly and with too little preparation; her will has not had the discipline of independent action, and her spirit has not been sufficiently toughened by the bruising contacts of daily life. It comes to her to punish presumption, the presumption that leads her to probe the mysteries of love and personality, of separateness. These mysteries are a part of the life force. The paradox of unity and isolation that lies at the heart of love and the doubleness that lies at the heart of personality cannot be made to yield up their secrets. We are their victims, and they make our fate. It is the essence of Miss Welty's wisdom to distinguish these forces and acquiesce in their influence upon our lives.

"For more than a century the territory ahead has been the world that lies somewhere behind us," Wright Morris has written, "a world that has become, in the last few decades, a nostalgic myth." The thesis of Morris' *The Territory Ahead* is that the American writer's imagination has been crippled by the nostalgia that drives it to a preoccupation with our mythic past. Miss Welty's *The Robber Bridegroom* (1942), her first novel, provides an opportunity to test this thesis. The book is backward-looking and myth-making, a relevant demonstration of the fascination the past holds for its author. It is both an act of piety and an impulse of simple nostalgia that impels her to possess the past, and those motives are indeed crippling. Miss Welty obviously has in mind a wider use of the past, but she fails, in my opinion, to define what it is. Her hints about larger meanings of the past are abortive. *The Robber Bridegroom* is a charming little novel that fails to exploit and realize its potential.

Much of its charm lies in its fairy tale elements as Miss Welty has domesticated them in early nineteenth-century Natchez Trace country. In the novel Clement Musgrove is the weak father whose second wife, Salome, is the wicked stepmother to beautiful Rosamond. Salome forces Rosamond to appear to Jamie Lockhart as a kitchen slattern. Jamie is the gentleman highwayman who destroys his enemies, reforms himself, marries Rosamond, and lives happily ever after with her, in prosperity. Here are the elements of the Hänsel and Gretel story and intimations of the Cinderella motif. The story also has elements of magic: the talking head of Big Harpe, the talismanic locket Rosamond wears, the ever-full milk pail she carries when Jamie kidnaps her on horseback.

In addition, Miss Welty works into this book much of the legend and lore of that time and that place, partly by bringing into her story Mike Fink and Little Harpe. The historical accuracy of her material can be checked by a reading of Robert M. Coates's *The Outlaw Years*, published in 1930. The strength and appetites and dress of Mike Fink are much the same in the Coates book and in the novel, down to the red turkey feather Mike wears in his cap. The same is true of details in the lives of the Harpe brothers, including the wrapping of a human head in blue clay. Both books tell of using berry juice and bearskins as methods of disguise, of evading American law on the Mississippi, of ornamenting petticoats in New Orleans with gold lace at the bottom.

The analogues to the fairy tales lend charm to the book, and the accuracy of historical detail constitutes an act of harmless piety. These two related aspects of the story are self-contained. But Miss Welty reaches beyond them toward a meaningful interpretation of the American past, and this further reach leads her to confusion. Clement Musgrove, for instance, is made into an Adamic man who figures forth the impregnability of innocence. No harm comes to him, although he constantly falls into the hands of evil forces: Mike Fink, who would rob and murder him; the Indians, who would torture and kill him; Jamie Lockhart, who would rob him; his wife Salome, who would rob him of his daughter and trouble his mind with her greed for land and things. Successful in staving off the assaults these people make upon him, he is nevertheless the unwilling victim of the westering impulse that has traditionally gripped Americans. He is not ambitious or a seeker after anything, he explains, "Yet it seemed as if I was caught up by what came over the others, and they were the same. There was a great tug at the whole world, to go down over the edge, and one and all we were changed into pioneers, and our hearts and our own lonely wills may have had nothing to do with it." This impulse, unconsciously felt, draws Clement as Adam into the West as Paradise. It is a search for continued earthly happiness that he pursues. He is unsuccessful. Paradise is corrupted by his greedy, proud wife and by the coming of other men. The spoliation of Paradise, even by those who seek it, is a paradox attendant upon the fall of man. It is a drama enacted in the history of the American conquest of the West, a history that reveals, on the symbolic level, the tragedy in the end of innocence. Unfortunately, Miss Welty does not reconcile the corruption of Paradise with her happy ending. She does not give us a deeply human Clement, matured through suffering and reconciled to the human lot. She begins to grope toward the archetypal meanings of her fairy tale, but she draws back from its total meaning. She accepts its happy ending without accepting or recognizing its great cost.

Miss Welty imposes upon this slight book the burden of another serious problem — the question of identity. This question is related to themes seen in the short stories, particularly the idea of doubleness and the paradox of love and separateness. The ambiguity of doubleness appears in this speculation by Clement about Jamie:

If being a bandit were his breadth and scope, I should find him and kill him for sure. . . . But since in addition he loves my daughter, he must be not the one man, but two, and I should be afraid of killing the second. For all things are double, and this should keep us from taking liberties with the outside world, and acting too quickly to finish things off. All things are divided in half — night and day, the soul and body, and sorrow and joy and youth and age. . . .

The question of Jamie's identity, which arises because he disguises himself and because he is both a gentleman and a robber, is pervasive throughout the book. Little Harpe comments, when Jamie's face is half-stained, that Jamie wears his two faces together. Rosamond is happy as Jamie's beloved, except that she does not know who he is because she has never seen his face. When she washes off the berry juice, at the instigation of her stepmother, Jamie leaves her: you did not trust me or love me, he says, you only wanted to know who I was. The urge for separateness in Jamie overcomes, for the moment, the power of love. The urge to banish the ambiguity about his identity impels Jamie to kill Little Harpe. "Not a man in the world can say I am not who I am and what I am, and live," he says. But the establishment of his identity and his separateness does not bring him the heart's ease he anticipates. He yearns for Rosamond, who he thinks is dead. When she appears as he is about to take ship for Zanzibar, they fall into each other's arms.

Why does Miss Welty raise the question of the inviolability of identity? The fully realized consequences of this self-conscious separateness, when it is entangled with the power of love, are, as in the case with the end of innocence as theme, tragic, dark, full of struggle. Again, the deepest implications of the fairy tale, of any tale which shows how mystery and magic are rooted in human experience, might have yielded up a meaningful resolution of the lover-separateness paradox. The yoking of the two demands a symbolic vision that penetrates to the depths of man's life. But Miss Welty, with a kind of failure of nerve reminiscent of Miss Gordon, does not in this novel force herself into those depths. *The Robber Bridegroom* only succeeds in raising more questions than it answers; it reveals a potential that Miss Welty is unwilling or unable to exploit. It is, in the end, no more than an affectionate effort to conjure up the romantic past, to play with legend rather than to plumb it.

Delta Wedding (1946), Miss Welty's second novel, is a far more rewarding book. Here, too, profound questions are raised, but the results, if they are not altogether successful, are much more satisfactory than is a reading of *The Robber Bridegroom*. Miss Welty's concerns here are not new: she is exploring the meaning of love — of familial and marital love. The conflicts Miss Welty uncovers lead her to an exploration of the self as it is involved in these relationships, so that the novel turns out to be, once again, about love and separateness, the subjects that Robert Penn Warren so perceptively saw at the heart of Miss Welty's work. She writes delicately and subtly, with a full awareness of the need to provide room for her probing, an awareness revealed when one of the characters is moved to reflect on how "deep were the complexities of the everyday, of the family, what caves were in the mountains, what blocked chambers, and what crystal rivers that had not yet seen light." Yet the promise of these metaphors is only partially fulfilled. Her great sensitivity inhibits the development of her power; her attention to delicate nuance lessens the possibilities for passion; and her habit of indirection narrows her range. *Delta Wedding* shows her suffering from the defects of her virtues. She is a prisoner of her limited experience. She cannot pass boldly beyond it.

But the experience she does choose to treat is finely shaped and warmly realized. The shaping is a triumph of unifying forces over diversification. The novel is told from various points of view, so that the narration of the story takes place simultaneously with an exploration of the individual consciousness of a given character. The method could easily lead to a series of scattered portraits, but Miss Welty controls the book by the use of two devices. One is the family, which in the present context functions as technique to hold things together. The other is the episode of the train crossing the trestle, which is told or thought about by several different characters in the course of the novel. Since it recurs so often and so crucially, it is a device which helps to unify the novel.

What is warmly realized is the idea of the family and the family place. The size, confusion, activity, things, fertility of the Fairchild family — all these are impressively rendered. These people draw their living from the land, occupying a large plantation with three houses; they have a numerous work force and an overseer. These facts about the novel have suggested to one critic that it is a pastoral, and certainly both the social structure depicted in the novel and the important place given the rich cotton-bearing land which supports the life of the Fairchilds lend credence to this view. The family has been long on the land and is firmly established there, so that the fact of their past becomes a cohesive force in their lives. In such a family, tradition and ritual will play an important role. The past must be kept alive in order to preserve the identity of the family, to present a model to which the present Fairchilds must conform. As in most traditional societies, the task of preservation falls to the elder members of the clan. The old Fairchild aunts are the living keepers of the past. But the entire plantation is redolent of it and possessive of it. Portraits of the Fairchild forebears are hung about; their books and diaries are testament to the presence still of this one who built the first mud hut here on the bayou or that one who was murdered on the Trace or the other one who fell in the War Between the States. The ideals of the family are embodied in Denis, not long dead, who is regarded as a Chevalier de Bayard. The myth of the family centers upon Denis, who represents its vicarious claim to honor, beauty, grace, indeed perfection.

But all the Fairchilds are people of charm. Vibrant and attractive, they feel that what they are and what they do are important. Full of this confidence (but not a sense of self-importance), they compel fate: things wait for them to appear in order to happen. When the event takes place, then the Fairchilds are there, generously of the moment. Ellen Fairchild, the mother and mistress of Shellmound plantation, sees the happiness of the Fairchilds growing out of their exuberance and satiety. A special providence watches over the Fairchilds: trains may kill other people, unknown and vagrant, but trains do not kill Fairchilds. They are the darlings of destiny. They are a unit, a complex organism that one yearns to belong to. Thus the little cousin, at first excluded, is asked to live with the family at the end and feels "part of it all."

Miss Welty is far from content, however, to give us only the idealized pastoral view of this family as a totality. Its totality is a fact, but the irony and finally the point of this novel lies in the many deviations from the collective image of the family made by its individual members. Ellen and her daughters, Dabney and Shelley, all examine the family from the inside, so to speak. Robbie Fairchild, who has married the paragon George, the living Fairchild hero, examines the family from the outside. Out of their speculations arises the conflict between conjugal and familial love.

Dabney, who is to marry the overseer, is aware that her family thinks she is marrying beneath her. Her approaching marriage weakens her bond to the family and gives her perspective on it. She is able to think that the Fairchilds are indulgent and that they substitute indulgence for real understanding. They never "looked deeper than the flat surface of any tremendous thing." As a child she had wanted all the Fairchilds to care about nothing but the family. Now, on the verge of marriage, she is herself breaking the ties to the family, as she breaks the little night light that her aunts give her for a present. Smashing the light is an unconscious declaration of her independence from the Fairchilds. She has asserted the demands of love and marriage in the teeth of familial loyalty. The irony is that the continuity of the family necessitates its disruption. Dabney will marry, will create new life on the plantation, will establish a vital relationship to its land and its creatures with her husband. The novel is about this process: the family *must* lose Dabney to a man, to love, to life itself.

Shelley, the oldest daughter, fears men and life. The fact of the male, the hovering sexual impulse, holds Shelley to the family. She wishes the family to preserve its wholeness. She approves the action of her brother George on the trestle. He had refused to jump to safety when the train approached because he was trying to free a niece who was trapped there. Shelley thinks that George's selfless act is justified by the solidarity of the family: a heroic Fairchild must be willing to die for the Fairchilds, without giving thought to his own life. Yet Shelley is perceptive enough to see that while the family presents a solid wall to the outside, each member of it is a very private person and very lonely. This observation is important because it justifies the technique of the novel — the presentation of events through the separate consciousnesses of the characters — and it reminds us once more of Miss Welty's attitude toward the mystery of personality and the separateness of people.

Robbie Fairchild also plays a part in the conflict between love and marriage. She wishes to possess her husband fully. She says she did not marry *into* the Fairchilds; she married George. Her difficulty in winning him away from the rest, as she understands, is that the Fairchilds love only themselves. They love themselves in each other, and this is why they idolize both Denis and George. It is one of the sharpest observations about familial love that Miss Welty gives us in this novel.

Of the four women, Ellen Fairchild has vision of the deepest penetration. She has a suprasensitivity: channels of knowledge are open to her through dream and intuition or even revelation. She is not happy at losing her daughter to the overseer; the loss is symbolized in the loss of a garnet pin her husband had given her — here is love twice lost. She is not happy with George's marriage. Yet as she watches George she comes to see that he has his own kind of detachment. George is ready to accept his fate. It was inevitable that he should risk his life on the trestle because he would not contest his destiny. Nor would he contest the destiny that makes him love Robbie. Through this understanding of George, Ellen comes to a critique of the Fairchilds. Their legend is happiness. But George has reached an acceptance of life which is more profound than the superficial aim of the family as a whole. George is alone, as Shelley knew each of them had to be. Alone, he shows that a man must search for his own fate and accommodate himself to his own reality. He cannot permit the family unit to absorb all experience into itself and so muffle it and make it meaningless in the static, secure bosom of the family. The meaning of marriage in the novel and the conflict of loyalties come finally to this — the need for both love and separateness. Ellen, now possessed of George's knowledge, realizes he is one who "relieved the heart's overflow" for her.

The Golden Apples (1949), Miss Welty's third novel, is an impressive book, representing a great increase in power and passion without sacrifice of subtlety or control. The several chapters of the novel appear to be short stories, but they are fused into an ordered whole by a chronological time scheme, by characters or families who appear prominently or fleetingly in all, and most of all by the community of Morgana, which is the most persuasive unifying factor. Within this rather unorthodox novelistic framework, Miss Welty employs the same themes that appeared in her earlier fiction, but she achieves here more intensity and a larger dimension than she has hitherto. Predominant among the themes is the conception of the outcast within the community — the irony of the lonely crowd. Miss Welty gives us her most profound rendering of this theme in *The Golden Apples* because she has most deeply felt and projected a sense of the community here. Clustered about this central theme are others, familiar but ancillary: the search for love and the failure to find it; the appetite for life; the desire to know the self.

"Shower of Gold," the first story or chapter, introduces this pervasive sense of community. The town functions here as a protective device; it is a unit that absorbs Snowdie MacLain and insulates her against her wayward husband. Her neighbor Miss Katie Rainey, a passing Negro, any person, acts in a common cause which is understood even though unexpressed. This solidarity of the community, which will recur, acts to shut out King MacLain, the husband, although it is true that he has chosen to alienate himself from the community. King, as the title suggests, is like a mythical fructifying force — a Zeus to Snowdie's Danaë —

and he cannot be contained in a prosaic community of ordinary mortals. He is a man who presses against the limits of life, in pursuit of himself. He does not know who he is, and in this story, quite literally, even his own sons do not know him.

In "June Recital" the community functions in the same way to exclude those who will not bend to its will or conform to its mores. It manifests itself in bodily form in the procession, like an animated frieze stately and well-ordered, of the ladies of the town who march off to their afternoon Rook game in the beginning and then march back again at the end. Their order and their serenity give the tone and create the frame for the chapter. These are the ladies who have shut out Virgie Rainey and Miss Eckhart. Virgie is like King MacLain, an *isolato*. She is different, as a child, from the other little girls: independent, unattached, wild, lower-middle-class. Miss Eckhart is different. In Morgana, Mississippi, she is a German, a Lutheran, a spinster, a cook who prepares unheard of and outlandish dishes. And so the community makes of Virgie a little tart and drives Miss Eckhart to madness. They become two human beings "terribly at large, roaming on the face of the earth" like lost beasts. They are unloved. Miss Eckhart, who did not know how to attract the love of a man, had wanted at least the love of Virgie, her best piano pupil. But Virgie had been unable to return that love.

The revelation that these two are lost comes to Cassie Morrison, a young girl, through whom we see a part of the action in the story. It is Cassie, too, who intimates that the community is guilty. These two insights represent Cassie's expanding perception and understanding. The story is about her growth too, as Cassie makes clear to us near the end, when she thinks, I am not my young brother Loch or Virgie. "She was Cassie in her room, seeing the knowledge and torment beyond her reach. . . ." Cassie is learning about herself and about the pain of life. She is learning about the difficult quest for love. In contrast, Loch, who also observes the action, understands nothing and learns nothing from it. This expansion of the limited vision of a growing girl is both a thematic and a technical device that Miss Welty uses again in the "Moon Lake" chapter of this novel.

There the expanding consciousness of Nina Carmichael, which is the center of the story, feeds and grows upon two of Miss Welty's typical preoccupations: relationships between the male and female worlds and the isolation of the outcast who is in pursuit of the self. In a predominantly female world, made up of town girls and orphans who are at camp with women counselors, one Boy Scout, Loch Morrison, bugler and life guard, makes his presence felt. He lives at the periphery of the camp, at the periphery of the girls' minds, but they are nevertheless aware of each other. In the most dramatic episode of the story, he dives into the water to rescue Easter, an orphan; he drags her out and gives her artificial respiration. As he straddles her, pumping vigorously, all the female onlookers are uneasy and Nina faints away. She does not consciously retreat from the sight of Loch apparently violating Easter, but surely the sexual overtones of this scene and the helplessness of the female are what overcome her. At the end of the story, Nina and Jinny Love Stark catch a glimpse of Loch's naked body, and again the sex of the male intrudes upon their minds. They run off, saying they will never get married.

Easter is the leader among the orphans and the most determinedly alienated among a group of outsiders. Nina wants to help her, but it is a synthetic reaction born of sentimentality. Easter rejects all offers of sympathy. Her personality is hard and depthless. Nina is forced to face the fact of Easter's alienation, even though she yearns to penetrate Easter's being and try for the "fiercest secrets." Like Cassie Morrison earlier, Nina must learn about the frustrations and the hardness of life. As for Easter, alienation and orphanage lead to puzzlement over identity: who is an orphan? Easter cannot answer the question and must, as a consequence, blindly struggle to create an identity.

The next two chapters concern the MacLain twins, the boys in the first story who failed to recognize their father. Both of them are in travail, now that they have grown to manhood. One is cut off from his wife and his father. He cries out to his father and his twin brother, who have both left Morgana, "What you went and found, was it better than this?" His special pain is the loss of his father to whom, as narrator, he addresses his story. This desertion is the chief fact in his isolation. His brother, who now lives in San Francisco, is even more an outcast upon the world. He feels himself unloved and he is cut off from his native ground in Mississippi. He spends one whole day with a Spanish guitarist, a man with a deep, mysterious trouble. They wander aimlessly over the city and by the sea, unable really to communicate with each other, both of them lost.

It is the condition of man, Miss Welty is saying in this book, to be lost, as the last chapter makes poignantly clear. Here, in "The Wanderers," she has completed the wide circle which her book describes. Miss Katie Rainey, the neighbor of the first story and the mother of Virgie, is dead. The community draws together to confront death and to honor Miss Katie now as its members never had when she was alive. The solidarity of the community is felt at the end of the book as it was at the beginning. Now that Miss Katie's contemporaries are old, a conviction sweeps over them that all men are outcasts in the world, and the fate of Virgie and King, so surely seen, is in reality the fate of all men, who must search and reach for what they will never achieve. As they look at Miss Katie dying, they are "reminded vaguely of themselves . . . now that they were old enough to see it, still watching and waiting for something they didn't really know about any longer, wouldn't recognize to see it coming in the road."

But King and Virgie, among all these people, have most pointedly typified man's lot. King, a very old man, is now home with his wife to stay. He is not satisfied. He is still a driven man, one who feels animosity at everything. Virgie is allied in spirit with him. They are people who have resisted and have been outside the pale. At the end of the story, Virgie, who seems always to have hated Miss Eckhart, has almost turned her hate into love. She remembers a picture Miss Eckhart had of Perseus holding the head of Medusa, and somehow this memory leads her to see the need of absorbing the past into one's experience so that one could go on in life. Miss Welty imposes upon that picture the burden of her ultimate meaning as Virgie comes to see it. "Cutting off the Medusa's head was the heroic act, perhaps, that made visible a horror in life, that was at once the horror in love, Virgie thought — the separateness." The meaning absorbed, Virgie is ready to meet the challenge of life, which she had faced as a young girl when she had run away from Morgana and which she must face now and always. For she feels what King must have felt, that life is a prison, a wall, that one must beat one's way through. The task is complicated by the ambiguities of life, which so many of

Miss Welty's characters recognize — notably Clement Musgrove in *The Robber Bridegroom*:

. . . that all the opposites on earth were close together, love close to hate, living to dying; but of them all, hope and despair were the closest blood — unrecognizable one from the other sometimes, making moments double upon themselves, and in the doubling double again, amending but never taking back.

In Morgana, the immutable patterns of life are repeated over and over again. The continuity of time, like the continuity of birth and death, gives life a stability men reluctantly accept since they can do no other. They know they are imprisoned in Time, but that life is meaningless without it. They know they cannot strike through the mask, but they cannot happily reconcile themselves to a doctrine of acceptance. The human dilemma, in short, victimizes Morgana, as it operates everywhere. Miss Welty transcends provincialism with *The Golden Apples*, and speaks to the world in delicate accents of penetrating impact.

Paul Bowles and the Passionate Pursuit of Disengagement

In Paul Bowles the gothic imagination had a life outside the South in the forties. Instead of the South, he used lands of primitive peoples and barren landscapes, Latin American or Arab-African civilizations, equally hospitable to the gothic. Bowles is closely related, then, to Capote, Mrs. McCullers, and Miss Welty, even though his provenance is not southern. He is also related to that nihilistic strain which we saw in the war novel, represented, for example, by Vance Bourjaily. But while these reference points help to locate him, they do not give us his unique quality. That lies, I suggest, in the intensity of his flight from the realities of the Western world. Bowles's characters are far more concerned with flight than with quest. The recognition of the failure of the West is more acute in them than their desire to find the self. It is a measure of the intensity of Bowles's nihilism that his people have, in comparison to Capote's characters, for example, so little interest and even less success in saving themselves. In an article he wrote for the *American Mercury* in 1951, Bowles has suggested, in describing the new lost generation, what his own fiction is about. This lost generation has been learning to take dope, not to achieve self-expression but to reach a state of ecstasy related in no way to intellectual or artistic endeavor. More and more Americans, Bowles said, are coming to Tangier ". . . in passionate pursuit of one thing: an absolute detachment from what is ordinarily called reality."

Reality is defined for these Americans by Western civilization, and its bitter failure is spelled out in a variety of ways in Bowles's work. He believes, it is clear, that contemporary civilization makes for alienation from the self; the flow of one's spiritual and emotional life is frozen within the benumbed consciousness. He believes that the value systems of the West have failed. The skid into moral relativism, a tactic of compromise, cannot salvage our morality or our belief. Faith in Christianity strikes him as a ludicrous refuge. The overwhelming achievement of Western civilization is to have made victims of practically everyone, to have prepared a cage for every man to occupy. Indeed, in his pessimism, Bowles finds that finally everyone, everywhere, is a victim, in the primitive civilizations as well as in the West.

Bowles's use of African and Latin American civilizations and natural settings repudiates two recognized notions in our intellectual tradition while reinforcing his own dominant view of human experience. Bowles is absolutely contemptuous of primitivism. His underdeveloped lands are not peopled by noble savages living in a harmonious relationship with Edenic nature. Primitivism originates in a revolt against a sophisticated culture. Writers who have embraced the view in the past have used natives of one place or another as a living criticism of the West. But although Bowles rejects his own culture, he does not find noble natives in another. They are simply savage. The harder environment in which they live is not superior to the West's in its moral climate. And this assertion leads to the second idea, a related one, that Bowles repudiates. The Westerner, sick with the ills of his culture, has sometimes fled to a simpler milieu to establish life-giving relationships with elemental forces. Bowles rejects the proposition that the unsophisticated culture and a "natural" environment will revivify or save Western man. Instead, in his fiction Africa and Latin America are places where men die. Or where their spirits are finally crushed. It is an expression of his total pessimism to deny the saving possibilities in primitivism and the therapeutic values of a simple life in a simple culture. That pessimism sees that nothing endures in man but evil, no matter where he is. But Africa and Latin America make the evil more palpable, more dramatic. Bowles derives power to drive home his point partly because he frustrates the sentimental expectation of salvaging the self in a primitive land. A primitive society in a desert place awakens and encourages, in his work, the savagery and mindlessness that lie at the inner essence of human beings. It is easier for Bowles to sense and communicate the real presence of evil in these places than to deal with it elsewhere. These locales are congenial to the sensibility of shock. Nature, in these climates, reveals more starkly than elsewhere its blind, indifferent face, its unconcern with the destiny of man. Bowles makes the absence of motion that he notices in the great heat of Africa correspond to the absence of life in his characters. Unfortunately, Bowles's imagination sometimes seems the feverish victim of that same heat which drives his characters to death or madness. And the wild sadism or sexual perversions of his people seem on occasion less a manifestation of the indigenous behavioral patterns than a descent to sensationalism.

The first novel Bowles wrote, *The Sheltering Sky* (1949), illustrates many of these generalizations in its story of Port and Kit Moresby, who come to North Africa searching for sanity and for each other. Port, who has ceased to love his wife, thinks that only in solitude and proximity to the infinite can he find himself. He conceives of Africa as a purgative force that will heal the wounds he has suffered in a decadent civilization. Africa proves anything but health-giving. Flies, filth, dust, and disease are everywhere. In one town is a dead fig tree wound about with barbed wire, an obvious sign of the dessication and infertility of Africa. Port dies of typhoid in this harsh country. He has not allayed his self-doubt. He has not been able once more to love his wife. Feeling alone, lost, abandoned, hopeless, and cold, cold at the very core of his being, he cannot recover the sense of purpose in existence which he had lost in the West. He represents the collapse of the intelligent and sensitive man for whom there is no place and no value that will sustain life. His soul is worn out, as we learn from his dream, and he dies from this too; this exhaustion is as much a cause as the typhoid.

Kit is a woman in whom there is a latent atavism. Her fate is to be possessed by atavistic impulses and to sink into nature, that is, into the life of the senses where she loses whatever it is that distinguishes man from the other creatures. She does not suffer from the sense of loss that afflicts her intellectual husband. She loves him and she waits for him to come back to her. When he does not, because he cannot in his spiritual bankruptcy unstop his sexual energies, she grows irritable. She needs the physical satisfactions of sex. As the West has robbed her husband of the power to love, and thus deprived her of the normal appetitive fulfilment of marriage, it has made her fearful of life. It has induced an imbalance in her life which demands righting, and is righted to such excess as to induce an imbalance on the sensual side. When her husband dies, Kit unaccountably wanders into the desert. Thought processes leave her, and she reverts to a kind of animal state. In this condition she is picked up by Arab merchants leading a caravan. They assault her; one of them takes her home with him. She lives now only for the hours of love with him. She never thinks and she hardly ever speaks. When her Arab lover, now her husband, does not come to her as often as she wishes, she breaks out of his house to seek gratification anywhere, now the victim of a burning and insatiable itch. It is fair to say that the West has destroyed in her a durable sense of balance between thought and emotion, making her the victim of a compulsive sexual urge. The sheltering sky of the title is for her an irony; under the vicious assault of that cruel sun and that blank, motionless sky, she has shed her humanity and merged with nature, where no moral judgments exist.

The meaning of the novel is conveyed in the fate of its two leading characters. The West can satisfy neither the intellectual nor the physical needs of human beings. And such people, in a state of fatal imbalance when they come to Africa, will be destroyed there. The minor characters contribute very little that is good to the novel. Tunner accompanies the Moresbys, makes love to Kit, and tries to save her after her husband's death. He serves to induce in her feelings of guilt toward her husband which contribute to the insolubility of their marital problems. He survives in Africa, as the other two do not, but Bowles fails to explain why this conventional young man deserves so kind a fate. The Lyles, mother and son, are a pair of unlikely British wanderers in the desert who seem to be sleeping together. I suppose they reinforce Bowles's conviction about the decadence of white civilization. They, and Kit's almost indefatigable Arab lover, whose cloying sexual exercises have all the horrid fascination of *The Sheik*, are hard to take seriously.

The Delicate Prey and Other Stories (1950) is dedicated to the author's mother, who first read to him the stories of Poe. The acknowledged kinship with Poe is neither with the romanticism nor the psychology of that writer. It lies in the sense of felt terror that Bowles finds as immediate and as pervasive in life as Poe did. It lies in the deliberate manipulation of horror and nightmare that both are capable of; it lies in the recognition that man is alien and alone in society and nature; and to put the best face on the matter, it lies in the courage they share in looking steadily into the real face of evil. These short stories demonstrate all the dimensions of that kinship. At the same time, Bowles goes so far in conceiving the world as amoral, in accepting the demonic and embracing the irrational, that he approaches excess; he out-Poes Poe.

Bowles conceives man as depraved and murderous in these stories. The real fellowship of men is established in their shared brutality. The real motive force in man is an anarchic sex drive that breaks out at any moment in any odd way. And since it is a force as real as any other in nature, Bowles reports its manifestations with the same objectivity that another man might apply to recording a snowstorm. In an inland Latin American town, under a blank sky, except for a vulture or two, a native with a blank mind and a blank face smokes his *grifas*, rapes a white woman, and goes home. Or a spinster in her forties suddenly takes to exposing herself and trying to seduce young Indians. The most extreme refinement in Bowles's treatment of sex is in "Pages from Cold Point," where, with great delicacy and restraint, the story is told of how a man and his son have homosexual relations and the son blackmails the father. The real fate of youth is ultimate corruption, usually coming sooner than later. The real condition of man is to be alone, for communication can never be established. The last two stories in the volume, "The Delicate Prey" and "A Distant Episode," sum up Bowles's view of man. The first, a story in which the horror mounts to nightmare proportions, shows that man preys upon man, and the second reveals a motiveless malignity. The shock of violence in these stories is the last desperate tactic by which Bowles thinks to press home his vision of a world now dead and holding no promise of life in the future.

The weakest of Bowles's first three books is *Let It Come Down* (1952), which concerns still another deracinated character who makes still another quest in Africa to find self and meaning in life. He fails, of course. He is told that since he has an empty life, he is safe from being saved. This man, Dyar, makes a greater effort at directing his life by exerting his will and making choices than any other character in Bowles's fiction to this point. But he inhabits the same world as the hollow men and his fate is theirs: "Between the idea / And the reality / Between the motion / And the act / Falls the Shadow." The absence of purpose in his life expresses itself in the demoralizing sense of motionlessness that he feels: he is trapped in the cage of cause and effect to which he has no key. He feels, as a consequence, that he is not alive, that he is beside reality instead of in it. When, at the end of the book, he senselessly kills a man, he feels he has achieved the optimum kind of participation in life: by this destructive act he has made a relationship with the rest of mankind; like everyone else, he is now beyond redemption. The novel is clumsily and inefficiently arranged, and its themes are stated explicitly rather than dramatized. But in it Bowles brings us inexorably to the country he most comfortably inhabits. It is a rock-strewn hell as barren as Eliot's waste land where love and faith and courage and honor are all impossible. Here Bowles's characters live, having chosen not to strive or suffer or endure in the real world that men commonly know. From that world they have fled, they have been forced to flee, to the hashish dream or the fruitless homosexual orgasm. This is total negativism. No one in his generation makes a more complete denial of life than Bowles.

Many of the short stories in Shirley Jackson's *The Lottery, or The Adventures of James Harris* (1949)[1] resemble closely the kind of new fiction written by Bowles, and by Capote too. Where Bowles

[1] Some other stories in this collection and the two novels she published in the period, *The Road through the Wall* (1948) and *Hangsaman* (1951), indicate she has a range beyond the gothic new fiction. A full account of her work would have to take into consideration especially her concern with old-fashioned liberal ideas.

is strident and melodramatic, she manages a low-keyed and quiet nihilism which is nonetheless almost as pervasive as his. Where both men force us to look into the uncovered face of evil, she quite matter of factly assumes its presence everywhere; indeed, her healthy-looking, apparently normal children reveal a particular appetite for contemplating violence and horror. Seemingly content to deal with ordinary experience in an ordinary way, she is always aware of the other side of consciousness, of the lurking figure, real or imagined, who leads her characters out into a strange nowhere. Her unpretentious and rather colorless prose is a suitable vehicle for the laconic expression of an equation of disintegration: as the culture seems to be going to pieces in some of these stories, so does the human personality. Her fiction is created out of this play on the incongruity between the ordinariness of her manner and the unreality of the reality that she perceives. Her dedication to a pessimistic view of experience is everywhere explicit, but occasionally it is obscured by the manipulation of her paradoxes.

THE CHILDREN OF HENRY JAMES

In the history of American fiction, the line from Henry James runs through Edith Wharton and Ellen Glasgow up to the forties and the writers of the new fiction whom I am about to discuss. The great revival of interest in James, which was in large part an enterprise pushed forward initially by critics rather than writers of fiction, began in the forties. In the preceding decade, little attention had been paid to James. The kind of realism that he had worked out and the interest in the life of society, in modes of social intercourse as a way of expressing moral attitudes — these aspects of the novel of manners fell into the hands of writers like John O'Hara and J. P. Marquand. They are not the legitimate sons of Henry James. But if we examine their work briefly — and it is appropriate to do so since they continued to publish throughout the forties, and beyond — we may discover what the novel of manners was like as it limped into the forties. We may then see, in the work of the new fiction writer, what differences were wrought from the dependence upon James.

It would be more reasonable, I suppose, to speak of O'Hara, who published four volumes in this decade,[2] in the same breath

[2] *Pal Joey* (1940), *Pipe Night* (1945), *Hellbox* (1947), and *A Rage to Live* (1949).

with Hemingway, or Ring Lardner, or even Damon Runyon than to link him to the writers of the new fiction. But the characteristic of his work I wish to point to as relevant is the knowledgeable treatment he can give to a wide variety of social phenomena, ranging from the entertainment world to the total structure — ethnic, social, political, moral — of an observed community. It is as a social historian that he carries forward, however haltingly, the tradition of the novel of manners. In O'Hara's treatment, a patina of cynicism often overlays condemnatory judgments of the superficiality or emptiness of the cherished goals in American society. The difficulty is that his work suffers from a failure of aesthetic responsibility. It is sentimental despite O'Hara's pose of hardboiled objectivity. He gives little depth to some sound insights because he cannot make his stories whole. They are fragmentary in structure, and so in meaning, because he has not the technical resources or the imaginative profundity to round them out.

Marquand, a more substantial writer, continued into the forties what he had initiated with *The Late George Apley*. His social satire, while it is repetitious, is an eminently suitable genre for an examination of the good and bad in the New England life he writes about. He studies the workings of tradition, the influence of family and place, the weight of one's total heritage. He sees the values of stability and continuity in the lives of his characters against the inertia and monotony they must suffer and the way they protect themselves from the challenges of life. He understands how societies that degenerate from experimentalism to stasis by clinging to a tradition no longer valid may become the victim of what Toynbee has called the nemesis of creativity: that is, once creative societies, suffering a setback, are unable to adapt to new conditions and assume once again a creative role. He balances the idolization of the ephemeral self against the genuine contributions of moral integrity and responsibility that came from the past. In short, Marquand commands a fruitful tension between the attraction and repulsion that he feels toward New England. There are some affinities, in this work, to the James of *The Bostonians* or of *The American Scene*, in addition to the more generalized kinship in the shared participation in the novel of manners.[3] I should add here that Gerald Warner Brace bears a

[3] The two novels of particular relevance to my discussion that Marquand published in our period are *Wickford Point* (1939) and *H. M. Pulham, Esquire*

similarly tangential relation to James. In his most successful book, *The Garretson Chronicle* (1947), he appears, however, to derive directly from Marquand. Brace's novels [4] seem always to show an unsteadiness of purpose, as much when they deal with the ambiguous meaning of the past as when they offer the idiosyncrasies of regionalism.

It is hardly necessary to say that no one of these writers matches the sensitivity or the profundity of James's psychological penetration. No one of them has depicted with such fine discriminations the life of moral intensity that James reveals to us in page after page of his fiction. The exquisitely cultivated sensibilities of his characters might have provided a model for anyone concerned with the condition of the interior life, but these writers did not learn such a lesson from James. It was his gift that he could bring alive the moral character of a type or a class, even a nation. And much of what he did successfully was the result of an unparalleled dedication in America to the craft of fiction. Those who made a real attempt to follow him were sharply aware of the great contributions he had made to the writing of fiction. They do not equal him, either. But many of them made an effort, more or less self-conscious, to imitate him, and to make important for them what had been important to him. They are careful writers, therefore, paying attention to style in a way that makes the work of O'Hara and Marquand appear rough by comparison. They cherish the psychological insight and concentrate attention upon the inner life of their characters, as the master did. The range of their fiction tends to be more narrow than his and the moral intensity less well sustained. But they are nonetheless clearly inside the Jamesian tradition instead of being on the far side of its periphery as O'Hara and Marquand are.

But it will not do to conceive that tradition too narrowly. James will have to stand as a symbol of the new fiction, too, a symbol of the revolt against naturalism and the social realism of the propaganda novel. He is the symbol of the turn toward myth and tradition, toward the investigation of the personalities of children.

(1941). Others to appear were *So Little Time* (1943), *Repent in Haste* (1945), *B. F.'s Daughter* (1946), *Point of No Return* (1949), and *Melville Goodwin, USA* (1951), referred to in the chapter on the war novel.

[4] In addition to the title above, they include in our period *Light on a Mountain* (1941), *A Summer's Tale* (1949), and *The Spire* (1952).

Frederick Buechner illustrates this need for a more inclusive conception of the Jamesian tradition in his *A Long Day's Dying* (1950), which belongs there, especially in its stylistic indebtedness, but which also draws upon a traditional religious notion of absolution and T. S. Eliot's ideas for the use of myth. It is enough merely to mention this novel here, since it has been analyzed by John W. Aldridge in *After the Lost Generation*; the only cavil I have with Aldridge's discussion is that it devotes more space to the book than it merits. In its reworking of the Tereus and Philomela story, the novel conveys the impression of a formal exercise in the techniques of the new fiction. It fails to give the myth the immediacy that would justify its use in our time. In fact, the book seems to deal almost perversely with what is not-life in such a way as to exclude the possibility of genuine involvement with human passions or ideas.

The new fiction is much dependent upon the psychological *aperçu*. For this reason it is attracted to the themes of maturation and the initiation into evil. These are handled by dealing with the interior life of the characters, who are of course children. William Maxwell and Mark Schorer share interest in such matters. Maxwell has written a novel in which he traces the growth of a young boy. At the beginning the boy is an incipient homosexual, dependent on a friend who represents both mother and father to him. At the end the boy achieves spiritual independence, signified by a dream of the death of his friend. Schorer reveals in his short stories a sympathetic understanding of the relationship between parents and children, conveying the felt sense of the difficulties of communication between the generations and the hazards of so unequal a dialogue. He is sensitive to the way in which children may be victimized by the pressures in the lives of adults. The effect of his preoccupation with children is to domesticate the problems of the social scene; his stories gain, in this way, in particularity but they lose in breadth. They are cloistered but manageable. Louis Auchincloss' particular psychological interest, in the one volume he published in this period, is in the outsider whose responses fail to meet normal expectations and fall outside the pattern as given. In addition, Auchincloss has taken over the fictional domain once so ably governed by Edith Wharton; he is a novelist of manners with a sensitively developed moral sense.

His people are well-placed New Yorkers, and his locales range from good city clubs to Bar Harbor, Maine. None of these writers made a deep impression upon the forties, nor did they produce a sizable body of work. They seemed to be what the forties had produced for the next decade. They should have pointed out the direction American fiction would take in the fifties. But the promise of the new fiction was not in them fulfilled.[5]

Schorer knows that the quality of life is not summed up in the facts of life. He understands further, even if his stories do not well convey it, the imperative need to engage oneself in the experience of life, a need so memorably recognized by James. What he has momentarily grasped, Brendan Gill has managed to express with subtlety and irony in an admirable novel, *The Trouble of One House* (1950). The irony so characteristic of the new fiction is embodied here in the character of Elizabeth Rowan, a dying woman who is yet a vital force. She is at the center of the book, and her influence radiates out from her bed to affect the lives of all who know her. She is quick and clever, with a mind that sees through hypocrisy to the unspoken. She has a wit and charm that compel us to accept the tough-mindedness she shows in facing truth, particularly the fact of her own imminent death. She is a woman with the kind of intuitive wisdom that reminds one of Mrs. Wilcox in E. M. Forster's *Howards End*. As a mother, a wife, and a friend, she is life-giving. And she is love-giving. When she dies, the Monsignor, who has loved her, finds that he has lost the main support in his life and that he is suddenly an old man. Her young confessor is awakened to the meaning of love. Her cynical and empirical nurse and her repressed doctor are released into love for each other by her example in life and by her death. But her husband and her sister hate her for her perfection. In this perverse reaction is a second irony that must balance the first. For these two characters have found perfection a reproach to their own shortcomings. Their rejection of Elizabeth, while it is a measure of their incapacity for love, is at the same time an all-too-human response to unassailable virtue. Gill knows enough to introduce discord where life is apparently perfect, and he has

---

[5] The discussion in this paragraph is based on *The Folded Leaf* (1945) and *Time Will Darken It* (1948) by William Maxwell; *The State of Mind* (1947) by Mark Schorer; and *The Injustice Collectors* (1950) by Louis Auchincloss.

given Elizabeth a husband who cannot return her love and who brings on her death. For Gill, evil is the failure to love, which is the denial of life. The triumph of such evil is destruction, as her husband destroys Elizabeth, but the rewards of evil are alienation of the self and isolation from the warm community of men. Elizabeth's husband discovers this in the end, when, alone, he must face his children in the knowledge that they will grow to hate him. The work of virtue, on the other hand, is the affirmation of life. The radiance of virtue shines forth even in apparent defeat, since even in death Elizabeth reveals to others the moral and emotional possibilities in life.

The Two Worlds of Jean Stafford

Jean Stafford is the finest exemplar of the Jamesian tradition in her generation. A true daughter of James, she gathers together various strands in the fictional practice of her contemporaries, writing social satire that is reminiscent of Marquand and exploring the maturation theme as Schorer and Maxwell do. But these superficial resemblances to others do not convey the quality of the exquisite sensibility that she has dedicated to the pursuit of psychological realism in her work, an approach which James showed her the way to and which Freud, as she acknowledges, both deepened and illuminated for her. "To be writers, then," she has said, "we must be good psychologists, and this is only another way of saying that we must be experts in the study of reality and cool judges of our own natures." In this enterprise of studying and judging, writers are indebted to Freud, for he has "made our moral attitudes more humane and he has modified our habits of observation, making us more alert to our conduct and to the patterns and symbols of our experience, enriching our insights, sharpening our sense of meaning." This psychological vision, which she so intensely cultivates, is one of her chief aids in drawing the fine distinctions that characterize her work and link her in still another way with James. These distinctions arise out of her concern with the interior consciousness of her characters, where much of the action in her fiction takes place, and issue in the moral relations she establishes among her people. James and Freud join forces, then, to teach her how to see, from a psychological and moral point of view, what must be the consistent business of the novel, which is always concerned, she says, with "emotional motivations and their intellectual resolutions, with instincts and impulses and conflicts and behaviour, with the convolutions and complexities of human relationships, with the crucifixions and solaces of being alive."

She has had other teachers as well, to join those two, who only appear to be an odd combination. Dostoevski, whom Nietzsche regarded as a great psychologist, makes his presence felt especially in the first part of her first novel, although he has a continuing influence upon her. His special ability to summon his imaginative resources for a scene of excessive emotionalism or of erratic human behavior seemed to present Miss Stafford with a model of power in the writing of fiction. She seems also to have been moved by Dostoevski's penetration to the dark truths that lie below the surface of human reason. She knows from Dostoevski that rending mixture of love and hate in the human personality which makes for the complexities of human relationships. Although she did not mention Proust in a list of favorite authors she once compiled, her manipulation of time and her sharp awareness of the presentness of the past remind us readily of this writer. And finally she has drawn upon Jane Austen's accomplishments in the drawing room. She gives a more muscular and less disciplined account of life there than Miss Austen does, but it is nonetheless laced with the sharpness of wit and the depth of perception that so consistently marks the writings of Jane Austen.

The uses to which she puts her mixed and celebrated literary heritage are very much her own. The prevailing pattern in her fiction is to exploit a conflict in contrasting spheres of experience; her stories emerge as the fruits of the tension thus generated and of the differences thus exposed. The process is not a dialectic, because Miss Stafford is not intent upon a synthesis. But this is not to say that her fiction is static. The movement, the development, in her stories takes place independently within each sphere, and sometimes simultaneously. This pattern of conflict prevails in two major areas in her work: it may take the form of a clash of cultures, or it may be seen in the division of the self represented by the conscious and the unconscious levels of human experience. The two worlds of her fiction are the social world of cultural differences and the psychic world. And within the social world are many contrasts: between national groups, Americans and Germans, for example; or between regional groups, representing New England and the West, for example; or between outsiders, like European immigrants, and insiders, like the Boston aristocracy; or between the world of the adult and the world of the child. Often, as she manages the conflicts that arise from differing cultural allegiances and moral standards, she is at the same time slipping back and forth between the conscious and unconscious minds of her characters to record in depth the impact of these conflicts. It is the carefully traced and felt intricacies of this complicated procedure that give the depth and intensity to Miss Stafford's fiction.

Her first novel, *Boston Adventure* (1944), is an exciting if not altogether successful examination of two such social worlds — the European transplanted to America and the Boston aristocracy — treated in such a way as to conjoin in one work the manner of both Dostoevski and James. The heroine of the book is Sonie Marburg, the child of German-Russian parents who have come to Massachusetts. She is the first of many outsiders who people Miss Stafford's fiction. She yearns to cast off what is to her an unsavory and unclean European heritage and to identify herself with Boston. The book charts her movement from one world to another, a movement marked by explosions of consciousness at critical moments that bring her to knowledge and a sense of her self. Sonie finds that the world she had longed for will admit her only to its fringes and that to exist in it at all she must surrender her will and the hope of love and marriage. In Miss Stafford's work, the pursuit of cherished goals or the escape into zones of greater brightness or freedom than one had previously inhabited is inevitably accompanied, when successful at all, by a recognition of the cost and the vanity of human striving. It must be clear that Miss Stafford writes about her characters with an air of detachment. Her special forte, the fruit of maintaining her disciplined distance from them, seems to be a vision capable of capturing them in three-dimensional perspective.

The first part of the novel deals with the displaced Europeans. The vital forces of the Marburg family are dissipated in a chaotic effort to survive in an alien culture. The family collapses because, in its undisciplined and heedless way, it surrenders whatever stabilizing elements it might have brought from the Old World and clings to that part of its heritage which has the least survival value in America. The father has renounced his Catholicism, which might have been a refuge in Puritan Massachusetts. He thus inflicts upon Sonie a sense of guilt and alienation from both God and man. He persists, on the other hand, in an ideal of craftsmanship, an anachronism in a mass production society, which brings his family the meanest kind of poverty and makes Sonie feel apart from the dominant culture. The precarious position of the family and the deep psychic disturbances felt by its members (including Sonie) account for the monumental quarrels that work to destroy it. Sonie detests her family and wants to escape from it. Her alienation is thus double: from the culture in which she is a stranger and from the family from which she is essentially estranged. It is this condition which induces in her the daydream in which she meets a Harvard student named Andrew Eliot Cabot Lodge, who falls passionately in love with her. She does not want to be outside the dominant culture, but inside.

Miss Stafford has made no frontal attack on the problems of the foreign-born in this novel, or on the question of acculturation. She has said that the novelist is not a social-political messiah, any more than he is a doctor, an evangelist, or a crank. She is not a sociologist. This first part of the novel, however, demonstrates how the perceptive imagination may open to our understanding the nature of a sociological phenomenon. The scope of Miss Stafford's achievement in *Boston Adventure* is enlarged by the inclusion of this social dimension. But that achievement is only partially recorded in the account of the Marburgs; it broadens when we turn to the second half of the book for a consideration of the Boston aristocracy.

There, in an effort to identify herself with the dominant culture, Sonie makes a liaison with Miss Pride, a wealthy Boston spinster who lives in Louisburg Square. Miss Stafford arranges such a fate for her in order to cast a cold eye upon a Boston dominated by a Puritanism from which the religious element has long since departed. Miss Pride is a latter-day Puritan who is convinced that the stewardship of the elect properly maintains control over the totality of society. But while the Puritan will to leadership survives in Miss Pride, and the externals of behavior dictated by

Puritanism, as well, the deep-lying moral impulse of the **Puritan** has evaporated. And the Puritan regard for the works of the **mind** has become in Miss Pride a complacent anti-intellectualism.

Miss Stafford has not been kind to Miss Pride as the Boston patrician. Her examination of proper Boston society as a whole sometimes takes on the air of parody as she conducts her comedy of manners with a good deal of exaggeration, laying about her with broad strokes and broad comments. Her Bostonians utter platitudes so firmly and courteously that their opinions seem indisputable. Miss Stafford wants us to see that these self-appointed gods have feet of clay. She is content to show us the limitations, even the decay, of this native American culture, just as she revealed the disintegration of a displaced European culture. Yet she makes Sonie, who knows the superficiality and the evil in it, choose the former, because the half-life of tradition it offers her represents the ballast that will hold her to sanity.

The promise and dimensions of Miss Stafford's achievement are foreshadowed in *Boston Adventure*. The sensitive exploration of Sonie's interior castle, where, in her psychic depths, she fights the fear of madness, is an indication that Miss Stafford has committed herself to psychological techniques in fiction. These she will develop in succeeding novels and stories as she works toward her own particular mode of writing. The Puritan conscience, which is here given a satirical treatment reminiscent of that in Marquand's work, is a subject to which she will return, although in another vein. The Jamesian manner in the second part of this novel she will come to dominate more successfully later on; here she lacks the finish, the subtlety, and the assurance of the master, and, as a consequence, often overextends her prose — makes it too rich and too complicated — in an effort to attain a density of tone and meaning that she is not yet ready to command. The writing of this novel may have convinced her that she lacks the direct, brutal force of Dostoevski, and his is an influence that diminishes perceptibly in the course of her career, although it does not entirely disappear. Finally, the strategy of contrasting worlds, applied here to give both range and tension to her fiction, is carried forward in other books.

The Mountain Lion (1947), Miss Stafford's second novel, revolves around two themes: the necessary separateness of human beings, which is achieved in the process of maturation and individuation, and the conflict between polar worlds, one inhibiting growth and life-awareness and the other free with all the dangers attendant upon freedom. Again we have the alienated personality, wandering through the uncharted territory of the inner self in search of definition. The mountain lion, used in the resolution of the novel, represents Miss Stafford's effort to introduce a symbolic level of meaning into her story; the use of a large-scale symbol is a departure from her practice in the first novel.

The attack on the maturation theme is double, since it is the growth of two children that this novel charts. They are bound together in the beginning in their mutual hostility to their mother and two older sisters. Ralph and Molly are thus estranged from their family and made into outsiders. They turn to each other in a relation of love and dependence, which for a while satisfies a great need, especially in Molly. But such love cannot withstand the processes of growth, and Ralph in particular begins to feel the necessity for aloneness and the demands of his ego for freedom; he comes also to some dim consciousness of his sex. The more intensely introverted Molly, who wants to marry her brother, senses his disengagement. She tries to disfigure herself with acid in order to punish him. The destructive rage generated by the tension in their relationship turns in upon itself in Molly. In the end, full of hatred for everyone in her estrangement, she comes of course to self-hatred. But the hatred that Ralph feels for Molly, mingling with his love for her, begins to lead to an unconscious wish for her death. She comes to represent for him, all unknowingly, the feminine principle that stands as the obstacle to the full expression of maleness. In the inevitable assertion of his manhood as a part of the individuation process, he kills his sister, shooting at the mountain lion, in an accident that is the unconscious expression of his wish.

That fatal act, which declares Ralph's independence and growth, is the culmination of a maturation process that Miss Stafford has carefully prepared. That process is accompanied by feelings of embarrassment and guilt as the demands of sex begin to insinuate themselves into their lives. The decisive moment in which the knowledge of good and evil comes to them, the moment when their childhood ends, is figured forth in a Freudian metaphor of a tunnel. The children are born into the world, so to speak, emerging from the railroad tunnel as from the trauma of birth. They come into the valley, where the knowledge of life awaits them.

The growth of the children, especially of Ralph, is made possible by their breaking away from the world of their mother and entering the world of their Grandfather Kenyon and Uncle Claude. The mother stands for a safe, cloistered, effete, respectable, merchant world. (Merchant, obviously, is a pejorative word in Miss Stafford's work.) Although she lives in California in a world of nature, she clings to the conventional, urban standard of St. Louis, which her father had represented to her. The atmosphere of her home is full of moral and cultural uplift and only a little hypocritical. It is a feminine, middle-class home whose air is stultifying to the two children. They look with unclouded vision at the ugly truths in it that the older people can no longer recognize. Miss Stafford has made her critique of the artificial and the pretentious in middle-class life through the irony of giving true perception and wisdom of a superior order to the young.

Grandpa Kenyon, by contrast, has the vitality and the appetite of a god. His son Claude inherits much of his simplicity and directness. Ralph and Molly are drawn to them. Life on Claude's Colorado ranch is on a scale which at first frightens the children when they visit for a summer. The mountains overpower them, the food in its rough amplitude sickens them, and the behavior of the others, so independent of law and restriction, amazes them. But in time Ralph especially grows to love this ruggedly masculine and freely appetitive life, learning to shoot and watching the cows calve. It fosters growth in the open air. It is during the year that the children are left by their mother on the ranch with Claude that Ralph kills Molly. In a sense, then, her death is the consequence of being deprived of parental supervision, an action on the mother's part as unconscious as Ralph's own motives in the shooting. In another sense her death is a sign of the cost of growth in an environment of undisciplined nature to which she is abandoned. Her death is the toll exacted by the freedom of that environment. And here is where the mountain lion enters as symbol. For it must stand, in one way or another, for the random, uncontrolled forces of nature which are neither predictable nor governable but with which one must take his chances. Man must contend with them in order to win to a healthy life, but they are just as likely to take life as to give it. But I advance this interpretation of the mountain lion rather tentatively, because I feel that Miss Stafford has not sufficiently realized its symbolic meaning. This mountain lion as symbol is pretty much a failure when compared to the symbolic lion in Walter Van Tilburg Clark's *The Track of the Cat*, which I shall discuss in the next chapter. Miss Stafford's lion does not make its presence felt throughout the book, and so is not prepared to carry the burden of thematic resolution that is imposed upon it. Nor does it contain a range of meanings or give rise to serried implications as the well-wrought symbol should.

If the book fails on the symbolic level, it succeeds elsewhere. In its depiction of the adolescent outsider as victim — for Molly is this, a child who can survive in neither the genteel air of her home nor the free air of the ranch — Miss Stafford has conveyed once again her sense of the tortured impasse that life can bring us to. Molly's is the tragedy of the maladjusted personality whose journey toward selfhood will never be completed. Her story is part of the maturation theme as Ralph's is. His growing up is attained at great cost, almost as though, Miss Stafford might claim, one has to exchange a partial life for a whole life. And it is that yearning toward completeness in life that Ralph represents in his urge to be a defined and whole individual. This urge links the growth-and-individuation theme in the novel to the conflict-of-two-worlds theme. For the children instinctively reject a world which imposes a rigid pattern upon them, their mother's world where the personality must maim or twist itself in order to fit properly in a proper niche. The world of freedom, even if it brings death, is better than this when one must search out the secrets of growth.

On the whole, *The Catherine Wheel* (1952) is better than the two novels which precede it. It does not have the range or the violent energy of *Boston Adventure*, but it achieves greater solidity by replacing the occasional note of farcical comedy in treating an aristocratic milieu with an assured approach to the same matter that yields greater understanding. Miss Stafford's mastery of the Jamesian moral tradition in this later novel is demonstrable in her treatment of the treachery and guilt that stand at its very center. She here penetrates to the heart of the Puritan consciousness, whereas in *Boston Adventure* she had managed only a rather stylized formulation of this theme. As this novel has a moral intensity that neither of the others has shown, it also reaches a psychological depth that neither of the others has plumbed. In this respect, too, she draws closer to the master, capturing the reality that lives wildly in the secret recesses of man's being. In place of range, then, it has the merits that arise from intense and concentrated cultivation. The fruits of such cultivation are nowhere more apparent than in her handling of the major symbolic device in the novel. The catherine wheel as symbol does virtually everything that the mountain lion failed to do. This novel is dedicated principally to the investigation of the complex relationship between moral guilt and the psychic life. It is built on the two-world pattern — here opposing and combining two generations, age and youth, as well as the past and the present — that serves usually as Miss Stafford's structural device. It is the finest example of its kind that the new fiction produced in the years after the war. *The Catherine Wheel* is a disciplined and completed book.

The story concerns Andrew Shipley, another of Miss Stafford's adolescent outsiders, who comes to spend the summer with his Cousin Katharine at her ancestral home, Congreve House, in a town called Hawthorne. But he is not happy because his best friend in Hawthorne, Victor Smithwick, is caring for a sick brother and is not free to play with him. Andrew begins to wish for the brother's death so that Victor will be free. His Cousin Katharine is once more deeply involved with John Shipley, Andrew's father, whom she had loved and lost many years ago. She had wished for the death of John's wife, and now she wishes for Andrew's death because she is afraid that he has perceived her guilty relationship with his father. Andrew and Katharine bear their burden of guilty wish through the summer, suffering increasing pain as the days pass, until Katharine is killed at a fireworks display. The moral life of the book takes place, then, inside the characters and is manifested in judgments they pass upon themselves; we get minimal public expression of the moral crises they undergo. Nor do they commit immoral acts during the summer in which the action of the book takes place. External action is of little consequence in this novel. It is the interior drama that we must fasten our attention upon. It is the kind of dark story, in its moral and psychological life, that Nathaniel Hawthorne might have written, a name that comes readily to mind in this New England locale.

Andrew is made an outsider so that his alienation may produce his guilt. He is estranged from his fellows at school because he is too small to play their games. He is estranged from his family at home. His parents are troubled by a sense of their disintegrating marriage, although his father, a self-centered man, had never helped him, and his twin sisters seem naturally to shut him out. At Hawthorne he is shut off from his anticipated companionship with Victor. It is when he is disappointed, bored, excluded from society that he begins to wish for the death of Victor's brother. He comes to see the brother as the embodiment of all his frustrations and loneliness. But he cannot entertain this wish for the brother's death without a sense of guilt. He thinks that Katharine knows what he is wishing, that she hears the voice in him saying, "Charles Smithwick, die." He suffers from the almost intolerable intensity of his guilt feeling.

The moral assumptions in this boy's life are unquestioned. They come to him, we must suppose, from the tradition in which he has been raised. When we turn to Cousin Katharine, we are able to understand the impact of the past upon the characters in the novel. Katharine's refined and civilized way of life is a heritage from the past, and so is her code of conduct. Her tradition demands self-control over tightly disciplined emotions. It demands that she confront her unhappy fate with courage: she must face up to her lot in life. It demands that she give up the man for whom she has been hungry through a lifetime, for will must triumph over appetite and order over inclination. It demands that she suffer for her sin and go on suffering to the end, because man is never free of his sin. Her moral code, obviously, comes from the Puritans. Her failure to live up to it is destroying her. The Puritan past stands in stern judgment upon her, and she submits to it. The civilized way of life, which developed out of the wealth that Puritanism was able to accumulate and pass down to its heirs, reveals the past as irony. The manner is from the past, the sophisticated, literate manner of a sensitive aristocracy, but beneath the manner are the realities of sin: Katharine's assignations, during the preceding winter, with John Shipley; her treachery to his wife, who innocently confides in Katharine about the affections of her husband that Katharine has alienated; the secret wish, that eats at her bowels, that Andrew die.

Katharine loves the past because, she thinks, it is completed. It has the charm of old ways and things. She lives with it, feeling that it is unchanging, but not in it; she is not old-fashioned. But to live with the past is to live with the wounds that mark one's own history. If she wishes to enjoy the stability and dignity of her heritage, she must also suffer from the memory of her rejection, in the past, by John Shipley. The past keeps intruding into the present. Her spinsterhood now is the result of what happened to her in the past; she has, in other words, deprived herself of fulfilment in marriage because of the past. And the malevolent pain that she feels now, she has lived with since John Shipley rejected her. It is a gift from the past. The generations have labored to make of her a polished shell, a thing of grace and beauty, but inside the shell she is going to pieces, the victim of pain and guilt furnished by the so-called finished past.

Andrew and Katharine, deeply troubled through this summer, are guilt-laden souls tortured by their own consciences. The trouble of each, caged within, makes each feel the other suspects him. They are locked the summer long in a loving relationship of unadmitted, mutual suspicion, an intensely dramatic relationship in which they prey upon each other. They suffer from insomnia, nightmare, fainting fits, nagging voices they hear within, all signs of the deep psychic disturbances that guilt has induced in them both. Still another irony of the book is uncovered in the mortal antipathy these two feel, since, instead of enmity, it has always been Andrew's experience that Cousin Katharine would offer him her unchanging affection in beautifully unchanged Congreve House. But the generations find themselves, despite themselves, at war — with themselves and with one another. The escape from guilt, for Katharine, is to give up John Shipley and thus renounce the adultery and the hypocrisy that now threaten her; and to burn her diary, in which she has fully recorded the pain of her loss through the lonely years. She will rise purified from the ashes of the diary, but such a purgative ritual, she knows, will not really free her. It is she who must burn. Fire will free her then.

Miss Stafford prepares Katharine's doom with great care. The voices of guilt within her are the messengers of her destiny. It is with some dim sense of an overwhelming fate that she orders her tombstone, a *memento mori* that consoles her in much the same way that Sam Sewall, that old Puritan merchant, found solace in the stored and ready coffins in his barn. And Miss Stafford uses the people of the town like a monitory Greek chorus, a public voice muttering of the tragedy to come. Katharine gives a party, the climax to be a fireworks display in which catherine wheels will be set off. Victor's brother, now recovered, is to light the fireworks. His hair catches fire as he tries to light one wheel. It seems he will perish after all, in accordance with Andrew's wish, by Cousin Katharine's catherine wheel. But Cousin Katharine dashes in to put out the fire, catches fire herself, runs screaming in a circle, a living catherine wheel, and dies.

Catherine of Alexandria was tortured on a catherine wheel in the fourth century. And it was by the light of a catherine wheel in a fireworks display that Cousin Katharine had seen that John Shipley had no eyes for her, but only for her cousin, whom he will marry. Miss Stafford introduces two literal meanings of the term, then, into her story — it is an instrument of torture and a firework — and proceeds to work from this two-footed base into the realm of symbolic meaning. Providing herself in the beginning with a term rich in resources in its double meaning, she creates what E. K. Brown has called an expanding symbol, one which is built up and given layers of meaning throughout a work as are the various musical themes of Vinteuil in Proust. The Proustian character of this novel is to be seen not alone in Miss Stafford's manipulation of the past-present time relationship, which has already been discussed, but in her treatment also of a pervasive symbol which unifies her entire book. The price of her careful workmanship in the exploitation of her symbol is the danger of making her meaning too explicit. The symbol must not lose that necessary power of concealment and subtlety that gives mystery and ambiguity, as has a greatly rendered symbol like the white whale, say, in *Moby-Dick*.

Whatever its shortcomings, Miss Stafford's catherine wheel is an admirable symbol in many ways. As Saint Catherine was tortured in body upon it, Katharine is spiritually tortured on her imaginary wheel throughout the book by her loss of John. At

times it becomes a whirling wheel within her as her guilt and
her longing writhe together to create a profound spiritual disquiet in her. It is her own rueful self-analysis that moves her to
link her name and her fate with the wheel by having one engraved
on her tombstone. It is the kind she has lived on as on a rack,
not the kind she has seen by — seen disaster — and that will kill
her. For in life as in the act of dying, she is a living catherine
wheel. She is a wheel of guilty fire that consumes her spirit and
at the end a wheel of living fire that destroys her body. The wheel
rolls through the novel as the great moral agent in this tragedy
of guilt and sin. It is the inevitably rolling wheel that brings the
real purgation by fire, the total destruction that is the inescapable
end for the sinner.

In 1953 Miss Stafford published *The Interior Castle*, an omni-
bus volume which contained a collection of short stories called
Children Are Bored on Sunday. All these had appeared between
1945 and 1950. (In the same period she published additional
stories in various periodicals, but these have not yet been collected.) The stories in this volume have the brilliant surface sheen
that we have come to expect from the fiction that appears in
the *New Yorker*, where many of them were first published. But
they are not superficial. Built around the clash of two worlds, the
conscious and the unconscious as well as national or regional
polarities, they reach, especially in their psychological penetration,
far down into the recesses of the human personality. Sometimes one
has the feeling that they are nothing more than exercises in Miss
Stafford's talent for insight or for psychological empathy, as in
"The Interior Castle," a concentrated study of pain which in the
end is only a tour de force. In the stories involving a clash of cultures, Miss Stafford is ironic and disciplined, always giving her
loyalties conditionally in recognition of the universal fallibility
of man. "The Bleeding Heart" is a plant in the story of that name,
but the title refers also to a Mexican girl who deludes herself,
idealizes the New England character, and then must face the realities of an impoverished and decadent New Englander, who is
himself something of a bleeding heart. This story, where the irony
compels our perception of the difference between reality and
appearance, is one of the few that presents a fully rounded form.
Many are wanting in a design for the whole that gives the aesthetic

satisfaction of completion. Few are astir with the moral overtones of Miss Stafford's imagination when it burns most brightly.

Charles Feidelson, Jr., has argued that modern American literature began with the turn toward symbolism in the mid-nineteenth century. Miss Stafford's work is the expression, in the forties, of that continuing tradition in which the moral life of the novel has centered in its symbolism. I have not been able to speak of her fiction without reference to Hawthorne and Melville. Her achievement has been to carry on what they started. Finding in James a similar morality, she might have passed him over. But he offered her a different manner, and this was decisive. It is what makes her a writer of the new fiction, a writer for whom style always counts, and counts for more than it did with Hawthorne or with Melville. It is her style that is the enabling instrument in the fabrication of her irony and her symbols, that bares to us the truth of her psychological insights. She shows us, then, how the new fiction is in reality a continuation of a certain line in American fiction and has its roots in a past which still nourishes it. This is a different line from the one to which Capote and Bowles are attached, the one that runs from Poe. Seen together, the two lines place the new fiction in a proper perspective, confirm its Americanism, and demonstrate that its newness lies in making the old current

CHAPTER SEVEN

IN SEARCH
OF MAN
AND AMERICA

THE FICTION OF THE FORTIES AND THE
EXISTENTIAL CRISIS

In its largest dimension, the crisis in the culture of the forties was an existential crisis. The theme of self-discovery that runs through the fiction of this period reveals the intense preoccupation of writers with the problems of the self; it reveals the struggle to define and shape a relationship between the self and American culture. In one context or another we have seen, in the preceding pages, how writers dealt with these problems at a time when the culture seemed in many ways particularly inhospitable to the survival of the self. The writers I shall consider here make four different responses to the existential crisis as they test the proposition that alienation from the culture is the price one must pay for self-realization. Walter Van Tilburg Clark is overborne by this crisis and seems to reject man and accept the world of nature. Wallace Stegner represents a failure in the quest for the self because he has not resolutely cut his ties to the culture. Wright Morris searches for man under the dead weight of the past; he rises to the challenge of the crisis with an effort to remove the weight and find the man buried under it. Finally, Saul Bellow responds to the crisis by seeing the self as triumphant and free. He gives full expression to a seriously tried yet insistently romantic conception of the self as all in all.

In philosophy, European existentialism was the expression of this intensely felt need to reclaim man in a twentieth-century world that seemed bent on destroying him. Thus Karl Jaspers speaks of the necessity of engaging oneself in the human situation, without illusions, with full knowledge of suffering, conflicts, faults, bonds; he urges men to go forward as though the promise of an abundant life might nevertheless be realized. From quite different original assumptions, Trilling and Warren came to an understanding of this need. But neither Clark nor Stegner, as much as they are aware of the problem, can bring themselves to a face to face meeting with it. Sartre and Heidegger, rejecting God, make the main business of philosophy, as Marjorie Grene says, the inner odyssey of the self seeking the self. Each individual must forge his self and find his essence out of senseless circumstances and meaningless limitations. This view illuminates the position that Bellow works out in his fiction. I am not arguing for the influence of existentialism upon American fiction in the forties; surely there was precious little. But I am claiming, first, that Americans were trying to meet in literature the same dangers to the existence of man as man that Europeans were meeting in philosophy; and, second, that Americans were reaching, more or less independent of Europeans, similar conclusions. They pursued their task against an American background in which the history and geography, indeed the total life, of America played a part and colored their conclusions: the Far West is in the work of Clark and Stegner, the Nebraska town and plain in Morris, the great city in Bellow.

The existential problem, like existentialism itself, is not new. William A. Orton has suggested that the whole tendency of Bergson's philosophy in the nineteenth century and of Whitehead's in our own "is toward a revendication of personality against the encroachments both of a mechanically conceived universe and a collectively conceived society." The statement implies that the uncertain relationship of man to the cosmos and to his culture has a long history; it is an outgrowth of the disintegration of belief that began with the Renaissance, and of all the problems introduced by science, the emergence of laissez-faire economics, and the rise of the nation state. While these historical developments encouraged the growth of individualism, they also made the existence and stature of man in the modern world debatable questions. Simply to mention such developments is to catch a glimpse of the larger background which lies behind the impulse toward personalism or the self in modern fiction. As for existentialism, William Barrett has devoted a book to showing that this philosophy has a long history. Nevertheless, it speaks with particular urgency to the contemporary mind. If man has always been in a stage of crisis, he must have felt, he did feel, in the forties that he was in the throes of an especially deadly struggle. His culture threatened to obliterate him. Even his history might work to efface him or to bury him. It is against the background of this existential crisis that I believe we can profitably look at the four writers treated in this chapter.

WALTER VAN TILBURG CLARK: AMID CONFUSION, THE TRIUMPH OF NATURE

No writer belongs more firmly in the forties than Walter Van Tilburg Clark, if one is to judge from his thematic preoccupations and his literary strategies. Neither society nor ideology has any interest for him. In making a specific and energetic rejection of the whole complex of societal themes, he has turned his back on the spirit of urbanism and cosmopolitanism which ordinarily nourishes such themes. His work bears a superficial resemblance to the new fiction, but his emphases are ultimately quite different. True, he presents the sensitive and artistic young man and the poignant, stirring childhood experience. True, he offers a deliberate and extended manipulation of symbol. But when he writes of the maturation of characters who undertake a search for their identities, he moves away from the new fiction. His characters are impelled by the existential crisis. And they search for themselves by trying to discover their relationship to natural, cosmic forces. Clark moves in the open air that the new fiction seldom breathes. The ethical problems which he treats, probing the Laocoön-like entanglements of good and evil and the ambiguities of morality, bear a closer resemblance to the ethical realism of Cozzens, say, than to any moral quality in the new fiction. Finally, it must be said that Clark has withdrawn, that is, withdrawn from the world of man because he has given up faith in man. Such a surrender of faith lies in part behind Bowles's nihilism, but in Clark it has led to a kind of dualism. Withdrawing from the world of men, despite his interest in maturation, he has come, unsteadily and hesitatingly, to prefer the non-human world of nature. The values he admires, finally, are those he finds inherent in nature. The nature he deals with is the one he finds in the West.

The regional character of Clark's fiction is apparent at once, in his first published novel, *The Ox-Bow Incident* (1940). The novel deals with traditionally western matter: the pursuit of cattle rustlers by a posse and a lynching. But the regional quality of the novel is not its outstanding characteristic. Like much other fiction of the forties, *The Ox-Bow Incident* offers a deliberate commingling of social and moral issues. It is Clark's only fiction, except for the uncollected short story "Letter to the Living," in which he chooses a subject with specific and obvious social implications. But the social problem in this novel serves only as an occasion for what is essentially a philosophic investigation. Clark's interest here is in the moral nature and destiny of man, not in the social consequences of violence and injustice.

In this novel Clark views man critically and unsympathetically. Most of the characters are members of the posse, and some of them are simple stereotypes: the town drunkard and the deputy sheriff are moved only by an appetite for evil and violence. The leader of the posse, Major Tetley, is a vicious, predatory man. His son sees the father as one who must feed upon other men, killing them for sustenance. The major loves cruelty, and he yearns for power. The uncomplicated sadism of these characters is not matched by the majority of the posse. Most of the others are sheeplike victims of emotional appeals, to be sure; but since they are not committed to evil, some vestige of decency in them causes them to struggle with themselves, if only feebly, before they accept injustice. Being ordinary men faced with a challenge to direct action in the best western tradition of heedless virility, they do not have the courage to consult their own interests or inclinations, let alone to voice and act upon their own principles in a time of crisis. They are not so much cruel as weak, and their weakness is a function of their role as group men. Clark sees that man, acting in a pack, is brutal in defending the wholeness of the pack, eliminating anyone who, remaining outside it, is a threat to it. He sees, further, that man acting in a pack would rather be guilty of moral cowardice than physical cowardice. Every rider who appears in front of the saloon where the posse is forming immediately joins the lynching party in order to demonstrate that he is unafraid. But if, in the course of the pursuit or after the capture of the presumed rustlers, any man has doubts about the wisdom and justice of lynching, he swallows them. It is easier for man to live with an inner moral cowardice, Clark seems contemptuously to conclude, than to be charged by others with lack of courage to act.

So much for the weak or evil characters. The men of good will are impotent. Art Croft, the narrator, has a spectatorial attitude. A sensitive man, he is opposed to the use of force, but he does nothing to stop the lynching. In fact, he feels compelled to accompany the posse to protect himself, because as an outsider — he is a long way from his own range — he is himself under suspicion. The minister is totally ineffectual. Only Davies the storekeeper tries to redeem for the reader the image of man. Davies is the spokesman for the idea of orderly social justice. His attempts to prevent the lynching are futile, although he makes a strong case against the popular, frontier distrust of the uncertainties of the law. Extralegal justice, he argues, weakens the fabric of all law; time, precedent, and the consent of the majority are all on the side of the judge, giving sanctions to his decision; the law is precious as the conscience of society. But men, the mob, reject these reasonable propositions. When argument fails, action must follow; here Davies funks it dismally. He knows that he might have stopped the hangings if he had faced down Major Tetley with a gun. But to kill Tetley is to take the law into one's own hands and to do violence in order to prevent violence. This dreadful paradox Davies cannot solve. In fact, he evades altogether the moral issue posed by it. He fails to bring a gun with him and he refuses en route to accept one so that he cannot possibly involve himself in a moral showdown.

In giving us a full sense of the ambiguities of moral courage, Clark makes it clear that no man in the book is able to act decently and justly in a society of men. Or, to put it another way, those who live by action in that society will get their way, even if it leads, as in the case of Tetley, to moral bankruptcy and suicide. Those who live by moral principle must withdraw or be defeated. In making the men of the posse waver between the two conceptions of man — man as cruel, thoughtless, and angry, as represented by Major Tetley, and man as the repository of civilized institutions and traditions of justice, as represented by Davies — Clark sharpens the contrast between the two views and drives home his conviction, dramatized in the men's choice, that man is a mean creature. Heedless, thoughtless action triumphs over the anguished search for a moral certitude that might be applied to the desperate problems of men.

The Ox-Bow Valley in Nevada, where the action takes place, is a beautiful, isolated corner of the West. The time is spring, and Croft reports the trilling bird song and the new growth on the mountains as he rides from the town of Bridger's Wells with the posse to hunt down the presumed rustlers. It is surely a deliberate irony that the violence of men bent upon a mission of death should be portrayed against the clean and open world of nature in the season of growth. As the posse rides through a high pass, it is caught in a late snowstorm. Is this nature, endowed with moral purpose, protesting against defilement by men of invidious intention? It is not an unreasonable speculation, I think, because Clark is to find man a stranger in nature on many occasions in his subsequent work. The world of man and the town and the works of men generally are a curse upon the earth. Art Croft, the lonely cowboy from the range who belongs to the world of nature, feels this revulsion against the society of organized men when he gladly leaves the town at the end of the book. Only in the out-of-doors can he review and sort out the experiences through which he has passed.

His departure closes a cycle, and the cycle is the principle of organization in the novel. The story begins when Art and a friend enter the town. It builds surely toward its central matter with news of murder and rustling. The issues are debated, the rustlers pursued, tried, hanged. The story proceeds to moral investigation and to adjustment to the moral consequences of the act. Then Art leaves for the open country again. This is the most severely organized novel Clark has written thus far, and he exhibits in it a control that grows from clarity of intention. His treatment of the point of view, whereby the narrator is both inside and outside the action, participating in it yet observing it, gives a legitimate double focus to the novel which both broadens its range and increases its impact. That impact rests principally on the chief irony of the "incident," that the men hanged were neither murderers nor cattle thieves.

Man's quest for justice, then, is doomed by the nature of man. Having demonstrated the futility of finding human morality in man's activities as a social being, Clark seems willing to drop any major consideration of society. He will henceforth localize his search for morality in individual man, especially in man's relationship to nature. In the story of American fiction in the 1940's Clark thus becomes one of the earliest figures to turn his back upon the social preoccupations of the thirties. And he does so because he clearly rejects the liberal's uncritical assumptions about the worth of human nature which informed so much fiction of the preceding decade.

The next novel Clark published, *The City of Trembling Leaves* (1945), takes no such mordant view of man and his pursuit of ideal values, precisely because man is here the isolated artist, struggling to adjust himself to his cosmic, not his societal, environment, and to find himself in relation to nature's scheme of things, not man's. It follows that this novel, which has the air of a first, autobiographical work, would demonstrate a greater interest in character than does *The Ox-Bow Incident*, where, indeed, no figure was drawn in the round. Since its protagonist, Tim Hazard, becomes a composer, what we have is a portrait of the artist as a young man; but this is an American artist very unlike Stephen Dedalus.

The first section of the novel tells of Tim's early search for knowledge and experience, his brief exultation and passion, and his fall. This movement is clothed in episodes tritely and sentimentally conceived: peripheral adventures in sex, athletic successes in track and tennis, an abortive bobby-sox love affair, the break-up of the family. The second part of the novel depicts Tim's struggle in the slough of despond as he plays in a honky-tonk dance band and his gradual climb to a plateau of artistic and emotional fulfilment. Released from the thralldom exercised by the girl he had vainly loved, Tim marries the patient Griselda of his childhood and writes the City of Trembling Leaves symphony.

This bald summary is not, I'm afraid, unfair to the novel. One critic has said that a part of Clark's failure is the result of the thinness of American experience and of his identification with the great American boy-man. The justice of these comments is apparent when we place Joyce's book beside this one. Joyce had the Church, the city life of Dublin, the history and myth and legend of Ireland to draw upon. Clark has Reno, Nevada.

Reno does offer, at least, mountain and desert. Tim's maturation draws in a large part on this world of nature, which Clark here views as a Transcendentalist might. Nature comforts and cleanses. Nature offers regeneration: one bathes in the mountain lakes ritualistically to cleanse the soul and shed the mean urges of the body, as Thoreau bathed in Walden Pond, thinking of King Tching-thang. Climbing in the mountains, Tim discovers that nature holds the key to the secret recesses of the soul. In the desert nature is harsh, but again regenerative. The desert tests the spiritual and physical qualities of Tim and his friend Black; it purges them of the crippling illness induced by the money and phony culture of the city (Beverly Hills) they have just fled. Tim wishes to merge with nature and become one with it in the ultimate mystic act of the orthodox Transcendentalist. He then will have penetrated to the cosmic secret of life. In essence, Clark is saying that nature is the norm and that man defines himself by reference to nature. This relationship, in which man is dependent upon nature and subordinate to it, is, in *The City of Trembling Leaves*, a further development of what Clark had already hinted in *The Ox-Bow Incident*. But it raises the most serious philosophical question to be found in the writings of Clark: is maturation, with its emphasis upon a defined sense of the self, compatible with the monism which is the logical consequence of Transcendental assumptions? On the face of it, the answer is no. In the novel, Tim manages to straddle the two worlds. He lives in the world of nature which has enabled him to find himself in the world of art or of men. Baldly put, it is an unlikely proposition.

Clark's confusion is seen in another way in this novel. Tim is the all-around all-American boy who strives to succeed in mutually exclusive areas of human endeavor and in mutually antagonistic areas of society. It is simply too much of a good thing that Tim should be star athlete and sensitive artist, but it is worse that he is never made to recognize the incompatibility of middle-class philistia and artistic bohemianism. He is not given to understand that the goals of one group will corrupt those of the other, and that striving in both areas will corrupt him. This is why one cannot believe in him when he professes to be an intellectual critic of Henry Adams or yearns to be a child of nature.

The writing in this book is inflated and pseudopoetic. Clark insists on taking a serious view of his hero's flatulent outpourings, as though he were a victim of his own sentimental rhetoric. Seeming to feel that every neural itch of his hero must be reported, he has failed to make a judicious selection of materials. Here is the crucial failure of method in a book to which Clark brought such intellectual conceptions that Diana Trilling called it, with some justice, a novel of boogie-woogie *Weltschmerz.*

The Track of the Cat (1949), in its thematic and technical assurance, reveals a great advance over *The City of Trembling Leaves.* The style of *The Track of the Cat,* a kind of symbolic realism, shows Clark at the top of his bent in the massing of tendentious detail, despite the prolixity of the book; this is a welcome contrast to the looseness of its predecessor. The method and structure of *The Track* are clear and controlled, again in contrast to *The City.* In the latter book Clark uses a wholly unsatisfactory narrator who is rarely present at the events of the story he reports; and he makes an abortive attempt to reproduce in the novel the structure of a symphony. In the later work the chief symbol is finely realized, while in the earlier the effort to make the leaves of the title symbolic is a flat failure.

One of the chief merits of *The Track of the Cat* is that the three brothers in it give us the full range of Clark's view of man. Arthur Bridges is the meditative man, comparable to Davies in *The Ox-Bow Incident.* Gentle and decent, he cannot impose his will upon men or situations and he cannot participate in violence. Tracking the cat that has been killing the family's stock, he refuses to carry a gun. His brother Curt has called him a monk, and the parka he wears looks like a monk's cowl. So unworldly and reflective a man, a *religieux,* always brooding on the "big secret" of nature and human destiny, like Tim Hazard, cannot survive in the harsh, frontier West. Lost in his own thoughts, he is killed on Cathedral Rock by the mountain lion; he is a man who invites his fate. Curt had told himself, "Don't think at all; it makes you blind." Arthur's blindness causes his death. But his death has another meaning. Extending the religious metaphor, one can see that Arthur is a martyr, and his death a propitiation for the guilt of the white man in despoiling the West. For Arthur shares in the double-edged guilt of Americans in the West who have deprived the Indian of what was really his and have, by imposing their own fat dream of wealth and power on the land, raped it of its pristine innocence and goodness.

Arthur's strength of moral purpose and courage in confronting the essential problems of life inform much of the book. In his effort to grasp the big secret and expiate the white man's guilt, as well as out of his humane impulses, Arthur befriends Joe Sam, the Bridges' Indian hand, and comes to a partial understanding of Joe Sam's mysticism and primitive mythology. But in vain, for Arthur fails as Davies had failed in the earlier novel. The literally fatal fact is that meditation robs Arthur of the capacity for action. Furthermore, his asceticism is sterile, since he is unfulfilled in love. This passive denial of love constitutes an implicit loyalty to the god of Death; it may also be related to the antipathy toward action. Arthur fails also, as the white man must, in establishing rapport with the world of nature. Most sensitive of all the Bridges, he is yet a stranger in nature. Once when he flushes two deer, who run from him, he thinks, "I smell strong of the curse of my breed right now. . . ." No matter how much he partakes of Joe Sam's rituals, the old sin of exploitation cannot be washed away. It follows that Arthur, sterile and unloved in human relationships and estranged from the non-human world of nature, cannot find the big secret and he cannot find or fulfil his self.

If Arthur shows us the inadequacy of thought in the thought-action dichotomy Clark so often establishes in his work, his brother Curt shows us, as did Tetley in *The Ox-Bow Incident*, the moral bankruptcy of the materialistic, sensual, unimaginative, power-driven personality whose life is summed in the act. Curt lives with violent success on the pragmatic level of life, but he dies, ironically, a victim of the myth and spirit he has so coarsely scorned. He is killed, not by the real cat, but by a plunge over a cliff induced by an imaginary, supernatural cat, the cat of Joe Sam's myth. There can be no question about the inadequacy of the man of action.

With Harold, the youngest brother, Clark takes up again the theme of maturation. Harold's growth proceeds from a careful synthesis of the best traits in his brothers. Objective and subjective, realistic and idealistic views of life fuse in him. He understands much of what Arthur yearned for, and actually has himself a moment of insight when he thinks he is about to grasp the big secret. In a scene with his fiancée, he sees the conflict between the god of Life, which is love, and the god of Death, which is any denial of love: Curt's flesh-centered egocentrism or his mother's crushing, simplistic Puritanism. The same gods appear to Tim Hazard in *The City of Trembling Leaves*. The problem of growing up, as Clark views it throughout his work, lies in learning to cope with these polar forces. Harold's response, once he has learned from Arthur, is to learn from Curt's world, the world of men, a healthy sexuality as part of his genuine love and a practical grasp of affairs which makes him competent in the sphere of action — it is he who, with Joe Sam, succeeds in killing the cat. He survives where his brothers have failed, now the master of the ranch; he is triumphant health, normality, balance.

In this view, Harold is Clark's finest embodiment of man, discoverer of his own nature. But he still falls far short of the demands, perhaps impossible demands, that Clark makes of men. From his triumph neither the wronged Indian nor pristine nature gets its due. White dominance in the West continues and is carried on in him as a rancher; the exploitation of nature for the fat dream is a necessary condition of ranching. Man is still a stranger in nature. Harold can no more avoid the guilt of his marauding heritage as a white man than he can successfully become one with the non-human world of nature. The seal is put indelibly on Harold's failure by Joe Sam. When the cattle-killing mountain lion is slain, the Indian refuses to accept it as *his* black panther, the creature who symbolizes for Joe Sam the instrument of vengeance on the white for wrongs done the Indians and the means whereby the old, natural order of freedom will be restored to the West, along with Indian supremacy. This sense of the white man's guilt, felt by Clark I am sure as by Joe Sam, is the same guilt feeling Faulkner expresses toward the Negro and the Indian in the South.

What Harold can do is mitigate his guilt and his alienation by love. This is only a partial solution, especially when Clark flavors Harold's triumph so obviously with economic gain. What Harold emerges with is a prosperous ranch and a little woman to share it. Curt might have been satisfied with this, if the girl were sufficiently attractive. Even in his most favorably conceived character, then, Clark reveals man's inability to come to terms with his experience both in history and in the natural world. Or is Clark the victim of his reluctance to face his own view of man's inadequacy?

The rest of the Bridges family, mother, father, and daughter Grace, are conceived in terms of themes already discussed. Grace is on the side of the angels, but, unmarried and unfulfilled, she is the unwilling victim of the denial of love. The absence of love, which characterizes the parents as well and in them amounts to a denial of humanity, is coupled with a disquiet in nature that the mother at least comprehends. She has forced the family to come into the valley and take up a ranching life. Her husband and Curt, however, are lured by the worldly and appetitive satisfactions of the city. She herself struggles for an orientation toward her pitiless God. None of them can adapt to the natural world about them. The consequence is a family life pregnant with tension and hatred.

Joe Sam, more symbol than character, stands for the defeated Indian way of life that was once at home in the world of nature. His being is in tune with transcendental powers, and he enjoys a life of the spirit nourished by ceremony. His conflict of value and motive with Curt is so sharp that Curt comes to believe, in the hallucinatory stage of his tracking of the cat, that Joe Sam is tracking *him* and will visit a retribution upon him for flouting the magic and ritual by which Joe Sam lives. On the other hand, Joe finds Arthur sympathetic to his belief in magic. Each winter Arthur carves a wooden figure of a mountain lion for Joe Sam, and the possession of this charm, a surrogate for the real cat, dissipates the spells Joe Sam gets at the change of seasons and when he senses danger or death in the air. The only character in the novel who seems to possess the secret of nature is thus an ancient, inarticulate Indian who will fade into time, having cast a dim light which seems to have destroyed Arthur as much as Curt, since Arthur's death was in a sense a sacrifice to a magic that he respected even if he could not make it work for him.

All this brings us to the cat, in which one must find the total meaning of the book. There are two cats. One is real: it kills the cattle and Arthur, and when it screams in agony and rage at being shot, it is more real than any human character in the novel. Harold kills this cat with real bullets, this cat belonging to the simple narrative level of the story. But there is another cat. For Joe Sam this cat is ambivalent. It means the end of things for the Indian — being driven out of his native place, the destruction of the family as his wife and daughter were in fact destroyed by a mountain lion. It also means a mythical creature that will wreak vengeance on the whites, and as such it demands blood rites. For Arthur the cat is the symbol for the good, wild, clean life that existed in the West before the white man came to despoil with settlement, imposing civilization upon it and milking it of its wealth. And it is also the carving of a cat he gives to Joe Sam. For Curt the cat is the angel of death. No wonder readers have thought at once of Moby Dick in connection with the black panther, for, like the white whale, the cat is a successful symbol in the dialectic sense that Charles Feidelson, Jr., outlines. In it the subject and the object "fade before the unitive reality created by the symbolic medium." This fusion of subjective and objective gives the cat an identity of its own. The symbolic cat is never conquered. Man does not penetrate nature or expiate his guilt. The best man can do is to create, by the same dialectic process that gives the cat its being, a fusion such as Harold represents. Living in love, aware and capable, Harold may make an accommodation to nature, but he will not achieve identification with it.

In 1950 Clark collected nine of his previously published stories in a volume called *The Watchful Gods and Other Stories*; the title story, a novelette, appeared in print for the first time here. The themes of the stories are the same as those of the novels: man's effort to grow to a sense of his personal identity; man's need, in this desire, to understand and merge with nature; nature's steady rejection of man as outside the rhythm of its cycle. The treatment of these themes reveals some of the unresolved problems with which Clark is concerned and at the same time throws a more sharply focused light on his major preoccupations than we sometimes get in the longer works.

The problem of the relationship between man and nature is at the heart of "The Buck in the Hills." Here again is the romantic and sentimental expression of Clark's hieratic attitude toward the western mountains. It is an expression partly vitiated, as in *The City of Trembling Leaves,* by Clark's unrestrained sincerity and a resultant fuzziness of thought. The two "good" hunters in the story feel, like Emerson, that nature has a divinity in it; and they bathe in a pool of melted snow to cleanse themselves of any guilt that might cling to them as a consequence of the "bad" hunter's cruel action in violating the canons of decent relationship between man and nature. The bath as a purgative ritual is a standard device in Clark's work for those characters who feel themselves close to nature. But, unlike Emerson, these men, close as they might be, do not feel at one with nature. They recognize the "something listening behind each tree" that "didn't like us." If even such men are forever alien to nature, then it must follow that all men must be. A frank recognition that the world of non-human nature and the world of men are separate orders of existence would certainly tend to diminish the reaction of outrage when man, acting like man, violates the order of nature. This story epitomizes Clark's metaphysical difficulties. He regards dualism as inescapable. Yet the monism of his Transcendental heritage constantly appeals to his consciousness as the way of human redemption. Unfortunately, a belief in monism leads to the elimination of man in an exaltation of nature. Clark is most reluctant openly to espouse this position.

The same difficulty haunts "The Indian Well," where man is only a transient phenomenon in the immemorial flow of events in nature. But the confusion is dissipated in "Hook," because in this story Clark virtually dispenses with man altogether. The story relates the life cycle of a superb hawk from the time he is hatched from the egg until he is killed by a dog. The hawk becomes supreme in satisfying his three driving urges — flight, killing, sex. His downfall begins when he is crippled by a Japanese farmer. Hook is portrayed as the very essence of hawkness, and Clark seems to accept, indeed to admire, all his acts and attributes — his killing and his courage, and the grandeur of his magnificent flight. Here is the world of nature, seen clear in the lonely ferocity of the hawk. Hook, fulfilling himself, demonstrates the absolute harmony and rightness of the world of nature in the cycle of his life from birth to death. Man appears here only as an incidental force, hostile to the nature of things and disturbing the natural cycle. This story has been called "the perfect expression" of what Clark most wishes to say. The judgment must be regarded as sound when we see that the world of nature for which Hook is the compactly beautiful and cruel symbol is perfect in its movement and inevitability. Man is a mere excrescence upon it. Neither confusion nor sentimentality marks Clark's conception in this story. ("Hook" appeared in the *Atlantic Monthly* for August, 1940. "The Rise and Passing of Bar," which is essentially the same story except that it concerns a wild horse and not a hawk, appeared in the *Virginia Quarterly Review* for January, 1943. Presumably Clark sensed that what he had said in "Hook" was worth repeating because it was what he wanted most to say.)

Yet Clark cannot altogether leave man alone as a subject. He may pause to comment, as in "The Portable Phonograph," that even the best men, those who need and cherish the arts when the world has been destroyed, are potentially treacherous and suspicious. Or he may show the perversity of man, as in a little story like "The Rapids," where the joy and play afforded by nature must be sacrificed to the sane world of business responsibility and regulated domesticity. Or (as in "Why Don't You Look Where You're Going?") he may even praise the individualistic man — not as a fully developed character, however, but as a kind of abstraction, a figure dimly seen; in this story the man's power comes from confronting alone the great forces of nature, the sea, and the great symbol of leviathan civilization, the ocean-going liner. Or he may condemn the man who is a willing party to the corruption of his own personality and the loss of his identity, as in "The Anonymous," where Peter Carr denies his Indian heritage and replaces his native culture with a superficial grasp of the white man's sophisticated and cosmopolitan culture.

Not satisfied with man as he is or with his potentiality as man, Clark has recourse to the great Transcendental paradox that man will be fulfilled when he merges with the vast Cosmic One. Then, of course, man won't be man. He will be part of nature and indistinguishable from it. Then Clark will have the monism he yearns for and toward which he murkily moves at the prodding of his unconscious. This vision of unity, linked to the theme of mat-

uration, is the subject of "The Fish Who Could Close His Eyes"
and of "The Watchful Gods." In the first of these stories Clark
seems to take a very unsteady view of his young protagonist, Tad.
Tad is a dreamer who is "always upon the verge of the final discovery which would lift him into unity with everything." Tad's method of getting at the secret of the universe is, as Clark says, to work
from the top down, while the scientists about him, trying to solve
the same problem, work from the bottom up, inductively. Clark
seems to me to admire Tad's aim and approve of his imaginative
and intuitive method, whereas he seems critical of the scientists'
method. But Tad is also depicted as a fool and a sentimentalist.
Obdurate nature will not yield up its secret to a person of his
sort. One wonders why Clark undertook to make it a fool's quest
to seek the essential unity if he himself really believes in the
necessity of achieving such unity?

That he does believe in such a necessity "The Watchful Gods"
makes clear. "The Watchful Gods," tedious as it is, affirms Clark's
romantic belief that harmony with the entire cosmos must be
man's aim, and that real maturity begins by recognizing the necessity to reconcile and compound the antithetical forces of good and
evil, light and dark, life and death. In this story of initiation,
twelve-year-old Buck receives an ardently desired twenty-two for
his birthday and kills a rabbit with it. The precious sign of maturity, the gun, is also an instrument of death. The rabbit as victim
and symbol of Buck's prowess merges in Buck's mind with a rattle-
snake, as evil aggressor, that had once almost bitten Buck. The
fog and the sun play around him on the mountains of the Pacific
coast, gods of darkness and vengeance and of light and hope. The
painful fusion of all these polarities forces from Buck at the end
of the story a recognition of his relationship with transcendent
forces: "O God, God!" he exclaims. It is not altogether clear that
Buck has seized the great secret. But it is clear Clark feels that man's
only hope lies in making the effort to do so.

I am convinced that Clark has not yet had the courage to say
consistently what he really believes, namely, that nature is the
norm and that man must conform to natural law; that reality is
dualistic, man being the immoral, evil force and nature the good.
His pious hope that man will merge into nature is only his way of

temporizing in face of his conviction that man must be condemned. Much of what I have said is to be found in a letter Clark wrote to George Bluestone:

I would say, even, moral law exists only within natural law — and among humans. Increasingly, I believe, however, man having come to dominate the world to such an unhealthy degree, that unless moral law is brought into accord with natural law, which simply cannot be broken for any length of time with immunity, which is to say, unless the moral law extends to pass judgment upon human evil where it affects other creatures, man himself will perish, via his sole concern for man, no matter how moral he may become as man to man.

Behind this rather turgid statement lurks the conviction that it will be a long time before man becomes moral to man, and even if this should occur, it would not make much difference.

Clark would like to retreat from man as he has retreated from man-in-society. It is an unhappy paradox, therefore, that a writer who is so distrustful of man should have made a major concern of man's quest for his identity. It is confusing that this writer should set as the condition of finding one's identity the necessity of losing it in a larger whole, and I hasten to remark that *that* paradox bears no analogy to the Christian doctrine of losing one's life in order to find it. It is unfortunate that this writer has not been tough-minded enough, first, to make the essential philosophical distinction between monism and dualism, and, second, to see and courageously stand by the implications of his choice.

WALLACE STEGNER: THE UNCOMMITTED

Wallace Stegner is like Clark in certain important respects, a representative writer in the Time of Hesitation whose work is more important to contemporary literary history than it is to literature. Both are western writers. In rejecting Marx, Darwin, and Freud, that is, radical social thought and deterministic science, Stegner has taken a position very similar to the one held by Clark. Both men are interested in the problem of identity. The important difference is that Stegner has sought to find a place for men in the world. No extreme position will do, either moral or social, because any such position is corrupted by cynicism and tyranny. Stegner searches for some middle way of viewing man and his cultural experience in which the possibilities of good and evil will be reconciled and the possibilities for variety will be recognized. He believes in man, whose will and morality, he thinks, are operative in our culture. He is at his best when he affirms the goodness of life even though his characters know it is latent with horror.

Stegner's first two novels, published in the late thirties, seemed to indicate a commitment to life at least so far as they attacked those forces that would deny the natural flowering of human life forces. But he is so far committed to undefined life forces that he comes to an evasion of moral responsibility, revealing an indecision that is to plague him in later work. His third novel, *On a Darkling Plain* (1940), makes a reasonably full statement of his characteristic position. It does so by examining the Thoreauvian case for solitary self-dependence and finding it wanting. The self-exiled protagonist of this book has decided that the world is a poisonous place, and the people in it are poisonous too. Yet despite the existence of a flawed man in a flawed society, Stegner permits a sense of brotherhood and community to triumph. Somewhere between Thoreauvian romanticism and Swiftian misanthropy we must come to the somber realization that "Men are brothers by life lived, and are hurt for it." This is a line from Archibald MacLeish which stands as the epigraph for the novel and describes its theme: man defines himself by accepting life among men.

In *Fire and Ice* (1941) we see again Stegner's fascination with the quest for identity and his inability to pursue to the end the logic of his situations. For Stegner throws away the opportunity that might lead his protagonist to self-analysis. Out of the suffering and punishment that should attend his situation (he is in jail for attempted rape), he might well have come to some evaluation of himself. But he is made to suffer very little, and he is punished hardly at all. Instead of anguished appraisal from him, we get a superficial analysis of the nature of campus radicalism.

In 1943 Stegner published *The Big Rock Candy Mountain*. It is his most intensive study of the problem of identity; and in it he has also fully shaped his vision of the American West. Stegner builds the first theme around the natural rebellion of the son against the father. The father's crude energies and moral cowardice fire hatred and contempt in the son. But when, late in the book, the hatred turns to pity, the son comes to understand the father. With this understanding he achieves self-knowledge.

For Stegner, the West is the home of the American Dream, where the big rock candy mountain beckons always with unfulfilled and receding promise. The novel chronicles the passing of the frontier and the delusive quality of its myth. The expansive air of the West seems always to promise more than it is prepared to deliver and to make the promise of the future more important than the reality of the present. Moreover, the frontier ethos demands that life adjust to a ruthlessly materialistic scale. The father of this novel is victimized by the rock candy mountain much as Willy Loman falls before his version of the American myth. But the son sees the West for what it is. Stegner links his two themes by making the son's accurate vision of the West dependent on the purging of the hatred for his father.

Many of the patterns of response already outlined in Stegner's work appear in his next novel, *Second Growth* (1947). This rather slight book is a study of characters who represent different facets of a New England village. Characteristically, Stegner rejects the self-reliance of the independent outsider in this novel for integration into the society, even if it is often a mean-spirited and narrow one. And he permits his young man to run away to a new life, escaping his sordid past, escaping the challenge of the recalcitrant New England soil. In this fashion Stegner has it both ways.

He wants it both ways, too, in *The Preacher and the Slave* (1950). He wants to condemn the iww, but he cannot help admiring its revolutionary enthusiasm. He has claimed for himself, however, a neutral attitude in writing the book: he had hoped "to pose in dramatic terms the quarrel between the way of violence and the way of peace, between self-righteous revolutionary fervor careless of its means and Christian scrupulousness uneasy about its moral ground." But this very formulation of his problem reveals Stegner's bias. The novel bears out his preference for the preacher Lund whose anguished pursuit of truth is placed in opposition to the doctrinaire certainty of the Wobblies; for a Lund torn between compassion and morality in opposition to Joe Hill, the slave of unthinking piety; for a Lund who believes in whittling away at social evils in opposition to a Joe Hill who embraces violence as a legitimate instrument in the class war, even for its own sake.

The insight that perceives and articulates these images of the preacher and the slave can yield a profound interpretation of recent American experience. The conditioned reflexes of the Wobblies are not much different from the closed ideology of the Communist party. Changing the world by whittling away at it represents not only the historical ad hoc approach to social problems in this country but the current emphasis on improvisation and the suspicion of theory. Furthermore, the idea of man in these two images is revealing. Joe Hill's inadequacy is in his simple faith that all good men and true will recognize that the straight path of violence leads to social salvation. But the preacher, harassed by what is an existentialist agony, quickly recognizes the power of corruption latent in good intentions. He understands the terrible difficulties involved in making moral distinctions. The result is that Joe fails as a man, failing in the effort at self-discovery, because he is dishonest with himself and because he comes finally to share self-consciously in the making of the myth about himself.

Yet with all this understanding of politics and man that Stegner has mastered, the novel is not a success. Stegner reveals a confusing ambiguity toward Joe and the IWW. He is both attracted and repelled by them. This conflict in Stegner impairs his investigation of the legend of Joe Hill, for he wants to see Joe as a mythic character, but he is unwilling to validate Joe's hieratic and mythic qualities.

Stegner's short stories were first collected in *The Women on the Wall* (1950). Of the eighteen stories in that volume, nine concern children. Of these nine, six were incorporated in *The Big Rock Candy Mountain* and one became a section of *Second Growth*. For the most part these stories show a preoccupation with the father-son relationship that is well-nigh obsessive in Stegner. He seems under some compulsion to punish the father image and to define the child by repudiation of the father. Many of these stories are also exercises in the manipulation of illusion and reality. The staple of Stegner's technique throughout the volume is the moment of truth when illusion is stripped away or destroyed. It is dependent upon Stegner's treatment of blurred vision, the distorted or dishonest way in which his characters conceive experience. Reality is truth, the truth that shatters pretense, escapism, naïveté, the calm surfaces of life.

Stegner is capable of understanding the tangled depths of human experience and recognizing human limitations. But this leads him only to a timid, negative striving. He will not save man by giving him the kind of value system that Warren has worked out while taking a similar view of man's nature. He will not abandon man as Clark has done for the world of nature or as Bowles has done for a positive nihilism, if that is an acceptable paradox. He has brought man to a dead center. It is toward this dead center that American society has been moving, in the late forties and in the fifties, where the other-directed citizens practice togetherness and huddle in mutual anonymity. In their hands the polarities of American life are disappearing. Stegner, in refusing to make choices, speaks in an idiom that these uncommitted people understand. In the midst of his society, he has not so much seen it as experienced it. He has tried to record the life of man and society from within the given framework. But trustworthy vision and a true perspective come most often to the artist who is outside — especially when it is a non-traditional society, like Stegner's, that the writer is dealing with. In his failure, then, to alienate himself from his society is his failure to commit himself to the quest for identity. In *A Portrait of the Artist*, one of his friends says to Dedalus, "You're a terrible man, Stevie — . . . always alone. —" Joyce knew what Stegner has not learned: that the artist must be utterly independent. He must be alone.

WRIGHT MORRIS: THE ARTIST IN SEARCH OF AMERICA

Wright Morris is alone. He is his own man, embarked in his own way on the discovery of America. He resists cataloguing, yet the disenchantment with the American spirit and character which broods over his books is characteristic of the critical attitude of many other writers in the forties. Like them, he is engaged in a reappraisal of the American experience, because, as he says, "Reappraisal is repossession . . . ." What drives Morris is the need to repossess by understanding the past and, through the past, himself. He expresses the existential crisis by discovering the chief obstacle to self-realization in history. One might feel that this interest in the past attaches Morris to the conservative movement in American letters, as Warren, for example, has sought his answers in the past, but the truth seems to be that Morris is interested in the past because he feels that by possessing it he can purge himself of it. As I have pointed out, the burden of his critical volume on American letters, *The Territory Ahead*, is that the mythic, nostalgic past, while it has generated what is memorable in our literature, has now crippled the American imagination. In order to write his own fiction, it was necessary for Morris to uncover for himself this particular meaning of the backward glance, of the flight into the past, just as it was necessary for him to become aware of the American writer's love affair with raw material which tended to overwhelm the efforts of the shaping imagination. Morris' work through the decade of the forties represents the assessment he felt compelled to make of his own particular segment of the American past, his taming of raw material through technique, and so his freeing of himself from what he regards as the killing preoccupations of American writers. As he wishes to free himself, so he feels compelled to free his characters.

Looking back, he has been able to perceive his bondage, as a writer and an American, and to trace his liberation. "Raw material, an excess of both material and comparatively raw experience," he has written,

has been the dominant factor in my own role as a novelist. The thesis I put forward grows out of my experience, and applies to it. Too much crude ore. The hopper of my green and untrained imagination was both nourished and handicapped by it.

Before coming of age — the formative years when the reservoir of raw material was filling — I had led, or rather been led by, half a dozen separate lives. Each life had its own scene, its own milieu; it frequently appeared to have its own beginning and ending, the only connecting tissue being the narrow thread of my *self*. I had been *there*, but that, indeed, explained nothing. In an effort to come to terms with experience, I processed it in fragments, collecting pieces of the puzzle. In time, a certain over-all pattern *appeared* to be there. But this appearance was essentially a process — an imaginative act of apprehension — rather than a research into the artifacts of my life.

The realization that I had to create coherence, conjure up my synthesis, rather than find it, came to me, as it does to most Americans, disturbingly late. Having sawed out the pieces of my jigsaw puzzle, I was faced with a problem of fitting them together.

These revealing comments indicate the task that Morris faced, in his own view, as a novelist: to avoid the errors of the writers who had gone before him in America by escaping enslavement to the past, and to forge a style, a mercilessly disciplined way of writing, which would put him in full control of his material. The need to escape arises only from an enforced and involuntary imprisonment. The drama and interest of Morris' books throughout the forties lie in part in the process whereby he works his way toward freedom. The style that he evolves is the product of his struggle. It is indigenous to his native Nebraska, bearing the stamp of the plains, as he says, using a minimum of words and ornament. It has sparseness, using objects as both signs and symbols. It is cryptic in its effort to avoid the excesses of a Wolfe: Morris has said in an interview that "the important things are those that remain unsaid; . . . the problems of art are concerned with how we hint at them." The creative problem is to reveal but not to expose. The result of this style and this struggle is to impel Morris to a restricted and repetitive view of his own particular past, that is, the past present to his consciousness. That he is deeply troubled and challenged by it is evident from what can fairly be called his obsessive concern with certain elements in it. If it is possible to say that most authors write the same novel over and over again, of Morris it can be said that the same characters occur again and again, the same objects and symbols, the same events, in book after book. One can only guess that Morris is haunted, to use an overworked but precisely accurate term here, and that he needs to exorcise the ghosts of the past if he is to understand them and himself; this understanding will set him free.

As a literary man, he turns for his understanding to the imagination, which must process life and transform the raw material before it can be possessed. "In this transformation there is a destructive element," he says. "The artist must destroy, in this act of possession, a part of what he loves." Morris' critical creed, as here expressed, describes with startling accuracy his own literary practice in his Nebraska books. The imagination opens for us a life that is more real than life: this is the function of art.

As an American literary man, Morris, like so many of his contemporaries, wishes to discover himself by discovering his country. *The Inhabitants*, an experimental volume of photographs and text, is dedicated to the inhabitant "who knows what it is to be an American." The revolution, Morris says at the end of the book, is to discover America. And the method of discovery, as revealed in this book and in the fiction, is to puzzle out the figure in the carpet, to trace the pattern of advance into the West and retreat back to the East, to chart the desolation of the West and the waste land of the city in the East, to assess the freedom to fail that Veblen had pointed to as the corollary of the opportunity to succeed, to comprehend the loneliness of man in a sense deeper than any that Riesman saw in *The Lonely Crowd*. The quest for the real America and the real American in Morris' work involves the stripping away of nostalgia, of sentimentality, of the optimistic myth of success and progress that has maimed the American psyche. An anonymous character in this book sums up for Morris:

I say killin's hard, I say dyin's harder — but I say livin's hardest yet. Anybody likely to die for somethin', take a man live it out. Dyin' hurt bad once, livin' hurt bad every day. Every day have to get up, be killed, an' die all over again. Take a good thing make a man put up with somethin' like that. Take a good man to put up with a good thing.

Wright Morris' first novel, *My Uncle Dudley* (1942), is a slight book, derivative and backward-looking, confessedly autobiographical. Determined to write simply and sparely, Morris gravitates with unerring conformity toward Hemingway as a model for style. Dealing with carefully assorted types — too carefully assorted — who live outside the framework of respectable, organized society, Morris reminds us of Steinbeck assembling his carefree slobs in *Tortilla Flat*. Uncle Dudley, the really good character, is a con man with a heart of gold. He has the same faith in a common man who knows what he wants and who he is as Ma Joad has in *The Grapes of Wrath*. In a fine show of almost completely unmotivated rebellion, Uncle Dudley resists the forces of law and order in the name of what we are supposed to understand as human dignity — he spits in the eye of a brutal, unfeeling cop. Such rebellion, again reminiscent of Steinbeck, was in the thirties characteristically turned against the police as the symbol of authority.

If Morris reveals his debt to the literary and social past in this pleasant, picaresque book, he also begins to grope toward something that is his own and toward a way by which he might possess it. He begins here an investigation into the tangled web of characters and events that is his consuming and continuing interest in the novels that will follow. Who is Uncle Dudley? And who is his nephew, the other important but nameless character? This boy is Wright Morris himself, who, like the nephew in the book, made such a trip in the West in such a Marmon and passed through Pomona and vowed to go to college there and did. But the boy is also the character in later books, grown to manhood perhaps and given a name, whose compulsion it is to keep coming back, to return again and again until he is finally free. He belongs to that family that lives as much, I suppose, in Morris' mind as it does in Nebraska. In the next book the boy's uncle is named Kermit and he is named Agee; a picture exists showing them in a battered car that has returned from the Far West. The uncle, whatever his name, is the figure of the wanderer in the family. The boy or man, whatever his name, is the native returned, the narrator of the story, the central consciousness. He may not *be* Wright Morris, but he has the substance and the color that lead one to believe he speaks for Morris.

In *My Uncle Dudley* the movement is from Los Angeles back toward the East. Uncle and nephew explicitly reject the West and retreat from it. It is surprising that Morris' first novel should reveal this thematic consideration, as though his untutored imagination had grasped instinctively a feeling that became a conviction to be reiterated again and again in later work. Artistic fulfilment, Morris was to imply fifteen years later in his study of American letters, is not to be sought in the West but in the East, in the direction Henry James took, away from the destructive temptations of raw material and the cloying influence of nostalgia. The real discovery of America depends on movement toward the East.

In this novel we get a fleeting reference to a coin-operated mechanical violin which plays in a Japanese restaurant in Hastings, Nebraska. In at least two other books, Morris speaks of such a violin in such a restaurant, although the Nebraska town seems to have changed. Clearly the violin and the restaurant constitute a sign or a symbol for Morris. He does nothing with them in this first novel except to pull them out of his consciousness and put them on public view. Whether, to mention only two possibilities, this is preparation for their later more meaningful appearance or whether they rose out of his being in response to some associative act that can no longer be traced, I cannot pretend to know. Whatever the case, it seems to me that they have a meaning in the total context of Morris' work. This unlikely combination — the rootless, alien Japanese restaurant stuck in the heart of mid-America and the mechanical music-maker — is Morris' comment on the cultural tone and aspirations of the Middle West. This combination of the outrageously esoteric and barrenly mechanical is an index of the Midwest's conception of taste, of its pitiful quest for light and beauty. This same kind of criticism Morris will level many times, but he was not, in *My Uncle Dudley*, quite prepared to articulate it. The restaurant and the violin stand mute in this book, except for those who have read all the novels. Generally speaking, one must know the whole of Morris' work to understand any part of it.

My Uncle Dudley is a transitional book, looking backward to the thirties but suggesting Morris' unique and independent development in the forties. *The Man Who Was There* (1945), the second novel, belongs to Morris. His own manner shows forth here, not Hemingway's; he uses his own attitudes, not Steinbeck's. He understates everything but gives the impression always that beneath the scanty surface lie substantial meanings. His characteristic humor — sharp, dry, antiseptic — appears here, revealing a satiric talent not exercised earlier. His favorite enemies, I might say incidentally, seem to be funerals and morticians: in several books he treats the rituals of burial in America with a controlled savagery justified by what he sees as the commercialization of bereavement. More important, in this novel he enters fully into his struggle with the Nebraska scene, and he opens the question of the possibilities for love and art in our society.

The hero of this novel is Agee Ward, a painter, whose problem is the same as Morris' and whose impact as artist and person is what every artist could wish to achieve. The problem is to comprehend and absorb America. Agee tries to embrace the country by getting away from it, thus gaining perspective and sharpening his vision, as so many other American artists have done. And then by coming back, his perceptions heightened, he broadens if he does

not fulfil his vision of America. Agee does in miniature and painting what Henry James had done in *The American Scene*, a book
Morris admires extravagantly. He repossesses America and so can
reveal in his pictures the shadowless, depthless sterility of the
naked little Nebraska town; he can see the grim and dismal life
of the Nebraska farm; he can see the barren lives of the people
and their barren characters, in the Great American West; he can
see, in the structure and growth of the towns, the almost conscious
yearning toward the East which signalizes the bankruptcy of the
myth of the frontier. As Agee revisits Nebraska, sees it, and by
coming to understand it, purges himself of it, he is doing what I
think Morris himself had to do, and continues to do in subsequent
books.

As an artist and as a person, Agee frees men and women for
love, liberating their emotional and spiritual energies. His effect
upon them is mystical, ineffable, Morris' conviction being, apparently, that the barriers to the direct communication of love are
insuperable. Agee himself is not a lover, but he makes love
possible. Even when he is gone, missing in action in the war, it
is his influence, for example, that releases the spinster Gussie
Newcomb into the world, permits her to marry, and gives promise
of her fertility. He will be perpetuated in her children. Morris
reminds one of Sherwood Anderson in his belief that the passional
life of Americans has been muted or buried, that it must be
opened and expressed if people are to avoid destruction.

Agee Ward's father had been a station agent, probably for the
Chicago, Burlington, and Quincy Railroad. When Agee returns
to Nebraska, his Uncle Harry is still living on the farm, but his
footloose Uncle Kermit has disappeared. The barber in town
remembers that his mother had been Grace Osborn before her
marriage. Uncle Harry has a picture of the family, taken in 1892,
showing ten men and two women. In Morris' next book, *The
Home Place* (1948), an experiment with narrative text and photographs, Clyde Muncy is the name of the protagonist. He comes
back to the Nebraska farm of his Uncle Harry, who owns a
photograph showing fourteen members of the family, taken in
1892. The barber tells Clyde his mother was Grace Osborn, whom
he resembles as Agee did. We learn from a later book that Clyde's
father was an agent for the C. B. & Q., that he went in for raising

chickens, built a large house in the country, and took the girl who was to be his second wife to a Japanese restaurant where a mechanical violin could be played.

I submit that the characters in Morris' novels, up through *The Works of Love* (1952), belong, almost all of them, to one family. Uncle Dudley and Uncle Kermit are the same man. The father in this family is Will Brady, not named until *The Works of Love*, which is his story. The son is Clyde Muncy, Agee Ward, the nephew in *My Uncle Dudley*, the boy in *Man and Boy* (1951) — all are the same. The son is in search of his heritage, which means he wants to possess his past in order to be free in the present, and he wants, for the same reason, to find his father. This continuing drama of the relationship between father and son is complicated by the ineffable barriers to love that virtually destroy communication between the two. The father, also in search of love, is in addition the symbol of man's fate in recent American history. Born in the plains states, he has seen the frontier officially closed and the frontier virtues disappear. He has turned his back upon the barren land to go East, only to find the waste land of the city. Loveless, uprooted, confused, lonely, he has lived in hotel lobbies and tasted the strangeness of life. The American dream ends for Morris in the empty towns of Nebraska, inhabited only by the ghosts of men whose illusions had been swallowed up in the too big sky; or it ends in the oily waters of the Chicago canal, where Will Brady, the father, plunges to his death.

Morris has not worked out these interwoven relationships with precision, the dividing lines between the generations sometimes seeming to blur. But the relationships between father and son are constant, and the same themes are consistently, even indefatigably, pursued. In *The Home Place* we have the return of the native, of the city-dweller, to the country whence he came, to seek the figure in the carpet which will explain to him his own identity as an individual human being and as an American. "Home is where you hang your childhood," and where you look for the explanations you need. But Clyde Muncy discovers that you can't go home again. He is an alien now in Nebraska, but even though he is outside, his excursion into the past yields him an explanation of the meaning of Nebraska. He sees that life lived in a house gives the house its meaning, even though the house be unoccupied, just as when the rug is worn away, the figure begins to stand out. What he comes to is a meditation in a vacant house over an old pair of shoes which reveal the figure:

The word beauty is not a Protestant thing. It doesn't describe what there is about an old man's shoes. The Protestant word for that is character. Character is supposed to cover what I feel about a cane-seated chair, and the faded bib, with the ironed-in stitches, of an old man's overalls. Character is the word, but it doesn't cover the ground. It doesn't cover what there is moving about it, that is. I say these things are beautiful, but I do so with the understanding that mighty few people anywhere will follow what I mean. That's too bad. For this character is beautiful. I'm not going to labor the point, but there's something about these man-tired things, something added, that is more than character. . . . Perhaps all I'm saying is that character can be a form of passion, and that some things, these things, have that kind of character. That kind of Passion has made them holy things. That kind of holiness, I'd say, is abstinence, frugality, and independence — the home-grown, made-on-the-farm trinity. Not the land of plenty, the old age pension, or the full dinner pail. Independence, not abundance, is the heart of their America.

This passage is Morris' most eloquent tribute to Nebraska, as Uncle Harry, who typifies the virtues of the Protestant ethic, is his most sympathetically drawn Nebraskan character. "The carpet wears out, but the life of the carpet, the Figure, wears in. The holy thing, that is, comes naturally." So it is with Uncle Harry, who has endured in the semi-arid climate, who is wearing out so that the dry humor, the well-hidden capacity for love, the tenacity for life, the steady realism of his vision are now fully to be seen.

Morris' examination of the West takes a different course in his next novel, *The World in the Attic* (1949). Here we see that the Western promise has been frustrated and the Protestant ethic corrupted. An older generation, Uncle Harry's perhaps, had exercised its stern virtues of frugality and abstemiousness in such a way as to produce, paradoxically, an abundance that undermined its descendants. For abundance made possible mediocre respectability and bourgeois comfort. Clyde Muncy, still the returned native, is seized with what he calls small-town nausea upon first re-entering his native place. He is overwhelmed with the barren quality of the lives and minds of the people, of the physical surroundings. The sense of degeneration or of decline is dramatized in the death of Caddy Hibbard, who is a symbol for the early promise of the western town and whose death is the symbolic death of the town. Caddy personified the feminine grace and joy that might have tempered the Protestant virility of the early days. But the light that Caddy brought had for many years been shut up in her great house, because the town did not want it. She is frozen in her house, leading her life in death since she had not been able to sustain real life in the town. The town did not grow, literally, up to her house any more than it managed to grow up to her ideas of elegance and entertainment. It never reached the crossroad of Pioneer and Horace Greeley Streets, where Caddy's house stood under the magnificent city street light that bespoke expectations for the town that were never fulfilled. For the town stopped growing before it reached the light. The children left it, most of them to go East, yearning, says Morris, for what Jay Gatsby yearned for: an experience more highly colored than any available on the plains.

They left, one may assume, by railroad. Every Nebraska town in Morris' work is built alongside a railroad, and it becomes a vehicle of escape from the town just as it is a connection with the rest of the country. And it is more than this. The father works for the railroad, and so it is a means of earning a living. But it is also an instrument of death. Its potential for destruction is shown in the recurring scene of the man in the buggy, reining in his horse at the railroad crossing as the train approaches; its capacity for destruction in the number of people it actually kills or who use it, in despair at their empty lives in the empty West, as an instrument of self-destruction. Or it is a symbol of romance — of luxury and of flight — which draws the Gatsbys of the plains toward the golden East.

Man and Boy is the first of Morris' novels to be laid in the East; the setting is a Philadelphia suburb and the Brooklyn Navy Yard. The theme of the novel is the failure of love. Father and son, man and wife, are unable to make the proper connections with each other. The barriers to communication block their emotional satisfactions to such a degree that, having given up the pursuit of such satisfactions long ago, husband and wife have virtually given up verbal communication as well. It is the woman in this novel (and the one in *The Deep Sleep*, 1953, which has the same theme and the same Pennsylvania scene) who is the enemy to love. Her emotional life is throttled, like her husband's. She drives father and son from the house but yet makes for estrangement between them. In the inevitable movement of her overwhelming and indomitable personality, she emasculates her husband and alienates her son. Even though she is a real force in the national Congress as a lobbyist for bills to provide quail refuges and similar matters, she does not seem to love birds. She is the most determined but disengaged ornithologist in Morris' novels, where a feeding station, for some inexplicable reason, seems almost to be standard equipment. It appears to be Morris' view that such middle-class American women are in flight from love, and so have denied life and opposed joy. Ironically, the mother whom the navy honors in this novel has none of the feminine characteristics of gentle protectiveness and inexhaustible sympathy sentimentally associated with mother. Yet it is to the credit of Mother, as her husband quite significantly calls her, that if she is without love she is also without patience for the meaningless formalities and traditions of male institutions like the navy. Her very faults — her sweeping self-assurance and her calm capacity for domination — redeem her as the champion of democratic behavior in the face of naval custom.

The figure of the male systematically deprived of his prerogatives as husband and lover and exiled to the attic or cellar in his own house is more than the measure of baffled love for Morris. It represents his view of a relationship between the sexes that grows out of American society as he sees it. The hard Protestant virtues of the frontier put emphasis upon acquisition and endurance but did not provide a basis for love and understanding between a man and a woman. What Morris' repossession of the past tells him, then, is that it has created an America in which men are starkly alone and unable to bear the burden of their loveless state. Morris has freed himself from the past by accepting the bleak present which is his rightful but unhappy heritage.

The Works of Love makes clear this more or less integrated movement of Morris' fiction up to that date. This is the story of Will Brady, born in Nebraska, ". . . who was more or less by himself." It was God's country to his father but godforsaken for his mother. "Perhaps only Will Brady could combine these two points of view. He could leave it, that is, but he would never get over it." Will Brady is the father who never knows his son or his wives, whose painful, inarticulate search for love is successful neither in the plains nor in the city to the East. Some fright, some insecurity, grips him in Nebraska; he has only the comfortable prostitute to turn to. She understands this sort of thing in men, she has seen it so often, but she can give them only passing surcease. Will can nowhere find the love that will ease his loneliness and quiet his fear, but he does learn pity. Watching an old man chewing food and then feeding it to pigeons so that he feeds himself to the birds in a eucharistic parallel that Morris has used more than once, Brady hears a voice out of the sky telling him that there are no lovers in heaven: "Pity is the great lover, and the great lovers are all on earth." This sentiment describes the limit of the satisfaction he derives from his two wives.

As for his boy, an adopted son who is sent to him because of his capacity for pity, Will Brady is unable to make any vital connection that might express the love he feels. He searches for an avenue to understanding, but finds nothing better than the puerile observations of *Penrod* and the superficial mythos of athletics. He is forced into a relationship with his son which he conducts exclusively in his fantasy, since in the real world his loneliness is impenetrable. The final extension of this fantasy world occurs when he takes a job as Santa Claus, which opens to him a relationship with all boys and girls. He thinks it an enviable position:

To live in this world, so to speak, and yet somehow be out of it. To be himself without children, without friends or relations, without a woman of his own or a past or a future, and yet to be mortal, and immortal, at the same time . . . in the world it is evil for an old man to act like that. There is a law against it — unless the old man is Santa Claus. But for this old man these things are all right, they are recognized to be the things that count; and the children, as they do in such cases, all believe in him.

Since the reality of everyday experience cannot provide Will Brady with the love he craves, he must seek his satisfaction in a tired myth that takes him out of the range of such reality. But the satisfaction is artificial and illusory, as the sun-tan is that he cultivates by lamp to make his Santa healthy-looking and attractive. The spurious satisfactions reward him finally with death as, blinded by his sun lamp, he wanders off to drown in a canal.

The Santa Claus role acts on Will Brady the way a hotel lobby does. It is the only place that he feels at home, because the purpose of every lobby is to be both in and out of this world. It takes people out of themselves and gives them a public identity different from the real self, which is too painful to face. In *The World in the Attic*, Clyde Muncy's father used to have himself paged in the lobby of a big city hotel, as Will Brady does. But role-playing in a lobby offers no more ultimate satisfactions than the Santa Claus part. The lobby is for lonely people who seek substitutes in their lives or who need surrogate lovers. When the lost souls of the urban waste land must face the reality of this world, even in the lobby, nothing can hide from them the dreary dimensions of their lives.

The quest for love and the quest for America — one or the other or both — have fascinated writers in this country as different as Sherwood Anderson, Faulkner, and Saul Bellow. I choose these three because Morris has something in common with all of them, and perhaps most with Anderson. Anderson watched America emerging from a rural, small-town civilization into full-fledged industrialism. He regarded the scene much as Morris does the degeneration of the frontier and the overpowering presence of the city. In both writers the American character shows itself as lonely and inarticulate, with sensitivity inhibited or disguised and channeled toward inanimate objects instead of human beings. What Morris shares with Faulkner is a totality of vision, but in microcosmic scale. Faulkner's integrated view of all southern history in his epic of Yoknapatawpha County finds a minor parallel in the patterned repetition of Morris' novels of the forties. And as, in that decade, love and identity preoccupied Saul Bellow, who found them threatened, so with Morris, who, less interested in the threat, seems content to record their fate. The manner of his work, as I said at the beginning, is his own. He has a satiric humor that should make him the natural enemy of every mortician. He has a style that makes his novels read, sometimes, like autobiographical essays. Ambitious in understatement, he has not been rich in invention. He has not, then, written the great American novel, nor wanted to, but novels, small and contained, undeniably in the American grain.

SAUL BELLOW: MAN ALIVE, SUSTAINED BY LOVE

If it is the function of the novelist to give a sense of his own time, Saul Bellow has met the obligations of his craft. In a time when every major social phenomenon has shown the same drift toward human effacement and individual anonymity, Bellow has faced, in everything he has written, the problem of the relation of man to his society. I do not mean to suggest that he is a social novelist. But he knows the faceless, corporate world around him and has been ravaged by it. His characters know it too, as they struggle in the iron-bound landscape of urban America under the excoriating pressure of money. Like any artist he has reacted to what is actual in his own time. Yet for him it has been the plight of man, not society, that has demanded attention as the novelist's true subject; it has been the imagination and not the analytical powers that he has relied upon as the ordering and shaping instrument of his art. In *The Lion and the Honeycomb*, R. P. Blackmur, discussing the relation of literature to politics, remarks that "The true business of literature . . . is to remind the powers that be, simple and corrupt as they are, of the turbulence they have to control. There is a disorder vital to the individual which is fatal to society." Bellow in the role of writer would make and preserve the opportunity for the expression of this individual disorder.

To do so, he must set himself against the society around him. He has no difficulty in taking up this stance: it has been forced upon him. In his essay, "Distractions of a Fiction Writer," Bellow says society does not honor the imagination. He knows that the writer feels society does not need him, that he is held in contempt. He says that in modern times the writer has "gone counter to the general direction" of society. Bellow's friend, the late Isaac Rosenfeld, writing on the relation of the writer to his society, has said, I believe, what Bellow himself would accept. It is essential for the writer, Rosenfeld asserts, to stand aside from society and to refuse to be assimilated to the institutions and attitudes of society. The writer must reject the role that society gives him, since society always showers upon him a contempt, suspicion, hostility, and rejection that are beyond alienation. The writer must rise above all this to achieve his real fulfilment, which is to record life from his living perspective. Bellow, I feel, has gained this perspective. The distance he maintains from society has enabled him, paradoxically, to grasp the truth and meaning in it. The sources of his power are inherent in his position. Being outside the society, in contrast to Stegner, he can readily see what it is doing to man. And he can freely speak out, for he is committed to no one but himself.

As the writer is driven, willingly and in his own interest, out of the society, so men generally are alienated from it. What has happened to man in the desperate world that Bellow has known has not lessened the writer's interest in him. On the contrary, it has made all the more intense Bellow's assertion of the indomitable and insatiable attraction of man for his kind or the interest of man himself in himself. At the close of "Distractions of a Fiction Writer," Bellow quotes Simone Weil: "To believe in the existence of human beings as such is love." Here, I think, is the clue to Bellow. With Jean-Paul Sartre, Bellow could well say, "I choose man," for the writing of a novel in which the writer cares about his people, Bellow seems to imply, is in itself an act of love. The kind of power that the writer wields, the power of imagination, enables the writer to give meaning to the feebleness and servitude of man's life. This power must reveal to man his greatness and must enable him to complete his own life. In this way Bellow reclaims the individual through love; he brings him again a sense of his own identity. The novelist, he has said, is self-appointed and self-elected. It is to these great tasks that he is elected.

In discovering his purpose and his mission, Bellow has not laid a claim upon either the new conservatism or the revival of religion. As these movements outline and propagate the hard view of reality with its omnipresent evil and its innate depravity, they have failed to attract Bellow's allegiance. In what I believe to be a comment on the contemporary scene in *The Adventures of Augie March*, Bellow recognizes that Christianity is demanding, in some quarters at least, a harsh reappraisal of man, principally in terms of his culpability. Such emphasis on man's potentiality for evil, as we have seen, is a part of the reaction against liberalism that gave impetus to both the new conservatism and the religious revival. When Augie seems to be unaware of the fashionable tendency to place first in his self-estimate his own propensity for evil, he is chided by his friend Padilla, the Mexican mathematician: "The big investigation today is into how *bad* a guy can be, not how good he can be. You don't keep up with the times. You're going against history." Bellow is like Augie. He is fully aware of man's fallibility, but it has not prevented him from declaring for love. If he has found support for his declaration in any tradition, it is a tradition in keeping with his alienation. It is, of course, a Jewish tradition.

Leslie Fiedler apparently thinks that the Jew is no longer an alien in America. He has claimed, on the contrary, in what I can only regard as a self-deluding fantasy, that the Jew is now "in the process of being mythicized into the representative American," that he is living the essential American experience, which is urban, lonely, European-oriented, and disenchanted with communism. Bellow has emerged, he says, as the writer who can transform this experience into myth. I cannot agree with this view of Bellow's impact on the national culture, but I do think it has the virtue of calling attention to the undeniably Jewish quality of Bellow's work. I want to suggest that Bellow's basic attitudes — the overwhelming need for love and the joy in life — bear a remarkable similarity to the principles of Hasidism. Aware as he is of his Jewish heritage, accomplished as he is as a translator of Yiddish stories, Bellow yet offers in his work no evidence of either the theism or the mysticism characteristic of Hasidism. He is a secular hasid, whether he knows it or not.

In our time, Martin Buber has been the chief spokesman for neo-Hasidism. He has said that "The core of hasidic teachings is the concept of a life of fervor, of exalted joy," and that the movement has "kindled both its simple and intellectual followers to joy in the world as it is, in life as it is, in every hour of life in this world, as that hour is." Buber emphasizes the primitive vitality of the movement, which binds one man to another in a relation of love and responsibility. The hasid knows that men must endure intolerable suffering, but he believes, nevertheless, that "the heartbeat of life is holy joy." In the hasidic life, sin is possible, but man may be purified of sin and every man may be redeemed. The appetites, far from being despised, are encouraged. Hasidism, Joseph Lookstein writes, glorifies "life" as against the book; knowledge and the intellect are less important than faith. In the struggle between reason and the instincts, if we equate the latter with "life," Bellow is never satisfied with the simplistic view that the rational man shall achieve his goal (as *Dangling Man* makes clear) or that reason is even a decisive force in man's acts. As Augie says when he sleeps with Stella before he has disengaged himself from Thea, "After much making with sense, it's senselessness that you submit to." Here is an Hebraism Matthew Arnold would not have recognized. Having cast out the stultifying preoccupation with sin, it is at ease in Zion.

It remains to ask, what are the literary consequences of the hasidic temperament, assuming always that Bellow shares it? The question is framed by the polarities of order and disorder. Hasidism suggests that religious enthusiasm of eighteenth-century Protestant sects, an emotional phenomenon accompanied by a disorder of a kind fatal to sustained literary effort. Yet John Crowe Ransom, in a symposium on the state of American writing in 1948, found American literature constricted, rising out of tension and moral protest, whereas the condition of great artistic creation, he said, is a "kind of exuberance of animal spirits," a massive joy. Bellow, especially after his first two novels, has displayed a plenitude of animal spirits, an ingenuity of invention, a richness of imagination. He has seized voraciously upon the cult of experience that Philip Rahv says begins for American literature with Strether's cry to Little Bilham, "Live, live!" Bellow has carried beyond earlier writers who sought, according to Rahv, liberation from convention and taboo; he has sought liberation for the self. The lavish and disorderly characteristics associated with Hasidism may then be fruitful for literary achievement. And this is especially true when they combine in a literary personality who feels, as Bellow does, that the novelist may not know what order is but does know this: "A novelist begins with disorder and disharmony, and he goes toward order by an unknown process of the imagination. And anyway, the order he achieves is not the order that ideas have."

If *Augie March* is the most obvious expression of massive joy that Bellow wrote within this period, it is not to be supposed that this book sprang from its author's mind without antecedents and foreshadowings. Bellow's critics tend to overemphasize the differences between that generous-spirited novel and the two shorter, more tightly organized books that preceded it. Looking back on the fiction Bellow has thus far given us, one can see that *Dangling Man* (1944), his first novel, leads a kind of subterranean life. While Bellow seems to succumb to despair and his protagonist seems to welcome self-immolation and self-effacement in regimentation, Bellow's persistent assumptions throughout the book are the constants that appear in all his work. In *Dangling Man* the burden of what Bellow says is that freedom is the necessary condition for man if he is to pursue his chief end as a man — the knowledge of himself; successful in his quest, man's energies may then be released in love. It may well be an oversimplification to say that all Bellow is encompassed in these three terms: freedom, identity, and love; but I submit that it may be a fruitful oversimplification. At the same time that the book looks forward to a positive statement of what most engages Bellow, it looks backward at certain modes of behavior and expression that Bellow wishes to reject. It becomes, in short, a document in the cultural history of the forties. Take, for example, the opening paragraphs of the novel. Joseph, the protagonist, who tells the story in the form of a journal, records at the outset an attack upon the code of the athlete and the gentleman which stipulates hard-boiled reticence, banishes introspection as sentimentalism, and substitutes violent action for feeling and thought. The inner life of the mind and the emotions must come first. The meaning of these passages, I would suggest, is that Bellow is turning away from Hemingwayism, away from an aesthetic of understatement which had been dominant for two decades and which was inimical to that treatment of experience which finds it necessary to discover and lay bare, with little restraint, the thoughts and emotions of its subjects. Bellow does not thus establish a style, but he clearly repudiates one, and his is one repudiation among others — like that of the new fiction — combined to diminish the influence of Hemingway on postwar literature.

A second note on cultural history centers upon a scene in a

restaurant where Joseph meets a member of the Communist party who tries to ignore him: he is angry with Joseph who has left the party. Joseph has left it before the novel opens. For Joseph, and for Bellow too, radical political thought is already in the past; answers are not to be sought in it. In this repudiation of radicalism is implicit a larger rejection which encompasses all politics. As we have seen in the war novel and in the new fiction particularly, and even in the fiction of tradition, political ideologies have proved singularly unattractive to the writers of Bellow's generation.

It is true that at the end of the novel Joseph goes to his draft board and hurries his induction into the army. But he is not eager to fight the Fascists. On the contrary, he feels himself overwhelmed by the society that wishes everyone to fight the Fascists, that wishes everyone to recognize as the only reality a world in which men must fight. Joseph knows he lives in this world, but he lives also in a world of "ideal construction," which is "the one that unlocks the imprisoning self." Joseph lives, in other words, in two worlds, and is aware of the unbridgeable gap between them. The tensions in Joseph's life, then, are in part the result of being both inside and outside society. This dilemma he generalizes: all people struggle to free themselves; in all people the final quest is for the same thing — "the desire for pure freedom." If we could achieve what we would ideally like to be and have, then we would stop living exclusively for our own sakes. Joseph, who early in the novel says he must "give all his attention to defending his inner differences, the ones that really matter," is determined to seek out his own identity: "But I must know what I myself am." When he attains this self-knowledge, he is prepared to return to the real world from the ideal construction, and to be a citizen and a good man in it. For "goodness is achieved not in a vacuum, but in the company of other men, attended by love." Bellow has here expressed a sentiment in 1944 that he was to repeat in 1957, in the quotation from Simone Weil that I have already cited.

Joseph reaches for what Bellow was not yet ready, in 1944, to permit his characters to achieve. Joseph cannot reconcile his two worlds, and he cannot exist as a whole man with dignity in the real world. Augie March can do both. Worse than this, Joseph cannot exist in his own independent world, carved out of his own inner resources of mind and will and sensibility. Intransigent in the face of real experience, Joseph tries to spin a life out of his own spirit, having the opportunity to do this when he is in suspension between a regular job and induction into the army. He fails, and his failure leads Rueben Frank to conclude that the ideological center of the book is "the bankruptcy of a metaphysically derived humanism." It is true that Joseph aims at a life of reason and hopes to cultivate the ability to absorb suffering and pain without resort to any power outside himself. This is the humanism that Joseph cannot himself sustain and that his world will not permit him to enjoy. I accept Frank's view, as far as it goes, but I would add two thoughts. First, the reason for the bankruptcy of humanism lies, I believe, in its oversimplified faith in a rationalism that has no understanding of emotional needs. Second, Bellow did not choose a strong representative of that humanism by which to test its viability. Joseph is not a scholar or an artist; as an intellectual he is a dilettante. To throw the burden of proving the possibilities of humanism today upon such a character is to vitiate the value of the test.

Bellow is on sounder ground, I think, in drawing upon the sense of alienation. Intellectual or not, Joseph has tried to find a sufficiency of inner resources and of intellectual independence to confront his world and lead a life of reason and disciplined feeling. But in the social vacuum in which he finds himself as a rootless man, he fails. One reason is that the society will not accept him, as it rejects artists and intellectuals generally. Since these people do not perform in their narrowest sense, essential and productive functions, they have no status in the eyes of the respectable and productive members of the community. Or rather they have the status of children, tolerated and patronized by their elders who know a great deal more about the bread and butter problems of life. Not being privy to the mystery of business and finance and not seeming to care about that mystery, these children are outside the pale. Upon them fall all the suspicions reserved by the in-group for dissidents, the breakers of images. To refrain from joining in is to invite fear and hatred. These are convictions which Bellow has cherished and maintained since writing *Dangling Man*, for they too were repeated in 1957 when he published "Distractions of a Fiction Writer." In that essay, as I have already pointed out, he asserts that society does not honor the imagination, which is so important to the writer. The writer feels, then, that the society does not need him. The writer lives in a world where a man's work is supposed to be in the practical realm of things. Not being practical, the writer is held in contempt. In the novel Joseph's brother and his family document the antagonism of the middle class to those who, outside it, are searching for freedom and identity.

Another aspect of the alienation motif lies in the psychological reasons for Joseph's failure to sustain his own ideal life. His idleness tends to feed upon itself and has the effect of immobilizing him. He quotes Goethe: "All comfort in life is based upon a regular occurrence of external phenomena." The absence of regularity, like being jobless, robs Joseph of a place. By this I mean what I take it Marmeladov means in *Crime and Punishment*: not simply that a man must have a job or even a haven, but that he needs a sense of belonging to the community of man. For Joseph the notion of community is breaking down. As it goes, he begins to lose feeling for the people around him, to lose touch with the magnetic chain of humanity, the most serious sin in Hawthorne's lexicon. For Bellow and Hawthorne are alike in their reverence for humanity and alike in condemning the absence of love that permits a man to isolate himself. Fiedler comments on Bellow's recognition of man's essential loneliness as the state that leads him to rediscover his identity. He thinks this loneliness is a condition of the dissolution of any shared definition of man. But Bellow himself has denied that his work as a novelist is dependent on an agreed picture of man and the universe. Bellow's characters are lonely when they are deprived of love.

In this connection a comparison of the relation between Joseph and his brother Amos and the relation between Augie March and his brother Simon is illuminating. Amos and Simon are very much alike in their shrewd worldliness and success. Both have contempt for their ineffectual brothers. Joseph cannot accept his brother's inadequacies; he cannot credit Amos' good intentions. This relationship is ambiguous: it is never severed, but it is always uneasy and almost always hostile. Augie, in the later novel, suffers terrible gestures of rejection from Simon. But he can surmount Simon's opportunistic and harsh treatment to make an outright declaration of love for his brother and to accept him, despite their differences. Augie, knowing love, the love for his brother and the love for his wife Stella, finds himself and maintains his independence. Joseph is borne down, cannot become the sovereign individual he wishes to be, and so is forced in the end to seek in the army the supervision and regimentation that signalize his defeat.

The form of the novel, despite the inherent disadvantages of telling a story through successive recordings in a journal, is admirably suited to the main character and to the purpose of the novel. As Percy Lubbock remarked, any author who uses this devise is "engaged in the attempt to show a mind in action." The solipsistic tendencies in Joseph's life — in the life of reason he tries to live and in the psychological aberrations that overtake him — are perfectly expressed in a technique that makes him the commentator on his own condition. On the other hand, Bellow seems to realize the limitations of his method, since he introduces a section on the "Spirit of Alternatives" so that Joseph may carry on a kind of interior dialogue. In this way, a second, opposing point of view can be presented in the novel. It is partly the fault of the method, furthermore, that no character emerges vividly. Joseph is interested in himself only but, paradoxically, is not completely self-revealing. His wife, his relatives, and his friends are only dimly realized.

Bellow's first novel is organized in the Flaubert-James tradition. It is a manner that persists with the next book, *The Victim*, but thereafter Bellow wisely drops it. The economy of scene and tightness of structure seem compatible, in *Dangling Man*, with the intense introspection of Joseph; they seem compatible with the negative case for love, where we get the careful dissection of what it means to a man to be denied. The manner changes with *Augie March* because Augie is not demoralized and corrupted by a state of suspension; his emotional life is not brutalized and coarsened; his search for identity is not frustrated. Augie succeeds, and his success demands free and ample movement.

But before Augie comes Asa Leventhal of *The Victim* (1947). Joseph was a victim of undirected, almost static floating in the current of American life; he had no place. Asa the Jew is a victim not merely of anti-Semitism but of his own sense of insecurity, of his own conviction that he has muscled in on an alien world where his precarious position is daily called into question. He is deeply anxious about his place. Both men feel keenly a sense of differentness: the intellectual as outcast and the Jew as outcast. And attendant upon their alienation is aggravation, exacerbation, maladjustment, and violence. Their condition is not simply a consequence of what society or other men have done to them; it is a result also — and this is of even greater importance to Bellow — of their own shortcomings. Neither man achieves a full sense of what it means to be a mature human being. The specific problem of *The Victim* is this: that Asa is a man who falls short of love and understanding and humanity. He is self-engrossed, but blindly, not in a way that will enable him to discover the self. His plight is a function of the anti-Semitism, real and imagined, that he feels engulfs him. Loaded with these disabilities and thus in the worst possible condition to do so, Asa is asked to consider the nature and extent of one human being's responsibility to another.

Not that Asa is a bad man. He wishes, as much as Joseph, to be a good man. When his sister-in-law, in the absence of her husband, summons him in the crisis of a child's illness, he accepts the burden of responsibility. Later he thinks that the mother somehow blames him for her son's illness. His uneasiness leads him to reflect on what it is to be human, and he decides that it must mean to be accountable in spite of weaknesses. The idea has been broached in a conversation he had had earlier in which an old man, Schlossberg, had talked about acting. Schlossberg is in the novel to represent the concept of humanity that Bellow generally advances in his work and to provide a scale against which we may measure Asa's failure, as he himself does. Schlossberg, a responsible man himself, tries to answer the question, what is human? In doing so, he rejects the scientific view that would seek to define man by quantification. For him, a human life is a great thing, because it has beauty and dignity. In another conversation he says, "I have to be myself in full." He conceives the full range of human possibilities — "my mind can go around the world" — and the stern limits — man is born once and he will die once. It is to the degree that Asa fails to measure up to Schlossberg's standards that he fails to be a good man.

Bellow's strategy in the novel is to deny Asa that definition of the self that man must achieve in order to become a responsible human being. The difficulties inherent in the self-conscious effort to discover one's identity are complicated by Asa's relations with Kirby Allbee, an anti-Semite who poses problems for him of responsibility and guilt which he cannot resolve. Allbee, a descendant of the New England aristocracy (one of his forebears was Governor Winthrop), accuses Asa of having deliberately caused him to lose his job. Asa at first denies the charge flatly, but later comes to a grudging and partial acceptance of it. At this point, Allbee, who is a virtually penniless and unemployable alcoholic, moves in with Asa. The latter is thus forced to pay for his guilt by living intimately with a man who despises him. The charged ambiguity of this situation lies in determining which of the men is the victim.

Allbee's view is that he is the victim at once of social determinism and social displacement. His predicament, he says, is the result of blind movement and has nothing to do with his own efforts. The individual is "shuttled back and forth . . . Groups, organizations succeed or fail, but not individuals any longer." If no human agency is responsible for making the fate of individual man, it is difficult to see how any one man can be responsible for any other. What moral obligation, then, is Asa, a more or less successful man, supposed to have toward Allbee, if neither man has made the arrangements? Allbee attempts to get around this problem by making an argument based on the Old Testament. Asa, he says, must reject determinism as un-Hebraic. Asa must believe that if a man suffers, he deserves suffering, which comes to him as a punishment. Life itself is not evil, but man may be, thus bringing punishment down upon himself. This is the Jewish point of view, found everywhere in the Bible. By accepting, it, Asa frees himself of any blame for Allbee's ruin. From Asa's point of view the difficulty with Allbee's argument is that Asa is not sure whether he accepts it or not; he is confused and uncomprehending. Asa cannot establish a philosophical position or take the long view because he is submerged in his self, a frightened, insecure Jew.

If it is inconsistent of Allbee to use determinism as a protective rationalization for his own failure and at the same time to charge Asa with responsibility for his downfall, one must remember that Allbee is one of Bellow's plausible eccentrics, a madman loosed upon the world with a perfectly straight face and an unencumbered right to pursue his peculiar fantasy. Nevertheless, the problem of determinism which he raises is one of Bellow's enduring preoccupations. Always aware of the possibilities for social and biological determinism, Bellow seems little inclined to choose between them and free will.

The issue of social displacement is allied to Allbee's determinism, since he is able to exonerate himself from blame by believing he has been drowned in an irresistible tide of Jews. They have cultivated, in a metropolitan culture, survival qualities which are totally alien to the Anglo-Saxon sense of honor and fair play. The gutter virtues of opportunism, shrewdness, and calculation come naturally to the Jew in the competition for money and power. Usurpation of economic domination is bad enough, but when the Jew begins to take over the culture, the full bitterness of his failure sweeps over Allbee. He resents Jews who write books about Emerson and Thoreau or sing Negro spirituals; they represent the degradation of his heritage. Actually, Allbee has abdicated his position of leadership in the culture, as he admits when he says that he is not living up to his ancestors. Asa is by no means in a position to set the tone and character of the culture. What Bellow seems to suggest is the traditional flux that marks the open, democratic society of America. The danger of this condition, which he emphasizes, is that it makes a sense of insecurity pervasive in the culture so that the culture seems, in its loss of continuity, to belong to no one. Bellow also seems to suggest that Allbee is a victim of the status revolution in America that resulted in the displacement of the old Protestant families. In this respect, Allbee has much in common with James Gould Cozzens.

Allbee's anti-Semitism must be seen in the context of his beliefs in determinism and displacement. The tactics in his attack upon Asa vary from wheedling and cajoling to demanding and threatening, but the aim is always the same: to emphasize Asa's differentness and to crush him with a sense of guilt. His head is cluttered with stereotypes of the Jew. Jews do not drink, and they think all gentiles are drunkards; Jews resort to trickery, not to violence, to settle differences. In addition, he makes a great deal of the cultural disorientation of the Jew in America. But none of these approaches is as bad as the way he eats at Asa's spirit once he has insinuated himself into the Levanthal apartment. He reads the intimate correspondence between Asa and his absent wife. In Asa's absence he brings a whore into Asa's bed. He turns on the gas and tries to kill himself and Asa as well. In all these ways he goes beyond anti-Semitism to violate the sanctity of the human heart, to destroy the integrity and privacy of Asa's inner being.

So it follows that Asa is a victim of anti-Semitism, but not the lily-white sacrificial lamb of the socially conscious fiction. He *is* guilty. He has contributed to Allbee's downfall out of his own sense of insecurity and tendency toward paranoia, out of his own secret feeling that he is not worth much on the market, and even without knowing consciously that he is doing it. It is the fear inherent in Asa's very Jewishness, emerging in truculence and aggressiveness, that trips up Allbee and starts him on his slide. The other side of Asa's offensiveness is the economy of compassion and of sympathetic understanding that Asa feels forced to practice. He is afraid of his decency and good impulses. At the end of the novel, after he has forcibly thrown Allbee out of the apartment, it comes to Asa that Allbee must have experienced unspeakable horrors, things that would have been fatal to him; that Allbee had made his crazy demands on him in order to delude himself because he was frantic with self-hatred. A self-possessed man, confident in his own judgment, would not, in the first place, have permitted Allbee to make real the kind of fantastic situation he had foisted on Asa. In the second place, a secure man would have permitted his heart to be engaged by the miserable plight of a derelict like Allbee. Asa, a frightened man, could not afford compassion. His fear, his recalcitrance, his bellicosity — all these murder understanding and love.

Bellow's achievement is to have seen all around the theme of anti-Semitism in such a way as to elevate it into something of general significance. Or, to put it another way, Bellow understands that anti-Semitism is a superficial social phenomenon. He has succeeded in getting at the profound psychological and sociological truths that lie beneath the surface of anti-Semitism. In this downgrading, so to speak, of anti-Semitism as a theme Bellow reveals the same hard-nosed tendency to rip through surface manifestations to the essentials that he does in *Dangling Man* when he has Joseph say the war is only an incident because it will change nothing important, that is, man's effort to find love and dignity. These fundamentals, in *The Victim*, are drawn together in Bellow's vision of American life as dynamic, where the clash between the new and the old constantly creates tensions. Bellow does not advocate any easy answer like social tolerance. Solutions, if there are any, lie in time, when men like Asa will have achieved selfhood.

In 1953 Bellow published *The Adventures of Augie March*, his first popular success. Explaining in the *New York Times* for January 31 of the following year how he wrote the book, Bellow begins and ends his account with a quotation from Robert Penn Warren about writing abroad, " '. . . where the language is not your own, and you are forced into yourself in a special way.' " He comments on the paradox that, being away from home, he thought about home most of the time. One is reminded of Glenway Wescott in Paris remembering Wisconsin or Scott Fitzgerald in St. Raphaël finishing *The Great Gatsby*. In Austria, Italy, Paris, writing about Chicago before and during the Depression years, Bellow was in the tradition of the expatriate who had found Europe a stimulus to the examination of his native ground. But with Bellow there is a difference, or two differences. One is, as he says, that he was writing *Augie March* at a time when Americans were being told what they were and were not; as an American it was therefore a good time to look for a definition of the self. The other is that he sees himself self-consciously as rootless, or perhaps it is better to say as having roots everywhere. He is the son of Russian-Jewish immigrants and grew up in Montreal and Chicago. He wrote his novel in many places in Europe and the United States. It was a gesture meant to link the two continents, to show that he belonged nowhere and everywhere. He will not be condemned to a place or a time. "We are not born to be condemned but to live."

It is fitting that the author of *Augie March* should feel the necessity for self-discovery, should wander about on two continents, should exalt experience. Augie himself, the picaresque hero of his story, is an uncommitted wanderer upon the face of the earth, savoring experience for its infinite variety and cherishing his independence to seek it out where he may. He is full of the joy of living in a world where the opportunity for experiment is practically limitless. For Augie, the doctrine of life is in the act, not in the thought; the life of reason must be investigated, but no finalities, no ultimate satisfactions or motives, are to be found there. Yet Augie is not hostile or indifferent to ideas. In his scale of values he has simply placed ideas on a less than dominant level. Bellow has a conception of man so broad that ideas cannot dominate it. It is the imagination, which shapes experience, that launches Augie on "a campaign after a worth-while fate," the discovery of self, love, and the joy of living. Augie is successful, so far as any human being can be, where Joseph and Asa of the previous novels had failed; his story is the positive statement of Bellow's most persistent and deepest convictions.

Augie's "campaign" suggests an activist course. His friend Padilla tells him he is too ambitious, by which Padilla means that Augie is reaching for ideal happiness and good. The sense of quest involves the sense of a directed will. It is by no means clear, however, that Augie is pursuing his fate with a clear-cut conception of what it ought to be. He is not a young man who knows exactly where he is going, because such a straightforward conception of experience — as though life could be arranged on a taut line — is foreign to Bellow's feeling for the happenstance of life. Most of the time, in fact, Augie entertains experience as it comes to him, in a mood of uncritical acceptance. He is receptive and tends to be passive. Bellow conceives him as happily adrift on the flux of life and easily susceptible to manipulation. Stella, the girl he eventually marries, sees that he and she are alike in that both are persons who can be used by others. The world of experience is spread all before him, and he feasts upon it. But he eats of it only to live, for his quintessential life is, like Gatsby's, his Platonic conception of himself. This he guards always.

The best example of Augie's duality — his passive acquiescence in the aims of others and his last-ditch faithfulness to his image of himself as free — is in his courtship of Lucy Magnus, daughter of a wealthy family into which his brother Simon has married. Simon has urged Augie also to marry into this family, and Augie obligingly woos Lucy. But some stubborn will to resist, blindly to balk at being swallowed up, makes him slow in pushing on to marriage. When circumstances falsely cast him in the role of faithless lover, the Magnuses summon him for a solemn scene of rejection. "I was thrown for fair on the free spinning of the world," he says, and he likes it. He has lost a great deal of money. But he is freed from the threat posed by continued intimacy: that it will force him to betray himself. Here is Bellow's version of Miss Welty's love and separateness conceptions.

In this duality, to put it another way, the warp of Augie's life is exposure to experience, as is apparent from the very beginning of the novel. When Grandma Lausch finds Augie various jobs as a boy, he comments, "Saying 'various jobs,' I give out the Rosetta stone, so to speak, to my entire life." Shortly after this, he begins to mingle with all kinds of people: intellectuals and students, criminals and street loafers. It is the pattern of his life to meet and know a vast variety of people. Bellow scatters with prodigal hand a huge sampling of humanity through the pages of his novel. With his taste for the bizarre and the outré, which he somehow manages to present as ordinary and credible — simply by assuming that it is — Bellow gives us a range of character and experience fully in the tradition of the picaresque novel, greater in its variety than the adventures of Captain Farrago and Teague O'Regan in *Modern Chivalry* or of Huck Finn and Nigger Jim. He has a sense of the mystery and strangeness of people. Thus Augie has a lover who trains an eagle to hunt iguanas; he serves as general factotum to a many-sided, philosophic cripple conceived as a heroic, Napoleonic figure; he is a castaway in the company of a scientist who believes he has discovered the secret of life; he is research assistant to a millionaire who is writing a book on human happiness from the standpoint of the rich; he holds jobs as shoe salesman, dog currier, smuggler of aliens, labor organizer. In one of his uncollected short stories, Bellow's protagonist says he has "an idea that a man is bound to do everything in his lifetime." Augie has had a try at fulfilling this ideal, and all these apparently disparate experiences are made coherent and unified by the inexhaustible love of life that provides the initial and basic motivation for them.

One of his friends quotes to Augie:

> Les vrais voyageurs sont ceux-la seuls qui partent
> Pour partir; coeurs légers, semblables aux ballons,
> De leur fatalité jamais ils ne s'écartent,
> Et, sans savoir pourquoi, disent toujours: Allons!

This last was probably aimed at me and accused me of being too light of heart and ignorantly saying good-by. I seemed to have critics everywhere. However, for a cold day this had a very bright sun, the trains were passing in blackness over an embankment of yellow concrete, the kids were screaming and whirling over the whole vast play yard, around the flagpole and in and out of the portables, and I felt especially stirred.

The passage speaks for itself in its sense of exhilaration; it is to be noted especially that this is an urban scene that moves Augie. Bellow, however, is not to be conceived as committed to a simple optimism about experience. Augie is made to say that he understands as well, "how much disappointment is in the taste of existence."

A man submitting, but submitting only so far, to a variety of experiences defines his own character. He wants to discover what possibilities are open to the human being. He is like the character who wanted to do everything in the short story I referred to above; that fellow banged an Italian on the head with a bottle, without provocation, in order to discover what it meant to do something hateful and lousy. Robert Penn Warren is thus wrong, I believe, in saying that Augie is a man who has no commitments. This judgment, to be sure, reflects Augie's spirit of independence and confirms Einhorn, the philosophic cripple, who says that Augie has opposition in him, a desire to offer resistance and say no. But it overlooks the rationale behind Augie's experimental mood in embracing such a variety of experience. Augie is trying to find out who he is, to realize his self, and to this task he is continuously and perseveringly committed throughout the novel. In the cohesive but criss-crossed pattern of his life, this quest is the woof. The constant threat to his independence is his passivity, since he is exposed to numerous "persons who persistently arise before me with life counsels and illuminations throughout my entire earthly pilgrimage." They are people who would subjugate his will and twist his personality into some facsimile of their own. He is the chameleon man, taking his coloration from the strong characters around him, but he is always in the end the stubbornly reluctant recruit. He admires Einhorn, whom he meets at an impressionable age, but he says, ". . . if I were really his disciple and not what I am . . . ," because he has already learned to shun limiting loyalties.

The problem of maintaining independence in order to seek identity creates its greatest tensions when Augie falls in love. I have already indicated that he feels that the intimacy of marriage with Lucy Magnus might lead to falsehood, that is, to some distortion of his person made necessary by accommodations to marriage. Later, in a period of intensive self-examination he wonders if he is not totally confused, wanting to serve love and yet to preserve his independence.

The problem is insoluble, but laboring with it leads Augie to one of his most decisive insights into the nature of the self. He marries the beautiful Stella and discovers that if love conquers all, there is plenty for it to conquer and go on conquering, always and always. The hard work that all people have is to maintain themselves in their present positions in the face of the burden they are carrying, the pretenses and adjustments they must make, the things they must remember and forget. Augie and Stella live in Paris where life is supposed to be *calme, ordre, luxe, volupté*. But he realizes that Stella, like others, has work to do. Within herself she has come to combat the world and all in it, to justify her existence. This is everyone's toil: "Every precious personality framed dramatically and doing the indispensable work." This conception of the self, seen in terms of dramatic conflict, struggling to preserve inviolate its own integrity, is Bellow's most profound statement about the nature of man and the relation of the individual to the world.

In defining the self, Augie has occasion to draw a distinction between man and Mankind that reflects, I suppose, Bellow's reaction to the enterprises of society in his time. When Augie is in Mexico he runs into a man named Fraser, an intellectual he had known at the University of Chicago, who is working for Trotsky and who proposes to Augie a harebrained scheme for the protection of Trotsky. Augie's response is "Please God! . . . keep me from being sucked into another one of those great currents where I can't be myself." Augie sees that Trotsky is one of the great abstractions. He is Living History, he is important for Mankind,

but he will eat up a single man. Later in the book, Augie meets
Fraser in Paris. Fraser has been in military intelligence; he is
now with the World Education Fund. He is the emissary to the
world of affairs, and he talks about Paris as the City of Man. In
Augie's view, Fraser is not alive as a man and does not recognize
that others are so alive; Augie thinks Paris must be for men, for
human beings like himself. His own, particular experience is always more precious to him than any group experience. When he
is a C.I.O. organizer, he spends the Decoration Day of the Republic
Steel massacre in bed with his girl.

It wasn't even in my power to be elsewhere, once we had started. No,
I just didn't have the calling to be a union man or in politics, or any
notion of my particle of will coming before the ranks of a mass that
was about to march forward from misery. How would this will of mine
have got there to lead the way? I couldn't just order myself to become
one of those people who do go out before the rest, who stand and inter-
cept the big social ray, or collect and concentrate it like burning glass,
who glow and dazzle and make bursts of fire. It wasn't what I was meant
to be.

Late in the book Augie makes explicit the idea of quest for the
self: "You will understand . . . that I have always tried to become
what I am. But it's a frightening thing. Because what if what I am
by nature isn't good enough?" Then he adds, "I will never force
the hand of fate to create a better Augie March, nor change the
time to an age of gold." To which his friend replies, "It is better
to die what you are than to live a stranger forever." This determination in pursuit of an end recalls Ortega's definition of a hero
as ". . . one who wants to be himself. The root of heroic action
may be found then in a real act of the will."

The assumption necessary for the portrait of the hero thus becomes freedom of will. I have already indicated how Bellow moves
between the doctrines of passivity and activism in his depiction
of Augie. He seldom permits Augie to make a specific statement
about this philosophical conflict, which is, of course, the old
question of freedom versus determinism, but other characters in
the novel talk about it. A girl Fraser gets with child is determined
to have an abortion, even if it kills her — and it almost does. But
she knows what she wants: "You can't let your life be decided
for you by any old thing that comes up." She is as eager as Augie

to command her own destiny. Augie's brother Simon, in contrast, believes in biological determinism and explains what are to him Augie's sexuality and irresponsibility as a consequence of the same traits in their parents. Augie himself is led to reflect on this problem the first time he sleeps with Stella. He is helping her in a perfectly altruistic spirit to run away from an unpleasant situation when their car breaks down on a mountainside in the night. They give in to the circumstances, joyously, and Augie comments, "The inevitability that brought us together on this mountain of wet grass was greater than the total of all other considerations." It is about this incident that Augie had commented, "After much making with sense, it's senselessness that you submit to." The instincts in the end determine action and dominate life, while the reason's weakness is constantly exposed and the will's efficacy thus doubted. Much later in the book, Augie finds himself in the company of the mad scientist who would use reason alone to save man and the world. But Augie knows that the scientist is a distorted personality because he has neglected the heart.

Such discussion is not designed so much to establish Bellow's philosophical position — and this it would be difficult to do because of the apparent contradictions — as to clarify the meaning of the self. It is subordinate, in short, to the main business of the novel. So it is that in treating the problem of realism and idealism, Bellow's aim is to show how this philosophic question bears on Augie's conception of man. In one discourse to himself, Augie appears to reject idealism, thinking that while everyone tries to create a world he can live in, the real world is already created and he will have trouble if his fabrication does not correspond to the real world. The problem here is the adjustment of the individual to the world. Later on, when Augie is in despair, he tells himself he is no worse than anyone else. Everyone pretends to be what he is not, hiding his real self behind a mask. Mere humanity, "disfigured, degenerate, dark," is as confused as he. Everyone invents a man who can stand before appearances, for to expose his real self is to be exposed to shame — a thought that seems to echo the existentialists. Each man tries to recruit others ". . . to play a supporting role and sustain him in his make-believe." The leader invents a whole world, and this becomes his reality and the reality of his followers. Most people live in the invented world; they take

their place in it, and they are safe: they are types. But they muti-
late themselves to fit some one else's idea of reality. Because he
wishes to be an independent personality, Augie does not accept
the invented world, yet he knows that he has constantly sought
out from others protection against the chaos of the real world.
Augie's preference, then, is philosophic realism, but he understands that he is not always strong enough for it. To live with it is
to be alone in a confused place among creatures capable of great
evil.

Augie's activities range from this kind of philosophic speculation to the stealing of books as a regular business enterprise, and
his acquaintance ranges from University of Chicago instructors
to uneducated Jewish immigrants. The demands made upon Bellow's ear and upon his verbal ingenuity and inventiveness are
thus very great. He has chosen to confront his writing problem
with what I shall call the paradoxical multilevel style. Augie
commands the language spoken by small-time Jewish fight managers as well as "a speech enriched by the dialectic and joyful intellectual play of Jewish conversation," as Fiedler has said of Bellow's
style generally. Augie commands the language of the books he
steals, being attracted particularly to heroic expression. He commands the language of business and of upper-middle-class society.
But it is his whim, or maybe his failing, to mismatch stylistic level
and social or experiental level. Giving a gutter experience heroic
expression, he counts on paradox and unpredictability to convey
the quality of his apprehension of life and people. What is ordinarily deemed an appropriate mode of expression is only infrequently Augie's choice, partly out of ignorance and partly out of
sheer delight in paradox and shock. The style, then, is mixed. It
has a great range and splendidly rich resources. It is flamboyant
and experimental. It pulsates with the same rapid and erratic
beat that we have seen in Augie's life. In a word, Bellow has
achieved an organic style in the novel: it fits his protagonist and
it fits his theme. The style is Augie, who wrote the book, ". . . not
in order to be so highly significant but probably because human
beings have the power to say and ought to employ it at the proper
time."

The last word on *Augie March* must be a reaffirmation of its
vitality. Here and there, indeed, Augie looks into the deep, dark

pools of humanity. He recognizes potentialities for evil as well as good in human beings. Though he has found love in marriage to Stella, he is coming to some sense of its cost to himself. Whatever a man's condition in the scale of human growth and decay, Augie recognizes that he is still a man. Although he sees the bizarre and grotesque everywhere about him, they simply add to his undiminished appetite for life. His characteristic posture is joyful. At the end of the book, a smile comes unbidden to his lips. He has met experience, he will go on pursuing it, and he will never permit it to overwhelm him.

In the work I have here considered, and in the fiction published later as well, Bellow has been moving toward a hedged affirmation: an insistence upon the importance and possibility for each man of fulfilment in knowledge and spirit, with a recognition always of the cost of such fulfilment. In qualified terms he has revived the cult of personality and, paradoxically, given us the clue to the social history of the postwar years. Preoccupied with what it feels like, what it takes, what it means to be a human being, Bellow has made man the vital center of his work. No guiding philosophic conception shapes his image of man; he is concerned with man alive. Augie says, in one of his introspective passages, that he seeks simplicity, and one is reminded of Thoreau's "Simplify! Simplify!" and then of his famous declaration of faith, "I did not wish to live what was not life, living is so dear; nor did I wish to practise resignation, unless it was quite necessary. I wanted to live deep and suck out all the marrow of life. . . ."

So it is with Bellow, who wants no confining philosophy or myth, who has no patience with passing social phenomena, who finds the essentials of human experience in human beings seeking themselves and seeking love. And fleeing annihilation. That fate awaits the corporate, tabulated man whose identity has been surrendered. Bellow's fiction is surely a response to his need and ours to push back the many-faced leviathan. It is a reaction against the loss of community in modern America. In its ultimate atomization it is social history.

APPENDIX:
FICTION OF THE FORTIES

The list of authors and titles below, arranged by year, shows the chronology and quantity of fiction written in the period covered by this book. The list includes all titles of fiction discussed in the text and a few additional titles which, for one reason or another, seemed to merit a place here.

1939

John Dos Passos, *Adventures of a Young Man*
James T. Farrell, *Tommy Gallagher's Crusade*
J. P. Marquand, *Wickford Point*
Irwin Shaw, *Sailor Off the Bremen*
Robert Penn Warren, *Night Rider*

1940

Erskine Caldwell, *Trouble in July*
Walter Van Tilburg Clark, *The Ox-Bow Incident*
James Gould Cozzens, *Ask Me Tomorrow*
James T. Farrell, *Father and Son*
William Faulkner, *The Hamlet*
Ernest Hemingway, *For Whom the Bell Tolls*
Granville Hicks, *The First to Awaken*
Meyer Levin, *Citizens*
Carson McCullers, *The Heart Is a Lonely Hunter*
John O'Hara, *Pal Joey*
Upton Sinclair, *World's End*
Wallace Stegner, *On a Darkling Plain*
Richard Wright, *Native Son*

1941

Gerald Warner Brace, *Light on a Mountain*
Howard Fast, *The Last Frontier*
Caroline Gordon, *Green Centuries*
Andrew Lytle, *At the Moon's Inn*
Carson McCullers, *Reflections in a Golden Eye*

J. P. Marquand, *H. M. Pulham, Esquire*
Budd Schulberg, *What Makes Sammy Run?*
Wallace Stegner, *Fire and Ice*
Eudora Welty, *A Curtain of Green*

1942

Nelson Algren, *Never Come Morning*
James Gould Cozzens, *The Just and the Unjust*
Howard Fast, *The Unvanquished*
William Faulkner, *Go Down, Moses*
Granville Hicks, *Only One Storm*
Mary McCarthy, *The Company She Keeps*
Wright Morris, *My Uncle Dudley*
Irwin Shaw, *Welcome to the City*
John Steinbeck, *The Moon Is Down*
Harry Sylvester, *Dearly Beloved*
Eudora Welty, *The Robber Bridegroom*

1943

John Dos Passos, *Number One*
James T. Farrell, *My Days of Anger*
Howard Fast, *Citizen Tom Paine*
Joseph Freeman, *Never Call Retreat*
Wallace Stegner, *The Big Rock Candy Mountain*
Robert Penn Warren, *At Heaven's Gate*
Eudora Welty, *The Wide Net*
Ira Wolfert, *Tucker's People*

1944

Saul Bellow, *Dangling Man*
Harry Brown, *A Walk in the Sun*
Erskine Caldwell, *Tragic Ground*
Howard Fast, *Freedom Road*
Caroline Gordon, *The Women on the Porch*
John Hersey, *A Bell for Adano*
Granville Hicks, *Behold Trouble*
Albert Maltz, *The Cross and the Arrow*
Jean Stafford, *Boston Adventure*

1945

Richard Brooks, *The Brick Foxhole*
Walter Van Tilburg Clark, *The City of Trembling Leaves*
Caroline Gordon, *The Forest of the South*
William Maxwell, *The Folded Leaf*

Wright Morris, *The Man Who Was There*
John Steinbeck, *Cannery Row*
Harry Sylvester, *Dayspring*
Glenway Wescott, *Apartment in Athens*

1946

Robert Coates, *The Bitter Season*
James T. Farrell, *Bernard Clare*
Howard Fast, *The American*
Alfred Hayes, *All Thy Conquests*
Robert Lowry, *Casualty*
Carson McCullers, *The Member of the Wedding*
J. P. Marquand, *B. F.'s Daughter*
Ann Petry, *The Street*
Irwin Shaw, *Act of Faith*
Gore Vidal, *Williwaw*
Robert Penn Warren, *All the King's Men*
Eudora Welty, *Delta Wedding*

1947

Nelson Algren, *The Neon Wilderness*
Saul Bellow, *The Victim*
Vance Bourjaily, *The End of My Life*
Gerald Warner Brace, *The Garretson Chronicle*
John Horne Burns, *The Gallery*
Erskine Caldwell, *The Sure Hand of God*
Howard Fast, *Clarkton*
Andrew Lytle, *A Name For Evil*
Vincent McHugh, *The Victory*
Willard Motley, *Knock on Any Door*
J. F. Powers, *Prince of Darkness*
Mark Schorer, *The State of Mind*
Budd Schulberg, *The Harder They Fall*
Jean Stafford, *The Mountain Lion*
Wallace Stegner, *Second Growth*
John Steinbeck, *The Wayward Bus*
Harry Sylvester, *Moon Gaffney*
Lionel Trilling, *The Middle of the Journey*
Robert Penn Warren, *The Circus in the Attic*

1948

Truman Capote, *Other Voices, Other Rooms*
John Cobb, *The Gesture*

James Gould Cozzens, *Guard of Honor*
William Faulkner, *Intruder in the Dust*
Norman Mailer, *The Naked and the Dead*
Wright Morris, *The Home Place*
Irwin Shaw, *The Young Lions*
Peter Taylor, *A Long Fourth*
Ira Wolfert, *An Act of Love*

1949

Nelson Algren, *The Man With the Golden Arm*
Harriette Arnow, *Hunter's Horn*
Paul Bowles, *The Sheltering Sky*
Truman Capote, *A Tree of Night*
Walter Van Tilburg Clark, *The Track of the Cat*
John Dos Passos, *The Grand Design*
James T. Farrell, *The Road Between*
William Faulkner, *Knight's Gambit*
John Hawkes, *The Cannibal*
Shirley Jackson, *The Lottery*
Alfred Hayes, *The Girl on the Via Flaminia*
Mary McCarthy, *The Oasis*
Wright Morris, *The World in the Attic*
John O'Hara, *A Rage to Live*
Eudora Welty, *The Golden Apples*

1950

Louis Auchincloss, *The Injustice Collectors*
Paul Bowles, *The Delicate Prey*
Frederick Buechner, *A Long Day's Dying*
Walter Van Tilburg Clark, *The Watchful Gods*
William Faulkner, *The Collected Short Stories*
Brendan Gill, *The Trouble of One House*
William Goyen, *The House of Breath*
John Hersey, *The Wall*
Mary McCarthy, *Cast a Cold Eye*
Budd Schulberg, *The Disenchanted*
Irwin Shaw, *Mixed Company*
Leon Statham, *Welcome, Darkness*
Wallace Stegner, *The Preacher and the Slave*
                 The Women on the Wall
Peter Taylor, *A Woman of Means*
Robert Penn Warren, *World Enough and Time*

1951

       Robert O. Bowen, *The Weight of the Cross*
       Truman Capote, *The Grass Harp*
       John Dos Passos, *Chosen Country*
       Caroline Gordon, *The Strange Children*
       James Jones, *From Here to Eternity*
       Carson McCullers, *The Ballad of the Sad Café*
       Norman Mailer, *Barbary Shore*
       J. P. Marquand, *Melville Goodwin*, USA
       Wright Morris, *Man and Boy*
       Irwin Shaw, *The Troubled Air*
       Herman Wouk, *The Caine Mutiny*

1952

       Paul Bowles, *Let It Come Down*
       Ralph Ellison, *Invisible Man*
       Granville Hicks, *There Was a Man in Our Town*
       Mary McCarthy, *The Groves of Academe*
       Wright Morris, *The Works of Love*
       Jean Stafford, *The Catherine Wheel*

1953

       Saul Bellow, *The Adventures of Augie March*
       Jean Stafford, *The Interior Castle*

NOTES

CHAPTER ONE

p. 1 John Berryman spoke of the forties as a "decade of Survival" in a symposium on "The State of American Writing, 1948: Seven Questions," *Partisan Review*, XV (Aug., 1948), 856. William Van O'Connor may have been the first to apply the label, Age of Criticism, to the forties; see Ray B. West's contribution to the survey, "The Postwar Generation in Arts and Letters," *Saturday Review of Literature*, XXXVI (March 14, 1953), 12. West himself had earlier pointed out the establishment, at last, of a critical tradition as a development of the forties; see "Truth, Beauty, and American Criticism," *University of Kansas City Review*, XIV (Winter, 1947), 137–48.

p. 2 Bishop's remark is in Edmund Wilson (ed.), *The Collected Essays of John Peale Bishop* (New York: Charles Scribner's Sons, 1948), p. 75.
F. O. Matthiessen suggests dividing American literary history into decades in "The Pattern of Literature," in *Changing Patterns in American Civilization* (Philadelphia: University of Pennsylvania Press, 1949).

p. 3 Fitzgerald's dating is cited by Robert Gorham Davis, "In a Raveled World Love Endures," *New York Times Book Review*, December 26, 1954. For establishing terminal dates for the forties see Norman Holmes Pearson, "The Nazi-Soviet Pact and the End of a Dream," in Daniel Aaron (ed.), *America in Crisis* (New York: Alfred A. Knopf, 1952); Granville Hicks, "The Shape of Postwar Literature," *College English*, V (May, 1944), 407–12, and Hicks, "Fiction and Social Criticism," *College English*, XIII (April, 1952), 355–61.
See Goldman, *The Crucial Decade: America, 1945–1955* (New York: Alfred A. Knopf, 1956), chap. v.

p. 7 The writer's attitude toward religion and politics is discussed by Judah Goldin, "The Contemporary Jew and His Judaism," in Stanley R. Hopper (ed.), *Spiritual Problems in Contemporary Literature*, Religion and Civilization Series (New York: Harper & Brothers, 1952); G. S. Fraser, *The Modern Writer and His World* (London: Derek Verschoyle, 1953), pp. 116–17, shows that British writers of the forties also entertained equivocal attitudes toward religion.

p. 8   See Arthur A. Ekirch, Jr., *The Decline of American Liberalism* (New York: Longmans, Green, 1955), chaps. 16–18, for the growth of governmental powers during and after the war. See C. Wright Mills, *White Collar* (New York: Oxford University Press, 1951), especially the "Introduction."

MacLeish followed *The Irresponsibles* (New York: Duell, Sloan & Pearce, 1940) with *The American Cause* (New York: Duell, Sloan & Pearce, 1941), in which he held that artists and writers as such must take part in the American mobilization for war by interpreting the democratic spirit for the world.

p. 9   The MacLeish–De Voto–Brooks position found a powerful academic voice in Howard Mumford Jones, "The Limits of Contemporary Criticism," *Saturday Review of Literature*, XXIV (Sept. 6, 1941), 3–4, 17.

Gide is quoted by Robert Liddell, *A Treatise on the Novel* (London: Jonathan Cape, 1947), p. 71, n.

p. 10   Macdonald, "Kulturbolschewismus Is Here," *Partisan Review*, VIII (Nov.-Dec., 1941), 442–51. Cowley, "The War Against Writers," *New Republic*, CX (May 8, 1944), 631–32. Even before the controversy over cultural nationalism broke out, men of letters like Allen Tate and James T. Farrell took the position that the writer as writer has no responsibility during wartime; see the symposium on "The Situation in American Writing: Seven Questions," *Partisan Review*, VI (Summer, 1939), 25–51.

John Lydenberg summarized the appeals for postwar nationalism in literature in "Mobilizing Our Novelists," *American Quarterly*, IV (Spring, 1952), 35–48. Wilson's review is reprinted in *Classics and Commercials* (New York: Farrar, Straus & Co., 1950), pp. 275–79. Examples of the disquiet stirred up by Steinbeck's novel are to be found in James Thurber's review, *New Republic*, CVI (March 16, 1942), 370, and the editorial comment and correspondence columns in the March 30, 1942, issue of the *New Republic*; see also Clifton Fadiman's review, *New Yorker*, XVIII (March 7, 1942), 59–60.

p. 11   Hook, "The New Failure of Nerve," *Partisan Review*, X (Jan.-Feb., 1943), 2–23.

p. 12   Dewey, "Anti-Naturalism in Extremis," *ibid.*, 24–39. Benedict, "Human Nature Is Not a Trap," *ibid.* (March-April, 1943), 159–

64. Hook, "The Failure of the Left," *ibid.*, 165–77. Wheelwright, "Dogmatism — New Style," *Chimera*, I (Spring, 1943), 7–16; see also Kenneth Burke, "The Tactics of Motivation," *ibid.*, 21–33. Allen Tate comments on the failure of the positivists in "The Hovering Fly," an essay published in 1943 and included in his *Collected Essays* (Denver: Alan Swallow, 1959).

p. 13   Ortega y Gasset, "Notes on the Novel," was originally published in the twenties; it first appeared in this country in 1948 and was reissued as part of *The Dehumanization of Art and Other Writings on Art and Culture* (Garden City: Doubleday & Co., 1956). Eliot, "*Ulysses*, Order, and Myth," appeared originally in the *Dial* in 1923; it is reprinted in William Van O'Connor (ed.), *Forms of Modern Fiction* (Minneapolis: University of Minnesota Press, 1948).

Jean Stafford, Ralph Ellison, and William Styron, among others, were protesting as late as 1955 that the novel was by no means dead; see "What's Wrong With the American Novel?" *American Scholar*, XXIV (Autumn, 1955), 464–503. William Faulkner gave it as his opinion that as long as people continue to read novels, people will continue to write them; see Malcolm Cowley (ed.), *Writers at Work: The "Paris Review" Interviews* (New York: Viking Press, 1958), p. 137. See Trilling, "Art and Fortune," in *The Liberal Imagination* (New York: Viking Press, 1950). The argument for the debilitating effect of a fragmented culture on the writer is made by Edwin Berry Burgum, *The Novel and the World's Dilemma* (New York: Oxford University Press, 1947), and by John W. Aldridge, who seems to follow Burgum, in *After the Lost Generation* (New York: McGraw-Hill Book Co., 1951). The opposing view with respect to the novel is developed by Alex Comfort, *The Novel in Our Time* (London: Phoenix House, 1948). See Max Lerner, *America as a Civilization* (New York: Simon and Schuster, 1957), pp. 71–73.

p. 14   Historians of the American novel who have utilized the idea of polarities and disunities include Richard Chase, *The American Novel and Its Tradition* (Garden City: Doubleday and Co., 1957) and Marius Bewley, *The Eccentric Design* (New York: Columbia University Press, 1959); Harry Levin uses the same conception in a specialized study of American fiction, *The Power of Blackness* (New York: Alfred A. Knopf, 1958). See Ralph Ellison, "Society, Morality, and the Novel," in Granville Hicks (ed.), *The Living Novel: A Symposium* (New York: Macmillan Co., 1957). For the origins of the novel, and its development in America, see the opening pages of Frank O'Connor, *The Mirror in the Roadway* (New York: Alfred A. Knopf, 1956); Harry Levin, "Society as Its Own Historian" in *Contexts of Criticism*, Harvard Studies in Comparative Literature, No. 22 (Cambridge, Mass.: Harvard University Press, 1957); the introductory section to Leslie A. Fiedler, *Love and Death in the American Novel* (New York: Criterion Books, 1960); and two suggestive essays in Trilling, *The Liberal Imagination*: "Manners, Morals, and the Novel" and "Art and Fortune."

p. 15 Chase, *The American Novel*, Levin, *The Power of Blackness*, and Fiedler, *Love and Death*, all deal with the gothic.

p. 16 See Ernst Cassirer, *Language and Myth*, translated by Susanne K. Langer (New York: Harper & Brothers, 1946), and Susanne K. Langer, *Philosophy in a New Key* (Cambridge, Mass.: Harvard University Press, 1942).

p. 17 On the avant-garde see Paul Goodman, "Advance-Guard Writing, 1900–1950," *Kenyon Review*, XIII (Summer, 1951), 357–80, and Dwight Macdonald, "By Cozzens Possessed," *Commentary*, XXV (Jan., 1958), 36–47.
See the suggestive comments on the hero in W. H. Auden, *The Enchafèd Flood* (New York: Random House, 1950), section three. Robie Macauley presents a regional pattern in "Fiction of the Forties," *Western Review*, XVI (Autumn, 1951), 59–69. Frederick J. Hoffman sees a four-part pattern for the novel of the forties: the novel of the war, the work of established writers, the naturalistic novel, and the work of those concerned with form in fiction; see his *The Modern Novel in America, 1900–1950* (Chicago: Henry Regnery Co., 1951), chap. 7.

p. 18 Fiedler's view is in his contribution to the symposium on "The State of American Writing, 1948," *Partisan Review*, XV (Aug., 1948), 870–75.

CHAPTER TWO

p. 22 Malcolm Cowley, *Exile's Return: A Literary Odyssey of the 1920's* (New York: W. W. Norton & Co., 1934), pp. 47, 50–51.

p. 24 Denis W. Brogan, No. II of a series, "The American Temper," *Manchester Guardian*, February 3, 1953.

p. 25 Quincy Wright, *A Study of War*, I (Chicago: University of Chicago Press, 1942), 261.

p. 26 A good, brief statement on the influence of Hemingway is to be found in Charles A. Fenton (ed.), "Introduction," *The Best Short Stories of World War II* (New York: Viking Press, 1957). See Philip Young, *Ernest Hemingway* (New York: Rinehart & Company, 1952), especially pp. 136–43. Kenneth Burke, *A Grammar of Motives* (New York: Prentice-Hall, 1945), p. 268.

p. 28 The critic is Ray B. West, Jr. See "Ernest Hemingway: The Failure of Sensibility," in William Van O'Connor (ed.), *Forms of Modern Fiction* (Minneapolis: University of Minnesota Press, 1948).

p. 30 See Kenneth Burke, *A Rhetoric of Motives* (New York: Prentice-Hall, 1950), "Introduction."

p. 31 Frederick J. Hoffman, "From Surrealism to 'The Apocalypse,'" *English Literary History*, XV (June, 1948), 153.

p. 33 In my discussion of Mailer I have drawn upon Norman Podhoretz, "Norman Mailer: The Embattled Vision," *Partisan Review*, XXVI (Summer, 1959), 371–91.

p. 40 See Philip Rahv, "The Cult of Experience in American Writing," *Partisan Review,* VII (Nov.-Dec., 1940), 412–24.

p. 41 Joseph Warren Beach, *American Fiction, 1920–1940* (New York: Macmillan Co., 1941), especially pp. 41–44.

p. 42 For a provocative view of Jones's novel see Leslie A. Fiedler, "James Jones' Dead-End Young Werther, The Bum as American Culture Hero," *Commentary*, XII (Sept., 1951), 252–55.

p. 45 I use lines from the original version of Auden's poem. Burke, *A Grammar of Motives*, p. 84.

p. 46 Jean-Paul Sartre, *Existentialism*, translated by Bernard Frechtman (New York: Philosophical Library, 1947), pp. 24–25.

p. 49 Trilling speaks often of the relation between literature and ideas; see especially "The Meaning of a Literary Idea" in *The Liberal Imagination* (Viking, 1950).

p. 50 Sartre deals with Manichaeism in *What Is Literature?* translated by Bernard Frechtman (London: Methuen & Co., 1950), p. 53. For the Fadiman and Thurber reviews see notes to p. 10, above.

p. 54 Sartre, *What Is Literature?* p. 162; Saint-Exupéry is cited on p. 164.

p. 57 Susanne K. Langer discusses gesture and symbol in *Philosophy in a New Key* (Cambridge, Mass.: Harvard University Press, 1942), chap. ii.

CHAPTER THREE

p. 62 Charles Child Walcutt, *American Literary Naturalism: A Divided Stream* (Minneapolis: University of Minnesota Press, 1956), gives a full-length treatment of the subject.

p. 63 See Rahv, "Notes on the Decline of Naturalism," in John W. Aldridge (ed.), *Critiques and Essays on Modern Fiction, 1920–1951* (New York: Ronald Press, 1952).
Winters discusses this fallacy in *Primitivism and Decadence*, which is published as part of *In Defense of Reason* (Denver: Alan Swallow, 1947), pp. 61–62.

p. 68 Bone, *The Negro Novel in America*, Yale Publications in American Studies, 3 (New Haven: Yale University Press, 1958), p. 157. Wright in Richard Crossman (ed.), *The God That Failed* (New York: Harper & Brothers, 1949), p. 130.

p. 69 Wright, "Urban Misery in an American City" and "A World View of the American Negro," *Twice A Year*, XIV–XV (Fall-Winter, 1946–47), 339–48. Cayton, "Frightened Children of Frightened Parents," *Twice A Year*, XII–XIII (Spring-Summer, 1945 and Fall-Winter, 1945), 262–69. Wright, "How 'Bigger' Was Born," *Saturday Review of Literature*, XXII (June 1, 1940), 3–4 ff.

p. 71 See Ralph Ellison interview, *Paris Review*, VIII (Spring, 1955), 57–71. Baldwin, "Everybody's Protest Novel," *Partisan Review*, XVI (June, 1949), 585.

p. 72 Williams, *Culture and Society, 1780–1950* (New York: Columbia University Press, 1958), p. 280.

p. 74 Algren in Malcolm Cowley (ed.), *Writers at Work: The "Paris Review" Interviews* (New York: Viking Press, 1958), p. 245.

CHAPTER FOUR

p. 86 See Hicks, "Fiction and Social Criticism," *College English*, XIII (April, 1952), 355–61. See Cassirer, *The Myth of the State* (Garden City: Doubleday & Co., 1955), Pt. I. Guérard, *Testament of a Liberal* (Cambridge, Mass.: Harvard University Press, 1956), p. 49.

p. 87 Crossman (ed.), *The God That Failed* (New York: Harper & Brothers, 1949), p. 4. Fast tells the story of his break in *The Naked*

God: The Writer and the Communist Party (New York: Frederick A. Praeger, 1957).

p. 88 See Hicks, "On Leaving the Communist Party," *New Republic,* C (Oct., 1939), 244–45. Farrell, "The Cultural Front," *Partisan Review,* VII (March-April, 1940), 139–42. Dwight Macdonald devoted a special insert to "The Waldorf Conference," *Politics,* VI (Winter, 1949), 32A–32D; Daniel S. Gillmor (ed.), *Speaking of Peace* (New York: National Council of the Arts, Sciences and Professions, 1949), gives an edited report of the conference.

p. 89 Rahv, "Proletarian Literature: A Political Autopsy," *Southern Review,* IV (Winter, 1939), 616–28. Representative examples of Marxist criticism are Howard Fast, "American Literature and the Democratic Tradition," *College English,* VIII (March, 1947), 279–84; Fast, *Literature and Reality* (New York: International Publishers, 1950); and Sidney Finkelstein, "The 'New Criticism,'" *Masses and Mainstream,* III (Dec., 1950), 76–86.

p. 91 The critic is Richard O. Boyer, "Making of an American," *New Masses,* LX (Aug. 20, 1946), 3–6.

p. 92 Bell, "The Background and Development of Marxian Socialism in the United States," in Donald Drew Egbert and Stow Persons (eds.), *Socialism and American Life,* I (Princeton: Princeton University Press, 1952), 396.

p. 94 Podhoretz, "Norman Mailer: The Embattled Vision," *Partisan Review,* XXVI (Summer, 1959), 371–91. Dwight Macdonald reports Mailer's comments in the *Politics* article on the conference (see notes to p. 88, above).

p. 95 Bixler, *Conversations With an Unrepentant Liberal* (New Haven: Yale University Press, 1946), p. 11. Kallen, *Art and Freedom,* I (New York: Duell, Sloan and Pearce, 1942), 10. Orton, *The Liberal Tradition* (New Haven: Yale University Press, 1945); see especially p. 190. Cohen, *The Faith of a Liberal* (New York: Henry Holt, 1946), p. 439; I draw upon the concluding essay in this volume: "The Future of American Liberalism."

p. 96 For a further discussion of the garrison state concept see Harold D. Lasswell, "The Universal Peril: Perpetual Crisis and the Garrison-Prison State," in Lyman Bryson, Louis Finkelstein, and R. M. MacIver (eds.), *Perspectives on a Troubled Decade: Science, Philosophy, and Religion, 1939–1949* (New York: Harper & Brothers,

1950). Two other relevant discussions are Bert Andrews, *Washington Witch Hunt* (New York: Random House, 1948), and Alan Barth, *The Loyalty of Free Men* (New York: Viking Press, 1951). See O'Brian, *National Security and Individual Freedom* (Cambridge, Mass.: Harvard University Press, 1955), especially pp. 22–29.

p. 97 Eliot, *The Idea of a Christian Society* (London: Faber & Faber. 1939), pp. 16–18.

p. 98 Howe, *Politics and the Novel* (New York: Horizon Press, 1957); see chap. i, especially pp. 17–19.

p. 102 See the *New York Times*, May 24, 1951, for an account of Schulberg's testimony before the committee.

p. 105 Kazin, in a review in the *New Yorker*, XXVI (Nov. 4, 1950), 154. Schulberg's essay on Fitzgerald appears in Alfred Kazin (ed.), *F. Scott Fitzgerald: The Man and His Work* (Cleveland and New York: World Publishing Co., 1951); see pp. 110, 112.

p. 106 Gibbs, in a review in the *New Yorker*, XXIII (Aug. 16, 1947), 86

p. 110 Shaw expresses his suspicion in "If You Write About the War," *Saturday Review of Literature*, XXVIII (Feb. 17, 1945), 5–6. He discusses the fundamental point in *The Young Lions* and speaks of himself as a recorder in an interview in the *Paris Review*, IV (Winter, 1953), 27–49.

p. 112 Barth, *The Loyalty of Free Men*, chap. i.

p. 114 Viereck's essay appears in Daniel Bell (ed.), *The New American Right* (New York: Criterion Books, 1955). The status revolution is discussed by Richard Hofstadter, "The Pseudo-Conservative Revolt," which also appears in *The New American Right*.

p. 118 Schlesinger, *The Vital Center* (Boston: Houghton Mifflin Co., 1949), vii.
See Popper, *The Open Society and Its Enemies*, I (London: George Routledge & Sons, 1945), chap. ix, where social engineering is opposed to utopian engineering. See Daniel Aaron's reluctant admission that the conservative hostility toward mass-man must, in large measure, be accepted: "Conservatism, Old and New," *American Quarterly*, VI (Summer, 1954), 99–110.

p. 120 Dos Passos, *Tour of Duty* (Boston: Houghton Mifflin Co., 1946), p. 329; *idem, The Prospect Before Us* (Boston: Houghton Mifflin Co., 1950), p. 116; see *idem, The Ground We Stand On: Some*

Examples from the History of a Political Creed (New York: Harcourt, Brace & Co., 1941), especially the discussion of Roger Williams and the summary statement, p. 401; *idem, The Head and Heart of Thomas Jefferson* (New York: Doubleday & Co., 1954), pp. 160–61.

p. 126 See Popper, *The Open Society*, I, chap. ix.

p. 127 Hicks, *Small Town* (New York: Macmillan Co., 1946), p. 47. Hicks, *Where We Came Out* (New York: Viking Press, 1954), p. 76.

p. 129 Two useful critical articles on Mary McCarthy on which I have drawn are Norman Podhoretz, "Gibbsville and New Leeds, The America of John O'Hara and Mary McCarthy," *Commentary*, XXI (March, 1956), 269–73, and Robert E. Fitch, "The Cold Eye of Mary McCarthy," *New Republic*, CXXXVIII (May 5, 1958), 17–19. Mary McCarthy in an interview, *Paris Review*, XXVII (Winter-Spring, 1962), 77.

p. 135 Trilling, *The Liberal Imagination* (New York: Viking Press, 1950), p. 283.

p. 136 *Ibid.*, pp. 219–22. Trilling, *Freud and the Crisis of Our Culture* (Boston: Beacon Press, 1955), pp. 33–34, 54.

p. 137 *Ibid.*, pp. 26, 58. *The Liberal Imagination*, p. 57.

p. 140 Cassirer, *The Myth of the State*, p. 70.

p. 141 Chambers, *Witness* (New York: Random House, 1952), p. 25.

CHAPTER FIVE

p. 147 The soundest account of conservatism is Clinton Rossiter, *Conservatism in America* (New York: Alfred A. Knopf, 1955); Peter Viereck has written *Conservatism Revisited* (New York: Charles Scribner's Sons, 1949), and *Shame and Glory of the Intellectuals* (Boston: Beacon Press, 1953); Russell Kirk, *The Conservative Mind* (Chicago: Henry Regnery Co., 1953), represents the far-out right. For Eliot see note to p. 97, above. Tate's comment was made in a symposium on "The New Criticism," *American Scholar*, XX (Winter, 1950–51), 89.
Chambers, *Witness* (New York: Random House, 1952), pp. 741, 742. Niebuhr, *The Children of Light and the Children of Darkness* (New York: Charles Scribner's Sons, 1944), "Foreword."

p. 148 Chambers, *Witness*, p. 491.

p. 149 "Religion and the Intellectuals," *Partisan Review*, XVII (Feb., 1950), 103–42.

p. 150 Ransom, *The World's Body* (New York: Charles Scribner's Sons, 1938), p. 41. De Voto, "The Easy Chair," *Harper's*, CXCVIII (Feb., 1949), 72–73. Bracher, *The Novels of James Gould Cozzens* (New York: Harcourt, Brace & Co., 1959).

p. 151 *Ibid.*, pp. 6–7.

p. 152 Richard Hofstadter uses the concept of status revolution in *The Age of Reform* (New York: Alfred A. Knopf, 1955); several essays in Daniel Bell (ed.), *The New American Right* (New York: Criterion Books, 1955) are built around this concept. Howe, "James Gould Cozzens: Novelist of the Republic," *New Republic*, CXXXVIII (Jan. 20, 1958), 15–19. Bell's essay is "Interpretations of American Politics"; Hofstadter's essay is "The Pseudo-Conservative Revolt."

p. 153 Cozzens' letter is cited by Richard M. Ludwig, "A Reading of the James Gould Cozzens Manuscripts," *Princeton University Library Chronicle*, XIX (Autumn, 1957), 4. See Eliot, *Notes Toward the Definition of Culture* (New York: Harcourt, Brace & Co., 1949) especially pp. 27–34, 40–42.

p. 155 Hyman wrote one of the earliest serious appraisals of Cozzens, "James Gould Cozzens and the Art of the Possible," *New Mexico Quarterly Review*, XIX (Winter, 1949), 476–97.

p. 156 This letter is also cited by Ludwig, *op. cit.*, pp. 6–7.

p. 160 The interviewer was Robert Van Gelder, "James Gould Cozzens at Work," *New York Times Book Review*, June 23, 1940.

p. 163 Walter has written the best brief attack on neo-conservatism that I know, "Conservatism Recrudescent: A Critique," *Partsian Review*, XXI (Sept.-Oct., 1954), 512–23; the quotation is on p. 518.

p. 164 Macdonald, "By Cozzens Possessed," *Commentary*, XXV (Jan., 1958), 36–47.

p. 165 See Grene, *Dreadful Freedom* (Chicago: University of Chicago Press, 1948), p. 6. For Dewey's ideas on morality and conduct see *Human Nature and Conduct* (New York: Henry Holt & Co., 1922), especially section four of part four.

p. 170 Walter, *op. cit.*

p. 171 Tillich is quoted by Charles I. Glicksberg, "The Myth of Nothingness," *Arizona Quarterly*, XI (Autumn, 1955), 226. O'Connor, *The Mirror in the Roadway* (New York: Alfred A. Knopf, 1956), p. 26. The critic is John Lydenberg, "Cozzens and the Critics," *College English*, XIX (Dec., 1957), 99–104.

p. 173 See Sylvester, *Atlantic Monthly*, CLXXXI (Jan., 1948), 109–13.

p. 178 See Woodward, "The Search for Southern Identity," *Virginia Quarterly Review*, XXXIV (Summer, 1958), 321–38; and Robert B. Heilman, "The Southern Temper," in Louis D. Rubin, Jr., and Robert D. Jacobs (eds.), *Southern Renascence: The Literature of the Modern South* (Baltimore: Johns Hopkins Press, 1953). Tate, "A Southern Mode of the Imagination," in *Collected Essays* (Denver: Alan Swallow, 1959).

p. 179 I am indebted in my discussion of Faulkner especially to Olga W. Vickery, *The Novels of William Faulkner* (Baton Rouge: Louisiana State University Press, 1959).

p. 186 Gordon, "Some Readings and Misreadings," *Sewanee Review*, LXI (Summer, 1953), 385.

p. 187 *The House of Fiction* (New York: Charles Scribner's Sons, 1950), vii.

p. 188 See Thorp, "The Way Back and the Way Up: The Novels of Caroline Gordon," *Bucknell Review*, VI (Dec., 1956), 1–15.

p. 199 Cowan, *The Fugitive Group* (Baton Rouge: Louisiana State University Press, 1959), p. 247.

p. 200 See Fraser, *The Modern Writer and His World* (London: Derek Verschoyle, 1953), especially p. 117.

p. 201 Carl Jung, *The Integration of the Personality*, translated by Stanley Dell (New York: Farrar and Rinehart, 1939), p. 281. *Ibid.*, p. 70. Jung's "The Spiritual Problem of Modern Man" appears in his *Modern Man in Search of A Soul* (London: Kegan Paul, Trench, Trubner and Co., 1933).

p. 203 Warren comments on the problem of identity in his essay on "Hemingway," *Kenyon Review*, IX (Winter, 1947), 27. See also his "Katherine Anne Porter," *Kenyon Review*, IV (Winter, 1942), 29–42. Warren, "Knowledge and the Image of Man," *Sewanee Review*, LXIII (Spring, 1955), 189–92. Warren, "Nostromo," *Sewanee Review*, LIX (Summer, 1951), 363–91.

p. 204 Warren, "Cowley's Faulkner," *New Republic*, CXV (Aug. 12, 1946), 177.
Warren in Malcolm Cowley (ed.), *Writers at Work: The "Paris Review" Interviews* (New York: Viking Press, 1958), p. 193. Warren (ed.), *A Southern Harvest* (Boston: Houghton Mifflin Co., 1937), xiv–xv.

p. 205 Warren, "Nostromo," *loc. cit.*, p. 376. See Warren, "The Love and Separateness in Miss Welty," *Kenyon Review*, VI (Spring, 1944), 246–59.

p. 206 Warren in *Writers at Work*, p. 190.

p. 210 See Bodkin, *Archetypal Patterns in Poetry* (London: Oxford University Press, 1951).
Hendry, "The Regional Novel: The Example of Robert Penn Warren," *Sewanee Review*, LIII (Jan.-March, 1945), 84–102.
Warren, "Introduction," *All the King's Men* (New York: Random House, 1953), iii, n.

p. 212 *Ibid.*, iii.

p. 214 See *ibid.*, v–vi, where Warren mentions Long.

p. 217 *Ibid.*, iii.

p. 219 Girault, "The Narrator's Mind as Symbol: An Analysis of 'All the King's Men,'" *Accent*, VII (Summer, 1947), 220–34; and Frank, "Romanticism and Reality in Robert Penn Warren," *Hudson Review*, IV (Summer, 1951), 248–58.

p. 228 An unfavorable view of Warren's style is taken by Wallace W. Douglas, "Drug Store Gothic: The Style of Robert Penn Warren," *College English*, XV (Feb., 1954), 265–72.

p. 230 Levin published this paper as "The Tradition of Tradition," *Hopkins Review*, IV (Spring, 1951), 5–14. Walter, *op. cit.*

CHAPTER SIX

p. 233 See Ortega y Gasset, the title essay in *The Dehumanization of Art and Other Writings on Art and Culture* (Garden City: Doubleday & Co., 1956).

p. 234 John Crowe Ransom, *The World's Body* (New York: Charles Scribner's Sons, 1938), chap. i.
Chase, *The American Novel and Its Tradition* (Garden City: Doubleday & Co., 1957), p. 53.

p. 237 Capote's statement about religion and politics is in Stanley J. Kunitz (ed.), *Twentieth Century Authors, First Supplement* (New York: H. W. Wilson Co., 1955), p. 168.

p. 243 Ransom's essay appeared in *Kenyon Review*, XII (Spring, 1950), 189–218.

p. 244 McCullers, "The Vision Shared," *Theatre Arts*, XXXIV (April, 1950), 30.
Buber, "Dialogue," in *Between Man and Man*, translated by R. G. Smith (Boston: Beacon Press, 1955), pp. 14, 31.

p. 245 *Ibid.*, p. 19. McCullers, "The Vision Shared," *loc. cit.*, p. 28.

p. 247 The case for Singer as a God-like character is made by Frank Durham, "God and No God in *The Heart Is a Lonely Hunter*," *South Atlantic Quarterly*, LVI (Autumn, 1957), 494–99.

p. 251 McCullers in Stanley J. Kunitz and Howard Haycraft (eds.), *Twentieth Century Authors* (New York: H. W. Wilson Co., 1942), p. 869.

p. 260 Miss Welty has written about her own work and method in "The Reading and Writing of Short Stories," *Atlantic*, CLXXXIII (Feb., 1949), 54–58, and *ibid.* (March, 1949), 46–49. Also in "How I Write, "*Virginia Quarterly Review*, XXXI (Spring, 1955), 240–51; the quotation is on p. 251.
Coleridge in Walter J. Bate (ed.), *Criticism: The Major Texts* (New York: Harcourt, Brace & Co., 1952), p. 386. Welty, "Some Notes on River Country," *Harper's Bazaar*, LXXVIII (Feb., 1944), 86.

p. 261 Welty, *New Yorker*, XXIV (Jan. 1, 1949), 50–51.
See Lodwick Hartley, "Proserpina and the Old Ladies," *Modern Fiction Studies*, III (Winter, 1957–58), 350–54.

p. 262 Miss Welty discusses the photograph in "Literature and the Lens," *Vogue*, CIV (Aug., 1944), 102–3.
Porter, "Introduction" to Eudora Welty, *A Curtain of Green* (New York: Doubleday, Doran & Co., 1941).

p. 263 *Ibid.*

p. 271 In this discussion of Jenny, and throughout this section on Eudora Welty, I draw upon Robert Penn Warren, "The Love and Separateness in Miss Welty," *Kenyon Review*, VI (Spring, 1944), 246–59.

p. 272 Morris, *The Territory Ahead* (New York: Harcourt, Brace & Co., 1958), xvi.

p. 276 See John E. Hardy, "*Delta Wedding* as Region and Symbol," *Sewanee Review*, LX (Summer, 1952), 397–417.

p. 283 Bowles, "Foreign Intelligence: No More Djinns," *American Mercury*, LXXII (June, 1951), 650–58; the quotation is on p. 654.

p. 290 Arnold Toynbee, *A Study of History*, I, abridged by D. C. Somervell (New York: Oxford University Press, 1947), 307–36.

p. 292 Aldridge, *After the Lost Generation* (New York: McGraw-Hill, 1951), chap. xiii.

p. 294 Stafford, "The Psychological Novel," *Kenyon Review*, X (Spring, 1948), 221, 216.

p. 295 *Ibid.*, p. 214.

p. 297 *Ibid.*, p. 223.

p. 305 See E. K. Brown, *Rhythm in the Novel* (Toronto: University of Toronto Press, 1950); chap. ii is devoted to a discussion of expanding symbols.

p. 307 Feidelson, *Symbolism and American Literature* (Chicago: University of Chicago Press, 1953); see especially chap. ii and the note on W. H. Auden, p. 239.

CHAPTER SEVEN

p. 309 Jaspers is discussed by H. J. Blackham, *Six Existentialist Thinkers* (London: Routledge & Kegan Paul, Ltd., 1952), p. 56. Grene, *Dreadful Freedom* (Chicago: University of Chicago Press, 1948), p. 41. Orton, *The Liberal Tradition* (New Haven: Yale University Press, 1945), p. 190.

p. 310 Barrett, *Irrational Man* (Garden City: Doubleday & Co., 1958).

p. 314 Vernon Young, "Gods Without Heroes: The Tentative Myth of Van Tilburg Clark," *Arizona Quarterly*, VII (Summer, 1951), 110–19.

p. 316 Trilling in her review, *Nation*, CLX (June 23, 1945), 703.

p. 320 Feidelson, *Symbolism and American Literature* (Chicago: University of Chicago Press, 1953), p. 53.

p. 322 See Herbert Wilner, "Walter Van Tilburg Clark," *Western Review*, XX (Winter, 1956), 103–22, where this claim is made for "Hook."

p. 324 Clark's letter appears in Bluestone, *Novels into Film* (Baltimore: Johns Hopkins Press, 1957), p. 193.
Stegner discusses the novelist's function and heritage in "Is the Novel Done For?" *Harper's*, CLXXXVI (Dec., 1942), 76–83.

p. 326 Stegner, *New York Herald Tribune Book Review*, October 8, 1950.

p. 328 Morris, *The Territory Ahead* (New York: Harcourt, Brace & Co., 1958), xiv.

p. 329 *Ibid.*, pp. 14–15.

p. 330 Morris was interviewed by John K. Hutchens, *New York Herald Tribune Book Review*, June 3, 1951. Morris, *The Territory Ahead*, p. 148.

p. 341 Blackmur, *The Lion and the Honeycomb* (New York: Harcourt, Brace & Co., 1955), p. 41. Bellow, "Distractions of a Fiction Writer," in Granville Hicks (ed.), *The Living Novel: A Symposium* (New York: Macmillan Co., 1957), p. 9. See Isaac Rosenfeld, "On the Role of the Writer and the Little Magazine," *Chicago Review*, XI (Summer, 1957), 3–16. "Distractions," p. 20.

p. 343 Fiedler, "Saul Bellow," *Prairie Schooner*, XXXI (Summer, 1957), 105.
Buber, "Introduction," *Tales of the Hasidim*, I, translated by Olga Marx (New York: Farrar, Straus and Young, 1947), 2, 3, 10.

p. 344 Lookstein, "The Neo-Hasidism of Abraham J. Heschel," *Judaism*, V (Summer, 1956), 248–55.

p. 344 Ransom, "The State of American Writing, 1948: Seven Questions," *Partisan Review*, XV (Aug., 1948), 879. See Rahv, "The Cult of Experience in American Writing," *Partisan Review*, VII (Nov.-Dec., 1940), 412–24.
Bellow, "Distractions," p. 6.

p. 347 Frank, "Saul Bellow: The Evolution of a Contemporary Novelist," *Western Review*, XVIII (Winter, 1954), 105.

p. 348 See Fiedler's *Prairie Schooner* article, cited above, p. 343.
Bellow goes so far as to chide critics for shutting the door on multiplicity in the "Distractions" essay.

p. 349 Lubbock, *The Craft of Fiction* (London: Jonathan Cape, 1960), p. 152.

p. 354 Bellow, "How I Wrote Augie March's Story," *New York Times Book Review*, January 31, 1954.

p. 357 Warren, "The Man With No Commitments," *New Republic*, CXXIX (Nov. 2, 1953), 22–23.

p. 359 Ortega y Gasset, "The Nature of the Novel," *Hudson Review*, X (Spring, 1957), 34.

p. 361 Fiedler, "Bellow," *loc. cit.*, 104.

INDEX

Aaron, Daniel, 368, 375
Abrahams, William, 51–52n.
Accent Anthology, 270
Adams, Henry, 150, 247, 316
Adams, J. Donald, 10
Aldridge, John W., 292, 370, 373, 381
Algren, Nelson: 64, 71, 73–85, 373; *Chicago: City on the Make*, 81; "Kingdom City to Cairo," 81; *The Man With the Golden Arm*, 81–85; *The Neon Wilderness*, 80–81; *Never Come Morning*, 77–80; "Poor Man's Pennies," 81; *Somebody in Boots*, 76–77, 81; *A Walk on the Wild Side*, 77
Alien Registration Act, 95
Altgeld, John Peter, 92
American Mercury, 283
Ames, Fisher, 161
Anderson, Sherwood, 246, 334, 340
Andrews, Bert, 375
Androcles and the Lion, 56
Arnold, Elliott, 39n.
Arnold, Matthew, 344
Arnow, Harriette, 71, 72–73
Atlantic Monthly, 68, 322
Auchincloss, Louis, 292–93, 293n.
Auden, W. H., 45, 371, 372, 381
Austen, Jane, 151, 295

Baldwin, James, 71, 373
Balzac, Honoré de, 155, 207
Barrett, William, 310, 381
Barth, Alan, 112, 375
Basso, Hamilton, 113n., 114
Bate, Walter J., 380
Beach, Joseph Warren, 41, 372
Beck, Warren, 113n.
Bell, Daniel, 92, 152, 374, 375, 377
Bellamy, Edward, 126
Bellow, Saul: 5, 29, 74, 308, 309, 340, 341–62, 382; *The Adventures of Augie March*, 345, 349, 354–62; *Dangling Man*, 344, 345–49, 354; "Distractions of a Fiction Writ-

Bellow, Saul (continued)
er," 341, 342, 347–48; *The Victim*, 152, 349–54
Benedict, Ruth, 12, 369
Benét, Stephen Vincent, 48
Bennett, Richard M., 126
Bergson, Henri, 309
Bernanos, Georges, 173
Berryman, John, 368
Bewley, Marius, 370
Bishop, John Peale, 2, 368
Bixler, Julius, 95, 374
Blackham, H. J., 381
Blackmur, R. P., 341, 382
Bluestone, George, 324, 382
Bodkin, Maud, 210, 379
Bone, Robert, 68, 373
Boone, Daniel, 48, 187
Bourjaily, Vance, 26, 28–29, 51, 283
Bowen, Robert, 58–60, 172n.
Bowles, Paul: 16, 231, 232, 236, 237, 283–88, 307, 310, 328, 381; "The Delicate Prey," 287; *The Delicate Prey and Other Stories*, 287–88; "A Distant Episode," 287; *Let It Come Down*, 288; "Pages from Cold Point," 287; *The Sheltering Sky*, 285–87
Bowman, Peter, 51n.
Boyer, Richard O., 374
Boyle, Kay, 39n.
Brace, Gerald Warner, 290–91, 291n.
Bracher, Frederick, 150, 151, 377
Brand, Millen, 116n.
Brogan, Denis, 24, 371
Brooks, Richard, 30n., 32–33
Brooks, Van Wyck, 9, 369
Brown, Charles Brockden, 15–16
Brown, E. K., 305, 381
Brown, Harry, 41
Brown, John, 199
Browne, Lewis, 113n.
Bryson, Lyman, 374
Buber, Martin, 16, 244–45, 343, 380, 382

Buechner, Frederick, 292
Burgum, Edwin Berry, 370
Burke, Edmund, 148, 153, 161, 199, 210, 216
Burke, Kenneth, 26, 30, 45, 60, 370, 372
Burns, John Horne, 21, 40–41

Caldwell, Erskine, 51n., 64, 66–68, 68n., 263
Calmer, Ned, 47n., 52n.
Capote, Truman: 16, 177, 231, 236, 237–43, 244, 283, 288, 307, 380; The Grass Harp, 241–42; "Miriam," 241; Other Voices, Other Rooms, 237–40; "Shut a Final Door," 240; A Tree of Night, 240–41; "William Wilson," 240
Carter, Hodding, 116n.
Cassirer, Ernst, 16, 86, 140, 234, 371, 373, 376
Cather, Willa, 151, 174
Catherine of Alexandria, 305
The Catholic World, 10
Cayton, Horace, 69, 373
Chamberlain, John, 10
Chambers, Whittaker, 141, 147, 148, 376
Chase, Richard, 234, 370, 371, 379
Clark, Walter Van Tilburg: 259, 308, 309, 310–24, 328, 382; "The Anonymous," 322; "The Buck in the Hills," 320–21; The City of Trembling Leaves, 314–16, 318, 321; "The Fish Who Could Close His Eyes," 323; "Hook," 321–22; "The Indian Well," 321; "Letter to the Living," 311; The Ox-Bow Incident, 4, 311–14, 315, 316, 317; "The Portable Phonograph," 322; "The Rapids," 322; "The Rise and Passing of Bar," 322; The Track of the Cat, 301, 316–20; "The Watchful Gods," 323; The Watchful Gods and Other Stories, 320–23; "Why Don't You Look Where You're Going," 322
Coates, Robert, 38–39, 273
Cobb, John, 21, 55–58
Cohen, Morris R., 95, 374
Coleridge, Samuel Taylor, 260, 380

Comfort, Alex, 370
Communism: as Americanism, 92; as basis for social-protest fiction, 86; Dos Passos rejects, 119; in America, 8, 87; in fiction of the forties, 87; linked to liberalism, 147; young writers rejected, 94. See also Communist (s), Communist party
Communist(s): and Fast, 88, 91; identified with liberals, 147; in McCarthy's The Groves of Academe, 134; and racial equality, 70; and theory of conspiracy, 3; in Trilling's The Middle of the Journey, 136, 141. See also Communism, Communist party
Communist party: and American writers, 11, 88; and Bellow, 346; and closed ideology, 327; declines, 86; in Dos Passo's Adventures of a Young Man, 121; and The Grand Design, 123; and Fast, 93; in Hicks's Only One Storm, 127; and Schulberg, 102; and Wright, 68. See also Communism, Communist (s)
"Confessions of Jereboam O. Beauchamp," 225
Conrad, Joseph, 44, 54–55, 203, 204, 205
Conservatism: in Cozzens, 151, 152, 154, 160, 165; in Faulkner, 185; and fiction, 148–50, 231; and religious fiction, 173; shift to, 153; and the South, 150, 177–78; summarized, 148; in Warren, 198. See also Conservative (s), New conservatism, New conservative (s)
Conservative(s): and Cozzens, 150, 153, 158, 163; and Lytle, 193–95 passim; task of, 147. See also Conservatism, New Conservatism, New conservative (s)
Cooper, James Fenimore, 15, 150
Cooper, John C. See Cobb, John.
Counterattack, 112
Cowan, Louise, 199, 378
Cowley, Malcolm, 10, 22, 23, 38, 88, 369, 370, 371, 373, 379
Cozzens, James Gould: 15, 149, 150–

Cozzens, James Gould (continued)
71, 174, 310, 352, 377; *Ask Me
Tomorrow*, 154, 156, 157, 158–60,
161; *By Love Possessed*, 150, 153,
169, 170–71; *Guard of Honor*, 21,
55–56, 150, 156, 164–70; *The Just
and the Unjust*, 160–64, 168, 170;
The Last Adam, 154–58, 169;
Men and Brethren, 156, 158
Crane, Stephen, 26
Crossman, Richard, 87, 373
Cultural and Scientific Conference for
World Peace, 88, 94
Cummings, E. E., 22

Daily Illini, 76
Dante, 138, 143, 210
Darwin, Charles, 324
Davis, Robert Gorham, 368
De Forest, John, 15
De Voto, Bernard, 9, 47, 150, 369, 377
Dewey, John, 12, 153, 168, 369, 377
Dos Passos, John: 4, 29, 40, 41, 118,
119–25, 375; *Adventures of a
Young Man*, 121–22; *Chosen
Country*, 121, 124–25; *District of
Columbia*, 121; *The Grand De-
sign*, 121, 123–24; *The Ground
We Stand On*, 120; *The Head
and Heart of Thomas Jefferson*,
120; *Number One*, 113n., 121,
122–23; *The Prospect Before Us*,
120; *State of the Nation*, 123;
Three Soldiers, 22; *Tour of Duty*,
120; *U.S.A.*, 124
Dostoevski, Feodor, 246, 295, 296, 298
Douglas, Lloyd, 172
Douglas, Wallace W., 379
Dreiser, Theodore, 62, 210
Durham, Frank, 380

Egbert, Donald Drew, 374
Eisenhower, Dwight D., 4
Ekirch, Arthur A., Jr., 96, 369
Eliot, George, 151
Eliot, T. S., 13, 16, 97, 147, 153, 200,
288, 292, 370, 375, 376, 377
Elliott, Arnold, 47n.
Ellison, Ralph, 14, 70–71, 370, 373
Emerson, Ralph Waldo, 352

Fadiman, Clifton, 50, 369, 372
Falstein, Louis, 39n., 46n.

Farrell, James T.: 4, 64–66, 88, 369,
374; *Bernard Clare, Ellen Rogers,
Father and Son, My Days of An-
ger, The Road Between*, 64–66;
Tommy Gallagher's Crusade, 113
Fast, Howard: 87, 90–93, 373, 374;
*Citizen Tom Paine, Freedom
Road, The Last Frontier*, 91;
The Unvanquished, 92
Faulkner, William: 29, 150, 178–86,
198, 204, 223, 246, 318, 340, 370,
378; *The Collected Short Stories*,
179; *Go Down, Moses*, 179, 194;
The Hamlet, 179, 182, 183; *In-
truder in the Dust*, 179, 182;
Knight's Gambit, 179; "Knight's
Gambit," 183, 185
Feidelson, Charles, Jr., 307, 320, 381
Fenton, Charles A., 372
Fiedler, Leslie, 18, 343, 348, 361, 371,
372, 382, 383
Fields, Arthur C., 30n.
Finkelstein, Louis, 374
Finkelstein, Sidney, 374
Fitch, Robert E., 376
Fitzgerald, F. Scott, 3, 28, 105, 106,
158, 354, 368, 375
Flaubert, Gustave, 1, 16, 187, 233, 349
Forster, E. M., 293
Fortune, 10
Frank, Joseph, 219, 379
Frank, Rueben, 347, 382
Franklin, Benjamin, 48
Fraser, G. S., 200, 368, 378
Freeman, Joseph, 100
Freud, Sigmund, 57, 102, 129, 136, 137,
294, 324
Fridley, William C., 39n., 47n.
Fuchs, Klaus, 134
Fugitives, 199

Gelfant, Blanche, 82
Gellhorn, Martha, 51n.
German-Russian pact. *See* Nazi-Soviet
pact
Gibbs, Willa, 116n.
Gibbs, Wolcott, 106, 375
Gide, André, 9, 369
Gill, Brendan, 293–94
Gillmor, Daniel S., 374
Girault, Norton, 219, 222, 379
Glasgow, Ellen, 15, 151, 289

Glicksberg, Charles I., 378
Gluck, Christoph Willibald von, 188
The God That Failed, 68
Goethe, 348
Goldin, Judah, 368
Goldman, Eric, 3, 368
Goodman, Paul, 371
Gordon, Caroline: 172n., 185, 186–93, 195, 196, 197, 232, 275, 378; "All Love the Spring," 190, 191; "The Brilliant Leaves," 190–91; *The Forest of the South*, 189–91; *Green Centuries*, 187–88, 194; *The House of Fiction*, 187; *The Strange Children*, 191–93; *The Women on the Porch*, 188–89
Gothic: beginnings in America, 15–16; and Bowles, 283; and Caldwell, 68n.; and Capote, 237; and culture heroes in the forties, 16; defined, 235–36; and Goyen, 243; and McCullers, 245, 254, 258; and new fiction, 236; and Welty, 258–59, 262
Goyen, William, 243
Grene, Marjorie, 165, 309, 377, 381
Greene, Graham, 58, 149, 173, 175
Greenglass, David, 134
Guérard, Albert Joseph, 30n.
Guérard, Albert Léon, 86, 373

Haines, William Wister, 46n.
Hardy, John E., 381
Hartley, Lodwick, 380
Hawkes, John, 21, 31–32
Hawthorne, Nathaniel, 16, 60, 132, 159, 233, 303, 307, 348
Haycraft, Howard, 380
Hayes, Alfred, 39–40, 51n.
Heard, Gerald, 12
Heidegger, Martin, 309
Heilman, Robert B., 178, 378
Hemingway, Ernest: 2, 4, 21, 23, 25–26, 29, 41, 205, 246, 290, 331, 333, 345, 372; *Across the River and Into the Trees*, 21; "Big Two-Hearted River," 190; *A Farewell To Arms*, 22; *For Whom the Bell Tolls*, 28, 59, 115–16; *In Our Time*, 22; *To Have and Have Not*, 59
Hendry, Irene, 210, 379

Hersey, John, 21, 39n., 47n., 52
Heym, Stefan, 33n.
Hicks, Granville: 86, 88, 118, 125–28, 129, 368, 370, 373, 374, 376, 382; *Behold Trouble*, 128; *The First to Awaken*, 126, 132; *Only One Storm*, 126–28; *Small Town*, 127; *There Was a Man in Our Town*, 128; *Where We Came Out*, 125–26
Hill, Joe, 327
Himes, Chester, 116n., 117
Hiss, Alger, 3, 134, 147
Hitler, Adolf, 92, 108
Hobson, Laura Z., 116n.
Hoffman, Frederick, 31, 371, 372
Hofstadter, Richard, 152, 375, 377
Hook, Sidney, 11–12, 369, 370
Hopkins, Harry, 124
Hopper, Stanley R., 368
Howe, Irving, 98, 152, 375, 377
Howells, William Dean, 15
Hunt, Howard, 46n.
Hutchens, John K., 382
Huxley, Aldous, 12
Hyman, Stanley Edgar, 155, 377

Identity: and Algren, 83–84; and Bellow, 348, 349; and Capote, 239, 240, 241; and Clark, 320, 322, 324; and Dos Passos, 121; and the organization man, 97; quest for, 117; and Statham, 54–55; and Stegner, 324, 325; threatened by society, 95; and Trilling, 136, 138, 140, 142; and war novels, 51; and Warren, 199; and Welty, 275. *See also* Self, idea of, Self-knowledge
I'll Take My Stand, 193, 199
IWW, 326, 327

Jackson, Shirley, 288n., 288–89
Jacobs, Robert D., 378
James, Henry, 15, 16, 20, 40, 44, 187, 191, 196, 232, 233, 234, 289, 290, 291, 293, 294, 296, 307, 332, 334, 349
Jaspers, Karl, 309, 381
Jefferson, Thomas, 48, 120, 125, 144
Jonas, Carl, 52n.
Jones, Howard Mumford, 369
Jones, James, 21, 26, 41–44, 372
Jones, Jesse, 124

Joyce, James, 4, 13, 16, 71, 187, 233, 246, 315
Jung, Carl, 201, 202, 210, 378

Kafka, Franz, 16, 31, 71, 93, 233
Kahler, Alfred, 25
Kallen, Horace, 95, 374
Kazin, Alfred, 105, 375
Kierkegaard, Søren, 12, 16, 63
Kinsey, Alfred, 130
Kirk, Russell, 146–47, 376
Kunitz, Stanley J., 380

Langer, Susanne K., 16, 57, 234, 371, 372
Langley, Adria Locke, 113n.
Lardner, Ring, 290
Lasswell, Harold D., 374
Lea, Luke, 213
Lerner, Max, 13–14, 370
Levin, Dan, 46n.
Levin, Harry, 230, 370, 371, 379
Levin, Meyer, 99, 101–2
Lewis, Sinclair, 116n., 155
Liberal (s): challenged by conservative position, 148, 152; and Clark, 314; defined, 95; and democratic orthodoxy, 39; dilemma of, 96–97; and Dos Passos, 120; and Freeman, 100; identified with Communists, 147; and M. Levin, 102; and McCarthy, 135; and Mailer, 35, 36; and Shaw, 110, 111, 112; and Sinclair, 99; on trial, 3; and Trilling, 136, 139, 143; and Warren, 213
New liberal (s): and McCarthy, 135; and neo-conservatism, 145; and religion, 172; and Trilling, 143. See Liberalism
Liberalism: attack on, 97, 229; and Caldwell, 68n.; and Cozzens, 151, 152, 160; failure of, 4, 7, 11, 12, 86, 95, 147, 173; and fiction of the forties, 113; and M. Levin, 101; and McCarthy, 132; and Mailer, 37; outdated in forties, 98, 153; persistence of, 94; reexamined, 118; and Schulberg, 102–6 passim; and Shaw, 112; and Steinbeck, 101; and Trilling, 139, 140, 143, 144; and Warren, 199

Liberalism (continued)
New liberalism: alternative to old liberalism, 146; defined, 119; and Dos Passos, 119, 120, 125; emerges in forties, 87, 118–19; as fictional response, 18, 19; and Hicks, 88, 125–26, 128; and McCarthy, 129, 133; and Trilling, 135, 137, 144
Old liberalism: and Dos Passos, 125; in fiction, 87, 144; in ill repute, 17; literary inadequacy of, 99; and McCarthy, 135; passing of, 19, 146; and Trilling, 137, 138. See Liberal (s)
Liddell, Robert, 369
Life, 10
Literary nationalism: debate on, 8–11 passim; and war novel, 26
Locke, John, 14
Long, Huey, 214, 379
Lookstein, Joseph, 344, 382
Lowell, Robert, 88
Lowry, Robert, 21, 26, 30–31, 39n., 51
Lubbock, Percy, 234, 349, 382
Ludwig, Richard M., 377
Lydenberg, John, 369, 378
Lytle, Andrew: 193–96; At the Moon's Inn, 194–95; A Name for Evil, 195–96

Macauley, Robie, 371
McCarran Internal Security Act, 96
McCarthy, Senator Joseph, 8, 96, 107, 114, 134
McCarthy, Mary: 88, 118, 128–35, 376; Cast a Cold Eye, 133; The Company She Keeps, 129–31; "The Genial Host," 130; The Groves of Academe, 133–35; "The Man in the Brooks Brothers Shirt," 130; Memories of a Catholic Girlhood, 133; The Oasis, 132–33; "Portrait of the Intellectual as a Yale Man," 130, 131, 132
McCullers, Carson: 16, 236, 237, 243–58, 259, 283, 380; The Ballad of the Sad Café, 256–58; "The Ballad of the Sad Café," 256–58; The Heart Is a Lonely Hunter, 4, 245–51, 255; The Member of the Wedding, 254–56; Reflections

McCullers, Carson (continued)
in a Golden Eye, 251–54; "A Tree.
A Rock. A Cloud." 256
Macdonald, Dwight, 10, 164, 369, 371,
374, 377
McHugh, Vincent, 21, 47–49
MacIver, R. M., 374
McKenney, Ruth, 89n.
MacLeish, Archibald, 8, 9, 47, 54, 325,
369
Mailer, Norman: 26, 42, 88, 372, 374;
Barbary Shore, 93–94; The Deer
Park, 93; The Naked and the
Dead, 21, 30n. 33–38, 64, 73
Malraux, André, 113
Maltz, Albert, 39, 49–50, 89n.
Mann, Thomas, 113–14
Mannheim, Karl, 119
Marquand, J. P., 46n, 289, 290n., 291,
291n., 294, 298
Marvell, Andrew, 225
Marx, Karl, 93, 102, 157, 201, 324, 382.
See also Marxism, Marxist
Marxism: and Algren, 75; and reality,
63; and Schulberg, 104; and Tril-
ling's The Middle of the Journey,
140; failure of, in America, 3, 86,
90, 93, 94; ideology of thirties, 6.
See also Marx, Marxist
Marxist (s): and Algren, 76, 77; and
democratic orthodoxy, 39; and
Dos Passos, 120; and McCullers'
The Heart Is a Lonely Hunter,
249. See also Marx, Marxism
Mather, Cotton, 163
Matthiessen, F. O., 368
Mauldin, Bill, 24
Mauriac, François, 173
Maxwell, William, 292, 293n., 294
Melville, Herman, 16, 46, 48, 233, 305,
307
Merrick, Elliott, 52n.
Merrick, Gordon, 29, 30n.
Mill, John Stuart, 95
Miller, Arthur 116n.
Miller, Merle, 112n.
Mills, C. Wright, 8, 369
Milton, John, 220
Modern Chivalry, 356
Modern Language Association, 229
Morris, Wright: 5, 121, 308, 309, 328–
41, 380, 382; The Home Place,
334–36; The Inhabitants, 331;

Morris, Wright (continued)
Man and Boy, 335, 337–38; The
Man Who Was There, 333; My
Uncle Dudley, 331–33, 335; The
Territory Ahead, 272, 329; The
Works of Love, 335, 338–40
Motley, Willard, 68, 70, 71
Mussolini, Benito, 106

Naturalism: 5, 18; and Algren, 74, 78,
84; and Caldwell, 67–68; defined,
62–64; and Ellison, 71; and Farrell, 66; and Mailer, 33; and the
Negro novel, 70; and novelists of
the forties, 71; revolt against,
291; and war novel, 26
Nazi-Soviet pact, 3, 86, 87, 88, 92
Neo-conservatism. See New conservatism
Neo-conservative. See New conservative (s)
The New American Right, 152
New conservatism: alternative to liberalism, 146; attacked, 230; place
in the forties, 229–30; and southern writers, 149; and Trilling,
137. See also Conservatism, Conservative (s), New conservative (s)
New conservative (s); and liberalism, 97; and the new liberal, 145;
and Trilling, 138; and Welty, 259.
See also Conservatism, Conservative (s), New conservative (s)
New critic (s): and new fiction, 232;
Warren as, 224
New criticism: indifferent to politics,
11; and James and Flaubert, 16;
and Marxists, 89; and neo-conservatism, 149; and new fiction,
19–20, 233–34; and new liberalism, 144; and Taylor, 196
New fiction: 5, 18, 19; and American
literary tradition, 307; and
Buechner, 292; and Clark, 310;
and Cozzens, 151; defined, 231–35;
and Gordon, 187; and the gothic,
236; James as symbol of, 291;
and literary nationalism, 11; origins of, 232–33; and Stafford, 307;
and subjectivism 13; and Taylor,
196 and Welty, 259
New liberal (s). See Liberal (s)

New liberalism. *See* Liberalism
New Republic, 50
New Yorker, 261, 306
New York Times, 354
Niebuhr, Reinhold, 147, 200, 376
Nietzsche, Friedrich, 295
Norris, Frank, 74
Novel of manners: 289; and Auchincloss, 292; and Cozzens, 151; and McCarthy, 129; and new fiction, 20, 231, 233

O'Brian, John Lord, 96, 375
O'Connor, Frank, 171, 371, 378
O'Connor, William Van, 368, 370, 372
O'Hara, John, 289n., 289–90, 291
Old liberalism. *See* Liberalism
Ortega y Gasset, José, 13, 36, 55, 233, 359, 370, 379, 383
Orton, William A., 95, 309, 374, 381
Orwell, George, 118

Paine, Tom, 91, 92, 144, 160
Paris Review, 74, 204, 206
Partisan Review, 11, 149
Pearson, Norman Holmes, 368
Penrod, 339
Persons, Stow, 374
Petry, Ann, 68, 70, 71
Podhoretz, Norman, 93–94, 372, 374, 376
Poe, Edgar Allan, 16, 195, 240, 261, 287, 307
Popper, Karl, 118, 129, 375, 376
Porter, Katharine Anne, 203, 202, 263, 380
Powers, J. F.: 149, 172, 174–77; "The Forks," 176; "He Don't Plant Cotton," 176; "Jamsie," 177; "The Lord's Day," 176; "Prince of Darkness," 176; *Prince of Darkness and Other Stories*, 174–77; "The Trouble," 175
Proust, Marcel, 246, 295, 305

Rahv, Philip, 40, 63, 89, 344, 372, 373, 374, 382
Ransom, John Crowe, 5, 150, 194, 196, 200, 234, 344, 377, 379, 380, 382
Red Channels, 112
Riesman, David, 331
Ripley, George, 132

Roberts, Elizabeth Madox, 73
Roosevelt, Franklin D., 95
Rosenfeld, Isaac, 341, 382
Rossiter, Clinton, 147, 161, 376
Rubin, Louis D., Jr., 378
Runyon, Damon, 290
Ruskin, John, 54

Sacco-Vanzetti case, 125
Saint-Exupéry, Antoine de, 54, 372
Sartre, Jean-Paul, 46, 50, 54, 309, 342, 372
Schlesinger, Arthur, Jr., 118, 375
Schneider, Isidor, 89n.
Schorer, Mark, 292, 293, 293n., 294
Schulberg, Budd: 102–6, 107, 144, 375; *The Disenchanted*, 102, 104–6 *passim*; "Fitzgerald in Hollywood," 105; *The Harder They Fall*, 103–4; *What Makes Sammy Run?*, 103–5 *passim*
Selective Service Act, 95
Self, idea of: and Algren, 85; and Bellow, 346, 354, 357, 358, 360; and Bowles, 283–85 *passim*; and Capote, 237, 244; and Clark, 315; and existentialism, 308–10; and fiction of the forties, 1–2, 5, 20; and Himes, 117; and new fiction, 232; and Trilling, 136–42 *passim*; and war novels, 51; and Warren, 198–229 *passim*; and Welty, 274, 279, 281. *See also* Identity, Self-knowledge
Self-knowledge: and Bellow, 346; and religious fiction, 172; and Stegner, 326; and Sylvester, 174; and Cobb, 57; and Ellison, 71; and Trilling, 140; and war novels, 28. *See also* Identity, Self, idea of
Sewall, Samuel, 305
Sewanee Review, 194, 214
Shakespeare William, 211, 212
Shaw, Irwin: 21, 39, 49, 106–13, 117, 129, 144, 375; "Act of Faith," 110; *An Act of Faith and Other Stories*, 107n., 107–10 *passim*; *Bury the Dead*, 107; "The City Was in Total Darkness," 108; "The Climate of Insomnia," 108; "Main Currents in American Thought," 107–8; *Mixed Com-*

Shaw, Irwin (continued)
    pany, 107n., 107–10 passim; "The
    Passion of Lance Corporal Haw-
    kins," 112–13; "Residents of
    Other Cities," 108; Sailor Off the
    Bremen and Other Stories, 107–
    10 passim; The Troubled Air,
    110, 112, 134; "Weep in Years to
    Come," 108; Welcome to the City
    and Other Stories, 107n., 107–10
    passim; The Young Lions, 47,
    47n., 50, 110–11
The Sheik, 287
Silone, Ignazio, 98, 113, 118
Sinclair, Upton, 99–100
Skidmore, Hobert, 51n.
Smith, Henry Nash, 187
Smith, Lillian, 116n.
Southern Agrarians, 193, 199, 200
Southern Renaissance: and conserva-
    tism, 177; and Cozzens, 151; and
    Faulkner, 179; and neo-conserva-
    tism, 149
Southern Review, 199
Speier, Hans, 25
Stafford, Jean: 5, 15, 231, 232, 233,
    294–307, 370, 381; "The Bleeding
    Heart," 306; Boston Adventure,
    296–98, 301; The Catherine
    Wheel, 301–6; Children Are
    Bored on Sunday, 306–7; The In-
    terior Castle, 306–7; "The Interi-
    or Castle," 306; The Mountain
    Lion, 298–301
Statham, Leon, 54–55
Stegner, Wallace: 308, 309, 324–28,
    342, 382; The Big Rock Candy
    Mountain, 325–26, 327; Fire and
    Ice, 325; On a Darkling Plain,
    325; The Preacher and the Slave,
    326–27; Second Growth, 326, 327;
    The Women on the Wall, 327
Steinbeck, John: 4, 48, 100–101, 333,
    369; Cannery Row, 101; The
    Grapes of Wrath, 4, 185, 331; The
    Moon Is Down, 10, 50–51, 100–101;
    Tortilla Flat, 331; The Wayward
    Bus, 101
Stendhal, 116, 207
Stevens, Thaddeus, 93
Studies in Social Psychology in World
    War II, 24

Styron, William, 370
Sylvester, Harry, 172, 173–74, 378

Tate, Allen, 147, 178, 187, 369, 370,
    376, 378
Taylor, Peter: 196–98; "A Long
    Fourth," 197; A Long Fourth and
    Other Stories, 196–97; "The
    Scoutmaster," 197; A Woman of
    Means, 197
Thoreau, Henry David, 42, 315, 352,
    362
Thorp, Willard, 188, 378
Thurber, James, 50, 369, 372
Tillich, Paul, 17, 171, 200, 378
Time, 131
Towner, Wesley, 33n.
Toynbee, Arnold, 290, 381
Trilling, Diana, 316, 381
Trilling, Lionel: 13, 49, 118, 135–44,
    174, 309, 370, 371, 372, 376;
    "Freud and Literature," 137;
    Freud and the Crisis of Our Cul-
    ture, 136–37; "Manners, Morals,
    and the Novel," 136; "The Mean-
    ing of a Literary Idea," 135–36;
    The Middle of the Journey, 135,
    136, 137–44
Trotsky, Leon, 160
Turner, Frederick Jackson, 187, 199
Twice a Year, 69

Van Gelder, Robert, 161, 377
Van Praag, Van, 30n.
Veblen, Thorstein, 331
Vickery, Olga W., 378
Vidal, Gore, 26, 29
Viereck, Peter, 114, 147, 375, 376
Virginia Quarterly Review, 322

Walcutt, Charles Child, 373
Waldorf Conference. See Cultural and
    Scientific Conference for World
    Peace
Wallace, Henry, 124
Walter, E. V., 163, 170, 230, 377, 379
Warren, Robert Penn: 5, 150, 185,
    186, 188, 196, 198–229, 232, 259,
    275, 309, 328, 329, 354, 357, 378,
    379, 380, 383; All the King's Men,
    56, 113n., 121, 212, 214–23, 224;
    At Heaven's Gate, 210–14, 222;

Warren, Robert Penn (continued)
  Band of Angels, 228–29; "Blackberry Winter," 223–24; Brother
  to Dragons, 202, 203; "A Christian
  Education," 223; "The Circus in
  the Attic," 224; The Circus in the
  Attic and Other Stories, 223–24;
  "Confession of Brother Grimes,"
  223; "Goodwood Comes Back,"
  224; "Knowledge and the Image
  of Man," 203; Night Rider, 4,
  206–10; "The Patented Gate and
  the Mean Hamburger," 223, 224;
  Segregation, 202; A Southern
  Harvest, 204–5; "When the Light
  Gets Green," 223; World Enough
  and Time, 224–28
Washington, George, 92
Waugh, Evelyn, 149
Weil, Simone, 342, 346
Wells, H. G., 113
Welty, Eudora: 205, 236, 237, 258–83,
  356, 380; "At the Landing," 264,
  271–72; "Clytie," 267; "A Curtain
  of Green," 269–70; A Curtain of
  Green, 262–72; "Death of a
  Traveling Salesman," 269, 271;
  Delta Wedding, 264, 275–79;
  "First Love," 268; "Flowers for
  Marjorie," 269; The Golden
  Apples, 279–83; "The Hitch-
  Hikers," 269; "How I Write,"
  260; "Ida M'Toy," 270; "June
  Recital," 280; "Keela, the Outcast
  Indian Maiden," 263–64; "The
  Key," 263, 268; "Lily Daw and
  the Three Ladies," 263; "Livvie,"
  271; "A Memory," 267–68; "Moon
  Lake," 280–81; "Powerhouse,"
  177; The Robber Bridegroom,
  272–75, 283; "Shower of Gold,"
  279–80; "Some Notes on River

Welty, Eudora (continued)
  Country," 260; "A Still Moment,"
  264–66; "A Visit of Charity," 270–
  71; "The Wanderers," 282–83;
  "The Whistle," 269; "Why I Live
  at the P.O.," 262; The Wide Net,
  262–72; "A Worn Path," 264
Wernick, Robert, 30n.
Wescott, Glenway, 10, 21, 53–54, 354
West, the idea of the: and Clark, 311,
  313, 316, 317, 318; and Gordon,
  187–88; and Lytle, 196; and Mc-
  Hugh, 47–48; and Morris, 331,
  332, 334, 336; and Stegner, 325,
  326; and Warren, 199, 201, 222,
  227; and Welty, 273–74
West, Ray B., 368, 372
Wharton, Edith, 15, 151, 233, 289, 292
Wheelwright, Philip, 12, 370
Whitehead, Alfred North, 309
Whitman, Walt, 42, 47, 48, 49, 77, 123,
  243–256
Williams, Raymond, 72, 373
Williams, Roger, 376
Williamson, Scott Graham, 30n.
Wilner, Herbert, 381
Wilson, Edmund, 10, 261, 368, 369
Winters, Yvor, 63, 373
Wolfe, Thomas, 4, 49, 330
Wolfert, Ira, 51n., 71, 72, 88
Woods, William, 30n., 50
Woodward, C. Vann, 178, 378
Woolf, Virginia, 4, 13
Wouk, Herman, 46–47
Wright, Quincy, 25, 371
Wright, Richard, 64, 68–70, 71, 373

York, Sergeant Alvin, 213
Young, Philip, 26, 372
Young, Vernon, 381

Zola, Émile, 62